ATLAS OF THE
GREEK WORLD

For Deirdre

Editor Graham Speake
Text editor Bill MacKeith
Art editor Andrew Lawson
Picture editor Polly Friedhoff
Map editor Liz Orrock
Design Adrian Hodgkins
Production Clive Sparling
Index Sandra Raphael

Published by Phaidon Press Ltd,
Littlegate House, St Ebbe's Street,
Oxford

Planned and produced by
Elsevier Publishing Projects (UK)
Ltd, Oxford

© 1980 Elsevier International
Projects, Amsterdam

British Library Cataloguing in Publication Data
Levi, Peter
    Atlas of the Greek world.
    1. Greece – Maps
    1. Title
    911'.38   G2000
    ISBN 0–7148–2044–X

Origination by M.B.A. Ltd,
Chalfont St Peter, Bucks.
Chapman Brothers, Oxford.

Filmset by Keyspools Ltd,
Golborne, Lancs.

Printed in Italy by Officine Grafiche di
Arnoldo Mondadori Editore, Verona, Italy

Frontispiece Maenads dancing for
Dionysos. The god is represented
by his xoanon, a draped post.
Freely adapted and colored from
a vase painting by Hieron in the
West Berlin Museum.

ATLAS OF THE
GREEK WORLD

by Peter Levi

Phaidon·Oxford

CONTENTS

Special Features

Site Features

List of Maps

CHRONOLOGICAL TABLE

	3000 BC	2000	1500	1000	800	600
AEGEAN AND GREEK MAINLAND	early Cycladic civilization	Cretan palace civilization	shaft graves at Mycenae; explosion at Santorini; fall of Knossos; fall of Mycenaeans	iron introduced from E, then reaction to bronze; rise of great families	population increases in Greece; chief period of colonization to E and W; international festivals established; tyrants in control of many cities	first Greek coins; increasing power of cities; beginnings of democracy at Athens; Sparta dominates Peloponnese

Cycladic female figurine in white marble, 2600–2200 BC.

The so-called mask of Agamemnon from Mycenae, 1550—1500 BC.

The "warrior vase" from Mycenae, early 12th century BC.

Geometric amphora from Athens, c. 750 BC.

The "peplos kore" from the Athenian acropolis, c. 530 BC.

	Bronze Age			dark age	archaic	
POTTERY STYLE	Helladic and Minoan			sub-Mycenaean; protogeometric	geometric; Orientalizing	archaic (black-figure)
ART AND ARCHITECTURE	Cycladic sculpture	great palaces in Crete; Santorini frescoes; great beehive tombs; figurines, fine working in gold and semiprecious stones (e.g. sealstones)			monumental vases; rectangular plan of buildings; Olympia tripods; first stone temples	kouroi and korai
LITERATURE, PHILOSOPHY, SCIENCE			Linear A tablets; Linear B tablets; Phoenician alphabet		Greek alphabet; Homer; Hesiod; lyric poets	beginnings of tragedy and comedy; Pythagoras; Aischylos; Pindar; Sophokles;
EGYPT, ASIA MINOR AND THE EAST	Egyptian Old Kingdom; great pyramids	Hittite empire in Anatolia; Babylonian empire	Egyptian New Kingdom; great temples; Tut'ankhamun	Miletos, then other Ionian, then Black Sea colonies; Assyrian empire at most powerful; Assyrians lose power to Medes and Babylonians		Darius founds Persian empire; Persians conquer Egypt
WEST MEDITERRANEAN				Phoenicians spread W	Carthage founded; Greeks found colonies in Sicily, Italy, France, N Africa; in Spain; Rome founded	
ELSEWHERE IN EUROPE		Stonehenge and other late megaliths raised		Early Iron Age (Hallstatt period) in central Europe; beginning of Celtic dispersal		

	400	300	200	AD	AD 500	1000	2000

...ian invasions
...hens dominates
...elian league
...ge of Perikles
...Peloponnesian war

Athenian revival
unification of Greece
rise of Macedon
campaigns of
Alexander

rise in power of
Achaean and
Aetolian leagues

Macedonian wars
Macedonia becomes
Roman province
Achaea becomes
Roman province

Greece remains cultural and
intellectual center of Mediterranean

Alexander the Great at the
battle of Issos. Detail from the
"Alexander mosaic" found at
Pompeii, copy of a Greek
painting of c. 300 BC.

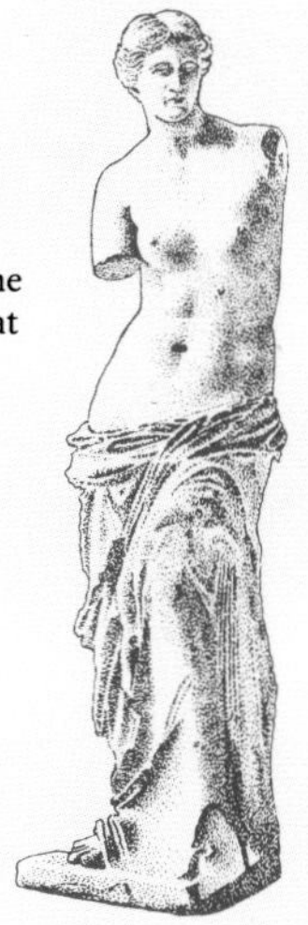

Coin of Hadrian,
2nd century AD

...he Parthenon
...t Athens,
...ompleted
...47–432 BC.

The Venus de Milo,
a 2nd-century BC marble
statue from Melos.

...ical | Hellenistic | Roman empire | Byzantine empire | 1500–1821 Turkish domination / 1821 independence and revival

south Italian painters

...igure

...ater; temple of
...at Olympia;
...thenon; Erechtheion;
...eidias, Polykleitos
...sculptors);
...olygnotos (painter)

Praxiteles (sculptor);
mausoleum at
Halikarnassos

Hellenistic baroque

altar of Zeus, Pergamon
Winged Victory of Samothrace
Venus de Milo

Roman copying of
Greek sculpture and
architecture

Hagia Sophia built

...dotos; Euripides;
...rates; Hippokrates;
...ucydides; Aristophanes;
...lato; Aristotle; Epicurus;

Theokritos;
Euclid; Archimedes

creation of library
at Alexandria

Horace

Pausanias

...rosses Hellespont
...vades Greece

Alexander conquers
Asia Minor, Egypt,
Persia, NE India
successor kingdoms,
Ptolemaic, Seleucid dynasties
Gauls settle in Galatia
Parthian empire founded

Rome defeats Antiochos
of Syria
Pergamon becomes
Roman province
Egypt becomes
Roman province

Sasanian empire
founded in Persia
Byzantion refounded
by Romans (Constantinople)
Arabs besiege
Constantinople

...epublic
...d
...rthaginian defeat
...t Himera

expansion of Roman
power in Italy

Pyrrhos of Epirus
defeated in Italy
three Punic wars, ending
with destruction of Carthage
Rome controls N Africa;
Spain; Gaul

start of
Roman empire

...e cultures

PREFACE

The history of mankind had a crisis in the 5th century BC, an explosion of light which affected everything and still does so today. Europe is the result and Greece is the key. What happened in Greece in the 5th century was part of a long process.

It is impossible to understand Greek history or art or poetry at all well without a strong sense of the prehistory, of the landscape, the climate, the mountains and rivers and the conditions of life. For this understanding it is necessary to have some acquaintance with the ruins and places of the Greeks; and getting to know them is an attractive process, even in the pages of a book. This book is an attempt to make sense of the ancient Greeks, of their spiritual and mental world as well as the physical world of their experience, of their history and their travels and expansion as well as their arts and their achievements. Those include philosophy, medicine, natural science, the theatrical arts, marble architecture, a new economic system and the rule of law.

For this simple-sounding but in fact rather vast enterprise of making sense of the Greeks, pictures and plans as well as maps and a continuous text are not a luxury, they are actually necessary. The medium of an atlas is ideal; but even so it is not possible to include everything. No one has visited all the Greek ruins in the world. Very few scholars have seen all the antiquities even of Greece itself, inside and outside the museums. Certainly no book includes them all. No attempt to make sense of this mass of material, and of the many hundreds of years of Greek history, can have absolute authority. A new one will naturally have the personal quality of the passion and knowledge that went into it; and yet that is not quite enough. Such a book should at least offer a coherent history, and not conflict with the evidence where real evidence exists. The marriage of text and illustrations and the overall planning of this book, which are the work rather of the publisher than the author, or rather of both together, are meant to support the expression of this coherence and this truthfulness as far as possible.

Of course the planning was a selective process, and selection always entails compromise. We have tried to present some fresh and unexpected images, but there are also certain famous ones it would be perverse not to offer. Equally selective has been the inclusion of certain themes and anecdotes in the continuous text.

I could produce here a very impressive list of those great men by whom I was taught, but I am aware that this book is very far from being the sort of sustained scholarly contribution that would do them credit. I hope it does contribute to scholarship here and there, but its principal purpose is different: it is meant to explain, to instruct, to excite curiosity, to challenge contradiction, to stir the imagination of readers I have never met. It is also meant to tell my wife, who knows no Greek and little Latin, and my stepson, who is nine years old, as lucidly as possible about what has interested me and moved me so much in the history and the world of the Greeks. I think it is the Greeks' world rather than their history that inspires my passion, but history is needed to make sense of the world. So I have tried to discuss art and literature, and even such large themes as law and science, as parts of history.

When one is constantly turning over in one's head the material of a life-time's study, it is hard to predict what will come uppermost at any particular moment, for instance the moment of writing. Here the length of time it takes to produce a book is a great restorer of balance. So are the contributions of more knowledgeable scholars, in the case of this book particularly Thomas Braun of Merton College, Oxford, who gave advice on matters of history, and John Boardman, who advised on art and archaeology. Mr Braun also provided cartographic information and wrote the captions for the maps; Professor Boardman wrote the special features on the development of vase painting and on the sculptures of the Parthenon; Dr Colin Kraay wrote the feature on Greek coinage; and Dr Richard Witt the feature on music. From time to time in revision I neglected learned advice, having got the bit between my teeth. That is my own fault. I beg the reader therefore not to treat this book as a perfectly respectable and efficient guide. Although it remains within its limitations as reliable a guide as I could make it, it is meant, at a deeper level of feeling, to excite, engage and amuse. There are libraries of books about the classics more sober than this one, though few, I believe, more seriously intended.

PART ONE
THE LAND IN CONTEXT

THE GEOGRAPHY OF ANCIENT GREECE

Social patterns are sometimes imposed by the landscape, either in obvious or in subtle ways. The same human patterns occur in the same landscape again and again. It is not surprising that the great plain of Thessaly was a breeding ground of horses in the ancient world, and the Thessalians were strong in cavalry, nor that the social organization of these fertile lowlands was somewhat feudal. The heartland of the Spartans is both very rich, in the Eurotas valley, and very wild in the mountains – hollow, craggy Lakedaimon, as Homer calls it. It is understandable that this mountain-encircled sanctuary was the cradle of a dominating people. It is easy to realize the nature of the great international shrines of the Greeks, the mysterious oracles at Dodona and Delphi which must have been at first the holy places of mountain herdsmen, and Olympia in the big bend of a powerful river, a meeting place for games and a natural theater for races.

But there are more difficult questions. How much forest was there in the 8th century BC? By the 4th century the Athenians were buying their timber from Macedonia and the Black Sea, and Plato and Theophrastos lamented the loss of forests, but it may have been only the great increase in population in the late 8th century BC that caused the devastation of the trees, and certain useful trees never grew in Attica. Were the flora and fauna ever as dense as early Greek visual art suggests? We know that there were wolves, and sacred woods, and some very ancient trees, but we know little of the continuum of natural history, let alone the migrations of bustards and egrets. How few trees would a landscape need to have in order to look deforested to Plato? We know of woods destroyed in time of war, but a wood might grow again. Plato's Academy was a training ground for naked exercise beside the river Kephisos, a short walk outside Athens. It had fine plane trees. That area was deeply covered in dried alluvial mud, hence its suitability for a training ground, and hence the plane trees. In the Middle Ages and down to the last century it lay under new mud and an immense grove of olive trees. Fifteen years ago that area, where it was not built over, was a flat, muddy ground where a football team trained, between a brick works and a field of cabbages. If we could live another 1,000 years, we might see the plane trees again, just as in Crete there were cypress forests in the Middle Ages where it seems there were none in late antiquity.

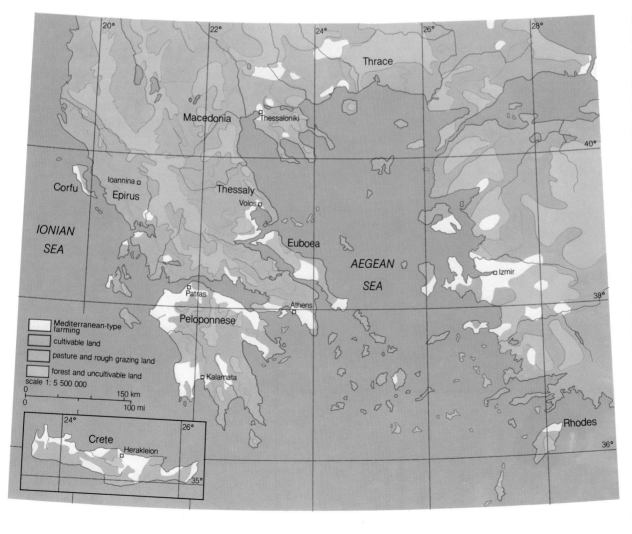

Left: The vegetation of the Greek world today
Even today Greece is not as treeless as some people think; for example Mount Athos, Thasos and Samothrace are thick with trees and Attica has been replanted with pines. But the forests were certainly more extensive in antiquity. Great tracts of Crete and the Pindos mountains, for instance, were wooded then, and there was a great deal more game. The best firs for ship building grew in the north, which is one reason why the Athenian empire of the 5th century tried to keep in with the kings of Macedonia and attached much importance to the colony at Amphipolis.

In mainland Greece upland pastures entailed the spring migration of sheep. Water meadows with grass all the year round, for which Argive territory was famous, were a rarity. Horses would normally have to be stall-fed and were a sign of wealth. The Greeks worked with oxen, mules and donkeys, fattened enough stock for the occasional sacrifice, but in coastal areas were better supplied with fish.

Mediterranean crops are those that thrive on winter rainfall and need no rain in summer: wheat (though Athens and other parts of Greece never grew enough for themselves and depended on imports), barley, olives, grapes, figs and pomegranates. Melons, peaches and lemons were not introduced until the Roman period and oranges were not known until after the Portuguese voyages of the 16th century, whence the Greek word *portokali*.

Map legend:
- Mediterranean-type farming
- cultivable land
- pasture and rough grazing land
- forest and uncultivable land

scale 1: 5 500 000
0 — 150 km
0 — 100 mi

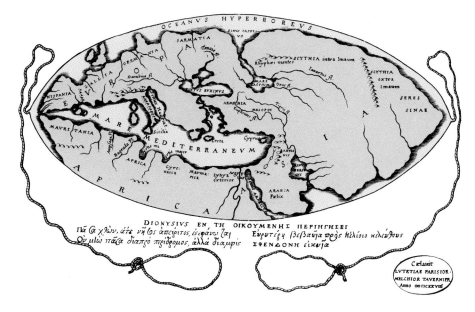

The regions of Greece

Thrace and Macedonia in the northeast were wild; Epirus, extending westward to the Ionian Sea, was wild and isolated until after the death of Alexander; and Arcadia was the remotest part of the Peloponnese, with the oldest-sounding dialect, the strangest religious cults, and the most primitive reputation, until the 4th century BC. But Greece has many different kinds of landscapes, and one of the most crucial elements in its make-up is a rich diversity of conditions with little communication between them. There were still, a few years ago, villages in the Peloponnese where a foreign traveler on foot who came from across the local mountain would be greeted as an explorer or arrested as a spy. Toward the Albanian frontier, or high in the Cretan mountains, or even in Euboea until recently, some shadow has lingered of the isolation of ancient times. The isolation of the mountains has not altered much. The Pindos, the rocky backbone of northern Greece, is still crossed by only three roads.

Climate, calendar and farming

Three-quarters of Greece is mountainous, and only one fifth of the land can be cultivated; but the coastal plains and certain inland areas are very rich – parts of Crete are almost unbelievably so, as Homer knew. The olive and the vine have long flourished, but not quite always and not quite everywhere. I have met a Greek, brought up in this century in a mountain village, who had never seen an olive (or a fish or an orange) until he was 12 years old. The Greek colonists in Sicily took some time to establish olive trees; for several generations oil was imported into Sicily. It has been said that the Greeks spread in the end as far afield as the olive will grow, and the Romans as far afield as the vine. That is roughly true, but one should remember that even mainland Greece itself was never completely colonized. Wheatfields in mainland Greece were never very big. Small wonder that its human population shifted and struggled over the riches between rock and rock.

The average temperature differs from one part of Greece to another, with hot summers and mild winters in coastal and most southern areas but cold winters in Macedonia and the mountainous interior. Rainfall is high in the west (up to 130 cm per year) but much lower on the eastern plains (38 cm in Thessaly and Athens). The differences between seasons are dramatic. Winter is shorter than in northern Europe, but in the mountains winter is very hard and summer is stupefying. Spring is fresher and more delicate, and autumn kinder and much longer than in northern Europe. All this has affected human societies in Greece, from the patterns of the festivals of the gods and the moving of herds to questions of war and peace and the details of colonization.

Of course the calendar of months and festivals, by which the cycles of the moon and the great cycle of the sun were built into a single, more or less international Greek system, was a gradual development; Homer seems to know only of seasons. The calendar of the ancient Greeks was based on Babylonian mathematics, and at least at Athens it needed to be empirically adjusted year by year to avoid contradictions. From mid-March to mid-May two months were sacred to Artemis, and from mid-

ADRIATIC SEA

ITALY

BULGARIA

YUGOSLAVIA

ALBANIA

Macedonia

L Megali
Prespa

L Vegorritis
2061▲

Thessaloniki

Chalkidike

Drama

Xanthi

Kavalla

Thasos

Thra

Nestos

1770▲

Strymon

Axios

Aliakmon

Vijose

▲2637

Olympos ▲
2917

L Volvi

Athos ▲
2033

Corfu

Ioannina

Pinios

Lemno

Corfu

Dodona

PINDOS
MOUNTAINS

Larisa

Epirus

Thessaly

Volos

N SPORADES

AEGE

Arachthos

SEA

Leukas

Spercheios

Skyros

IONIAN

Acheloos

L Trikhonis

Thermopylai

Euboea

2457▲

Kephisos

1743▲

Evinos

Delphi

Chalkis

Kephallenia

Thebes

ISLANDS

Patras

GULF OF CORINTH

1413▲

Marathon

Attica

2376▲

Corinth

Athens
Peiraeus

Ar

IONIAN SEA

Zakynthos

Olympia

Peloponnese

Alpheios

Tripolis

Kea

Kythnos

Hydra

CYCLAD

Pa

Kalamata

2407▲

Sparta

Eurotas

Melos

2000m

1000m

200m

0

▲   spot height in meters

scale 1:2 900 000

SEA OF CRE

MEDITERRANEAN SEA

0   150km

0   100mi

Herakle

2456▲

Cr

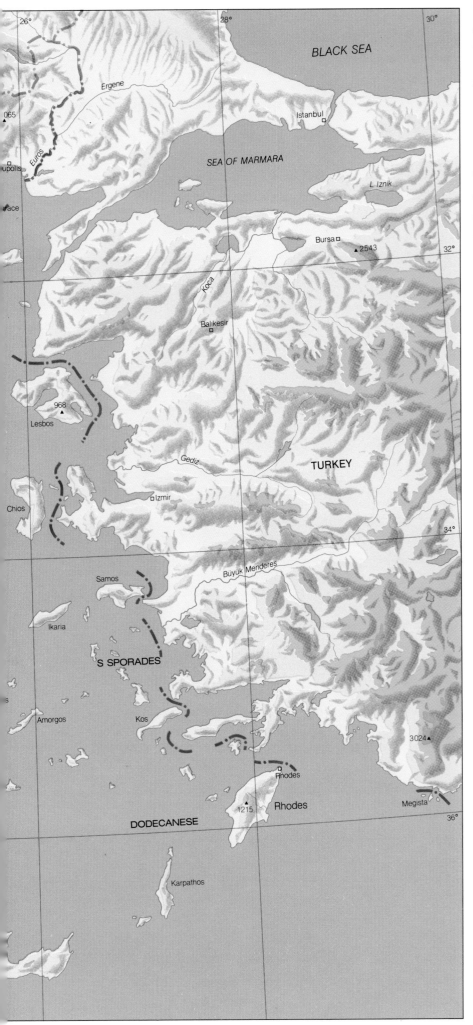

May to mid-November six, with perhaps one exception, were sacred to Apollo. The first and the last of his festivals in that long summer had to do with vegetation. The four remaining months of the year, from mid-November to mid-March, belonged to roaring Zeus, to Poseidon the god of earthquakes, to Hera the goddess of marriage, and to Dionysos, at whose festival the dead were commemorated and the year's new wine opened.

Until recently Greece was full of herds of sheep and goats that moved partly at random, partly on traditional tracks, twice a year, to have summer grazing in the mountains and winter grazing well below the snowline. This pattern of movement is very ancient all over the world; it has been observed and studied in every country from Spain to Afghanistan. Transhumance involves a complete way of life, and it nourishes a system of values and a social organization of great interest to scholars of the ancient world. Indeed, John Campbell's study of the modern Greek Vlachs, *Honour, Family and Patronage*, and Juliet du Boulay's *Portrait of a Greek Mountain Village*, both of which draw very close connections between geography and behavior, have implications of the greatest importance for our understanding of ancient history.

Mythology is full of stories of cattle raids, and so is history, down to the first campaigns of the Peloponnesian war. Homer tells us of the herds of the island king Odysseus wandering on the mainland. We know from an inscription of a small grazing fee payable at a temple on the Isthmus for herds that must have been passing across. Now and then in history, a shepherd sees an army from his mountainside. The cattle sacrificed at Athens in the 5th and 4th centuries must have been immensely numerous. Where did they graze? Are the cloaked boys who manage the cattle on the Parthenon frieze herdboys?

We know at least how the story ended. When Atticus the friend of Cicero lived his retired life in Athens he was a rich man, and he lent money to both sides in Roman politics. The substantial source of his wealth, apart from banking, was in cattle; we are told he controlled the grazing of all Epirus in the northwest. Later still, we know from complaining inscriptions that on island after island sheep farming and agriculture were annihilated by huge flocks of goats, protected by gangs of armed thugs and owned by very rich men a long way off. Overgrazing by goats is more destructive of the landscape, and has done more to shape the eastern Mediterranean as our grandfathers knew it, than any other single element: more than earthquakes or forest fires.

Caves, watersprings and rivers

The importance of the watersprings, the caverns and the rivers of the great limestone system of Greece has been fundamental. Rivers were boundaries, because each side grazed its flocks and watered them to the same limit, but in winter no one could cross. Caves were mysterious, religious places, associated in mythology with secret love-making and with secret birth, and in religion with simple and rustic fertility cults. Springs of pure water had powerful influences; sanctuaries of healing and oracles of worldly help would center on a waterspring. The gods of even small rivers had a

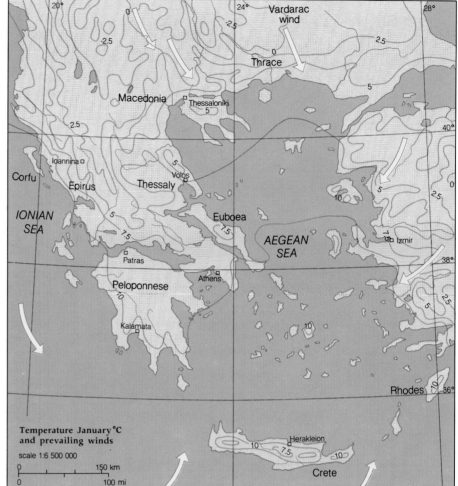

Temperature January °C
and prevailing winds

scale 1:6 500 000

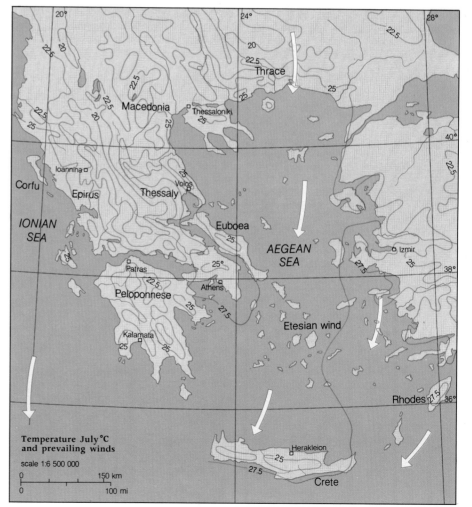

Temperature July °C
and prevailing winds

scale 1:6 500 000

considerable dignity, and the initiation of adolescent boys into manhood involved a river ceremony in ancient Greece, as it does to this day in parts of Africa. In more than one rocky river gorge there were oracles of the dead.

It is hard to avoid making ancient religion and society in its own landscape sound like a poem, a resonant, self-enclosed world of freshness and strangeness. That is partly because any social system simpler than our own, and defined by technical conditions so limited, will appear to us like the small, amazing model world of a poem. But the ancient world was everyday and open-ended: by a slow continuous process it resulted in the modern world. The principal way in which the physical geography of tall rocks and misty sea surfaces affected the ancient Greeks was economic. Even in the idylls of Theokritos, a freshly romantic picture of country people painted for city intellectuals, fishermen are miserable, only their pathos is attractive. For a Greek in the 5th century, what romantic scholarship now sees as the sacred landscape of Vergil, or of Pausanias, or of a Roman wall painting, was the difficult earth where he made his living, and most of its gods were difficult gods. At the popular level, Greek religion was fearful, envious and desperate.

Serfs and slaves

The ancient Greek economy was limited not only by its material resources, but further by lack of knowledge of those resources. The silver mines that made Athens rich in the 5th century had been known to the Mycenaeans, but their techniques of recovering and refining silver were by no means sophisticated, so that the best deposit, what Aischylos calls "the waterspring of silver, the earth's ancient treasury," came to light only in the early 5th century. Even then the mines were exploited haphazardly, by means of short-term mining leases and constantly changing slave labor. In fact the Greeks accomplished rather few great public works at the time of their flowering, and it is worth asking why.

The vast Lake Kopais, north of Thebes in Boeotia, which has been drained in modern times, was drained at least partially by the Mycenaeans. It went back to water, reeds and eels in the dark ages after the fall of Mycenae. No attempt to cut the Corinth canal was successful in antiquity. Schemes like the harbors of Corinth and Athens indicate the extreme limit of Greek resources of manpower. There were slaves enough in the silver mines of 4th-century Athens, but they were not publicly owned. The Syracusans in the 5th century were already using slaves on a vaster scale than Athens ever did, and Sparta held down a large part of southern Greece by a system of serf labor. But at least until the 5th century, when imperialism led to suicidal war, the Greeks were unable to attempt any enormous disturbances of nature. To rear a stone temple was for them a colossal project. The great temples of the 6th century were even more impressive to the Greeks than they are to us.

It is still disputed to what extent agriculture was carried on by means of slaves. In the *Odyssey* the relations are patriarchal, but the world of the Trojan wars (c. 1200 BC) as portrayed by Homer 600 years later is homelier than what was to follow it.

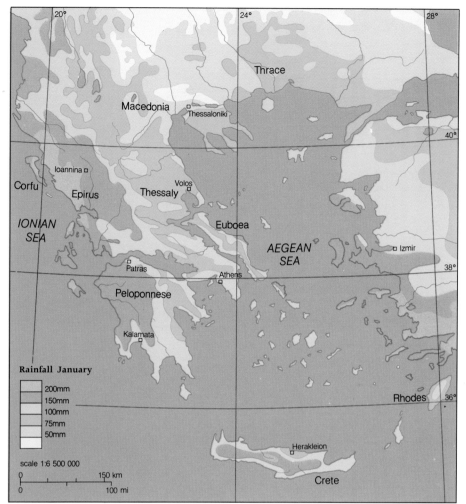

Rainfall January

- 200mm
- 150mm
- 100mm
- 75mm
- 50mm

scale 1:6 500 000

0   150 km
0   100 mi

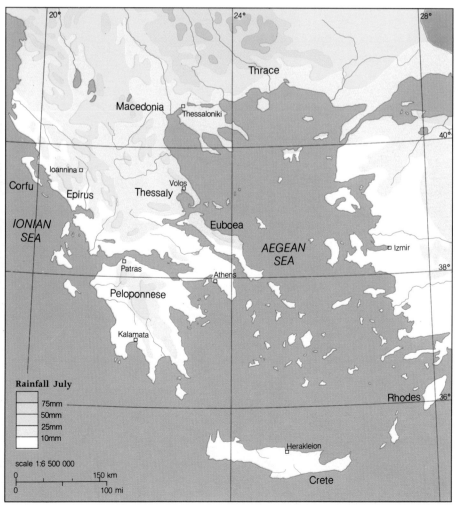

Rainfall July

- 75mm
- 50mm
- 25mm
- 10mm

scale 1:6 500 000

0   150 km
0   100 mi

Telemachos, the son of Odysseus, dances for his father's victory in the palace with the swineherd and the other herdsman, and Laertes, Odysseus' father, works himself on his own land. In the early 5th century Solon interfered in Attica to redeem the impoverished peasants from actual slavery. In the 5th and 4th centuries only the most wretched Athenian would live without any slave at all, but the idea of leaving all farmwork whatsoever to slaves was a Utopian dream, an Aristophanic joke. For what the information is worth, in the 20 years from 340 BC, when we know the names and professions of about 80 Athenian slaves who were set free, only a dozen were farm laborers. There were also farm servants, hardly differing from slaves; they seem almost to have vanished at one time, around 400 BC, but at the end of the 4th century 10,000 or 20,000 Athenian citizens, deprived on grounds of poverty of their citizen rights, either emigrated or sank back into the laboring life of their ancestors in the Attic countryside.

Patterns of settlement

The rise and fall of cities repeated itself for the same reasons, just as the rise and fall of individuals did. Corinth was rich because it was nearly impregnable, and because of its position and its two ports, commanding the Isthmus and the trade of the eastern and the western sea. The Romans destroyed Corinth (146 BC) and built up Patras in its place, but in late antiquity Corinth once again overshadowed Patras. Ten years ago the same rivalry still existed. Another pattern is the alternating movement of towns uphill to sites on rock refuges in bad times, and downhill to attractive trading positions in periods of peace. These movements occur in Greece, particularly in Crete and the islands, as they did later in Italy. In the same way the remote hill towns of Arcadia were abandoned to build Megalopolis in the 4th century; today the upper villages of Arcadia are being deserted to increase the population of the cities, not quite for the same reasons but under a similar pressure.

The growth of modern towns on ancient sites is not always a matter of continuity or of chance. From the center of modern Corinth, for example, it is five kilometers to the village of Palaia-Korinthos, which covers part of the site of the ancient city. There are ancient sites without even a village, and some modern towns, like Pyrgos in Eleia, which are not built on ancient sites. But the position of Corinth, the harbors of Athens and of Corfu (Kerkyra), the site of Kalamata, where the Messenian plain meets the sea, and the positions of certain islands make it inevitable that human settlements will occur there. Within the period of antiquity there seems to be a similar connection in certain cases between Mycenaean and Classical Greek settlements. At Thebes and at Athens the continuity was minimal, but there as elsewhere an important archaic and Classical city arose just where a Mycenaean palace had stood. The reason why the same cannot be said for Mycenae itself is that the site of Mycenae lacks logic. To control the plain, Argos is just as logical, and its water supply is better.

The place of Greece in Europe

From time to time in history Greece has seemed to belong to the east; indeed we should remember that from before the 7th century BC until the 1920s continuously the western coast of Asia was predominantly Greek. At other times Greece has seemed, by definition against the Persian or the Turkish world, to be the frontier of Europe. It can be said that Greece both is and is not part of the Balkans.

It is as well to notice that these simple-sounding generalizations have a sound basis in geography, since they certainly have a resonance in history. Most of the offerings at Dodona down to the Classical age were the simple pottery of more northerly Balkan people. Athenian relations with Thrace in the northeast were an essential element in the culture and consciousness of both peoples in the 5th century, even though, and indeed because, in Athens in Classical times, the Thracians were considered to be barbarians.

The relation of Classical Greeks to their northern neighbors needs to be approached through the preexisting, prehistoric relation of Greece with the north as well as with the east. The paradox that best illustrates this is the treasure of Vix in central France, whose prize item is a vast 6th-century bronze vessel, massively and finely worked and as high as a man, made, perhaps in south Italy, by a Spartan (see p. 68). The interpenetration of the Greek with other worlds in the archaic age was often more productive than in later times of more aggressive relationships.

Around the year 2000 BC, when Greek-speaking and identifiably Greek people become visible to archaeology, the same social and economic system seems to have prevailed right across Europe: the

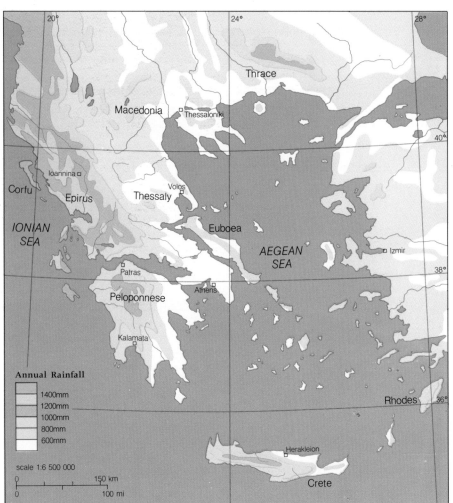

Annual Rainfall

1400mm
1200mm
1000mm
800mm
600mm

scale 1:6 500 000

0 ——— 150 km
0 ——— 100 mi

tribes were ruled by a heroic warrior class, patrons of bronze, living by the values celebrated later in epic poems, and buried in state. As a class system, with a fighting and hunting gentry living in great houses, that lasted nearly 4,000 years, perhaps until 1914. The houses that went with it, with their porches, their great halls and their inner rooms, existed already before 2000 BC, in Anatolia and in eastern Europe as well as in Greece, but it was in Greece that the great halls of this kind of house became the impressive centers of palaces. Yet Greek

architecture at that time was not the most ambitious in Europe, and Troy itself was smaller than Stonehenge.

What happened in Greece was a special, but never quite an isolated development. The Mycenaeans of the late 17th century BC took their treasures of gold and silver, and the sacredness and perhaps also the very use of horses, from the east, their ornaments of amber from the north, their weapons from Crete or the Levant. But weapons spread swiftly, and it was a Mycenaean helmet copied in Germany that became the standard battle helmet of the west. The Mycenaeans measured their wealth in weapons; 90 bronze swords were found with only three bodies in one of the shaft graves at Mycenae. As far away as Brittany at the same time the rich and powerful were buried with bronze daggers in the same extravagant numbers.

Although no palaces have been found in the rest of Europe like those of Greece, the warrior graves are equally rich in many places; the 15th-century treasure from Borodino to the northwest of the

Communication by mule-track and droving track spread like a spider's web far across the rocky surface of the earth. By the 6th century BC Chinese silk and Greek bronze were to be found together in the tomb of a prince buried near Stuttgart.

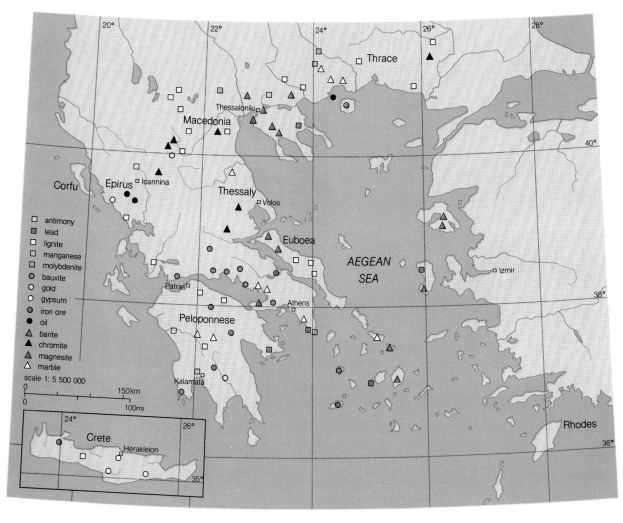

Map legend:
- □ antimony
- ▣ lead
- □ lignite
- ▢ manganese
- ▢ molybdenite
- ◍ bauxite
- ◉ gold
- ○ gypsum
- ◉ iron ore
- ● oil
- △ barite
- ▲ chromite
- ◮ magnesite
- △ marble

scale 1: 5 500 000

Map labels: Thrace, Thessaloniki, Macedonia, Corfu, Epirus, Ioannina, Thessaly, Volos, Euboea, AEGEAN SEA, Izmir, Patras, Athens, Peloponnese, Kalamata, Rhodes, Crete, Herakleion

The mineral resources of modern Greece

The great breakthrough which brought bronze tools and armor had taken place at the beginning of the third millennium BC, but even after iron came into common use, bronze was still needed for many purposes. Cyprus was the archetypal source of copper for Greek bronze. The copper ingot symbolized Cypriot trade. But more copper would be brought down to the Levantine ports from such regions as Tabal near modern Kayseri. The tin which is an essential constituent of bronze came from even further away. By the 6th century it was being brought by middlemen from Cornwall, up the Seine and down the Saône and Rhône valleys to the Greek port of Marseille. Even for iron, Greek mariners were prepared to travel huge distances at the beginning of the colonial period. Pithekoussai was settled in the 8th century for the sake of iron from Elba. The Chalybes in northwest Asia Minor are also a famous source of iron. Silver, as well as tin from Galicia and further north, came to the Greek world from Tartessos in southern Spain from about 630 onwards, brought by Phocaean seamen. But silver was the one ore with which the Greek homeland was well supplied. The Athenians struck it rich in their own mines at Laurion from the early 5th century. Silver and gold made the fortune of the island of Siphnos. Kroisos' wealth in 6th-century Lydia came from the alluvial gold of the Hermos valley. Gold was also exploited in Mount Pangaion and Thasos.

Black Sea contains spears of silver, axes of jadeite and mace heads of alabaster. Everywhere in Europe gold and silver and imported finery were buried with dead soldiers. Mycenaean gold cups were imitated in Cornwall. In Romania there were silver battle-axes that were surely not for use, and a single gold dagger weighing three pounds of solid gold has been found. The trade of the world ran in a sense uninterrupted from Britain to Mongolia.

That the Greece of the Mycenaeans had such formidably wide horizons is due to the physical position of Greece in the world. In both ancient and modern times Greece has been doomed by the place it occupies on the map to be a doorstep between Europe and Asia; whenever one or other of its obvious geographic links has weakened for a time, it has always revived later. At the beginning of the 5th century BC Greece was almost but not quite swallowed up by the Persian empire, a situation that Alexander reversed. From the west the Roman empire overwhelmed Greece for a time; but Greece revived and, as part of the Byzantine empire, became subject to Oriental influences, while at the same time its cultural tentacles reached Anglo-Saxon England. The comparative obscurity of Greek relations with the barbarian north is equally the effect of geography, of mountains and of forests. Influences moved more swiftly on the roads of the sea, and there is no time except perhaps immediately after the fall of the Mycenaeans when Greek ships were not fingering the surface of the western Mediterranean.

How much the Mycenaeans contributed to Europe must remain uncertain in the absence of written records, but it was surely more than techniques of fighting and weaponry, or ornamental scratches on amber beads. From the point of view of the general pattern of human geography within which the ancient Greeks must be studied, it is fascinating how prehistory repeated itself in Greece. Shortly before 1000 BC, when the level of material culture in Greece had sunk to the less spectacularly sunken level of the rest of Europe, something like a new beginning occurred again in the Aegean, which prepared that explosion into form and light we call Classical. It is no derogation from the splendid achievements of the Celts in gold and bronze, and in many arts now inevitably lost – their music for example, their poetry and their wooden architecture – to claim something special for the Greeks in the 1,000 years before Christ.

It is interesting that the Iron Age started earlier in Greece, at the end of the Mycenaean period, than in Celtic Europe. The reasons for the introduction of iron are uncertain. If it was smelted from meteorites, as sometimes it was, it may have had a magical value. Once the technique of forging it was mastered, not an easy step, it was cheaper and more abundant than bronze. It seems likely that the beginnings of the Iron Age in Greece were connected with a failure in the supplies of bronze from the east, together with the arrival of the necessary techniques, from the same direction. Iron is heavier than bronze, even though its edge is less sharp, at least until the technique of tempering iron into steel has been mastered. That skill was certainly available in Greece before the 5th century BC, since swords of that date have shown under analysis a tempered steel cutting edge applied to a bronze weapon. An early iron ax head with bronze rivets from the very beginning of the Greek Iron Age suggests that, independently of the shortage of bronze, iron was preferred to bronze for some purposes.

In that dark age, when Greece was as poor as the rest of Europe or poorer, light came from the east, from more developed peoples. The closeness of the Phoenicians and the Egyptians, the Syrians and the Hebrews, constitutes an influence sufficient in itself, if there were no other, to account for the development of the Greeks, for their superiority to the Etruscans and the Gauls. From the Phoenicians came the alphabet, from the Egyptians came sculpture, and from the whole Levant architecture. Even the individuality of what grew up in Greece – the continual insistence on interpreting every foreign influence, however overwhelming, in Greek terms, so that Greek statues were stepping out freely when Egyptian ones were still as stiff as ramrods, and Greek decorative art achieved a lucid formality and a final quality otherwise unknown – is due to the physical nature of Greece, the not quite complete isolation of so many vigorous communities, the mountains and the islands.

The Classical Greeks were still using Mycenaean roads, and even in the Roman period Greek road making by no means attained the military grandeur of the same period in Britain and France. The only great Roman road in Greece ran east across the far north, the Via Egnatia, the military route to Asian wars. Some of the Classical Greek roads survived until recently as mule and drovers' tracks. The diversity of Greek provincial styles, even within the rather narrow limits of geometric art, is a product of this trickling system of communications; so perhaps are the wars between city-states, and so I conjecture are the racial theories of the Greeks. The chauvinistic kind of division of mankind, into Hellenes and barbarians, is not specially Greek; such divisions are almost universal. But the Greeks of the Classical period developed a mythical history of racial conflicts of Greek against Greek, Dorians and Ionians and Achaeans, following roughly the evidences of ancestry and dialect, which was the charter of later wars and alliances, and of the quarrels between great families.

These racial theories may well have been entirely false. It is at least not contrary to the evidence we now have of Mycenaean and later Greeks to suggest that the growth of dialects was post-Mycenaean. They may well be the product of the mountainous divisions and isolated developments of the dark age. If that is so the racial consciousness of Dorians and Ionians was a false consciousness. One should remember that the division of the Peloponnese into states was incomplete even in the 5th century. The southernmost towns were independent until the time of Augustus, it was obscure to whom Triphylia in southern Elis belonged, Arcadia itself was hardly unified, and between Sparta and Argos there were semi-independent tribes. Even to have sailed a few times around the stormy southern point of Greece was an achievement worth recording on a gravestone as late as the Roman empire.

The dialects of ancient Greece
In Classical times there were still some survivors of pre-Greek languages in isolated places: Eteocretan in Crete, Lemnian spoken by the native people of Lemnos, and in Cyprus the Eteocypriot of Amathous. The Doric dialect with its broad *as* was spoken where it was said that Dorian invaders had taken over. Non-Dorians in these areas, even if conscious of being racially distinct, spoke Doric too. The Thessalian and Boeotian invaders brought their Aeolic dialect with them. On the mainland the Athenians, never vanquished, retained Attic, their dialect of Ionic, whose literary prestige eventually conquered the whole Greek-speaking world. The *koine* of Hellenistic times was a popularized version of Attic. In western Asia Minor the stylized language of epic poetry was evolved, never a medium of ordinary speech. What people did speak was Aeolic in the north, which the poets of Lesbos used for their songs, and Ionic in Samos, Chios and the coastal Ionian cities. This was the language of the first prose writers. The physicians of the Hippokratic school at Kos and the historian Herodotos of Halikarnassos wrote Ionic, although they were Dorians. Mainland northwest dialects are known from inscriptions but not from literature. In Arcadia an archaic dialect survived, with striking affinities to the kind of Greek the first settlers had taken to Cyprus, c. 1200, and continued to write well into Classical times in their ancient syllabic script. In the Pindos mountains there were people speaking a language unintelligible to Greeks and eating their meat raw. The Macedonian language was related to Greek.

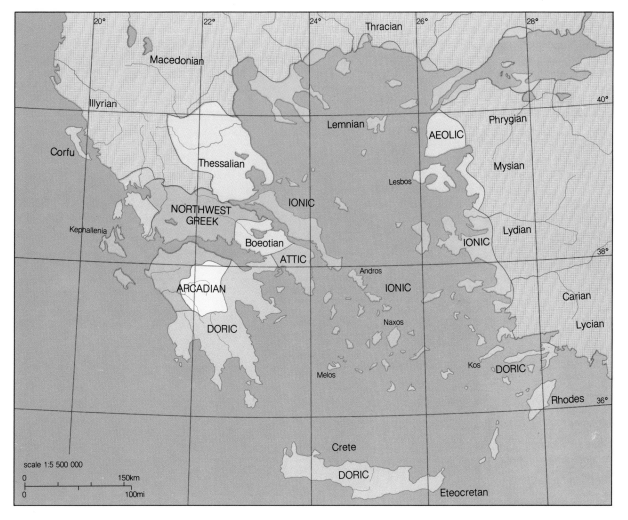

THE STUDY OF ANCIENT GREECE

The study of the Greeks is an inseparable part of European cultural history, and even the archaeology of Greece has a history of its own. It is worthwhile taking a careful look at that long process, and at the different motive and bias of each successive generation, because they have certainly left traces on what we think of today as the available or the most important knowledge of the ancient world.

Greece and Rome

When the Greeks were swallowed up into the Roman empire, their prestige remained immense. The Rome that swallowed them was partly Greek. The literature, the philosophy, all the fine arts, even most of the religious mythology that the Romans valued were Greek. The Greek language had the highest prestige. The Romans were overawed by Greek athletics, by the conveniently remote notion of Greek liberty, even by idyllic notions of Greek peasants and shepherds. The Romans even seem to have believed that Greek personal, physical beauty was greater than theirs. The foundation of our own attitude to the Greeks rests heavily on Roman literature and romantic Roman understanding. Politically, the Romans both despised and admired Greece extravagantly, and in most other ways they idealized the Greeks. Eduard Fraenkel, one of the greatest of all scholars of Roman literature, has observed that the deeper any Roman writer was as a man, the more deeply he was penetrated by what was Greek. That is also true, but the Roman feeling for, and conception of, the Greek world are not embodied only in deep humanity or in great literature.

Already in the Roman period there were nostalgic historians like Plutarch, there were accepted notions of art history, which in writers like Pliny the elder, author of the famous sentence "art at this time ceased to exist," had an immense influence, and there were even archaeologists, of a kind, like the Asian Greek Pausanias, whose *Guide to Greece* is an uneven but a thorough and comprehensive description of the cities and monuments of religion and art that survived in mainland Greece in the 2nd century AD. But down to the late Renaissance, it was through literature, and chiefly Roman literature, that western Europeans understood the Greeks. Pausanias was seldom copied and little read. When by chance he came to light in the 15th century, one Italian scholar remarked to another how this text showed that only through the power of literature could monuments survive.

No one thought of excavating at that time. Archaeology began in Rome, and Greek archaeology began and long continued as an extended version of Roman treasure hunting. The first great collectors of Greek antiquities took their inspiration from Italy. As late as the end of the 18th century Athenian painted pottery, because it was first known in Italy, was thought to be Etruscan. It was in Italy, in the 17th century, that Milton took a notion to visit Delphi, and in the 18th, under the patronage of Cardinal Albani, that Johann Joachim Winckelmann (1717–68) planned to excavate Olympia. It was from Rome, not from London, that the British Society of Dilettanti sent out in 1764 its first Greek expedition, which found the site of Olympia. Giovanni Battista Piranesi's drawings of the ruins of Paestum, made in the year of his death in 1778, and James Stuart and Nicholas Revett's *The Antiquities of Athens* (1762–1816) are extensions of a conventional Roman taste.

Travelers and despoilers

The first serious survey of ancient monuments in Greece after Pausanias of which we have any record was by that intrepid traveler, merchant, diplomat, scholar and eccentric, Cyriaco of Ancona (1391–1455). Already in court circles and in learned monasteries here and there in Greece, there was some interest in identifying the ancient cities named

Below In the 15th century AD Cyriaco of Ancona made a drawing of the 4th-century BC stone dancers from Samothrace shown in the photograph *opposite*. Already the Renaissance imposed its own expectations on what it discovered.

Piranesi's impression in 1778 of one of the famous temples of Paestum, not long after their rediscovery. They stood at one time in shallow water at the edge of the sea. Later, when the sea receded, they were stables for water-buffaloes for the making of mozzarella cheese. Paestum was more undisturbed than most Greek sites until this century.

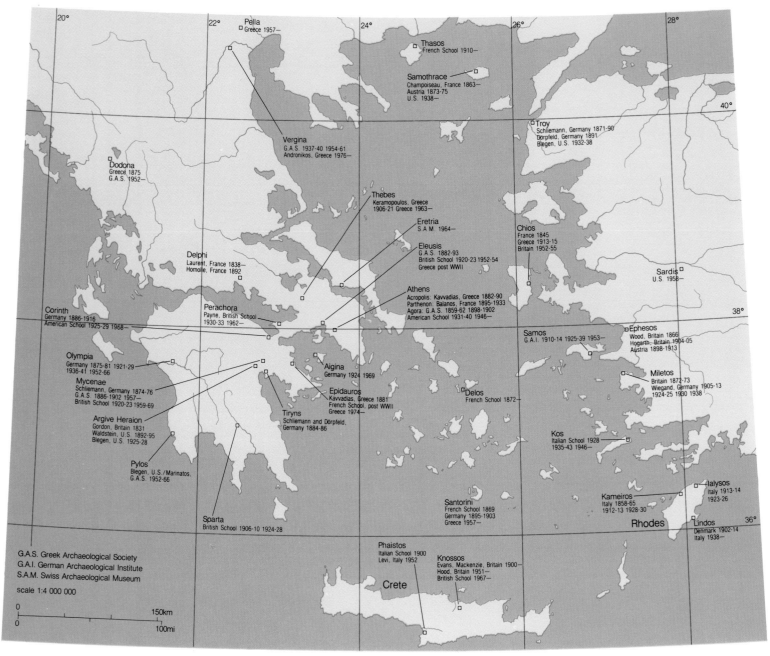

Pella
Greece 1957—

Thasos
French School 1910—

Samothrace
Champoiseau, France 1863—
Austria 1873-75
U.S. 1938—

Vergina
G.A.S. 1937-40 1954-61
Andronikos, Greece 1976—

Troy
Schliemann, Germany 1871-90
Dörpfeld, Germany 1891
Blegen, U.S. 1932-38

Dodona
Greece 1875
G.A.S. 1952—

Thebes
Keramopoulos, Greece
1906-21 Greece 1963—

Eretria
S.A.M. 1964—

Chios
France 1845
Greece 1913-15
Britain 1952-55

Delphi
Laurent, France 1838—
Homolle, France 1892

Eleusis
G.A.S. 1882-93
British School 1920-23 1952-54
Greece post WWII

Sardis
U.S. 1958—

Athens
Acropolis: Kavvadias, Greece 1882-90
Parthenon: Balanos, France 1895-1933
Agora: G.A.S. 1859-62 1898-1902
American School 1931-40 1946—

Corinth
Germany 1886-1916
American School 1925-29 1968—

Perachora
Payne, British School
1930-33 1962—

Samos
G.A.I. 1910-14 1925-39 1953—

Ephesos
Wood, Britain 1866
Hogarth, Britain 1904-05
Austria 1898-1913

Olympia
Germany 1875-81 1921-29
1936-41 1952-66

Aigina
Germany 1924 1969

Miletos
Britain 1872-73
Wiegand, Germany 1905-13
1924-25 1930 1938

Mycenae
Schliemann, Germany 1874-76
G.A.S. 1886-1902 1957—
British School 1920-23 1959-69

Epidauros
Kavvadias, Greece 1881
French School, post WWII
Greece 1974—

Delos
French School 1872—

Argive Heraion
Gordon, Britain 1831
Waldstein, U.S. 1892-95
Blegen, U.S. 1925-28

Tiryns
Schliemann and Dörpfeld,
Germany 1884-86

Kos
Italian School 1928
1935-43 1946—

Pylos
Blegen, U.S./Marinatos,
G.A.S. 1952-66

Ialysos
Italy 1913-14
1923-26

Kameiros
Italy 1858-65
1912-13 1928-30

Sparta
British School 1906-10 1924-28

Santorini
French School 1869
Germany 1895-1903
Greece 1957—

Rhodes

Lindos
Denmark 1902-14
Italy 1938—

G.A.S. Greek Archaeological Society
G.A.I. German Archaeological Institute
S.A.M. Swiss Archaeological Museum

scale 1:4 000 000

0 — 150km
0 — 100mi

Phaistos
Italian School 1900
Levi, Italy 1952

Knossos
Evans, Mackenzie, Britain 1900—
Hood, Britain 1951—
British School 1967—

Crete

Classic excavations

by Pausanias and in the more jejune accounts of Strabo (c. 63 BC–after 21 AD) and Ptolemy (2nd century AD) with modern villages. Few if any names had survived unmangled, and most cities were the merest ruins. Some sanctuaries had become fortresses: part of the temple of Zeus at Olympia had become a castle, the rotunda of Asklepios at Epidauros had been a keep, the Parthenon a church and the rest of the acropolis at Athens an Italian palace. By the time of Cyriaco's journeys most of the reused monuments had again been abandoned and now lay in ruins. The acropolis of Athens was in use, but it had still to face the worst part of its history. Cyriaco drew what he saw, recorded ancient inscriptions, hoarded information and annotated, sometimes lavishly, the manuscripts he owned. But he had no followers.

The first learned travelers and despoilers appeared before the end of the 17th century, from France and from England. The Venetian expedition against the Turks at the end of that century did appalling damage in Athens, and it was still true down to 1700 that the artists and amateurs who recorded Greece saw almost exclusively what they expected to see. Francis Vernon, who died by violence in 1677 and is buried in Isfahan, wrote voluminous notes on his Greek travels which lie still unpublished in the library of the Royal Society in London. He was as much interested in flora and in the fortifications of castles as in antiquity. The first great change occurred in the 1760s, when lucid architectural drawings and exact landscape records taught Europe for the first time to see Greek realities without Italian spectacles. At the same time one ought to admit that a romantic preoccupation with oppressed peasants and a certain picturesque and rococo interest in the Turks did color the attitudes of the travelers. Nor had the Roman influence died out; when Lord Elgin sold the spoils of the Parthenon to the British state, in 1816, the established connoisseurs still argued down their value in comparison with the Roman work for which they felt a more familiar affection.

It may be that today the only remaining effect of those centuries of delusion is that we define Greek originals too sharply against Roman copies, that we neglect those warmer and easier qualities to which both Greek and Roman art aspired from time to time, exaggerating starkness and strength. It takes a lifetime to disentangle the past within one's limits.

Archaeology and modern perceptions of Greece

In 1804 William M. Leake, an English officer with secret orders from his government to intrigue against the French in this way and that, was lent to the Turks to study the defenses of southern Greece. In the course of this task he made the first and still the most sympathetic survey of Greek ruins and sites. The slightly later French scientific expedition to the area did excellent work of the same kind.

During the 19th century, eagerness for the physical details of antiquity increased. Archaeology, however incompetent in its own techniques, began to overwhelm art history with the variety of its examples, and European taste, having battened on the Periklean age, began to adventure further. By the end of the century, the new and immense prestige of prehistoric archaeology had begun to be felt. Heinrich Schliemann

cient societies, a more active criticism of Plato, of the historians, even of the epic heroes and the dramatic poets. Excavation is more precise, more probing, and more concerned with the analysis of information than the recovery of objects. Even art history has settled among minute details of stylistic change and the attribution of complex works; the main lines of the art historian's method were laid down before 1939, and not even the abundance of new material alters them. There has been only a gradual shift of focus, backward in time from the 5th century toward the 8th, as new generations of scholars grow up who are familiar with more and more of the early material, particularly sculpture, which began to appear in the 1890s in Greece itself, and is still appearing. It was only between the two world wars that the first adequate studies of archaic Greek sculpture were published. One should remember also, so far as public taste is concerned, that it was a luxury and an adventure to visit Greece until the 1950s, nor has it always been easy even for scholars to study the vast collections for which the

Stuart and Revett published this temple as the Theseion in *The Antiquities of Athens* (1762–1816), but it was in fact the temple of Hephaistos. It is one of the best-preserved of all Greek temples. Only its roof was wrecked in the 18th century by a Turk in pursuit of the honey of wild bees.

had been digging in the 1860s to 1880s for Homer's Troy and Homer's Mycenae, but Sir Arthur Evans dug at Knossos in 1900 for a world which to the Greeks had been merely fabulous, for a pre-Greek script and a pre-Greek language.

Evans found the evidence he was looking for of an early script within a fortnight, but it was more than 50 years before the language was deciphered as an early form of Greek. In the meantime, Mycenaean and Cretan excavations have spread far beyond the scope of Homeric studies, and although it is hard to understand a history without written records, we know by now enough about the Cretan palace civilization, about the Mycenaeans, and even about much earlier stages of Greek prehistory, to be more careful in our estimates of the admittedly unique arts and graces of the 5th century BC.

There have been other changes in this century. First, the idea of a Classical education as aristocratic has withered in Europe. It is no longer specially usual for a Classical scholar to be a "gentleman" or a "lady"; therefore several silent assumptions of generations of scholars have silently disappeared. There is more anthropological questioning of an-

Greek archaeological service is responsible.

As a result, archaeology has become terribly bewildering. Works of art which, if they had been recovered 100 or 200 years ago, would have had immense influence, and would have modified the idea of ancient Greece when that idea was thought to have unique value, are nowadays neglected. Greek religion and mythology have lost their definition in a welter of comparative studies. History is argued in learned journals, but there has been no single convincing exposition of the whole history of the ancient Greeks since the last century, and there was never anything about the Greeks to touch Mommsen's *History of Rome* (1854–56) or Gibbon's *Decline and Fall of the Roman Empire* (1776–88). Marxist analysis has been more productively applied to late than to early Greek history. Archaeology today is making its greatest intellectual efforts in an area in which no one showed interest until 20 or 30 years ago: the darkness between the end of the Mycenaeans and the first glimmer of archaic Greece.

Some of the results of 20th-century excavation have been the inevitable consequence of the time

and money spent. We know a great deal more about certain types of problem, the centers of great cities and the extent of great fortifications, than our predecessors. Easier travel has brought useful comparative studies of colonial and trading sites, of architecture, town planning and so on. Ancient machinery has its experts and its devotees. On any great site one should remember that archaeology has been forced to deal with some things simply because they were there. A hundred years ago those who excavated were more aristocratic, they dug where they chose and neglected what they scorned. They were often precious and falsely aesthetic in their choice, and no doubt the modern fault is more on the right side. Opportunities once neglected will not recur. There is plenty about Olympia we shall now never know, and there are very few places, if any at all, where the field system of an ancient town, or even the graveyard system, can be found intact. If work now being done at the clearance of every one of the graveyards of Megara Hyblaia in Sicily is ever completed, it will be the first time we have ever had such complete information for any Greek settlement. Yet in the 19th century it would have been simpler to do such a job than it is today, for many sites then intact are now disturbed or hidden.

There is still a prejudice in favor of cities with known names, that are historically famous. This has affected prehistorians in the past as badly as it still affects classicists. It is pleasant to dig in a place mentioned by Homer, and almost everywhere is mentioned by Pausanias. The word "city" may be a misleading description of what was sometimes smaller than a modern village, and we grossly mislead ourselves by using the same word both for the tiny fortified villages of the Peloponnese and for Athens. In other ways, we exaggerate the importance of Athens, largely because it is the modern capital, and many archaeologists and scholars prefer it to the provinces. At least the sites are known of most of even the smaller towns of ancient Attica; the rest of Greece was not so comparatively underpopulated as it is today underexcavated.

The dashing Arthur Evans (*above*) had a fine collection of antiquities, and the passionate Heinrich Schliemann (*right*) dressed his Greek wife in the gold treasure of Troy (*far right*). These forceful personalities contributed greatly to prehistoric archaeology in Greek lands. Their excavations were on a huge scale and much of what they recovered was magnificent in quality.

Opposite The 15-meter-high interior of the treasury of Atreus (14th century BC) at Mycenae, drawn by the Englishman Edward Dodwell during his travels 1801–06. This is perhaps the finest of the great corbeled beehive tombs built at Mycenae from c.1500 BC

The work of Evans in Crete was marked by flair, personal splendor, and the highest professional standard of his times. He worked closely with his Cretan laborers and later controversies suggest he missed little that was in the ground.

Prehistorians, because they have always been forced to depend less on literature, are technically sharper than classicists, and more committed to the proper disciplines of archaeology. In this century they have finally rid themselves of the incubus of Homer and are losing interest in mythology. Only when the results of archaeology began to emerge in some quantity, independent of any suggestion in the text of Homer, did it become possible to see in what way Homer and prehistoric Greece are related. While one was studied by means of the other, confusion prevailed. It is likely that Classical archaeology has still to undergo a similar process, some shrugging off of famous names and associations, a concentration on physical evidence, on what the stones themselves want to tell us. It needs to be more sociological than it has sometimes been.

Some of the things we still do not know after so many centuries will surprise the non-specialist. There is still no complete study of the use of Greek marbles. The ancient sources of bronze, and even of gold, are still largely a matter of conjecture. We have almost no statistical studies of any kind. The physical history of nearly every great sanctuary in Greece, in one or other of its crucial phases, is in doubt. The only near exceptions to that generalization are the Athenian acropolis and perhaps Delphi.

Successive generations of scholars have made different aesthetic mistakes. The Minoan restorations that Sir Arthur Evans commissioned in the 1900s have, to put it politely, an Edwardian air. His draftsman Piet de Jong's reconstruction drawing of the throne room in a Mycenaean palace is like a rejected design for the foyer of a 19th-century railway hotel.

To consider the aesthetic misjudgments in our own time, much of the recent photography of archaic Greek sculpture has made it look indecently pretty. It is only now, when it is almost too late, that Pindar and his values are coming into focus, and at a time when we are telling ourselves to value ancient poems as poetry, comparable with other poetry, translation, at least in English, is frequently weak and berserk, though it is better in French, and in Italian it is often excellent.

PART TWO
THE AGE OF BRONZE

THE PALACE CIVILIZATIONS
OF CRETE AND MYCENAE

By now the accumulation of archaeological evidence year after year has made clear many details of life between 2100 and 1100 BC when Knossos and Mycenae flourished. There were Indo-Europeans in Greece well before 2000 BC. But some of the most obvious questions are still unanswered. Embittered controversy on some subjects, and the spreading thin over others of evidence which is suggestive rather than conclusive, have made events in those 1,000 years even harder to interpret. The time scale which archaeologists have used (see Chronological Table), for lack of precise knowledge and dates, differs slightly for Crete, for the other islands, and for the mainland. But by the end of the period, when Crete had become a great international influence, the time scale of development in all the Greek lands has become unified, and much of Greece begins to have a single history.

In the southern mainland, the first dynasty of the Mycenaeans, the first people we know to have spoken Greek, appeared comparatively late, about 1700 BC, when the palace civilization of Crete already existed and Cretan influence had spread through the islands and into the Levant. The first entrance of the Mycenaeans into modern consciousness of history was spectacular: it comes with the great circle of shaft graves at Mycenae. No palace of that period has been found there, and maybe none existed. Elsewhere in Europe at that time there were no palaces associated with warrior graves. The first lords of Mycenae may have lived, for all we know, in tents or in wooden huts. The city of Mycenae that survives in ruins was built later, and was not fortified until the 13th century BC. At that time rich outlying houses at Mycenae were ruined by fire, and the deep wells were dug there, and at Tiryns, and below the acropolis at Athens. The Mycenaean palaces we know best – Mycenae, Pylos and Tiryns – were built toward the end of the Mycenaean period, not at the beginning.

Crete before 2000 BC

At Knossos there was no fortification and curiously the palace has no fitting graves to go with it. Since arguments from archaeology to history depend heavily on cultural and physical continuities and discontinuities, that is inconvenient; but the recent theory that Knossos itself was a fake, uninhabited city, a giant grave, is certainly untrue. Knossos grew slowly and the palace, unlike the later one at Mycenae, stands on the deep debris of earlier human settlements. The Cretans came originally

Above Late Mycenaean art is economic and sometimes humorous. A pair of griffins feed their young in a bird's nest on this pot from Lefkandi in Euboea.

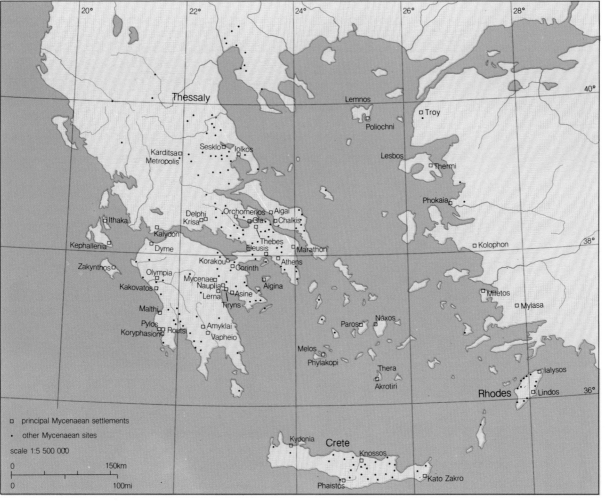

Settlements of the Mycenaean world

The citadel and splendid shaft graves and beehive tombs of Mycenae are matched by the great castle of Tiryns, a few kilometers away. Clay tablets in syllabic script, found at Mycenae and in the palaces of Pylos and Knossos, were deciphered in the 1950s and proved to be Greek. They are all inventories: unlike the tablets of the same period found in the Hittite capital, they tell us nothing about political history. But from archaeological finds we at least get an impression of the spread and variety of Mycenaean culture. Small beehive tombs are found in Kephallenia, to the west; there are huge ones in Thessaly. Mycenaean pottery was exported beyond the confines of this map to near Tarentum in Italy and to the Levant. These far-flung trade connections lapsed with the fall of Mycenaean civilization, to be resumed by the Greeks of the colonizing period. It is a surprise to find Mycenaean pottery and beehive tombs on some sites in western Asia Minor and its offshore islands, well in advance of the Greek migrations of c. 1000 BC. We cannot be sure that the users were Greek.

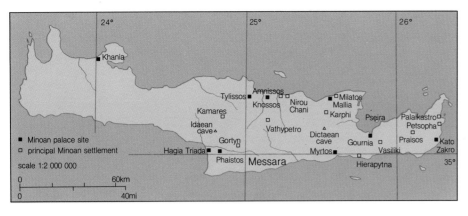

Minoan sites in Crete
The Classical Greeks remembered the labyrinth of Minos at Knossos. Excavations in this century have revealed the sprawling palaces of the second millennium BC of which Knossos is the grandest. After the destruction of Knossos c. 1450 BC, it was occupied by Mycenaean Greeks in the same tradition of grandeur.

from somewhere in the Levant, possibly as refugees from the disturbances in Egypt, possibly from further east, but the 7-meter pile under Knossos demonstrates that the site had been inhabited for some 4,000 years before those Cretans who laid out the palace c. 1900 BC. We know even that they had metal, since an ax made of copper, presumably a gift or an import, was found in one of the houses in a Neolithic level at Knossos.

Soon after 2800 BC the Cretans were already an influence in the Aegean and already at that time they had developed their characteristic tombs, domed like old-fashioned beehives. The style lasted more than 1,000 years, although not one has survived intact in Crete itself. The walls were thick, and the shape recalls mud-brick architecture. They were up to 13 meters across, and the circles with their long forecourts are surely the formal imitation of what had once been the shapes of houses. Up to 2000 BC the Cretans still had no knowledge of

writing, though that existed in the Levant. Egyptian stone vases have been found in Crete in some numbers even at isolated settlements; they were made in the centuries around 3000 BC, but there is no evidence that they entered Crete until much later. Did they really survive in Crete as heirlooms from the beginning, or can they be the loot of the royal and noble graves of the Old Kingdom in Egypt, despoiled about 2300 BC?

The context of the great palaces

The earliest examples of writing in Crete date from 1900 BC. They are hieroglyphic or pictographic. The script, the art of working stone vessels and the engraving of stone seals probably came to Crete from Syria, perhaps from Ras Shamra, on the coast opposite Cyprus. The arts seem to have been carried, in this case as in others, by refugees. The great majority of surviving examples of written language from this whole period – the Minoan Linear A script – are purely administrative records, and only the slightly later Mycenaean Linear B script has been deciphered, but the shape of certain early clay tablets from Knossos suggests that writing began on palm leaves. Among the Mycenaeans after 1450 BC there may well have been a written literature in Greek. In the same way we have statues of musicians of this date and earlier in simplified marble shapes from small Greek islands, but of course we have none of the music or poetry of the central Aegean islands. At the same time as the visual arts emerge in greater quantity in Crete (and in the islands Crete dominated), the artists themselves are intensely conscious of stone and its colors, of shells and of everything to do with the sea. Everywhere in that world, on graves and granaries and ritual vessels, there were decorations of close spirals. In the development of art, what developed was the conscious expression of natural forms such as shells and fishes, but the best design was as tight as William Morris's willow-leaf wallpaper, which in a way it recalls, although he never knew Minoan art.

The great palaces of the heyday of Crete between 2000 and 1400 were at Knossos, Phaistos, Mallia and Khania. The last is still largely unexcavated. There are a number of smaller palaces, some of which have yielded splendid material, but none of them, except perhaps Kato Zakro, can challenge the great centers.

Knossos and Phaistos were destroyed about 1700 BC, Phaistos perhaps more thoroughly. Both palaces were rebuilt and Mallia is built to a smaller plan. Knossos in its most flourishing period was about 160 meters square, the size of a small Oxford or Cambridge college or a small medieval monastery; it owned about the same number of sheep as Bolton Abbey did in 1300 AD. That at least is the excavated Knossos; outlying areas have been discovered in the last few years; to know them thoroughly we should need the wealth of Sir Arthur Evans.

In the mid-16th century BC, at the high noon of the Cretan palace civilization, the nearest of the Cyclades, the volcanic island of Santorini (Thera), exploded. On Santorini devastation was complete; the palace on the island had been abandoned in time, and only a few animals were caught by lava in the empty rooms, but a complete palace was buried and preserved until today as perfectly as at Pompeii.

Above Linear script A in two examples from Hagia Triada; *right* Linear B from Knossos. Many of the signs in Linear A were adapted in Linear B, but Linear A has not yet been decoded.

The explosion must have been awe-inspiring, and there may have been terrible damage as far away as eastern Crete. In Crete the crops suffered severely, there were other earthquakes, and at some time in these or the following years Zakro and Mallia were destroyed and Knossos damaged. Only Knossos survived. Zakro was apparently abandoned before that destruction. But in spite of the thrilling attractions of explaining everything that happened by one impressive explosion, the exact order and connection of events remains doubtful. Starvation, disease and revolution may have played a part, but they are all hard to trace archaeologically.

It used to be vehemently denied but now appears to be certain that there was a Mycenaean occupation of Knossos around 1400 BC, but here again the circumstances are obscure. Between alliance, empire, federation, dynastic marriage and cultural domination, it is not always possible to choose. Conquest becomes evident only when destruction is followed by an imported culture.

The Knossos archive

The important archive discovered at Knossos tells us something of the economy of a Cretan palace. The clay tablets are inscribed in the script called Linear B, which occurs in Crete only at Knossos, although it was also the script of the Mycenaean palaces on the mainland. The still undeciphered Linear A script, of which Linear B may well be an adaptation, occurs all over Crete between c. 1700 and 1450 BC. It looks as if, rather typically of their emergence as a people in Greece, the Mycenaeans learned from Crete more than they offered; the time of their domination, which is that of the Knossos Linear B tablets (toward 1400 BC), was one of straitened circumstances, military preoccupations, the advance of craft and the decline of palace arts. The fresco painters on the palace walls turned their attention to soldiers and to scenes of war, weapons were better made and the fabric of pottery refined, but decoration began to be slapdash. Still, one must not push such impressions too far: there was an equivalent increase in militarism elsewhere in the Near East at that time.

The Knossos Linear B tablets reveal that agriculture underpinned all riches. Sheep were counted in fifties, wool was calculated in multiples of one tenth the number of sheep in a flock, or a quarter the number of rams. The ruler was a king, but in the distribution of grain or land a council of three taken together have an equivalent share to his and an official who ranks next after the king a similar share to theirs. It may be true, though it remains unproved, that this grandee exercised secular powers of kingship, and the king more religious ones. There were several lesser ranks or functions, and a number of specialized trades and services: shepherds, goatherds, huntsmen, woodcutters, masons, shipbuilders, carpenters and so on. Women ground and measured grain, but men baked. The luxuries of life had already called into existence goldsmiths and bath women and boilers of unguents. Slaves could be owned by individuals and they could follow their masters' trades; captive women played an important part in the labor force. Bread, oil and wine were common and the ordinary animals were kept, including the not so ordinary Cretan goat. The suggestion of a sealstone that these tall-horned, patriarchal creatures were even used in pairs to

draw chariots cannot be absolutely dismissed. Mycenaean vegetables remain obscure, but we know of a wide variety of condiments used, including mint, and that Mycenaeans at Knossos ate cheese. Knossos shepherds and goatherds grazed their flocks at a distance from the palace, and special collectors took from each herd its quota of animals and wool. There were very few horses, and not many cattle. Pigs were herded, and fat ones specially listed.

Mycenaean religion

By contrast, considering the amount that has been written more recently on the subject, it is remarkable how little we know for certain about Mycenaean religion. Tomb offerings, masks of gold, and at times pickling in honey, which were the destiny of the rich dead, suggest serious views about life after death. The fertility cults in Cretan caves, in which stalagmites of a phallic appearance were singled out for worship, account for one corner of the divine system. We know of other mountain shrines, difficult to approach, built high up among rocks. Altars, with the formal sculptural representation of horns of consecration, have survived; so have a number of sacred symbols, such as the double ax, which probably belonged to the sky god, and the representations of a pillar cult, of which the most famous example is the lion gate of Mycenae. The lion gate may well have been a griffin gate, but whatever they were before they lost their heads, these heraldic beasts rest their forepaws on twin altars on either side of a single pillar.

The fact that we have lists of gods from the Knossos and Pylos archives, and that these are more or less the conventional names of the Classical Greek gods, hardly advances matters. In the deciphering of this part of the Linear B tablets, and still more in their interpretation, hasty conjectures have had to be abandoned more than once. But it is interesting that there was a dove goddess, that Poseidon was important, and that the Iphigeneia of Greek tragedy, whom mythology relates to Hekate, started her career as a powerful Mycenaean goddess. The gods received offerings and owned possessions. It may possibly be that the phrase "servant of the god" in the Pylos tablets, which are later than those from Knossos, means farmer, or worker in the fields. Much more can be sensed about prehistoric religion from the visual art of the Cretan palaces and of the Mycenaeans, but it has often turned out that this sensation of immediate understanding is not reliable.

Still, something more can be said. There is a series of enormous gold rings with a common repertory of designs, which seem to me to illustrate related mythical scenes and to tell stories that overlap. Some of the same pictures occur in smaller versions on engraved gems. One of the most attractive of these shows a human figure enthroned with an eagle behind him and a line of splendid pantomime beasts advancing on their hind legs carrying liquid offerings. A very lively sky sparkles above with thunderbolts, solar wheel, moon and stars, and some figure-of-eight shields below. One could hardly wish for a clearer illustration of divinely sanctioned kingship. The throne room at Knossos, where a free-standing throne is flanked by griffins on the walls behind it, makes a similar point in heraldic terms

Gold cup (c.1500 BC) from a domed tomb at Vapheio, near the later settlement of Sparta. A wild bull is being trapped with nets and ropes in wild country. Two humans have perished in the enterprise, but the sympathies of the artist are with the bull.

Left The marine richness of this octopus flask from Palaikastro in eastern Crete is very characteristic of Minoan taste both in its delighted observation of wild nature and in its sensuous luxury. *Right* The gold thumb-ring is one of a growing series found in tombs, full of mythology and marvels. They are less formally organized as works of art than the Vapheio cup or the octopus flask, but the figures are stiffer, more heraldic. *Below* This inlaid lapis lazuli and silver games board belonged to a palace. The lapis came from Faizabad in Afghanistan. No one knows what the game was.

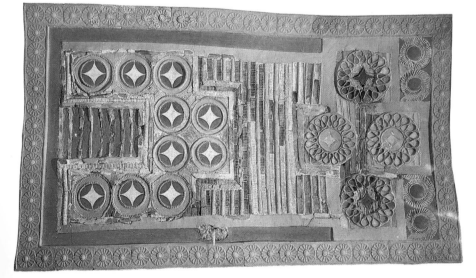

and we know that the tradition of such animal-guarded throne rooms goes back 7,000 years to the oldest known Neolithic town in Europe or Asia, Çatal Hüyük in the Anatolian mountains.

But most of the scenes on these rings show women or goddesses. One of the finest shows an ecstatic dance of female figures on a mountain, several show scenes of worship, while in others the story involves a sacred plant. This plant is discovered on a mountain, or carried on a ship, or revealed by a goddess. One scene seems to involve an eagle and a swarm of bees. Sometimes a small male god like a trophy of arms stands in midair. In one very full example, a lady in divided bell skirts, naked to the waist, surely a goddess, sits under the holy tree on a mountaintop, holding three poppy heads. Three other similar ladies, one tiny, bring offerings of leaves or flowers. The small male god stands in midair and the double ax presides. Another tiny lady is harvesting the tree. They probably derive, however freely, from the monumental paintings of a palace or a sanctuary; it appears from the heaviness and value of the rings and from their recurrence, since new ones are still coming to light, that what they expressed had special importance. The rings are too heavy for use in life; they are found only in the tombs of men.

Mycenaean secular art

If in interpreting arts like these there is much scope for individual intuition, we can also obtain a more precise taste of Cretan palace life from such objects as a games board inlaid with ivory and lapis lazuli.

Above A dagger-blade portraying a lion hunt, of bronze inlaid with silver, from a shaft grave at Mycenae. 1600–1550 BC. *Left* This goddess or priestess is painted ivory. She comes from the palace of Knossos, though figures like her have been found elsewhere. She has a cat on her head and waves snakes in the air. 1600–1550 BC.

There was only one source of lapis in the known world, the mines above Faizabad in Afghanistan; ivory must also have traveled from a distance, usually from North Africa where the African elephant was still at large. Crete was not isolated, it existed in a vast international context, just as Knossos existed in a landscape.

It was surely the secular brilliance of the Cretan palaces that attracted and perhaps civilized the Mycenaeans. The Cretans' spectacular objects of luxury, their many kinds of gems, their fine bronze and elaborate terracotta, their small sculpture, the imaginative paintings on their walls, their gold and silver, glass and lapis lazuli, could match for quality anything in the whole world at that time. Only in bronze work the Chinese, at the other end of the world, remained supreme. Some of the painting was imitative: there is a foreign influence at work in the ship fresco from Akrotiri on Santorini, just as there is later in the battle scene from Mycenaean Pylos. But the flying fish of Phylakopi, the Knossos birds and the Santorini landscape are highly individual masterworks. The intense vision of a Cretan early summer in the Santorini frescoes is something unique in human history.

Right The acropolis of Mycenae seen from the west. The 13th-century BC circuit wall encloses the great circle of shaft graves made some three centuries earlier and excavated by Schliemann in 1876. Further up the hill are the remains of 13th- and 14th-century houses and, in the upper area, the palace halls.

The well-known bull game, which may have had a religious aspect but does seem, from the realism with which it was depicted, to have taken place in real life, was a kind of acrobatics, a somersaulting over the bull's horns. It was performed by lightly dressed, unarmed young men, and on occasion the bull tossed them. Girls played some part, at least in art. We have a representation in gold (the Cretan cups found at Vapheio) of wild bulls being caught in rugged country, with the use of ropes and nets, and on an ivory box we have a somersaulting leap that uses the bull's horns like handlebars in the similar context of a hunt in wild country. If that interpretation is right, then the palace game, or representation of a game, may have more to do with the skills admired in real Cretan country life than it has with the contrived spectacles of the Spanish or Roman arena. It is hard to know whether an art that comes to us without language represents a divine or a human, a princely or a common, even a real or an unreal scene. There certainly exist unreal scenes in Cretan art, like a man wrestling with two lions at once, and scenes only obscurely related to reality, like the imitations of Egyptian pictures. The bull scenes, incidentally, are not confined to Crete; they occur also on the mainland.

Cretan animal art, in terracotta relief or engraved in miniature or painted lifesize, is sharply observed, finely executed and clearly designed. Indeed, it has many of the qualities of what we call the Classical art of 500 years later. Except in the case of heraldic animals, it is a lean man's art, laconic and invigorating, and at its best it is not restricted by conventions. In the context of Crete, I am inclined to treat human as a subdivision of animal art, because there is some similarity of treatment. Representation of the human body has some formal conventions, at least in court art, but the wasp waists, wide shoulders and hair-pin proportions of the young men and the generous modeling of the women are not necessarily far removed from nature, even though they may owe something to traditional representation.

Mycenae

The great city of Mycenae has yielded royal burials of extaordinary grandeur. The earliest graves, of the 17th and 16th centuries BC, were deep shafts in the ground. Later in the Bronze Age the massive architecture of the city, including a circuit wall built in the 13th century, matched the awe-inspiring ambition of the vaulted tombs, among them two known as the treasury of Atreus and the tomb of Klytaimnestra.

The influence and power of the Mycenaeans spread to Crete, to the Asian coast, to Sicily and some way north of Rome. Their possessions were luxurious; but they were a military people, and it is characteristic that the most glorious decorations should appear on an inlaid dagger hilt (*right*) of lapis lazuli, crystal and gold. The lapis had come a very long way, out of central Asia. The dagger, from a shaft grave, dates from the 16th century.

This simple vessel was probably for household use, but it was made in bronze in a tradition of excellent craftsmanship, and found in a chamber tomb at Mycenae. Bronze was the most useful of metals; it was also valuable.

The death mask of thin gold, symbol of kingly immortality (*right*), is the first of those found by Schliemann in the Mycenaean shaft graves and dates from 1550–1500 BC. Schliemann sent a telegram to the king of Greece saying "Today I have looked on the face of Agamemnon." Some of his wilder critics believed the Mycenaean gold was Celtic, or Byzantine, and it is only in living memory that the Mycenaeans were proved to have been among the earliest speakers of the Greek language. Agamemnon, whether or not he really existed, was worshiped at Mycenae from Homeric times onward.

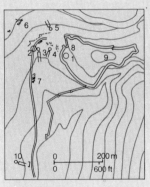

1 grave circle A
2 grave circle B
3 tomb of Klytaimnestra
4 tomb of Aigisthos
5 tomb of the lions
6 house of the wine merchant
7 house of the oil merchant
8 lion gate
9 palace
10 treasury of Atreus

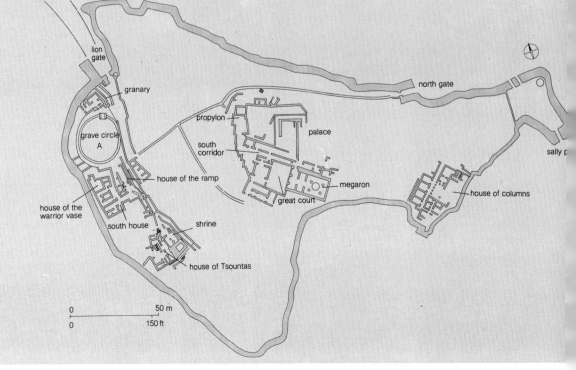

A hexagonal box with gold panels of which one face is shown (*bottom left*), the magnificent gold cup (*below*) which romantic scholarship in love with Homer has labeled "Nestor's cup," and the great entrance to Mycenae (*bottom*) called the lion gate (although the heraldic beasts may well have been griffins and not lions) give some impression of Mycenaean grandeur. Nowhere else have things of such quality and magnificence and in such quantity survived from the late Bronze Age.

Early drawings, like this one published in 1834 by the English traveler Edward Dodwell, and old photographs of Mycenae are best, since the continual activities of archaeologists, of tourists and of the restorers have altered those mighty ruins just as Stonehenge has been altered.

Knossos

Knossos was the greatest of the Cretan palaces and, later, the greatest city in Crete in the Classical period. It was excavated principally by Sir Arthur Evans, and its history is central to that of Bronze Age civilization in Greek lands. It was here that Evans first found what he was looking for, evidence of a written language in the Greek Bronze Age. The clay tablet archives that he discovered have enabled later scholars to build up a rather comprehensive picture of many aspects of Cretan society and economy. But the first impression of Knossos' princely culture remains, that it was very rich, but almost finer than it was rich, and also that it had its sinister aspect.

The site of Knossos itself continues to be excavated. Indeed it has been the focus of such concentrated work over generations that it is hard today for an amateur to control all the evidence and all the arguments that have accumulated. The palace was laid out about 1900 BC on a low mound comprising the debris of thousands of years of habitation. Knossos was more than once ruined, and in its last flourishing period toward 1400 BC it was under Mycenaean control. But even after the collapse of palace civilization, there was another Knossos, a town of about a square kilometer, that grew up just to the north of the ruins. Knossos in Classical Greek legends was the palace of King Minos, a king far greater than Agamemnon of Argos.

The site of the palace of Knossos still conveys the brilliance of wealth and at the same time great solidity. This view (*below*) is from the south wing, with Iuktas, where a peak sanctuary served the palace, in the background.

The curiously Edwardian or Victorian atmosphere of certain details is partly a matter of chance, a not uncommon freak of human nature, but partly perhaps an imprint of Sir Arthur Evans and his restorers.

The stone bull's horns, or "horns of consecration" (left center), are one of the commonest Minoan religious symbols.

This fragmentary but fine fresco (*above*) from the east wing shows what must surely be professional acrobats, though whether ritual or entertainment predominated in this dangerous sport it is difficult to say. It is worth noticing that the bull is a splendid animal, not unlike an old English longhorn. Much of the subject matter of Minoan palace frescoes is athletic or in the open air: they were more often decorative than religious. This one dates from 1600–1400 BC.

This early cup, made around 1800 BC, is a characteristic Minoan piece, both in its shape and in its decoration. The great beauty and high physical quality of the pottery of princely Crete in the Bronze Age are among the most remarkable signs of a consistently high level of material culture.

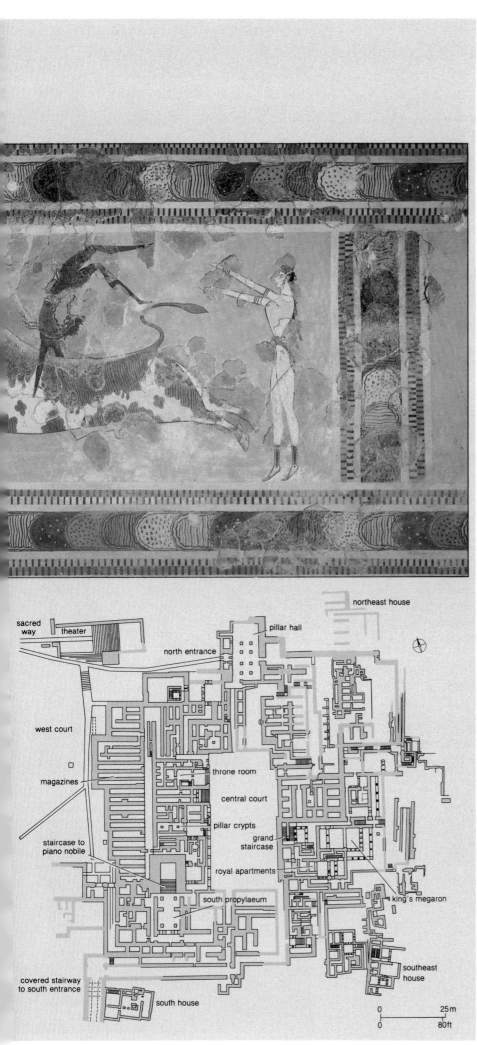

Late Mycenaean civilization

As the Bronze Age drew to a close, the surviving palaces of the Mycenaeans fulfilled more and more of the role of an exchange place and storehouse of goods and services, the center of a tottering community. Although we have some glimpses of social organization at Knossos, and a picture of something much more ramshackle in the last days of Pylos, we are unable to describe the decline accurately enough for diagnosis. Early in the 14th century, Knossos burned in Crete, and Thebes in mainland Greece; neither of these palaces was rebuilt. At the end of the 13th century several great fortresses were attacked. In the 12th century Mycenae was destroyed, Tiryns and Pylos perished by fire, and many smaller centers were abandoned. The palaces were dark hives lit by oil, there was plenty of wood in their construction, and the cores of walls were rubble; they were vulnerable to fire and earthquake. In the case of Pylos the archive has survived, baked hard in the final fire; it records an emergency distribution of rations to divided sections of the coastal defense force.

The Mycenaeans had attained to a life of some intellectual sophistication and great luxury. The massive and elegant architecture of their tombs makes these the most memorable of all Greek prehistoric monuments, and the formidable size and weight of their fortifying walls are disturbing reminders of what their power must have been like. Later generations attributed the building of Mycenaean walls to gods or demigods. In the Argolid alone there were at least ten stone settlements, seven in Attica, three in Boeotia. Their trade extended beyond Sicily and Lipari to Spain. Art and craft were more or less unified, and the whole Greek world had begun to have a single history, but the pottery stored in such profusion at Pylos, for example, was an inferior, provincial version of what was in use at Mycenae itself: such a unification of the world implies a metropolis. The bearded barbarians with the gold death masks and the interest in horses had founded a powerful people.

Spiritually, what bridges the age of the early palaces and their glitter to the world centuries later, yet more remote, in which epic poetry germinated, is a certain hard Mycenaean gaiety which is splendid rather than graceful. The stony riches of their palace decorations, the pillars of their graves and the elaborate styling of their body armor give some sense of a coherent taste, the projection of a society that can be understood. What brings early Mycenaean society to life for us are the inlaid daggers, the silhouetted battles and lion hunts, the leopards and wild geese. Their lapis and their ostrich eggs and no doubt all their best finery came to them through Crete, or more precisely through Tiryns (where, incidentally, a vast stone construction exists, almost unexcavated, underneath the Mycenaean palace). But the impersonal, almost inhuman presentation of so many scenes of conflict and bloody violence, which at the same time is continually almost human, continually fascinated by grace and by whatever is vulnerable, does foretell the future.

If the contents of the shaft graves could be called Homeric, the surviving stone marking one of those graves, carved with the earliest representation of horses in Aegean art, could be called Hesiodic.

Santorini

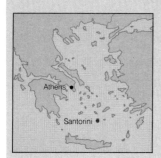

Santorini is the ancient Thera, a picturesque volcanic island not very far from Crete. The volcano exploded with great violence during the Bronze Age, preserving a palace in lava as wonderfully as Pompeii and Herculaneum were preserved by the explosion of Vesuvius. Excavation of the buildings under the lava, at Akrotiri in the south of the island, was begun in 1967, erosion by rainwater having revealed painted plaster.

The Classical city of Thera lies to the east, on a rocky promontory. It was occupied before the 9th century, and there are 7th- and 6th-century remains. But most of the ruins are from the time of the Ptolemies and later.

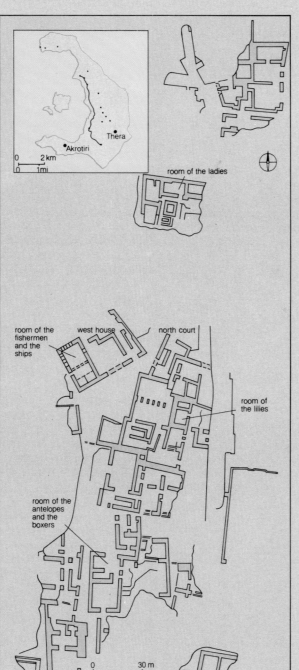

Above This mourning woman is an unsophisticated archaic figure of painted terracotta. She comes from Thera, but she could have come from anywhere in the Greek world. She is tearing her hair and scratching her cheek, the gestures of mourning that occur in a ritualized form on the geometric pottery of Athens. There is something touching in the contrast between the rather warm humanity of the big, incompetently contrived eyes and awkward arms, and the formal sobriety of the robe and hair and belt. The beauty of this little statue is perhaps a happy accident.

Left The Bronze Age fresco of fishermen from Akrotiri has the clarity of line and something of the dash and brilliance of the best Cretan palace work. The low life subject is particularly pleasing.

Seashells, flying fish, the octopus, fish of every kind, and seaweed, all attracted the attention of Cretan artists. The Cretans in the Bronze Age seem to have been fascinated by the sea, but this is still a rare subject. Can the fishermen be bringing the tribute of the sea to a god or to the palace?

Above The antelope fresco gives a far clearer and more powerful idea of what life was to a prince or an artist in Bronze Age Santorini than the excavated site can possibly do. The vigor of the animal and botanical drawing in the Santorini frescoes is striking; and the range of subjects, as well as that of color sense, is at least equally remarkable. Never before can such perfect works of art have been revealed so suddenly in such a perfectly beautiful island. The frescoes are now in Athens in the National Archaeological Museum.

Left The excavations under way at Akrotiri, where the 16th-century Minoan frescoes were discovered. Streets and houses, one of three stories, and rooms containing large storage jars have been uncovered.

Top The modern town of Thera is built on the western coast, on the lip of the volcano crater. The cliffs rise to 300 meters.
Over half the houses on this coast were destroyed in an earthquake in 1956.

The horses that decorate the grave-marker at Mycenae are rustic, clod-hopping creatures, and whoever carved them seems to have been more used to carving cattle. Yet when we first hear the Mycenaeans speak, in the Linear B tablets, their feelings about horse-drawn chariots turn out, as might be expected, to be closer to their feelings about leopards and about daggers than to the rusticity of that tomb carving. If there were what we should call peasants, preoccupied only with the struggle with season, beast and soil, in the Mycenaean world, they are inevitably silent.

Their chariots were light, with bent wooden frames and shallow bodies, and drawn by two horses, though in the 13th century the Mycenaeans figured chariots on their pottery, some of which were heavy enough to hold three or four riders. In a palace fresco at Tiryns two women travel in a crimson chariot picked out in white, with yellow wheels, blue tires and crimson reins. The same crimson leather is recorded in the Pylos tablets, one of which shows it apparently studded with metal. Chariots were built at Pylos in workshops that served a wide area; at Knossos one at least was recorded "from Phaistos, fully fitted, wooden pole, crimson paint, harness, leather and horn." Chariot harness was by modern standards terribly inefficient and at the same time cruel. The horses took the full weight on their throats, the bridle was a sort of noose with a nose band, and the only metal bit ever found (at Mycenae) has spikes inside its cheek pieces. The Mycenaean chariot is in some ways analogous to the most elegant of penny-farthing bicycles.

Although it was not dominant, Mycenaean trade and influence penetrated much of western Europe and the Levant. Mycenaean pottery, usually small vessels that must have held scent, has been recovered from Sicily, south Italy and Spain, and from many sites in Asia Minor. It is hard to know how that world system collapsed, but it seems likely that political changes in the Middle East determined other power changes, that there were raids, or a great raid, from the north, and that there was internal unrest in Greece. Nowhere can it be shown that there was anything so simple as mere dynastic

Pylos

The Mycenaean palace of Pylos lies in almost the furthest southwestern corner of mainland Greece, above a wonderful natural harbor and in rich, hilly country. One of the last outposts of the Mycenaeans, it survived the fall of Mycenae. The palace was luxurious, but not huge.

The palace has yielded Linear B tablets, frescoes and quantities of pottery. The original of which this fine fresco at Pylos was a variation was probably North African, but in its context in the last days of the palace it must have seemed to show a battle of Mycenaeans against barbarians.

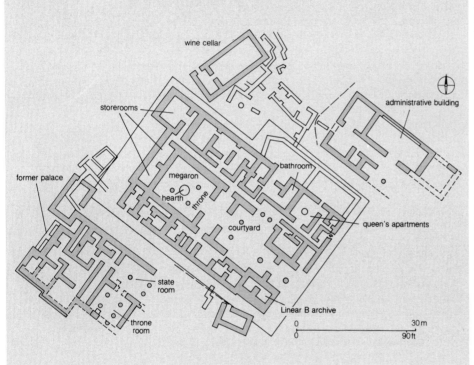

Opposite above This stone gallery at Tiryns (1350–1250 BC) hints at the force and the weight of Mycenaean architecture. Its effect is as impressive as it is gloomy. But the 16th-century stone relief on a shaft-grave marker from Mycenae (*left*), severely military as it is, has a strange, rhythmic beauty. It is either primitive art of extremely high quality or a sophisticated art transferred to the tougher medium of stone.

Far left This mysterious and rich piece of 13th-century carved ivory from Mycenae can be related to very ancient figures of mother goddesses, but we have little real idea of what it meant in its palace setting, except that it was religious.

change or the mere pushing out of one people by another.

It would be mistaken to underestimate the luxurious grandeur of even a small provincial palace like Pylos in its last days around 1250 BC or soon after. The frescoes and the objects of fine stone, and the wonderful situation of the palace, which seems not untypically to have been chosen on aesthetic grounds, speak of a society which has not surrendered. It is no longer the time of swallows and the best workmanship in the world, but the tribute of the villages is still coming in; the palace bath is not as fine as the finest Knossos bath, but still fine; even at the end ivory is still being inlaid into wood, and we hear of lions' heads of ivory, and of a ewer belonging to the queen which was designed like a bull's head decorated with seashells, although that may have been an heirloom.

Mycenaean religious art

Mycenaean religious art was at a much higher level of luxury and of sophistication. One ivory piece

from Mycenae in particular, a miniature carving of two women and a child, has the unusual quality of drawing one into a world of its own. It is not obviously beautiful but admirably designed or contrived, and so elaborate that its restraint is also astonishing. The sensuous curves, the balance of the small masses, the tranquillity and the casual motion, recall rather Buddhist sculpture than any other, and it may be relevant that the earliest Buddhist sculptors were ivory-carvers working in stone. The nostalgic strangeness of this little group owes something to precision and clarity in the peculiar details of dress, which seem to be Cretan and old-fashioned. Indeed, the clothing of one generation of royal women in Crete seems to have served for centuries as the dress of goddesses, in the same way as 6th-century men's dress survived in the conventions of 5th-century Athenian tragedy. The exact date of this ivory is unknown, since it was treasured in a palace store down to the last moment of Mycenae. A part of its attraction is the contrast of high art finely finished with some degree of formality, in the huge behinds of the goddesses, with the naivety shown in the child's feet and its proportions. We have no idea at all what this statue means.

The common religious statues of the Mycenaeans were made of pottery, small, simplified and very lightly painted. They may as probably be figures of worshipers as of goddesses, indeed more probably. The larger pottery figures used to be very rare, but they have now been found in good condition and in some numbers at Mycenae, Keos, Melos and elsewhere. A lady in a flat hat and with naked breasts (a similar figure in ivory, now at Boston, has gold nipples which are possibly modern, like the gold loincloth of her male companion piece at Oxford) waves a couple of snakes at heaven or at the worshipers. The painting on the pottery figure is fine and impressive, but not more so than that of the older-fashioned mother goddesses, who persisted in one form or another down to the last days of the Mycenaeans.

A great deal was made of mother goddesses in a bold and brilliant discussion, *The Prehistoric Aegean*, by the Marxist scholar George Thomson. His pioneering study has not been accepted as a whole, but some pieces of it have been digested, often without acknowledgment, by later writers. The sweep of his work, which was an attempt to apply anthropology and a wide range of other disciplines to what we know of Greek prehistory, is hard to deal with; it has therefore been neglected. He identifies his Minoan mother goddess with Demeter, and if she had a name that is as good an equivalent as any. Since he wrote before the deciphering of Linear B, he could not have known that Demeter's name was not used by the Mycenaeans, but that does not essentially weaken his position. The later pantheon did undoubtedly develop out of the earlier. What is not so certain is that the early society was matriarchal and matrilinear. The anthropological model that George Thomson was using is not now widely accepted by anthropologists. Whether or not his theory that the Mycenaeans came from the direction of central Asia is correct, analogies exist there for the dominant role of women, not only among the gods but in human society, that would confirm it.

MYCENAEAN SURVIVALS

The flourishing Bronze Age society of the 1,000 years from 2100 BC, to use rough dates, has left a disturbing contrast of bright illuminated points and awkward areas of darkness. Now, for some 300 years, the darkness becomes rather uniform. But it is a darkness of our knowledge, not necessarily of life. Agriculture did not cease, herds continued to graze, the dead were buried; the levels of luxury sank lower, but we know little of the levels of social organization, and nothing of those of happiness. We shall see in Part Three that a case has been argued for a dramatic and sudden increase in population at the very end of this period, in the late 8th century BC. The argument depends on the fact that we have not found what no one until very recently was interested in finding, that is, burials of the early dark age; but negative arguments of this kind are not absolutely compelling, even when they rest on comparisons of successive cemeteries in the same place. We know little of the populations of most of Greece after the fall of the Mycenaeans.

Population movements
About 1190 BC the Egyptians recorded that "the northerners were disturbed in their isles." New Mycenaean colonists arrived at this time in Achaea in the north Peloponnese, and on the Ionian island of Kephallenia, which had been for some reason outside their sphere, but where they now settled peacefully, side by side with the old Kephallenians. Handmade native pottery and Mycenaean pottery continued together there for some time. In Cyprus, particularly at the old capital Enkomi, there had already been colonizers, probably invaders, from the Argolid. But the rebuilding of Enkomi in a fine ashlar style was followed by another destruction, depopulation and a partial desertion of the site. At the same time the Mycenaeans who had nested much further east at Tarsus, in Cilicia on the Anatolian coast, died out. Other Mycenaeans, or perhaps it was the Mycenaeans of Enkomi, seem to have melted away among the Philistines, and ended enrolled into the tribe of Dan, as Jews.

Perhaps it is reasonable to ask where, if at all, the Mycenaeans did survive. If anywhere, they do seem to have survived at Iolkos near modern Volos in Thessaly. In Thessaly, even the old domed tombs continued to be built. To pin this survival to cavalry country, or to rich, well-watered fields, or to a social system loosely based on landownership that prevailed in Thessaly 400 years later, is simply to speculate. The survival of other Myceaeans in what are more like refuge sites, for example at Grotta on the island of Naxos, is easier to understand. But it is surely on Naxos that we must search for the mysterious trickle of worshipers who seem quite possibly to have kept open a Mycenaean religious center on nearby Delos down to the 8th century. Mycenaean life may well have survived longer in the islands than it did on the mainland, though archaeological evidence of a violent catastrophe does exist in a chain of eastern islands. The fall of Miletos, after one of those singular late Mycenaean flowering seasons we have noticed elsewhere, seems to mark the end of that story.

Miletos revived, or rather it was reoccupied by survivors, in cultural synchrony with Athens, with the same painted pottery, which is a poorer, simpler derivative of Mycenaean, and a fumbled beginning of the earliest geometric style of Greek decoration. The style of painted vessels found at Miletos indicates a reoccupation from Attica in the first half of the 11th century BC. It is not fanciful to say that the movements of peoples in the Aegean at this time were like the disturbed movement of waves, and must remain obscure to us, if only because we never can grasp quite all the factors. When Chaka, the 19th-century Zulu king, disturbed all southern Africa, the result was a series of movements and migrations of tribes and lesser units in a very far-reaching and complicated pattern. There have been similar disturbances in central Asia, at the fall of the Roman empire in the west, and all over Europe. In the case of dark age Greece the physical area is much more limited, and the language of the Mycenaeans, which is Greek, remained the same: the language had even extended its territory when the dark age came to an end.

This is the period when the mass of legends, superstitions and rationalizations that we know of as Greek mythology took form. A very few of these have genuine Mycenaean touches: the Minotaur, the labyrinth, the name of Hyakinthos, some part of the cult of Iphigeneia, perhaps the connection of honey with immortality. But the supposed historic legends, the lists of mythical kings and wars and invasions are mostly too late and too confused to be useful as historical evidence. It is better to ask what gave rise to them as stories than to peer about for historical realities that might correspond to them. That is true also of accounts of the early kings of Sparta and the mythical division of the Peloponnese as it is of the mythology of the Trojan wars. Greek mythology never ceased to be alive, or to alter. It is like a bucket of worms. There is no pure, early stage of the stories to which we have access. For us the darkest aspect of the Greek dark age is that it was illiterate. A story retold was a new story, so that consciousness of the past became an amazing jumble.

Kea, Delos, Cretan caves
The survivals of the Mycenaeans sometimes took strange forms. On the island of Kea, for example, just south of Attica, a small Mycenaean palace occupied most of a little headland. In one of the ruined rooms, of no great size or dignity, there were a number of religious statues, inexpressive figures 60 centimeters or more high. They were statues of goddesses or priestesses, a version of the usual lady with the snakes; they were the furniture of a late Mycenaean palace shrine. The palace perished, and

The linear late art of the Mycenaeans spread with them to Cyprus. It delighted in almost freakishly humorous drawings of animal life, combined in Cyprus with splendid blocks of color.

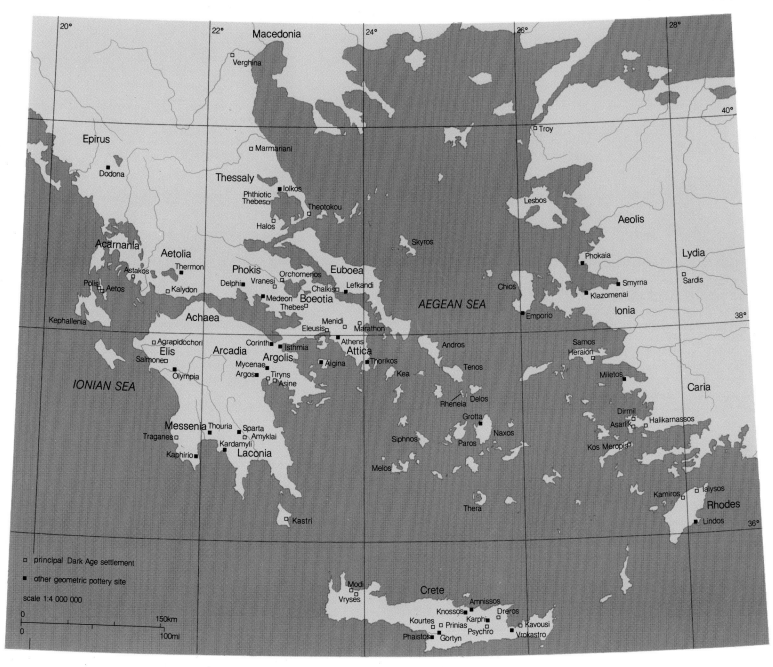

Dark age sites around the Aegean
Classical Greek legend concentrated on the Mycenaean period. The dark age that followed was illiterate and had hardly any known history before modern archaeologists began to analyze its tomb remains and votive offerings. Geometric pottery can now be classified by regions and dated. Nearly all Greeks made it except those of Lesbos and Aeolis, though the non-Greek Carians did so too. The years 1025–950 BC were a time of poverty and isolation, though migrations into western Asia Minor extended the Greek world to regions that remained Greek until 1923. From the 9th century on, renewed contact with the Levant, pioneered by Euboeans, brought gold jewelry to Lefkandi in Euboea and to Attica. Phoenician traders put in at Crete and Rhodes. But in Laconia and western Greece, still isolated and probably sparsely populated, the finds remain very scanty until c. 770 BC.

the rooms filled up with rubble. In the 9th century BC, certainly not earlier, just the decapitated head of one of the statues came to light, and someone set it up in a circle of stones on the rubble that then covered the floor. No attempt was made to excavate in the loose stones to find the other statues or the rest of this one. This head went on being worshiped until the 5th century BC when an inscription on an offering gives us the name of the goddess. She was apparently being worshiped as Dionysos, the beardless god. The sex change remains unexplained, though there is probably some connection with a nearby waterspring, Dionysos being often found among nymphs.

At Delos, on a late Classical wall, we have a number of graffiti of ships. One of them is almost exactly like the Mycenaean ship on a gold ring from Mochlos, where a sacred plant is being carried overseas by a priestess or goddess. On the wall at Delos, a tall lady stands on the ship, shedding light or influence with her right hand. She is Brizo, a birth goddess, worshiped in Crete as Britomartis. Brizo was an alternative name of Leto, the mother of Artemis and Apollo. We know that Brizo liked

offerings in the shape of ships. Her skirt in the graffito is surely the ancient Cretan skirt. How the construction of her ship was transmitted is a mystery. On the same wall there are two graffiti of Egyptian papyrus boats.

The case of this graffito is so paradoxical that we might prefer to ignore it, if it were not for the sacred deposit buried in the 8th century behind what became the temple of Artemis on Delos. The deposit is of very mixed material of various dates, and the pottery and small finds do not completely bridge the gap from the Bronze Age, unless the building from which they came, which might be a Mycenaean temple, had survived continuously in some sort of use until it was replaced. The palm tree of Delian cult does suggest a link with Mycenaean pillar worship, and the wolverine, the disguise of Leto, does suggest the prehistoric wolf cults of Lykosoura and elsewhere in the Peloponnese: there was some sort of a primitive stratum in common. But that is in itself no argument for continuity. The sacred deposit includes some Orientalizing ivories, perhaps from Cyprus, a curious gold plaque of a sphinx-like creature which is apparently Hittite, a

bronze double ax, fragments of pottery, some possibly (in my view probably) sub-Mycenaean terracottas, and a 13th-century bronze statue of a naked god with a round shield and a crooked weapon. Figures of this last kind seem to have a Hittite origin; they turn up not only at shrines in Asia and Greece, but as far afield as Schernen in East Prussia. They continue in a long series, and adapted into Greek myths they furnish the early statues of Zeus and I think also Apollo. I am personally inclined to credit the continuous use of the temple on Delos, but the argument is not complete.

The places where continuity of worship is most often claimed are cave sanctuaries, particularly in Crete. It is much easier to make such a claim where there is no need to demonstrate the continuous inhabitation of one place or maintenance of one building; and in fact the archaeological evidence usually turns out to be thinly spread across centuries, nor is it usual for the things recovered from caves to come out of stratified excavations. Around any object without a detailed archaeological context many doubts must hang. One exceptional site is the so-called ''Dictaean cave'' at Psychro on the high plain of Lassithi in Crete. Although it is probably wrongly named, that is, it is not the famous cave where it was believed that the child Zeus was reared, it was surely a Zeus cave of some sort. Its only inscription is in the Cretan Linear A script, on an offering table given apparently to the Great Mother. Its two main periods of activity are Bronze Age and 8th–7th centuries BC, which would fit the chronology of the Idaean cave (not the Kamares cave, also near Mount Ida) as well. From the 6th century onward it was neglected, and that too is not uncommon for archaic religious sites in Crete. There is no doubt about its being used in the post-Minoan period. The cult was of a birth goddess and of a child, with warrior offerings such as are found in other Cretan caves.

Artifacts and visual arts

When the palaces disappeared, there was certainly a discontinuity in visual narrative art, although that does not necessarily imply a discontinuation of older oral narratives. In an illiterate age, the question of inherited and transformed elements in stories inevitably remains obscure to us. But it is at

This small bronze figure is a dedication from the Dictaean Cave, one of a number of high mountain caves in Crete where the birth of Zeus was celebrated and supplication made for human childbirth.

Right The head of a Bronze Age statue from Kea. Found set up for worship among the ruins of the palace, on top of the rubble that covered other religious figures, she was worshiped as Dionysos, perhaps in association with the nymphs of a nearby spring.

Left The goddess on the golden ring is undoubtedly Minoan. There are a number of versions of this scene, one of which (*below*) seems to lie behind a late Classical graffito from a plastered wall in Delos covered with scratchings of ships, including papyrus boats from the Nile. The goddess still wears Cretan dress.

Right A Cretan terracotta of a goddess seated sidesaddle on a horse, now in the Herakleion Museum.

least suggestive that so much of the beginnings of narrative art, when it starts up again in the period of the geometric pottery style (about 1050 to about 700 BC), seems to adapt a new repertory of images from the Levant. Whenever an image is adapted, whether it be old or foreign, there must always be some degree of interpretation and shift of meaning, and the more complex the image, the wilder the adaptation, even to the point of grossness and contradiction. One of the most startling of the images of this period, in terracotta, appears to be a domed Mycenaean tomb with a divine figure revealed inside, being discovered from above by shepherds with their dog. That is not a certain, but must remain a persuasive, interpretation; there is no convincing alternative.

The emergence, or rather reemergence, of figure painting took a long time. By the early 9th century, sphinxes and lions glared, and wild-haired and shaggily dressed hunters pursued animals with spears across the shoulders of an early geometric pot. The similarity of figures at this time to earlier, Mycenaean figures is sometimes bizarre and perhaps fortuitous. A series of couples of men fighting with long daggers or short swords, arms crossed and holding one another by the hair, curiously recalls the two divine or princely boy boxers, if that is what they are, painted in Santorini 700 years earlier; but the Santorini fresco has been very much restored, and the problem of transmission of the image has no obvious solution. In what medium was it transmitted? The repertory of horse, bird and man was largely transmitted from the late Bronze Age to the 8th century in the conservative tradition of funerary art, and within that convention the changes were slower and more infrequent than one might expect.

Early physical objects undoubtedly survived; Minoan engraved gems and heirlooms were treasured as late as the 6th century BC, and early figurines were discovered and reburied, for example at Delphi from the area of the temple of Apollo and the altar of the Chians. On the island of Skyros, early Mycenaean gold disks have been found in early geometric graves, and even a Mycenaean jar in a grave of similar date at Athens. The sacred olive of the goddess Athene itself, on the acropolis of Athens, would not have had to be the oldest of recorded olive trees in order to date back to Mycenaean times. Ancient patterns lingered on textiles. The necklace of green beads, which was supposed to have belonged to legendary heroines and was kept at Delphi, was certainly to judge from its description Mycenaean. As for the evidence of later worship in Mycenaean tombs, it is overwhelming.

At one site, the sanctuary of Hera on the plain of Argos, groups of late offerings have been found in 15 out of 50 Mycenaean chamber tombs: was it thought that they contained the 50 daughters of Danaos, or the husbands they murdered, the 50 sons of Aigyptos? There was worship at the domed tomb of Klytaimnestra at Mycenae in the 8th century, and a full religious cult at a tomb at Menidi in Attica. At Phaistos, at Troy and at Mycenae the Greeks of the dark age built on old ruins. These phenomena of rediscovery and reuse illuminate the chasm that had to be crossed between the Mycenaean and later societies.

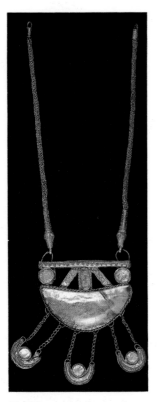

The fineness of Cretan jewelry does not entail the loss of sharpness. It retains to a remarkable degree the purity of its materials. This piece is in the Museum of Herakleion.

Continuity and discontinuity

The signs of that chasm include the disturbance of human settlements, the corruption not only of the decorative patterns but also of the shapes of pottery, followed by the transition to a new style with a brilliant development of its own, and other evidences of a new way of life. The pottery sequence developed extremely slowly: the development of geometric pottery took 400 years, and its emergence as a style perhaps the first 200 of those. This ought to be no surprise. Handmade as opposed to wheelmade pottery is rare in the Mycenaean period in Greece, but it does occur, and at the fall of the Mycenaeans it reemerges for a while. The phases of material culture overlap, they are not absolute. Only in a metropolis or a center of courtly patronage is the development of fashion swift, and the end of the rejected pattern absolute; but with the end of the Bronze Age courtly conditions had ceased to exist in Greece.

The one absolutely clear material change is supposed to have been the adoption of iron for swords, knives and plowshares. In the shape of the earliest Greek iron knives there is a suggestion of Cypriot influence, but the daggers of the last Mycenaeans and their successors have no parallel in Cyprus or the Levant. It is clear that by the time iron inlay had come to decorate bronze, when parts of iron completed parts of bronze, and when iron was used to repair bronze, the change was complete. But no such examples can be found in Greece until the 10th or 9th century, and inlay never. In fact, the detail of what occurred is complicated. It is certain that in most of the earliest geometric period, that is from about 1050 to 900 BC, in most places iron was in common use for nearly everything. At that time Attica seems to have set the pace of technology in metalwork as it did in pottery. A gradual reaction then took place in favor of bronze.

The disturbance of settlement patterns is evidence enough for the reality of that period. At the most recent count, which some experience of sites suggests is rather unreliable, but not utterly so, about 320 13th-century settlements were known, about 130 still occupied in the 12th century and about 40 in the 11th. Beyond these unreliable statistics, and the undoubted comparative poverty of at least the 11th century, all is speculation. In conditions of depopulation, it is true that skills are lost and horizons shrink. But if that did happen, then it seems a short time, a mere matter of two generations, before the scattered and poor communities recovered a degree of physical confidence. By the 10th century their painted decoration is splendid, the finest at that time in the Mediterranean and probably in the world. Even their imported luxuries and their gold earrings are respectable in the 9th. By 800 BC a necklace of gold appears in Crete with serpents' heads and a lunar shape of rock crystal, decorated with crystal and amber, brilliant and fine enough for a Mycenaean though not perhaps for a Minoan princess. Throughout this period Crete is rich, and more influential than is usually realized.

In Crete, the skills that survived were directly related to what had existed, precisely in Crete, long before. At 12th-century Karphi and Kavousi there were still builders working in stone, in a recognizably Minoan tradition. The rebuilders at

Left There is something strange about these two boy boxers from Santorini (c.1550 BC). If the restoration is correct their position is too stylized for any ordinary game. What is even more curious, the same problems recur over a series of silhouette figures from the dark age. Sometimes the figures grasp each other by the hair with one hand and use daggers with the other (*above*). The relationship of the series to the Santorini boxers is utterly mysterious.

Phaistos and the builders of Gortyn in the 12th century worked in the same tradition. At Karphi the streets were paved and the houses may well have had two stories. At Vrokastro, probably a little later, standards had fallen, but the tradition was the same. Such a craft can survive a long time: at Iolkos on the mainland, one of the few settlements where any comparable survival of skills has been recognized, a mason's mark from the Linear B script was still in use in the 9th century BC. Shipbuilding must also have survived; there was even some mining of silver. These survivals do not mean that the Greeks in the 11th century were not few and poor. The small treasures they valued, and carried to the grave, confirm that they were so.

Professor Snodgrass has offered (in *Archaeology and the Rise of the Greek State*, 1977) the important suggestion that the earlier, the essential Greece was a peasant community living from agriculture, and that in its burial customs, its pottery and its habit of life it reasserted its existence in the dark age. The Mycenaeans with their family tombs, their huge constructions, their big herds of animals and their pomp, he sees as aliens who vanished. To some degree this must be right: but 500 years may well have rooted the Mycenaeans deeply into Greece, just as 800 years turned the Norman invaders of the 11th century AD into the British peerage under Queen Victoria. The argument for an essential underlying Greece based on the evidence from individual burials is tempting but unconvincing, because the pattern of burial customs is confused enough to throw darkness on any significance one tries to give it. What emerges, after all, at the end of the dark age is startling, even spectacular, and quite different from anything the Mycenaeans would lead one to expect. We are confronted in the 8th century not only with economic, social and technical recovery, but with an achievement as tall as Olympos crowned with all its gods: the poems of Homer.

Mother Goddesses

The dominance of war and of male athletics in most people's notion of Greek civilization is partly a mistake projected backwards from our own world. From remote prehistory the Greeks had always shown a particular interest in a goddess who was a wife and a mother. Even Homer sees the *Iliad* and the *Odyssey* to some degree through women's eyes. Figures of a divine mother with a child were worshiped throughout the Classical period, and as late as the end of the Roman empire. They are often beautiful.

These stone women, reduced to geometric shapes, go back beyond Crete and Mycenae to small-scale societies of Neolithic farmers, without metal and at first without pottery. The same simplified shapes, which are characteristic of early sculpture ground down from stone rather than built up from clay, persisted for thousands of years. They survive here and there today in certain islands as the shapes of special loaves of bread with a red-painted egg for a head. The finely built lady (*right*) is over 7,000 years old. She was found near Sparta.

Left These three ladies were all built up with clay and fired as pottery, during the Bronze Age. The nearest (*left*) is from Crete; she is a nursing mother rather simply and awkwardly made, but somehow more moving, or more directly expressive, than the goddess or priestess of much grander design (*far left*) and more realistic craftsmanship, also from Crete. Her hands, which are raised in prayer (or blessing?) are well managed, her face is carefully modeled, and her head is ambitiously crowned with flowers and birds, but she has little charm.

The splendid lady who combines ornamental knickers with a clear sexual organ (*center*) is from Cyprus. She is now in the Louvre.

Below This seated, headless terracotta with the huge hands and feet is now in the Syracuse museum. She comes from Megara Hyblaia, and dates from the 6th century BC. For strength and beauty of modeling, this figure would be hard to equal. It combines the geometric purity of the earliest images with realism.

Below This lady, now in the Louvre, is Boeotian from perhaps the 8th century, in the geometric period, decorated with suns or stars and with water-birds eating snakes or eels. She carries ritual branches and her breasts are clearly marked. She is a goddess perhaps, certainly a religious figure.

Below and below right These two figurines are Mycenaean. The more finely decorated is a goddess from Mycenae 30 centimeters or so high, made in about 1300 BC. She and her like are handsome and dramatic and slightly awe-inspiring. The hands held to breasts indicate a nursing mother. The striped figurine is one of a series of small figures that were made and painted in enormous numbers. They are found not only in graves but also in houses, and being so numerous they were sometimes rediscovered, and recognized as holy, in the Classical period.

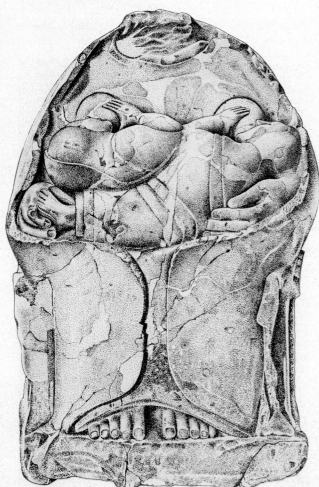

THE HOMERIC WORLD

The quality of life in the Greek dark age cannot be understood without its one overwhelming and living monument, the Homeric poems. They were not the only Greek epic poetry, and certainly not the first, since they refer often to earlier poems, the stories of earlier generations. The *Iliad* and the *Odyssey* are the earliest evidence we have of Greek poetry and of the world, at least the mythic world, that the Greeks lived in, and audiences understood, in the 8th century BC, when the long process of development and composition of these poems was substantially complete. From that time onward until the end of Greek antiquity, Homer was incomparably the greatest single influence on the Greeks, as the Bible has been for so long in western Europe.

Before the growth of modern comparative studies, it was thought in Europe that not only our religion, but our civilization itself was unique, with roots in the unique Greek world. Greek art and philosophy, Roman laws, Newtonian physics, and the Bible itself, all seemed to have an absolute value. In the same way, Homeric epic poetry was felt to be unique. We must now look more deeply and range more widely if we are to decide whether it was so. Until quite recently, the false and romantic sense that Homer was utterly unique was extended to the subject-matter of the *Iliad* and the *Odyssey*, so that one of the motives of archaeology in Greek lands was the rediscovery of Homer's world. That led to many doubtful and hopeful interpretations which have had to be discarded.

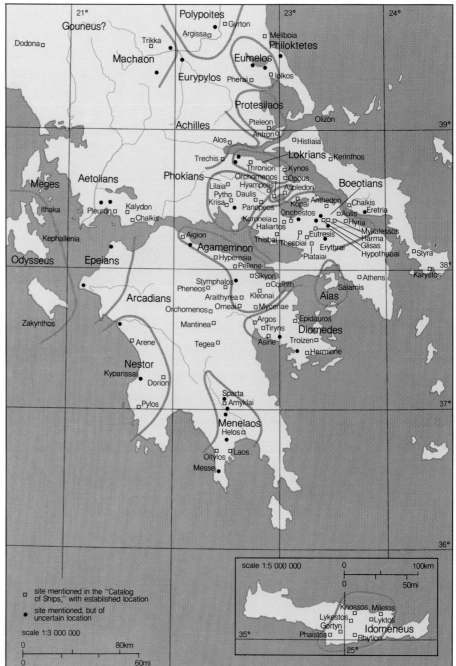

Homer's world

There is no reason to believe that the poets of the *Iliad* and the *Odyssey* were court bards. They must have wandered from place to place, like their successors and their equals in other cultures, settling now and then as they could. Hesiod had a mountain farm in Boeotia, about which he complained with epigrammatic venom, but Homer was probably more like Demodokos, a poet who figures in the *Odyssey*. He is a blind man, who lives in his own house, not in the palace, and when wanted he has to be sent for with a courteous request. When he comes he is given a good seat and well entertained. The audience appears to be mixed. When

Far left Heads of Homer like this Roman copy of a c.150 BC Greek original, which were produced in quantity in late Classical times, show a suffering face and a tragic vision of human life. The face is serious, the vision was the truth. Or so the sculptor believes.

Right Monuments like this were made for the rich and cultivated. They commemorate in stone the work of Homer as if Homer himself were a god. The work is 2nd or 3rd century BC, by Archelaos of Priene.

Agamemnon went to war it was a bard, not a blind one presumably, that he left to guard his wife, as one might have left a chaplain in the Middle Ages. Patronage did exist, and though the heroes themselves in Homeric poetry can play and sing, everyone hears a professional bard with special respect.

The life of the people is harder to characterize. The shield of Achilles was decorated with scenes of peace and war, the good and the bad city. One of the scenes is a harvesting, and the people are singing a folksong the refrain of which survived into Classical times and was then recorded. In the *Iliad* the men have a democratic assembly, which has an obscure relationship to royal decisions. Agamemnon is not so absolute a lord as Zeus, who is stronger than all the other gods put together, and the real degree of Agamemnon's supremacy is further confused by the necessary twists of the story. Princes, in both the *Iliad* and the *Odyssey*, have power only by exercising power. If they acquire honor and prestige by the exercise of power, their peoples are protected from invasion and piracy, and wealth and benefits and services in a closely interlocked system continue to hold the world together. The most

Homeric Greece
Book 2 of the *Iliad* contains the "Catalog of Ships," a detailed survey of the places in mainland Greece ruled by the heroes of the Trojan war. There is much debate on whether this survey reflects anything of the political geography of Mycenaean times. The Homeric epics also know of Troy and its allies in Asia Minor, Sidon, Cyprus, Egypt and Libya. In the Hesiodic corpus knowledge of more distant lands is shown. The *Theogony* speaks of a King Latinos ruling the Etruscans in remote islands. The "Catalog of Women" mentions Mt Atlas and the nomadic Scythians.

valuable objects in Homeric poetry, apart from weapons, horses and cattle, are useless in practical life, but their existence helps to hold the world in place, much as the morality of honor is not so much a private indulgence as a social binding force.

We have already seen (p. 17) that when Odysseus triumphs, his son Telemachos and the faithful swineherd dance together, because the right order of things has been restored. Odysseus finds his father Laertes at work on his farm, putting down dung around his pear trees. Nausikaa, the princess of the good kingdom of the Phaiakians, is discovered with her friends doing a great mass of palace washing in a river. Even one of the gods, and a number of demigods, are metalworkers, and Homer describes them hard at work. Thersites in the *Iliad* gives a different impression. He is a rebellious commoner, who speaks out against Agamemnon in the popular assembly.

The story of the *Iliad* is dispassionate and tragic. Its episodes are held in relation in the same way as clauses and phrases in a sentence. The language has relatively little syntax, and often depends on balancing clauses of equal status in the sentence. This affects everything in the *Iliad*, as it does in the earliest Greek prose, for instance the fragments we have of Charon of Lampsakos. Such a style rules out any extended passages of metaphysical construction or elaborate moral judgment, but it allows great freedom and subtlety, and the sharpest expressiveness. The sentences hold together more by their rhythm than by any other link.

Homer's world, in so far as it means anything to speak of a world of these great narratives, is imagined in the 8th century. Warfare is beginning to be scientific, there are some hints of regimental formation, but battle is still essentially a bloody personal conflict between heroes. The soldiers and lesser heroes are present only to be killed. War is felt to be tragic, but the best advice of a father to his son going to war is "always to be bravest and best and do better than the others, always to fight in the front rank," words that were echoed later on many inscribed gravestones. The great heroes have special arms and armor, sometimes strange or archaic. The gods interfere constantly, but they make nothing happen that might not have happened anyway. A weapon hits as it should, because a god helped, or someone escapes, because a god produced darkness or mist. Zeus is unable to save his own son, Sarpedon, from being killed.

The duties of hospitality are absolute; a breach of them, Paris' abduction of Helen, led to the war, and if links of hospitality are discovered to exist between two heroes in conflict, then they are not allowed to fight. The heroes ride to war in chariots, pursue one another in chariots. By exception they may spear an occasional charioteer, but in principle they fight one another on foot. No one except an acrobat can ride on the back of a horse. In the *Odyssey*, as in the *Iliad*, ships are light enough to be pulled up on the beach; they are mostly rowed, though sails are also used. We read that bread and meat are eaten, cheese is made, wine is drunk with water in it, and drugs are known, but associated with divine or magical healing. Helen in the *Odyssey* puts a drug into the drink for Menelaos and Telemachos, to cure them of sadness. Circe subdues men with drugs to turn them into animals, but the god Hermes knows that the antidote is a herb which grows nearby. The world of the *Iliad* and the *Odyssey* has many levels, as any world must have when it is fully imagined.

The Homeric context

The attempt to identify every city and island in the Homeric poems already caused controversy in the early Roman empire. Troy and Mycenae and Nestor's Pylos were great palaces in the Bronze Age, but in Homer's day Troy was almost certainly a ruin and Mycenae was no longer a great power. Homeric Pylos was sandy, but the palace recently excavated near Pylos is miles from the sea, and no palace has been found at the Pylos of the 5th century, which the Greeks of that time believed was Homer's Pylos. Homer does undoubtedly refer to real monuments as existing in his own day, he refers to cities, to famous tombs, and to the house of Erechtheus at Athens. His geography is formalized but full of detail. But the map of Bronze Age Greece that modern archaeology has revealed is not quite identical with Homer's world, though scholarly ingenuity and boot-leather have been generously expended in the attempt to bring them together. It is as much a question of what Homer leaves out as of what he puts in, and there is something to be said for the view that Homer's geography has as many roots in the 8th century as it has in earlier times.

Suppose that the stories from which the *Iliad* grew had their roots not only in other stories and in experience, as all stories do, but also in ruins and beliefs about ruins. Every village in the world, after all, invents a story of some kind to explain the local ruin. Homer's Greece has perhaps as many cities in common with 8th-century as with Bronze Age Greece. The attachment of the *Iliad* to the numinous ruins of Mycenae and of Troy should not surprise us. At Mycenae Agamemnon was worshiped, and at Troy there was a mysterious ritual in which Lokrian virgins were landed at night to serve the rest of their lives, if they reached sanctuary without being caught on the way, in the temple of Athene. We are told they were an offering of atonement for the sacrilege of Ajax of Lokri, who violated Kassandra at the altar of Athene in the sack of Troy. Is it not inherently probable that the myth was invented to explain the ritual, and did the *Iliad* not have wide-ranging roots in a huge mass of such stories?

These explanations are problematical for lack of exact, uncontroverted dates. We do know that in the last quarter of the 8th century BC a number of Mycenaean beehive tombs were opened for purposes of worship. Are the terracotta representations of what seems to be the discovery of such a tomb by shepherds, with a goddess in the tomb who resembles a Mycenaean figurine, indicative of a religious cult resulting from Homeric poetry? Or are they another expression of the strong feelings about remote, heroic ancestors on which Homer also drew?

Some of the physical things that Homer mentions do call for a Bronze Age explanation. A helmet, for example, is made of boars' tusks. Helmets of that kind were not used in Classical Greece, but they have been recovered in the excavation of Mycenaean sites. Representations of figures wearing them have also been recovered, one in fact from Delos. Did poet after poet describe these helmets for

hundreds of years? Did the trappings of the Bronze Age creep into 8th-century epic poetry because of the opening of tombs and the chance recovery of strange weapons associated with a heroic past? Was some outlying people still using those helmets later than we know? If we take all the Bronze Age props of the *Iliad* together, our choice of an explanation will still be linked to a literary question: how is epic poetry generated? Unfortunately, few archaeologists study comparative literature, and few scholars of epic poetry in all its ramifying traditions have any precise knowledge of archaeology.

Different explanations fit different cases. The great burials of the Bronze Age ceased in Greece long before Homer, but they continued in Cyprus. The long thrusting spears of the Mycenaeans had gone out of use and shorter throwing spears had succeeded them. Homer seems to know of the long thrusting spear, but he thinks the heroes threw it. That is surely the misunderstanding of an ancient object that had survived, but it might also be heroic exaggeration. Even among the heroes of the *Iliad* there is a sense that men were even stronger, and heroes more heroic, in an earlier generation than theirs.

Epic poetry in its full vigor embodies the self-consciousness, the memory and the identity of a whole people. The size of the Homeric world is astonishing, and so is its unity. Of course it has shadowy limits. The entry to the Underworld was very remote to Homer's audience, yet it seems clear that this was a real place in western mainland Greece, where there really was an oracle of the dead. Dodona, which is not far from the present Albanian border, was a mysterious and distant shrine to Homer's audience. The vast moral and intellectual horizons of Homeric poetry, its geographical, imaginative and historical horizons, must have been in the 8th century BC a more penetrating force for good than we can well realize.

Hesiod and the conventions of myth

The two great poems of Hesiod, the *Birth of the Gods*, or *Theogony*, and the long poem or amalgam of poems about morality and farming called the *Works and Days*, are near to being contemporary with the *Odyssey*, which itself is probably a little later than

A red-figure Athenian kalyx-krater by the Dokimasia Painter, 470–465 BC, apparently shows in formal terms how Agamemnon died. This is a man's world in which women merely lament and gesture. The conception of the same events in the *Agamemnon* of Aischylos is immeasurably more terrible.

Greek paintings, copied and recopied in the Roman world, have survived at Pompeii and elsewhere. This one shows a scene of conflict from the *Odyssey*. In these pictures the landscape is always dominant. The fact does convey an element of truth about Homeric poetry.

This small model of a building from Archanes in Crete must surely be a domed Bronze Age tomb opened for worship by the shepherds with their dog (?) who have found it and peer down through the roof. A series of these groups has survived.

the *Iliad*. However, the *Birth of the Gods* might even be older than the *Iliad*. The *Works and Days* shows a different world from that of the *Iliad*, but Hesiod formulates the same feeling about the past, more neatly and proverbially than Homer. The world has declined through a succession of ages, from the innocent Golden Age, through the Silver Age of demigods, the Bronze Age, the Age of Heroes and heroic war, ending with the present miserable Age of Iron. Hesiod's combination of the rules of agriculture with religious and magical rules, with country morality, and with the observation of seasons, is not a chance matter. At a primitive stage of agriculture every practical rule was a religious observance, and religious rules had the practical basis of making the crops grow. Once again, a modern analogy may be useful. In the 1920s an English professor attended the midnight celebrations at Greek Easter. He asked a peasant, "Do you really believe Christ is risen?" and got the answer, "Of course Christ is risen, otherwise how would the wheat come up?"

There is more of this sort of religion in Homer than most people notice, but in Homeric poetry agriculture is an undertone, and the popular morality of settled peoples asserts itself only towards the end of the *Odyssey*. Throughout most of the action, cattle raiding is normal, and the distinction between a merchant and a pirate is hazy. The *Odyssey* is a poem of return; its structure has a lot in common with the central Asian epic of *Dede Korkut*, whose oral tradition goes back at least to the 9th century AD. In both stories the hero returns from exile or imprisonment or foreign adventure, and has to win back his bride from other suitors. He must climb step by step on his own merit through all the levels of society. In the *Odyssey* he takes shelter with a swineherd and fights a beggar with his fists. The final trial in both poems is the shooting of a bow. The most obvious difference is that in the *Dede Korkut* poems neither the poet nor his audience has any idea of the sea. But the sea wanderings of Odysseus have almost nothing to do with the second half of the *Odyssey*. It seems that the Greeks simply added those amazing adventures to a story that already existed. Perhaps they were a variation on some lost version of the story of the Argonauts, the first ship and the golden fleece. There was certainly

an early epic poem about the Argonauts, but it has not survived.

The sea in the *Odyssey* is islands and shadows and distances. A ship can be blown very badly off course. Heading for the northern Peloponnese it can fetch up off the south coast of Crete. But other, luckier ships make the journey from Troy in reasonable time. There are islands almost no one has ever visited, with a wide repertory of magical or monstrous inhabitants. A number of the wilder stories seem to be set in Sicily and the west, although we are not told exactly how Odysseus found himself over there, and the geography of his wanderings is incoherent. In the *Odyssey* Egypt and Crete and Cyprus are real, and Odysseus has herds grazing in mainland Greece, on the coast opposite Ithaka. But in the west everything is fabulous.

Odysseus visits an island which is the home of the god Aiolos, who has charge of the winds. We know that the later Greeks localized this part of the *Odyssey* around the east coast of Sicily, where the Cyclops lived in a cave, and where Scylla and Charybdis raged in the straits of Messina. The Aeolian islands are a few miles north of Sicily not far from the straits. Lipari (ancient Lipara) in particular is a prehistorian's paradise, because its acropolis has been thoroughly excavated, and reveals a continuous succession of occupations from a very early period to the present day. Lipari is one of the few Mediterranean sources of obsidian, a volcanic glass which produces a fine cutting edge that was highly valued until the development of bronze tools, and maybe much later. The Mycenaeans traded there, and there are Mycenaean treasures in the Lipari museum. The moment the Greeks arrived at Lipari in the Classical period, they worshiped at a preexisting shrine, to Aiolos, god of the winds. There is little doubt that the story in the *Odyssey* is based on a religious cult, probably native before it was Greek.

The limits of reality

We must be careful about taking literally every later Greek identification of an ancient tomb or a ruin with the monuments of the heroic age. It is common among simple people to populate their landscape with a familiar story. I have been shown the cave of the Cyclops by a peasant in southern Crete, the ruins of the Temple of Solomon by villagers on a mountain in Afghanistan, and the pleasure-house where Menelaos of Sparta drank coffee at Kardamyli in southern Greece. In the 18th century it was believed by local people that the mount of Christ's Sermon on the Mount was near Nauplion in the Argolid, and that the ruined temple at Sounion south of Athens was a house built by Solomon for the Queen of Sheba. It is just possible that the localization of a whole section of the *Odyssey* around eastern Sicily happened in the same way when the poem was known, but I am inclined to believe that here the stories are local, transmuted by travelers into that vast assemblage of islands and events from which the *Odyssey* emerges.

The worship of ancestors is even more confusing. From their first emergence from the dark age, certain powerful families, like the Neleidai at Athens, are already claiming descent from the heroes of Homeric narrative and from gods. But the very fact that heroic ancestry was politically important, and that heroic narratives were used, and their true version sometimes disputed, in political quarrels, means that we can put little reliance on their historical value. The truth seems to be that heroes are a more powerful version of ghosts. They have a particular grave in a particular place, though Oedipus, for example, has three or four different graves. They are warlike, they do harm, they must be placated. Most of them died by violence.

Homer makes it plain that at least the graves at Troy antedate the composition of the *Iliad*. He even feels the need to explain away the non-existence in his time of what ought to have been a feature of the Trojan landscape, the great Greek ramparts in the

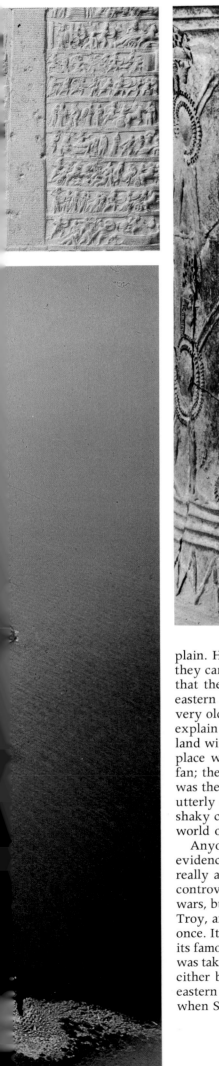

plain. He says that the gods were angry, and later they came and washed them away. It may even be that the curious cult of the grave of Penelope in eastern Arcadia, which is recorded much later, was very old and known to Homer. That at least might explain the task of Odysseus, to wander away by land with an oar over his shoulder until he found a place where people thought it was a winnowing-fan; there he should sacrifice to Poseidon. Arcadia was the only region in southern Greece which was utterly cut off from the sea at that time. These are shaky conjectures, but there was a whole shadow-world of strange stories Homer may have known.

Anyone who looks severely at the archaeological evidence is likely to doubt whether there was ever really a Trojan war; or to put the same truth less controversially, he will see that there were Trojan wars, but not *the* Trojan War. The Greeks did know Troy, and Troy was certainly destroyed more than once. It was immensely rich in the Bronze Age and its famous gold treasure, which disappeared after it was taken from Berlin during World War II and has either been broken up or is hidden somewhere in eastern Europe or in Russia, astonished the world when Schliemann found it in 1874. Rich and more

Above This archaic scene of the Trojan horse, who does not appear in the *Iliad* itself, is from the neck of a big pot from Mykonos, c. 675 BC, made about 50 years after the lifetime of Homer. The crowded stone relief (*above left*) is a piece of fantasy based on post-Homeric epic poetry that dealt with the Trojan war. This particular work is now in Rome; a whole series of these can be traced to one workshop.

Left Navarino bay is the site of the Classical Pylos; the coastline has altered greatly in this area, but we know what it was like in the 5th century BC from the historian Thucydides. The Bronze Age is more obscure to us, but the fine building called Nestor's palace high above the bay was in fact the center of a Bronze Age kingdom.

Overleaf Odysseus was separated from his home by "many glittering seas and many shadowy islands."

beautiful and more moving things have come from Mycenae and Knossos, but very little of comparable grandeur. Yet we have no sure archaeological evidence that the Greeks ever took Troy, and the huge expedition of so many Greek princes under the supreme command of one great king neither took place in the Bronze Age nor could have taken place in any later age until Alexander conquered Persia. Some grains of history half-remembered may have irritated the imagination of poets; that is all we can say. Neither the *Iliad* nor any other epic poem is pure fiction.

Growth of a legend

In an endless series of readaptations, the bones of a story, like the structure of folktales, grow stronger as the nucleus of fact grows weaker; reality continues to reenter the poem in other ways, for example in metaphors and images and dramatic tensions, but the scale of events alters utterly. The Serbian hero Marko the Prince was really a Turkish mercenary. Roland's battle at Roncesvalles was not very important, if it did occur. The central Asian hero Dede Korkut is as fabulous as Nestor, although his grave was identified and miracles of healing used to be worked at it until recently. It still, I believe, has a railway station named after it in southern Russia. The structure of the *Iliad* and the *Odyssey* yields little to any analysis that treats them as solid, deliberate works of literature. There was no word for literature then, any more than there was a word for fine art when the caves were painted at Lascaux. They are best studied as a petrified moment in an organic process, during which their structure never ceased to grow. They depend on generations of continuous reworking.

The *Iliad* is not the story of the Trojan war. It takes place during the war, which stretches away in time both backward and forward. The war is the situation and the scenery, and the condition of life. Both sides know how the war will end and heroes know their own fate. The power of the poem is in its detail and its language, the sudden focus on a minor character, the strange beauty of the gods, the effect of isolated lines in their cumulative context.

The instrument of this power is the hexameter itself. English has no meter so supple and so long. The Homeric hexameter was probably an east Greek development, but in Homer's time in the 8th century BC it had been perfected by many generations of anonymous poets. Indeed, the name Homer itself is a kind of anonymity. We are not able to say for certain even whether the same poet made the *Iliad* and the *Odyssey*. Long afterward epic and sub-epic poetry was still being made in the same verse. The so-called Homeric hymns are certainly post-Homeric; the last of them of any merit, the hymn to Pan, was probably written about 500 BC; but they have many characteristics of Homer, the same interest in places and *realia*, and much of the same skill here and there.

Epic morality

Genuine classical and folk epic poetry is transmitted by memory and adaptation, from singer to singer. It flourishes in an illiterate society, and its moral rules and traditions reflect the moral world of societies that are now rare on earth. Honor is paramount, and wealth is almost equivalent to honorable prestige.

The small archaic bronzes from Delphi and Olympia and many lesser shrines are the liveliest of Greek arts. Odysseus escapes from the cave of the blinded giant by hiding under the fleece of a ram. The same scene drawn on the shoulder of a jug from Aegina is sufficiently similar to highlight the slight differences of conception that go with the change of medium.

The prince protects his people, and he risks his life. The valiant die young. The rules of society, for example the duty of blood vengeance and the supremacy of physical courage, are absolute; epic heroes are like tin soldiers with human hearts and children's intelligence; for them it is unthinkable that society should be otherwise. Magnanimity is a rule in conflict with other rules. But of course societies are always altering, they are never quite stable. In the poetry of Homer, the heroes are almost free, the rules can be resented but not quite yet altered. The end of the *Iliad*, where Achilles gives up Hektor's body to his father, is immensely strong, just because compassion is felt to have overcome conflicting rules of the world. The power of the *Iliad* comes from this tension. Homer knows, and his characters are half-conscious of the fact, that the world of the Trojan war is appalling, hellish; but the poem proceeds remorselessly. The Trojans and the Greeks all speak Greek, and they say similar things. The gods fight on both sides.

Oral epic poetry uses a vast repertory of set phrases, adapted and readapted into new sentences and verses; a study of how they reappear tells us something about how the mind of Homer worked. The Greek prince Agamemnon says, "There shall come a day when sacred Troy shall perish." But Homer reuses this sentence later. He puts it into the mouth of Hektor, who is going out to fight, knowing that in the end he has to die. Even Achilles, the greatest hero, who survives the *Iliad*, has to know that he will die. He has chosen to be famous and to die young in battle. Without that darker tone, and without the compassion an avenging Homeric hero can hardly show, Achilles would be intolerable. It is

in order for Achilles to show compassion that the dead body of Hektor has to be begged back by his father, Priam. The *Iliad* ends not with the triumph of the Greeks, but with the burial of Hektor.

Small wonder we find it hard to know the origins of many Homeric conventions. We can see from Norse saga and from central Asian and from Irish epic poetry that in its long development every epic poem is organic, it puts out and it loses leaves and branches. Every retelling is for a different audience, every adaptation is a new attempt to make sense of given material. There are some obvious contradictions in the *Iliad*, for instance when the same hero eats a huge dinner twice in one evening; contradictions arise from reworkings. We are not even sure at what stage Homeric poetry was written down. What does seem to be unique in these among all the surviving epics of world literature is that they took a permanent shape, apparently in writing, when the tradition of epic composition and oral transmission was still in its fullest vigor.

The tradition of epic poetry composed and transmitted by word of mouth does not flourish when there is an audience that reads. Yet it is not exactly writing that destroys epic and traditional poetry, at least not in one generation. It is rather written law, new social organization, and all those transformations of a whole human society to which the spread of literacy is linked. As we look backward, Homer's world is cloudy to us. He stands on the edge of a great darkness. He has a crispness and a purity we associate with beginnings; yet if we are to do justice to the dark age, we should think of the *Iliad* as its evening star, not as the morning star of a later age.

PART THREE
THE
AGE OF
TYRANNY

THE 8th-CENTURY RENAISSANCE

Greek colonization of Asia Minor was well established in the 8th century. Al Mina at the mouth of the Orontes was a trading station, founded from Euboea before the end of the 9th century, and exploited by Corinth. Already by the 9th century the Phoenicians were expanding westward as the Greeks moved east. The resulting rivalry was fought out not in the Levant but in Sicily, since the Greeks moved west almost before they controlled the Aegean. Styles in the east intermingled, and what reached mainland Greece arrived usually in an adapted or impure form. The penetration of Greek art by these new influences transformed it utterly; this is simply the reverse image of that extraordinary expansion, intellectual as well as physical, loosely organized and resourceful, in which Greece boiled over. The increase of representational art in Greek lands is inseparable from the expansion.

It is curious that the styles we first detect as early as the 10th century roughly mark out what were to emerge as regional states: some by the dominance of one city, Argos or Thebes, some by aggressive policy ending in imperial adventures, Sparta for instance, some in leagues of cities like the 12 Ionian cities of the east, which combined in the 8th century, some by loose aggregation without a central city, like Elis, though never without a central sanctuary. The great international sanctuaries of Dodona, Delos and Olympia already existed at this time; they were oracular shrines or centers of common worship, implying and perhaps imposing a degree of common law and common language. Before the mid-8th century we know that at Olympia the first of the four great international athletic festivals had begun to be held (the others, at the Isthmus, Delphi and Nemea, became Panhellenic some 200 years later). Month and year and festival were to some extent synchronized all over Greece.

Painting, sculpture and architecture

Although painted decorations in the dark age were prone to international influences, in principle the styles were regional. Still they differed from one another less than the regional styles that followed them; no doubt the decay of Mycenaean patterns was a universal condition. A similar sub-Mycenaean style emerged in isolation as far away as Sicily for the same reasons, but with less later development. In mainland Greece, the painting and construction of pottery became by the 8th century a monumental art. The huge and shapely pots made at that time for Athenian graveyards stood as high as a man or higher. Their sober and intricate decorations of alternating tan-colored areas and black paint were executed in bold and complete schemes. The control and rigor of the early, simpler and bolder geometric patterns had taught an important lesson, and continued to teach it for generations, perhaps for centuries; it was not forgotten now. Greek painting never quite lost sight of the tightness, the formal and geometric organization of the 10th and

A monumental amphora from Melos of c. 625–620 BC, showing the Orientalizing style of vase painting.

9th centuries. Within its formal limits, Greek art had an astonishing and perhaps a seminal vigor in the 8th century.

This is the period of the first figure sculptures we know anything about after the Bronze Age: not only small cult-images in bone or ivory or wood, but some spirited and powerful bronzes. The decoration of the heavy bronze tripods of the gods at Olympia appears swift and vivid, in a dashing contrast to the heavy material, but at the same time it shows a strong feeling for the depth of the bronze, in its heavy curves and its long lines; the detachable figures, of a horse for instance, are richly and fully molded. The earliest Olympian warrior figures show an obvious Oriental influence, and a number of direct Oriental bronze imports have been found at the sanctuary. In fact the refreshed and reviving arts of Greece begin by Orientalizing. Still to come were the influence of Levantine stone-carving, the slow adoption of fine marble decorations for public building and the laborious adaptation of Egyptian human sculpture via the mathematics of eastern imitations. But already the new repertory of images was mostly Oriental.

In the course of that same century architecture also revived. The long apsidal or elliptical huts of earlier settlements gave way at least for sacred use to a smart, sharply decorated, rectangular style with a

Dodona

Dodona is the site of an ancient (reputedly the oldest) and mysterious oracle of Zeus on the northwest edge of the Classical Greek world, toward the Albanian border of modern Greece, some miles inland in a cranny under the Pindos mountains. According to Homer, its priests had unwashed feet and slept on the ground. They interpreted the noise of the wind in a great oak tree. There is plenty of evidence of late Bronze Age activity, but none of continuity of cult. Perhaps we ought to expect none. In Homer's lifetime Zeus was enthroned here with a goddess called Dione. There was some cult of an underground goddess, and some strange beliefs about sacred pigs. Dione is closely related to Demeter, it appears.

Dodona's buildings were poor and few until Hellenistic times, and most of the ruins visible today, which are very beautiful, have a late origin. Most prominent is the theater, built after the death of Alexander the Great, in the time of Pyrrhos of Epirus, and recently restored. Above the theater lies the walled acropolis; below it was a stadium of which the rounded end can be discerned in the center of the photograph (*below*).

Odysseus is supposed to have vistited Dodona, but he was a famous traveler. Most of the clients of the oracle seem to have been simple people; they came more often from nearby or from the remote north than from the center of the Greek world. The core of the sanctuary was the holy tree itself.

The site of Dodona retains something of its ancient remoteness and wildness. But even its smaller dedications were seldom rich or distinguished. Much of the pottery found there comes from the remote northern Balkans. The bronze warrior (*left*), which is now in Berlin, is a pleasantly ferocious piece, but it has little to do with Zeus. Like most such small finds, it could have come from any great sanctuary. Of the sanctuary buildings only the foundations survive.

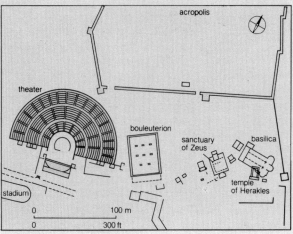

Left Vast commemorative pots such as this make plain their association with funerals. In atmosphere, they are not distant from the lamentations at the end of the *Iliad*; the same is true of their date. This example marked a grave in the cemetery of Athens on the road towards Eleusis.

Below The bronze bowl shows the heavy influence of Oriental art on the archaic art of the Greeks, in which formality and realism advanced hand in hand.

columned porch. Traces of the same geometric ornament that has been found on models have also been found at Corinth, on a bolder scale and in more colors, in the decoration of a real temple. Houses began to be square, built around their hearths, but apsidal houses and houses with curved walls did not die out at once. It is possible that on some of the islands Bronze Age building techniques, which had somehow survived, as they may well have done on Naxos for example, now came into their own again; alternatively, they may simply have been relearned from old buildings and readopted.

There are unsolved questions about the increase of population and of wealth, and about foreign relationships. The quantity of objects and styles that are recognizably Greek increases dramatically in comparatively few years. At first one has the sense that in every bronze statuette the relation of whole and parts and the balance of lines and masses are being worked out anew, as if for the first time. The same is true of terracottas, though only of types, hardly of individual figures. In the course of a generation that situation had altered. The variations within a received style, particularly when a big stone statue must take a solid six months of work and perhaps far longer, are considerable, and they are sometimes rewarding. Neither crispness nor originality dies out until the 5th century, although once the material is no longer felt to resist, originality loses its old sense, and geometric measurement relaxes. But in the visual arts in Greece it is open to us to set a high value, if we choose, on the remarkable period of adaptations from 750 to 650 BC for bronzes, and from 650 to 550 for the young men and women in heavy marble. Their cumbersome grace took longer than a century to go out of fashion, and that was still not the end of development; the strongest and the most fluid development of representational painting was from 550 to 450.

The big stone statues are grave monuments to individuals or dedications to the gods. The naked athlete statues that crowded the open-air sanctuaries where games were held were both portraits and dedications. The huge painted pottery of the ripe geometric period, the 8th century, represents the grave monuments of rich and powerful Athenians; nowhere else did these pots attain such a size or such a grandeur of design. It used to be thought that they belonged to an age of chariots, but chariots have only a heraldic role in early Athenian art; they were not used in the dark time, so far as we know. The point is worth making, since there has been a temptation to view the funeral scenes on these vases as terribly primitive, as an echo of the heroic world portrayed by Homer. I doubt whether that is right. The vehicles shown on some of these vessels are four-wheeled carts, and the dead man is laid out elaborately on a horse-drawn cart surrounded by mourners. The characters driving pairs of horses are not heroic warriors galloping around the tomb in chariots, they are only neighbors in farm carts.

Mainland Greece

At the same time certain great families, in Athens and elsewhere, were claiming ancient ancestry. The ancestors were mythical, half-divine, and it is uncertain when these claims were first made. But funeral monuments play an important part in the familiar solidarity of every aristocratic group, both by their show of material wealth and generosity, and by more precise affirmations.

The rise of these great families is easy to conjecture in the dark age, but it seems likelier that there was little room in that period for big social differences. With the coming of wealth, the politics of colonial expeditions, and the emergence of a literate state with written laws, the conflicts of family interests must have taken on a new importance. We know, as a matter of fact, that the distribution of wealth in Attica was more uneven than elsewhere. Athenian history in the 8th century was not a success story. Population increased, though faster in the countryside and perhaps partly by immigration. But overseas, Athenian commercial influence decreased, almost withered away. At home, the Oriental luxuries in graves were no longer direct imports, but local adaptations. Riches were as great in the countryside as in Athens itself, but the contrast of wealth and poverty between rich and poor graves was dire in the 8th century, and it became worse in the 7th.

The foreign aspect of this situation would be explained by defeat at sea, and Herodotos, three centuries later, does mention such a war and such a defeat. The interior situation of Attica is clear. Everything points in the same direction. The big baronial families, with a dazzling power of patronage and a solid basis of agricultural holdings, squatted on the riches of the countryside, presumably in rivalry to one another, and certainly to the detriment of those who were buried in the poor graves at Phaleron. The worship of the heroic and violent dead in the Mycenaean tombs, which began all over Greece about 725 BC, is another aspect. Every clan venerated the bones of legendary ancestors, usually somewhere in the countryside, where the clan held land. The evidence for individual cases is late, but the practice is at least as early as the 8th century. The epic poetry and the legends, the grave monuments and the hero-cults, the claims of the great families and their position in the countryside, at Menidi or Spata or Koropi or Anavyssos, are all parts of one situation.

The Argolid, the plain dominated by Argos, by contrast was powerful and outward-looking. At the end of the 8th century the fortress of Asine was utterly destroyed by King Eratos; the grave of a young soldier of that time reveals a splendid conical helmet copied from the east, and a bell-shaped corselet copied from central Europe. Most of the bronze cauldrons ornamented with bulls' heads that have been found in Greece are copies made in Greece itself or in Cyprus of Syrian originals, which were copies in their turn of the work of Urartu. The painting of vases at Argos was grand and monumental, as it was at Athens, with the same exception of cheap, mass-produced wares for the local peasants. The only center to produce fine wares for small shapes and everyday uses was Corinth, which produced also for export. Argive pottery did travel, at least as far as Sicily, Crete, Kythera, Corinth and the islands of Melos and Aegina, but never in such quantity. So far archaeology confirms what written history supposes. But in the case of Sparta there is an odd reversal. We hear of constant Spartan wars against Argos, but although Spartan pottery shapes have a genuinely native origin, the decoration is

Eleusis

Eleusis, home of the sanctuary of Demeter, lies on the seacoast west of Athens in what used to be idyllic countryside, now utterly swallowed up by industry. It was a Mycenaean, and an early archaic site; continuity of worship is perfectly possible, even perhaps likely. But we know nothing of any Mycenaean Demeter. Most of her shrines are in the country all over Greece, outside town walls.

Athens took over Eleusis in early historical times. The Telesterion, or temple of Demeter, is somewhat representative of building on the site, with a complex history of rebuilding from Mycenaean to Roman times. Eleusis has its own extremely rich museum.

Demeter was the goddess of grain, and the religion of Eleusis was based on the mysteries of the natural cycle of resurrection and rebirth. The laws of agriculture, of sex, of nature and of the gods were to the early Greeks one interwoven code. The Homeric *Hymn to Demeter*, which centers on Eleusis, is one of the most important documents we have for ancient religion. The relief carved on a lintel (*right*) is from Eleusis.

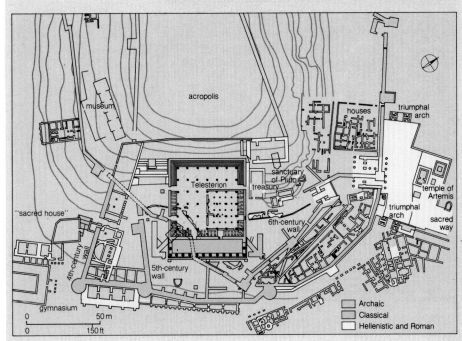

Map labels

ATLANTIC OCEAN

12° 8° 4° 0° 4° 8° 12°

Rhône

Po

Liguria

Etruscan City-States

Spina

Agatha

Massalia

Emporion

Corsica

Alalia

Gravisca

Tartessos, on the site of Sevilla, was taken over by the Carthaginians only in the 5th century, when Gadir (Cadiz) became a Carthaginian town.

Hemeroskopeion

Sardinia

Tharros

Kymai Neapolis
Pithekoussai
Poseidonia
Elea
Pyxo
L

Tartessos

Guadalquivir

Gadir

Malaca

Mainake?

Sexi

MEDITERRANEAN SEA

Sulcis Caralis
Nora

Hip
M
Panormos Sicily Lipara Mata
Soloeis Mylai
Motya Zank
Selinus Himera Katana
Minoa Leontinoi
Akragas Kasmenai
Gela Akra
Kamarina

Lixus

Mogador and Lixus: Phoenician trading posts, not necessarily settled all the year round, in the 7th and 6th centuries.

Mogador

Phoenician trading contacts by the 8th century.

scale 1:10 000 000

Carthage

Utica

0 300km
0 200mi

Hadrumetum

Melite

Leptis Ma
Kinyp

Tripolitania

The emporia were trading port Tripolitania, secured by Cartha before c.515, when Carthage ousted Spartan settlers from th abortive colony of Kinyps.

Legend

- Etruscan city - states c. 500BC
- Greek homeland in 11th-10th centur
- Mycenaean settlements of late 13th
- Greek settlements of 11th-10th cent
- 9th-century colonies
- 8th-century colonies
- 7th-century colonies
- 6th-century colonies
- □ Dorian colony
- ■ Ionian colony
- ○ Aeolian colony
- ● Achaean colony
- Achaean/Troizenian colony
- ◉ Lokrian colony
- ◇ East Greek colony
- ♦ Greek trading post
- △ Phoenician colony
- ◆ Phoenician trading post
- [□] temporary settlement

---

almost entirely Argive and Corinthian. Sparta, "lying low among the rifted hills" as Homer knew it, was not a trading power in the late 8th century.

The Greeks overseas

It is an old question whether it was land hunger or political unrest or trading enterprise that drove the Greeks into the western Mediterranean; no doubt there is no single exclusive answer. The Euboean settlers on the west coast of Italy close to the modern site of Naples were traders. The pottery they handled had a variety of sources: Euboea, Athens, Corinth, Rhodes, Crete, Etruscan, Apulian, Phoenician and Syro-Hittite; among finds at the sites of these Euboean colonies have been north Syrian seals, Egyptian scarabs and trinkets, and a bronze cauldron ornamented with bulls' heads. The quantities of the more exotic of these wares are very small indeed, but they do indicate a lively atmosphere of far-ranging trade. The local colonial artists imitated Euboean and Corinthian pottery. An entire local style arose in the hinterland, in which imitated Euboean birds and lozenges were applied to all shapes indifferently, whether native or Greek. Indeed the style spread over all southern Etruria in the late 8th century, and was followed by a local version of Corinthian. One cannot judge a human society by the commercial success of its painted pottery, but the process of Greek expansion, which was well under way in the 8th century, and in which the eastern products reached the western borders, was internationally important. It was as much the essential condition of life in mainland Greece as the Trojan war was the essential background for the duel of Hektor and Achilles.

Troy had been occupied by Greeks, perhaps from Lesbos but with some Rhodian presence, before 700 BC. It is close to the entry to the Black Sea. We know little about this early Greek Troy, because it was mostly destroyed to build a great sanctuary 300 years later. We do know that Troy had long been virtually deserted. It is usual for archaeologists to claim the ruins lay uninhabited for 400 years. That is probably an exaggeration, but it is immaterial to what extent Troy was involved in the disturbances at the very end of the Mycenaean world; sooner or later, it was certainly abandoned.

In the east the Greeks were in contact with Lydia and Phrygia in western and northwestern Asia Minor. The evidence of decorated pottery at Sardis in Lydia suggests not only an east Greek presence from 750 to 725 BC, but perhaps also a local style imitating the pendent semicircles of Greek pottery, drawn with compass and multiple brush, in the 9th century or the early 8th. The Phrygians were culturally in advance of the Greeks; it was their bronze bowls and bronze pins, and their imported or imitated Urartian cauldrons with the sirens or bulls' heads around the rims, that stirred the imagination of the Greeks in western Asia. It may be that Gordion, the capital city of the Phrygians, was a great trading center. At the end of the 8th century conditions were easy for such a long-range trade. Around the year 700 BC there was some influence of

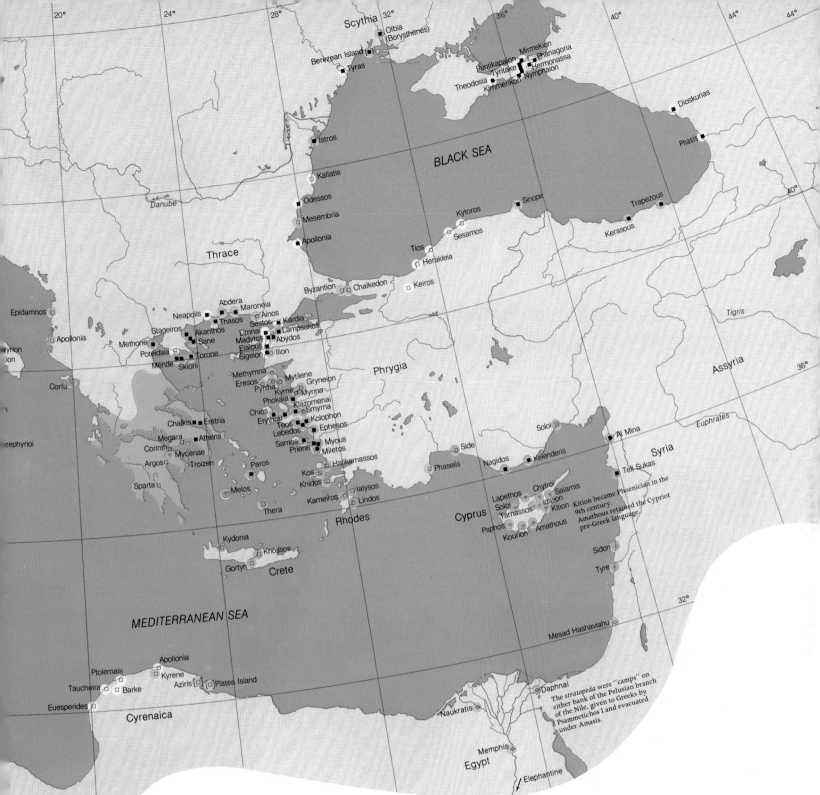

Greek colonization, 9th–6th centuries BC
From the 9th to the 6th centuries many Greeks settled far overseas, as traders, mercenaries in foreign service or colonists. As a rule they could not found major settlement colonies in the territory of established kingdoms such as Egypt, Assyria/Babylonia and the Etruscan cities. But populous Greek settlement colonies took over the best land in Sicily and south Italy, frequently at the expense of weakly organized native peoples. The colonies, mostly Milesian, around the Black Sea were small trading depots except for the great settlement of Olbia. The Ukrainian hinterland sent urgently needed wheat through these depots to Greece.

Phrygian pottery on the outline birds and animals that decorated amphorae on Paros and the nearby islands. It could almost be said that the Phoenicians and the Greeks alike were no more than tentacles of a Levantine octopus who was feeling his way toward the Atlantic.

Narrative motifs and the adoption of an alphabetic script

Meanwhile, before we have any literary versions of most of them, we can begin to make out familiar stories, or at least familiar story-patterns, among the decorations of painted pottery. Is the helmeted soldier handling a woman on a Cretan pot of around 700 BC Paris carrying off Helen? Is the murder of a child by a swordsman in the presence of an adult couple the death of Astyanax, Hektor's child? That is on a late 8th-century Athenian fragment; it seems less likely. We can recognize the Cyclops, and Zeus

with his thunderbolt, and various abductions of Helen. On the tripod leg at Olympia the two fine soldiers who struggle over a tripod must have been taken for Herakles and Apollo. Herakles (is it Herakles?) attacks Amazons under the gaze of an uninterested bird, on a round clay plaque like a shield from Tiryns. But the interpretation of some at least of the Levantine originals, for example a sheet of bronze figures at Olympia, must have been as obscure to the 8th-century Greeks as it is to us. Must every captive girl between two winged divinities be Helen carried off by the Dioskouroi? One can see in all these representations an abundance and a freedom of imagination of which the rigorous and burnished styles of the 9th century offered little promise.

In the whole structure of Greek life as it emerges into the half-light of early history, there are a few dominant factors which are so obvious that they are

The Archaic Moment

The short Classical springtime of Greek visual art was a simplification, a decorum, a restraint of abundant energy. The archaic period just before art became perfectly Classical, and long before it softened, swelled and languished, is full of obvious energy. Its devices are bold, its techniques ambitious, it sets out to astonish, it offers no permanent solutions or tranquil, everlasting forms. It appears constantly on the edge of breaking through into much later developments, even the baroque. It conveys a consciousness of the value of materials, particularly bronze, and of the fineness of tools: its swords and armor were like expensive shotguns. Its images expressed courage, physical daring and a certain combination of elegance and danger. At its best, it challenges comparison with anything being made anywhere in the world in the 6th century BC.

Offerings placed in sanctuaries or tombs were often made to a miniature scale like the glass amphora on the right. But occasionally a vessel of more than life size would be offered. The great late 6th-century bronze krater of Vix (*above*) was recovered from the burial mound of a Gaulish princess near the young river Seine, below the prehistoric hill-town of Mont Lassois.

Standing 1·64 meters high, weighing 208 kilograms, and with a capacity of some 1,200 liters, this vessel is the greatest masterpiece of Laconian, perhaps of all Greek archaic art. Seven men at arms and seven chariots parade ominously around its neck, molded in bronze like the massive Gorgon's-head handles, and applied; from the lettering

beneath the figures that marks their position, we know that the workman was from Sparta.

The weight and delicacy of the krater, the harmonious tension of its design of snakes and Gorgons, and the victorious plainness of the body, the crispness and the solemnity are hard to match. But how did it reach Mont Lassois, not far south of Paris? Was it the object or the craftsman that traveled? The beaten bronze of the body is in places only a millimeter thick: if it traveled it must have been transported most carefully. It may of course have been made in Italy, but besides Etruscan ware the grave also contained Athenian pottery and other Greek luxuries, among them a tripod and a cauldron ornament.

Above Always a luxury in ancient times and used primarily for trinkets and scent bottles, glass was never an important medium for Greek artists; but by the 7th century BC there were glassmakers at work in Cyprus and Rhodes and perhaps elsewhere in Greece. Like most miniature vessels, this little amphora (height 12 cm) imitates a Greek wine jar of the late 6th century. The attractive shape is cheerfully decorated, and pleasantly showy and unpretentious in contrast to the awkwardness of much monumentally intended vase painting and gem cutting of the same period. It was a modest offering for a grave, a gesture to suggest the pouring out of a whole precious amphora of wine.

This wonderful helmet is part of a hoard found at Archanes, in one of the richest parts of eastern Crete. The dedicatory inscriptions on the helmet and the *mitra* (belly guard) that goes with it suggest a date close to 600 BC. The helmet is a modification of the Corinthian type. The majestic mares have relatives in the relief decorations of big

Cretan storage pots of terracotta that were made in the second half of the 7th century, when Cretan representational art was the most competent in Greece, and in its calm, linear way perhaps the most beautiful. By contrast, the lion, a fabulous beast to the Cretans, is elaborate, a rich and fierce embellishment in Oriental style.

Left This Spartan bronze of c. 500 BC is unpleasantly successful. Its strictly sculptural interest lies in the abstract cloaked form and in the contrast of lines, the simple repeated lines of the drapery, the strange and formally highly effective crest, and the long locks escaping from the helmet. But the impact of this spooky warrior is immediate; this is representational art, and he provokes fear across 25 centuries. The sophisticated and mobile modeling is of an unusual quality, and so far as I know brilliantly original.

It has been suggested that the sideways crest is Italian Greek, but these crests occur also on Attic red-figure, and outside Athens on black-figure vases, and the Corinthian helmet itself

is common. It is not known where this warrior was found, but he seems to be Spartan. His feet are probably modern. This is a masterly piece, pushing outward on a small scale the limits of what sculpture could achieve.

Above These grave-faced early Classical youths (about 520 BC) are common enough in marble but rarer in bronze, at least on this scale, which is above life size. His hand held an offering, probably not the attribute of a god. He is more likely a gift to a temple than a grave monument. Found in the ashes of a Peiraeus warehouse where he probably lay awaiting export to Rome, when the Romans destroyed the port (86 BC).

Above This black-figure Athenian long-necked amphora is by the Daybreak Painter, a member of the Leagros group. The name of Leagros was written as a formal compliment on a great number of vases in the late 6th century, mostly red-figure. The black-figure vases, mostly decorated with scenes, sometimes obscure to us, from the Trojan war or the life of Herakles, have a fresh complexity, with bold incision of complicated groups. In this strange and dramatic scene perhaps Achilles' ghost does what Achilles did in life when he leaped ashore at Troy, and a waterspring broke out where his foot touched the ground – the famous Trojan leap.

sometimes overlooked. One is the adoption of an alphabetic script. Writing, like everything else, has regional variations in ancient Greece, but the alphabet is certainly a form of the north Semitic alphabet, learned from the Phoenicians, we have no idea where exactly or by whom. Of the regional Greek scripts, the Cretan alphabet is closest of all to Semitic, and there is no doubt of a special relationship between the Phoenicians and the Cretans, but the first adaptation may easily have occurred in some coastal trading station. The date of the introduction of the full alphabet is more easily determined, since alphabetic writing in Greek begins to appear in the mid-8th century, and never appears earlier. It is not only our present knowledge of the Greek world that the introduction of writing altered, but also Greek self-knowledge at the time. The sense that the world and events can be rationally controlled arises from rational description of how the world behaves, and what factors are involved. Writing created or intensified that sense among the Greeks, first among the deep social springs of morality and of human behavior, then in the whole field of history and politics, and finally in philosophy, in science and in religion. Perspective in drawing, the foundations of medicine, the procedures of legal argument and the shared exploration and description of foreign lands, are part of what depends on writing, on a literate culture.

Religion

Another dominant factor in the developments of the late 8th century is religious. The earlier history of Greek religion is hard to trace, but as the images emerge they are recognizable at once; they tell the same stories and embody almost the same values as those of the written literature set down at a slightly later date. Yet they are more solemn than Homer, and sometimes more terrible, although even the most primitive scenes are executed with a gaiety and glee which are remote from terror. The worst murders are almost heraldic, they are dreamlike in their naivety, just as the description of appalling events would be in the Homeric hymns. Two centaurs batter a human figure into the earth and he stabs them, or Perseus beheads Medusa, but these are dedications or *agalmata*, things in which the gods take pleasure; they are objects of delight, the toys of serious children.

Of course religion had a darker aspect. Polytheism continually corrects itself by proliferating, it is always alive at the edges, in its newer cults. There is some evidence that more or less professional prophets and holy men, whether by right of birth or by vocation, played an important role in Greek religion about this time. If so, it is worth noting that the same thing was going on in Israel in the same years.

The oracular shrines also existed, but their immense prestige was only beginning; still, it is remarkable how rich the offerings were both at Delphi and at Olympia at a relatively early date. Eleusis, just northwest of Athens, was certainly a settlement in the 8th century, and the cult of Demeter existed at Eleusis as it existed probably here and there all over Greece, though most of the evidence we have of the international fame of Eleusis is later. Yet the Homeric *Hymn to Demeter* is surely an early poem, of the early 7th century.

Kouroi and Korai

These statues have a family resemblance. They vary in size from ivory or bronze miniatures and small wooden idols to heavy stone figures raised on blocks, above life size. They have Greek ancestors in the 8th century BC, and remoter origins in Egypt and Mesopotamia. Their proportions were carefully worked out, and they were once boldly colored, though we know little about that, and even their proportions retain certain secrets. Each full-sized statue must have taken at least six months to make. Their season was from about 620 to about 480 BC. They were the memorials of the dead, or offerings to gods, or statues of gods or of heroes. There were occasions around the year 500 when particular statues were thought to have miraculous powers. Within the severe limits of their proportions a fascinating development can be traced through these figures, as the smile on their faces and the suppleness of their lines become more apparent, and they move their legs apart for the first time. This is not simply a matter of their severe charm, but a matter of mechanics, of the balancing of weight and the strength of materials.

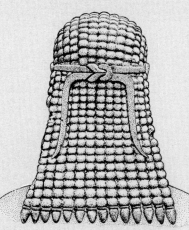

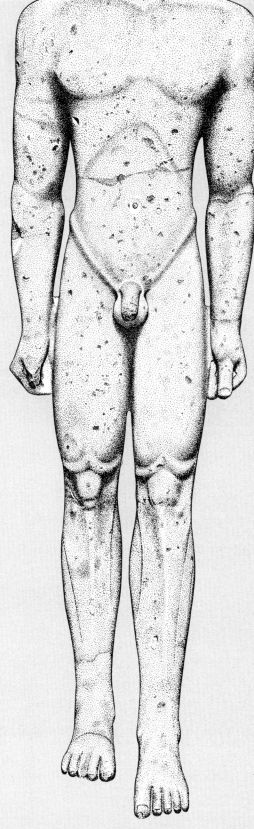

The slim boy from the island of Melos (*far left*) dates from the mid-6th century. He is made of Naxos marble. Archaic Melos has yielded work of wonderful quality to its excavators. His companion (*left center*) belongs to a slightly later development of the style. He was found in the countryside on the south coast of Attica. He is made of Parian marble, a silky and glittering white stone. On Paros, stone chests with human figures on them were being made for the Phoenicians in the 6th century. The larger drawing (*left*) is of an earlier figure, perhaps from the late 7th century, probably from the south coast of Attica. The line of the bone at the wrist of this early marble boy (*below*) is as formal as the tresses of his wig-like hair (*above*). His knees are like abstract decoration. This rather beautiful geometric analysis of the details of the human body is applied also to its private parts. It seems to be an inheritance from Mesopotamia.

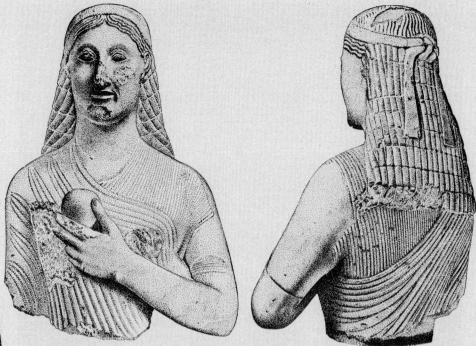

The dignified lady (*left*) holds a pomegranate and wears the hat of a priestess. She was found near Keratea in Attica, wrapped in a sheet of lead. She must date from the 570s, 20 years of so later than the impressive limestone head of Hera at Olympia. The folds of her dress are so heavy as to be dramatic, but the curls of her hair, the fine ornament of her hat, and the fruit in her hand do give her a certain delicacy.

The rear and front views of the head and bust (*above*) belong to another lady with a pomegranate, perhaps 10 or 20 years later again. She is made of Naxos marble and she was one of the offerings on the acropolis of Athens destroyed by the Persians. Her fine Ionic dress with buttons at the shoulders seems to speak of a different world, but it is only a local variation. Her hair also is delicately conceived, though less well executed.

The front and rear views (*below left*) are of one of the finest of all the Athenian statues. She was made in the late 530s and was also smashed by the Persians. The stunning quality of her close dress, with its severe ornamental playfulness, her face and hair and the beauty of her body combine to give the impression of irresistible joy. She had a painted necklace.

The other back view (*below*) belongs to a provincial version, a little old lady from an Etruscan tomb. Her face is a disaster, but her geometric elegance is undeniable. She is made of gypsum, and has traces of paint and gilding. Her bottom is partly restored.

Above Olympos was the home of the gods, the house of Zeus, god of the bright sky. It is visible from far to the south and from the sea.

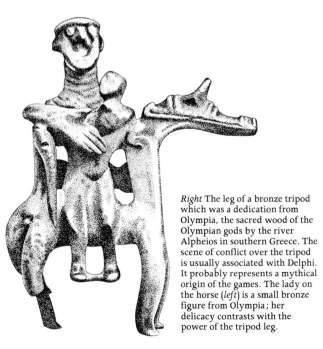

Right The leg of a bronze tripod which was a dedication from Olympia, the sacred wood of the Olympian gods by the river Alpheios in southern Greece. The scene of conflict over the tripod is usually associated with Delphi. It probably represents a mythical origin of the games. The lady on the horse (*left*) is a small bronze figure from Olympia; her delicacy contrasts with the power of the tripod leg.

By the early 7th century Eleusis was a holy place and a shrine of pilgrimage. Almost all we know of the architecture of Eleusis itself between the fall of the Mycenaeans and an oblong sacred building of the late 7th century is the construction of a terrace in what must have been the sacred area, and one small elliptical piece of wall.

It is worth wondering why the gods are Olympian. Olympia was named early, and Homer already records that Mount Olympos was the home of the gods. It is a commonplace that Zeus was the cloud god and the sky god, but why should his home be so far away? Since we know now that most of the names of the gods are Mycenaean, and since the name of Zeus in particular is closely linked to the names of the sky gods in the whole Indo-European family of languages, we may suspect the choice of Mount Olympos is 1,000 years earlier than 700 BC. It is at least likely that whatever people first colonized Olympos with gods had at one time lived in northern Greece, in the shadow of that mountain. On the other hand, Olympos is visible from the sea, and the home of the gods may have been put on the borders of the known world, to the north, just as it seems the entry to the Underworld in the Homeric poems is on or just beyond the western borders.

We can say for certain of 8th-century Greek polytheism that it was an open and ramshackle system of adaptations. There were no new gods with missionary religions, but a constant receptiveness to the gods on the borders of the Greek world, and a constant identification of foreign gods with existing names. Astarte influenced Aphrodite, Artemis is an Oriental Mistress of Animals, Aiolos the wind god was accommodated, and so on. But all this occurred without breaking the supple coherence of Greek mythology. It is impossible to tell on grounds of style whether any story as Homer handles it is new or old. Among the other results of this is that stories about the Mycenaeans, stories about distant people, folktales with magical themes, and the old religious mythology of the Greeks and of their neighbors became hardly distinguishable. All stories were told or portrayed equally under the same smiling sky, in the same atmosphere of hard-eyed gaiety.

The arts of the 8th century convey an irresistible energy, an invigorating sense that man controls, and almost sexually masters, much of nature. There is a fragment of painting at Argos where the ritual domination of a horse is applauded by a chorus of maidens with branches, and below the ground there are fish. The fish may be irrelevant, though hardly more so than the maidens, or they may indicate the presence of Poseidon, master of horses, earthshaker and master of the sea. Perhaps the horse is being broken in, perhaps for the first time in history, in a mythical scene. But many of the scenes of men and horses have something of the same spirit, one from Athens for example where one man holds two tall horses, and another where the same man is naked except for helmet, belt and sword. In harness, the horses are proud and long-legged. Still, the most sympathetic mount of all, and one that equally well expresses the vigor of the 8th century, is a statuette at Olympia, showing a small naked lady sitting sidesaddle on what looks like a horse. There are Mycenaean figurines of more or less the same kind, but the Olympian goddess (for she can hardly be human) is much more naive, and more spirited.

ARCHAIC RELIGIOUS PRACTICE

The decision to send out colonists and where to send them, the right behavior in a national emergency, even legal and constitutional questions, were all sometimes determined by oracle. They were religious questions before they were political, and this occasional power of oracles over politics lasted into the 4th century. Both at Delphi and at Olympia the dedications of ruling families and of nation states, some of them colonies of recent origin, were very rich, and they were permanently displayed in a static diplomacy of competitive prestige. Some of the athletic contests, at least the horse racing and chariot racing, were the sports of kings. As the conception of the temple as a glorious house for the cult statue of a god gained ground in the 7th century, the dedications at great temples became another kind of rich man's or rich nation's competition. The map of which cities made the greatest offerings at Delphi and Olympia in the archaic world is a suggestive indication of several kinds of history at once.

Delphi

Delphi was a herdsmen's shrine on an old Mycenaean site. In the 8th century it grew up where an impressive spring of water tumbled out of the lower rocks of Mount Parnassos, under tall cliffs. There is no evidence of continuous worship or continuous inhabitation; the earliest post-Mycenaean pottery is a few fragments from the 9th century. The sanctuary is on a steep slope, and the stadium for the Pythian games, one of the four great athletic festivals of the Greeks, is balanced further up on the mountainside. The whole site is a natural theater (the man-made theater was not built until the 4th century). The temple of Apollo was rebuilt more than once on the same site, but we know of no temple before the late 7th or the early 6th century. The ruins that stand today are substantially 4th century, with fine 6th-century work underlying them. The columns standing now, which were rebuilt by French archaeologists 30 or 40 years ago, are simply piles of ancient column drums of different dates.

Delphi is the most dramatic sanctuary in Greece. Eagles and white-tailed Egyptian vultures ride in the air above it, the waterspring is still abundant, it is a place of pilgrimage. It was at Delphi that peasants in the last century believed the first tourists were a pagan tribe called the Milordi, the descendants of the ancient Delphians, who had come back to worship their old stones. Euripides in the play *Ion* has a chorus of pilgrims arriving at Delphi, lost in wonder at the monuments. That play starts with a long scene of monologue. Ion, the bastard son of Apollo, begotten in a cave under the acropolis of Athens, has been brought up as a temple boy in the Delphic sanctuary. His job is to sweep and sprinkle water and to scare away the birds. The play begins at dawn and that scene more than any other in the writings of the Greeks

confirms that we are not wrong when we recognize at Delphi a special atmosphere.

Later in history, in the sunset of the place, Plutarch (c. 50–c. 120 AD) sets a leisurely dialogue at Delphi. The difference is great. In his day the priests are learned and cultured historians; they respect their shrine; intellectual curiosity and aesthetic pleasure play over the surfaces of stones; tourism and scholarship have begun. Delphi had played an important role in Greek history, and the remnants of many great historic monuments are still to be seen there. It was the richest and greatest of the oracles of Apollo, at least in mainland Greece; its only rivals were in Asia, and on the island of Delos. The Greeks had once believed that Delphi, not Delos, was literally the center of the world.

One can see what a mountain shrine and oracle of Apollo would be like without this degree of political importance and wealth at the Ptoion in Boeotia, north of the plain which was once Lake Kopais. It has a backdrop of rock, a fine spring of water, a few buildings, and the terraces for dedications. It is a wonderful place, it has an eerie and attractive quality and the great charm of being unexploited today; the hawks nest in the rock and goats wander through the ruins. But the scale of Delphi is more magnificent.

The monuments at Delphi are competitive. Both sides in the great wars of the 5th century built memorials at Delphi to their victories. In the Persian wars the Delphic oracle played an ambiguous part. Kroisos of Lydia had offered gold at more than one of Apollo's shrines, and Delphi was not unwilling to admit the effective presence of kings. When the great Athenian family of the Alkmaionidai was exiled from Athens, they maintained their grand position internationally by rebuilding the temple of Apollo at Delphi and running their horses in the Olympic games. One of the charges brought against Pausanias of Sparta at the time of his disgrace was that he made the victory dedication for the battle of Plataiai personal to himself by its inscription, which was then altered.

The base of that memorial still exists near the temple of Apollo. It was once a tall gilded bronze pillar of three entwined snakes. At the top the three heads looked outwards, with a gold tripod balancing on their three noses. It was taken from Delphi to stand in the hippodrome at Byzantion, where the twined bodies of the snakes still are. In the late Middle Ages it was made into a fountain. Pipes were run up inside it, so that a different liquid jetted from each of the open mouths. The twisted column was not destroyed until the 18th century, but all that is left of the snake-heads now is one menacing fragment in the Istanbul museum. It was Nero who first looted Delphi, but Rome was filling up with Greek treasures before his time. In the first two centuries after Christ the last great and lavish buildings were being constructed at all the great Greek international showplaces, but at the same

The dedication made by the Spartan general Pausanias for the victory over the Persians at Plataiai in 479 BC, as it appears in a Turkish manuscript. The memorial was taken from Delphi and set up in the hippodrome at Byzantion, where in the late Middle Ages it was converted into a fountain.

time works of art were disappearing. At Delphi it was Herod of Athens, a rich patron of scholars, who built the marble facade of the stadium in the 2nd century AD, and the theater, typically of Greek history, was restored in the 2nd century BC by a foreign king, and again under the Roman empire.

It is hard to isolate the earlier period; no great archaeological complex is the pure relic of any one moment in the past, least of all Delphi, which is vulnerable to landslides, earthquakes and falls of rock. The monuments have often been rebuilt and shifted from place to place. The most telling evidence of rebuilding is the marks of building clamps in the stones, which can be dated. Indeed it was in connection with the problems of rebuilding at Delphi that the most crucial work on the dating of these clamps was carried out. From the earliest Delphi we have a few bronzes and some foundations, and the two huge and charming statues of Kleobis and Biton. There is a naivety and heaviness about those two that speak of a more innocent age than anything to be encountered much after 600 BC.

The Delphic charioteer, of whom it has been unkindly said that he has the expressionless expression of the eternal cabdriver, loses terribly by his isolation. He was part of an immensely grand monumental group, and the strong vertical lines of his robe and the stillness of his pose are only one element in what was a tall monument, with the long legs of the horses, the high wheels of the chariot, and the proud heads. He expresses force, competence and victory, in the fifties of the 5th century. He is poised in fact on the edge of the era of flowering and of disasters. The liveliest sculptures at Delphi are earlier. They belong to a time of transition, they are inventive with no loss of archaic dignity, and mobile with no diminution of strength. They are as clever as a barrelful of monkeys, and as attractive. Their purpose is to decorate, not only to impress. They compete for attention but not for space. They are the stone frieze of the treasury of the Siphnians.

The island of Siphnos played little part in history, but it had gold mines and silver mines. Herodotos calls it the richest of the islands and speaks of a senate house and a marketplace of marble, but the precious metal ran out, at one place the sea broke in, and the fine buildings have never been found. Yet the Siphnian treasury at Delphi competes successfully with those of the greatest Greek cities. There were 16 of these buildings at Delphi, each the embodiment of city-state or national prestige, built to shelter the small, rich dedications to the god that Athens or some other great power might offer. The temple would not hold all the offerings, and the city-states liked to keep their own treasures in one place. The competition for prestige had its roots in the honor and shame system of Homeric heroes and of undeveloped peoples. Some of the cities were ruled by kings or tyrants. The wealth was not in the strict sense for use, but show was a use. It provoked the kindness of the god, it engaged the favor of the oracle, it bonded national self-respect and it asserted internationally the standing of Athens, Siphnos or other dedicators. The frieze of the Siphnian treasury was made about 525 BC, at a turning-point in the technique of sculpture. It is no exaggeration to say that in these figures one can watch the changes taking place.

Olympia

The most characteristic expression of archaic Greek religion is Olympia. Associated with a jumble of legends, Olympia was a grove, an open-air sanctuary with a dozen or more altars dotted around among the trees, some peculiar sacred relics, great dedicated wealth, a fine water supply and a huge extent of flat land suitable for an athletic festival. Sport had in Greek religion something of the same function as sculpture, which therefore often represents naked athletes; it was a display of strength and skill and animal quality in which the gods might delight; its obvious intention is to give them pleasure. Of course it was essentially competitive and it retained from the heroic society in which it began the quality of its principal reward – fame, an immortal and universal fame. In the wild version of polo, played with a dead goat stuffed with stones, swollen with water, half-buried and then tugged about by hand among the horsemen of northern Afghanistan, sport still has a similar social function; whoever scores is famous for life and attains heroic status. There is a continual gesture in Homer, and a more systematic, didactic attempt in the later poems of Pindar, to link this glorious status with breeding, ancestry and inherited wealth.

At Delphi, Kroisos king of Lydia dedicated enormous vessels of pure gold, but Olympia was not a shrine of pilgrimage like Dodona or Delphi; it had little political or religious power. It was a meeting-place, and so, of course, in virtue of their position, were Nemea and the Isthmus, the other international sporting centers. There was an oracle of Earth at Olympia and later of Zeus, but that fell silent early. The landscape of Olympia is not typical of Greece, but we know that to ancient taste it was the most beautiful in the world. Its central monument was not built until the 5th century, the gigantic and strangely shaped temple of Zeus, still unrestored today, and more impressive in its ruins than any of its better-preserved rivals. Pheidias' statue of Zeus was huge, of gold and ivory; ancient writers said it added something to human understanding of the gods.

Olympia lies in a bend of the Alpheios, a broad, powerful river coming down from the mountains of Arcadia. At Olympia this big volume of water is just about to break out into the fertile coastal plain; at one time it must have divided the upper from the lower grazing grounds, just as the same river divides Eleia from Triphylia and the old kingdom of Nestor at Pylos. When we first hear of Olympia, the Triphylians controlled it, presumably because the grazing grounds beside the Alpheios were theirs. From the ruins in winter you can see the snow on the Arcadian mountains, and from the nearest mountain you can see the sea. Today, as the road goes inland, it marks the end of the railroad and the beginning of the hills, and in winter the end of lamb and abundant fruit and the beginning of pork.

The altar of Zeus was made of the ashes of its own old fires. In the end it had become a huge construction with steps and a high core, but being nothing but solid ash it was all swept away in the Middle Ages by the floods of the Alpheios. The whole site was covered under 3 meters of mud; it was a long time before it was identified. The altar of Zeus has left no discernible trace; all that we can look for is where there was space for it. Monuments were not

These heads are made of ivory. Found at Delphi, they represent the poor ruins of a magnificent treasure. They may well have been finished off in gold, but it is the quality of their workmanship, not the glamor of their material, which marks them out.

These magnificent plaques from Delphi must have been the ornaments of a chest or more likely a throne. They were found with the ivory heads. It has been suggested that these are the fragments of a dedication by King Kroisos. However that may be, they are magnificently rich and they give great pleasure. The horns of the deer have an interesting remote resemblance to the animal style of southern Russia. The formal origins of all the figures are Oriental.

much moved about at Olympia as they were at Delphi, though there was some rebuilding. It must have been hard to find room in the 5th century for the big temple of Zeus; the sites of a number of older monuments are close to it. It does in fact seem to have crushed something under it, since pieces of an Ionic building have been found built into its foundations.

The floods that inundated Olympia have preserved piecemeal the fragments of great riches and of a few historic memorials. The river silt has confused the round-ended huts of the dark age and the traces of the Mycenaeans at Olympia. The finest early bronzes, the helmets dedicated after famous wars, and a wonderful golden bowl like half a pomegranate, stolen between the wars and now in Boston, are the spoil of the floods. So are the pediment sculptures of the temple of Zeus. They pose some problems for art historians, but whatever else is said, the important thing about them is their strength and beauty. Apollo's blank expression, which has been unhappily overstressed by inappropriate cleaning of the marble surface, has a terrible power. This is not a cult statue with a benign smile, it is the god of mythology. In several of these statues one can make out the beginnings of portrayal of human character and emotion, and of that attractive naturalism which degenerated so soon. The harmony of the limbs is both stony and bodily, the frozen action is a ballet of violence, like the wild arrested motion of the Bassai frieze a generation later, which gives the impression of a wind-blown stone dance. That was erected not far from Olympia in the Arcadian mountains and not very long after the Olympian sculptures, but the difference is already great. The solid and crisp strength of the marbles from the temple of Zeus marks the end of an epoch.

The workshop where Pheidias made the statue of Zeus still survives in ruins, as a Christian church, ruined in its turn. A cup that Pheidias marked with his own name has been recovered from it; so have some of the molds for the draperies of the statue. Some of the finest of the small finds from Olympia are the terracottas, the colored architectural decorations mostly of the long row of city treasuries that stood on a terrace below the hill called Kronion, at the edge of the sanctuary. The color is not garish, indeed some of the best are black and tan, from Pheidias' workshop, but their boldness and simplicity as an architectural scheme are stunning. On the big terracotta statue of Zeus with the boy Ganymede under his arm the colors are now fading badly. Fortunately it was photographed soon after it was found, when it was fresh as well as rich.

It is appropriate to add a word here about the Hermes of Praxiteles. There is no doubt at all that this famous statue is a fake, a copy made in the Roman period. But the excavators knew that Pausanias recorded a Hermes of Praxiteles here, and when they found this one in 1877 they were naturally excited. It is a brilliant copy, and the conception is fine, but to idealize it is false; it has a soapy taste. Once again it is better to use old photographs as the figure was damaged while it was being moved from the old to the new museum. The arguments against its really being the work of Praxiteles are too detailed to be set out here, but they seem to me overwhelming. They depend on fine points of sculptural technique.

There were an enormous number of victory statues at Olympia, and later political statues, and most of the greatest artists of the best period worked there, yet of all those masterpieces almost nothing has survived but the inscribed bases of the monuments and one ear of a bronze bull. The four horses of the Cathedral of San Marco which came to Venice from the sack of Constantinople started their journey at Delphi or at Olympia, at Corinth perhaps, or at Chios, assuming they were Greek.

But reflecting among ruins does not always make for very penetrating thoughts, and the contemplation of the loot of the ancient world, particularly when it is wrenched out of context, has a tendency to wither historical judgment. The evidence that tells us most about the archaic Greeks includes many fragments of their written literature, the cities in which they were beginning to live, their laws and institutions, and the always extending map of their activities. Delphi was hidden among mountains and Olympia was a sacred city with no permanent population; indeed, the Eleians had no city at all until a late stage in their history, and when one was built they were reluctant to live in it, preferring an old-fashioned life in the countryside. Is that not because water, with all its benefits, was comparatively abundant all over Eleia? The temple of Zeus is a monument of social transition; it was the first act of self-assertion of the first Eleian democracy. How interesting that it was built at Olympia and not at Elis.

Delphi

The Delphic oracle had quite a small sanctuary on a steep slope of mountain ledge under the cliffs of Parnassos, a little way inland from the sea on the north coast of the gulf of Corinth. It grew up where spring water broke in two places out of the mountainside. The Mycenaeans had known the same springs but Delphi was not continuously inhabited. The oracle gained rapidly in importance in the late archaic period. Greek cities sought its advice for their colonizing expeditions, and Delphi gained importance as a meeting-place with the establishment of the Pythian games about 590 BC.

In Classical times the sanctuary was a place of very high monuments, each craning up like a sunflower to be seen. Not surprisingly, they were frequently damaged by earthquakes. From the southeast corner of the walled *temenos* or enclosure, the Sacred Way wound up past the treasuries of the Greek city-states and the monuments they erected to mark victories and great events, to the temple and the oracle itself, and on to the terrace above.

In the sanctuary, as it survives today, the theater is a late (4th-century) addition, and the restoration of the columns of the temple of Apollo is particularly sketchy and inauthentic. Still, that is better than heavy-handedness. It is hard, but it is necessary, to relate the wonderful and intricate contents of the Delphi museum to the bare bones or bare stones out of doors. In this pure air, in this remote place, the masterpieces of many generations were crowded together.

This must have been a spectacular dedication when it was made about 475 BC, at the earliest moment of Classical art. It should be imagined high up on its base, the tall charioteer in his light car between its high wheels drawn by long-legged horses with fine heads. Chariots, and the breeding and training of their teams, were the accepted currency of magnificence.

The restored columns of the temple of Apollo (*above*); in front stood the altar and monuments including the Plataiai tripod. The archaic temple, built by the Alkmaiononidai in exile from Athens, was destroyed by earthquake in 373 BC. It was rebuilt, though on the same plan.

The treasury of the Siphnians represents a wealth that was shortlived. It perished when the goldmines on the island of Siphnos were overwhelmed by the sea. But the splendid marble decorations (made about 530 BC) of this building, the fineness of their proportions and their execution, and the frightening glee of their conception are among the masterworks of the archaic age. This bit (*right*) is a battle of gods against giants.

The round temple, or tholos (*left*), much restored and much hurt by earthquakes, is an outlying early 4th-century monument of Delphi. It had a peristyle of 20 Doric columns.

This sphinx (*left*) sat glittering on the very top of the pile of achievements of archaic art. Her smile is hardly personal; her lines are perfect; and she took a very long time to make, by the rubbing of hard stone day after day and week after week. But her triumph has lasted. She comes from Naxos, one of the earliest cradles of Greek sculpture, and dates from c. 570 BC.

The lady pillar (*right*) has the heavier, almost awkward grace of a more ambitious design. Supporting the porch of the treasure-house of the Siphnians, she was meant to impress and to amaze.

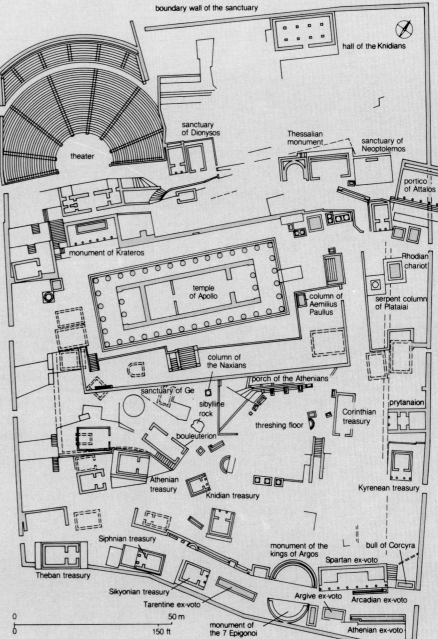

boundary wall of the sanctuary

hall of the Knidians

theater

sanctuary of Dionysos

Thessalian monument

sanctuary of Neoptolemos

portico of Attalos

monument of Krateros

temple of Apollo

column of Aemilius Paullus

Rhodian chariot

serpent column of Plataiai

column of the Naxians

porch of the Athenians

sanctuary of Ge

sibylline rock

threshing floor

prytanaion

Corinthian treasury

bouleuterion

Athenian treasury

Knidian treasury

Kyrenean treasury

Siphnian treasury

monument of the kings of Argos

bull of Corcyra

Spartan ex-voto

Theban treasury

Sikyonian treasury

Tarentine ex-voto

Argive ex-voto

Arcadian ex-voto

monument of the 7 Epigonoi

Athenian ex-voto

0   50 m
0   150 ft

The Oracle of Apollo

The importance of oracles to the societies we call "primitive" is inseparable from their religion, their social structure, their unity and their survival. Oracles control many human decisions about health and sickness, peace and war, colonization and migration, crime and punishment. Oracular shrines are places of vast international prestige where a grand dedication or the building of a temple comes close to an assurance of personal immortality, or for a city everlasting greatness. Who would ever think of the Siphnians if it were not for their treasury at Delphi? How did the Spartans and Athenians endure the sight of one another's monuments at Delphi or Olympia?

The great oracular shrines of the Greeks started very small, usually in difficult country with local clients, probably in many cases shepherds who moved their flocks over great distances. Delphi is essentially a mountain herdsmen's shrine, as are Dodona and the Ptoion. There are a number of others. The early records of the replies of the gods to the questions that were asked of them are inextricably entangled in folktales and embroidered stories of every kind. Oracular power was probably less dramatic than we used to think. But they were holy places, the essential symbol of the unity of the Greeks. International festivals grew up at oracular sanctuaries which already existed.

In their last stage, oracles embodied the conscious traditional wisdom of the Greeks, the final distillation of what it was thought the gods had to teach. The uninspiring but innocent precepts of the god at Delphi were copied and recopied far across Asia, on stone tablets as far away as the borders of Russia and Afghanistan. The sanctuaries themselves were places of pilgrimage and centers of learning even under the Roman empire. At the end of antiquity, there were Christian churches in many of the old oracular sanctuaries, but once the tradition of oracular wisdom had been broken, it was never revived. The society that had nourished it disappeared.

Above Apollo makes his offering. Hermes the messenger stands behind him and his sister Artemis, as elegant as Apollo is majestic, opposite. Behind her is possibly the Pythian priestess. Artemis has poured into Apollo's bowl. Apollo pours to the omphalos, the navel-stone at Delphi which was the center of the earth. This view of Delphi is Classical and Athenian but vague; it conveys only the grandeur of the gods and the fact that earth itself is even older, even holier, than they are.

Above right This large terracotta representation of the omphalos comes from Delphi itself.

Below left Oracle sites and dedicators of treasuries at Delphi and Olympia.

Below Soon after the victory of Marathon in 490 BC, the Athenians built this fine marble treasury, now restored, to contain the valuable dedications of Athens to Apollo at Delphi.

Right This is a Classical representation of the oracle of Apollo at Delphi; it is the decoration of a bowl made in the 5th century in Athens. Once again, there is no intention to be realistic. But the more realistic ancient drawings that survive of the Delphic sanctuary are confused and in their detail untruthful. This at least gives some idea of how the Greeks felt about the oracle and about its god. Details should not be taken literally. It was only by spraying the oracles with poetry that the Athenians could take them seriously at all.

Delphi

Olympia

dedicator of treasury to Delphi
dedicator of treasury to Olympia
oracle site

scale 1:12 000 000
0   400km
0   250mi

Olympia

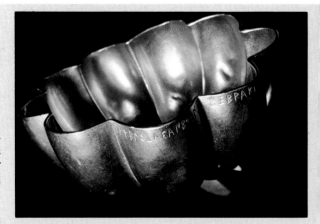

Olympia was a sanctuary, a sacred wood called Altis, in the unpoliticized countryside of western south Greece, on the banks of the powerful river Alpheios. It was named for the Olympian gods, and the hill that overlooked it belonged to Kronos, father of Zeus, and perhaps to his mother.

By the 8th century, Olympia had become an immensely rich and powerful holy place and the center of an international Greek festival of athletic games. The sanctuary has been painfully reconstructed fragment by fragment from the mud of the Alpheios floods which buried it. The altar of Zeus was made of ashes, and it was utterly dissolved. But his temple, built in the 5th century, has survived in colossal ruins.

There were cults of heroes, legendary human beings of divine ancestry, as well as of gods at Olympia; in the end the athletes themselves came to seem half-divine.

The gods were delighted with offerings. The sparkling quality of many of the small dedications has something to do with this intention to give pleasure; they are the toys of the gods. Zeus carrying off Ganymede (*below left*) commemorates a pleasant and not inappropriate story. The fine gold bowl (*above*), now in Boston, is a Corinthian offering dedicated by the sons of Kypselos, tyrant of Corinth, about 600 BC.

The glittering and rich color of these things was part of their meaning. Gold at least never fades, but the painted terracotta Zeus has unfortunately faded since its discovery and its reexposure to the light.

Along the south side of the temple of Zeus (*below*), the columns lie as they fell in an earthquake in the 6th century AD.

Looking over the site of Olympia (*right*), on the banks of the Alpheios, with the conical wooded Mt Kronos on its northern side.

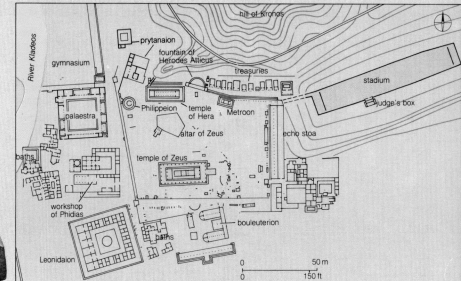

The tall stone figures that stood in the gables of the temple of Zeus have been restored from many fragments, and they have provided many scholarly controversies. The centaur (*left*) is carrying away a woman from the legendary tribe of the Lapiths. The occasion was the wedding feast of Peirithoos, the son of Zeus; the feast ended in fighting but the Lapiths won. Pausanias recorded in the 2nd century AD that the commanding central figure was Peirithoos. His account is based simply on Homer. Scholars prefer to take it for Apollo, since it carries a bow. There is a possibility that it might be the youthful, beardless Herakles, another son of Zeus of some importance at Olympia, who also used a bow and also defeated the centaurs. If so, this is a mixture of two stories, a new version of the myth.

The old man lost in contemplation (*far left*) comes from the gable at the other end of the temple. He is a prophet: he foresees the tragic outcome of the legendary chariot race just about to begin. Prophets by descent of blood still played an important part in Greek life down to the time the temple was built.

The Gods of Olympos

There are 12 great gods, but not always or everywhere the same 12; some important and interesting gods never join the 12, some of the 12 have multiple personalities. The gods shown here are at least authentic representations of the authentic 12 of 5th-century Athens.

Each city-state had its own patron or patrons, to be appeased and flattered, and a farmer would offer to Demeter for a good harvest, a sailor to Poseidon for safe passage. There were also countless minor gods, and in the country Pan and the nymphs were important. In later times the "mysteries" and more personal philosophies, and foreign deities such as Kybele from Asia Minor, Isis and the Greco-Egyptian Serapis gained in popularity.

Right Ares is the rarest of the great gods. He had only one country temple and almost no cult in central Athens, even though the greatest state council, the Areopagus, was named after his hill. This Ares is from Etruscan Todi. Ares is a god of war, but at Athens Athene held that role.

Artemis (*below*), the sister of Apollo, is a huntress, living in forests and on mountains among her nymphs, and a goddess of initiation. She was also Hekate, a death goddess, and had an interest in childbirth, though she was a virgin. The moon was hers.

Poseidon (*below right*) is the god of earthquakes and of the sea, and the god of horses.

Left Demeter is goddess of grain. Her mourning for her lost daughter causes winter; the daughter's recovery is the spring. Demeter was deeply entangled in rituals of death and rebirth, particularly at Eleusis, where her mysteries were perhaps the most august conception in Greek religion. To us, they remain obscure.

Athene (*right*) is the greatest goddess of Athens, patron of the young and brave, protectress of the city and of all arts and all crafts, and the war goddess.

Zeus (*left*) is the supreme god, whose throne is on Olympos, and god of the sky, its storms and thunderbolts. The master of the fates, or almost their master, he dispenses justice on earth as in heaven, by violence. He is best studied in Homer, in Aischylos, and in a very few representations like this.

Hermes (*below*) is the messenger of the gods, the conveyer of souls into the Underworld, and the god of herdsmen and shepherds, in the undisturbed countryside.

Apollo (*above left*) is the model of youthful strength. He is as passionate, as powerful and as dangerous as any of the gods. In his origins and essential nature he was a god of ritual purity and by development from that a god of oracles.

Hera (*left*) is the wife of Zeus and his first and last love, but he was not constant; few of the gods were. Hera had her own temple at Olympia (long before the mid-5th century when Zeus acquired his) and another, very ancient and magnificent, at Argos.

Aphrodite, the love goddess (*below left*), rose from the sea when it was sprinkled with the blood and seed of an earlier and darker generation of gods, but in the 5th century, even in Homer, Aphrodite is a playful, catlike goddess.

Hestia, goddess of the hearth (*below center*), had a very ancient role, but an utterly obscure personality. On the Parthenon

frieze her place was taken by Dionysos, god of wine. From his orgiastic festivals Greek drama ultimately developed.

Hephaistos (*below*) is the blacksmith god. At Athens he was closely connected with Athene as goddess of all crafts. In mythology Athene invented the metal trumpet and bitted the first horse with a metal bit, so metalwork was not alien to her.

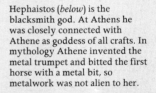

THE BIRTH OF CITY-STATES

The first laws

Early Greek laws seem to have been worded in two ways, one of them like the ritual laws of the Bible: "If a man shall do so and so, he shall suffer so and so, but if it be under such a condition then such a thing," a style implying an active lawgiver and an endless series of adjustments of a general principle. This is the style of the laws of Gortyn in Crete, a complete code of laws, inscribed only in the 5th century but dating back earlier. The other style owes its form to magic and ritual language, which long survived in the wording of epitaphs and curses. It was an inclusive language, because in a ritual no possibility could be left to chance. The annual ritual curses of Teos in Asia Minor take this form, much like the old Service of Commination which still nestles in the Church of England Book of Common Prayer: "Whoever works wicked magic against the Teians, their city or any one of them, death be to him and all his stock. Whoever hinders the import of grain, by whatever means or device, by land or by sea, or exports imported grain, death be to him and all his stock." At the ritual promulgation of the constitutional laws of the colony of Kyrene in North Africa, founded by Aristoteles of Thera (Battos I) c. 630 BC, there was a ritual burning of wax dolls. The all-inclusive formula, with its magical origins, became in the end the origin of the language of later democratic law, because of its tendency to accurate and equal definition, although conditional clauses of penalty also survived.

When written language was new, the recording of law was the task of a sacred official. The old laws had been known by heart, or they had been general principles like proverbs. With writing, the conscious elaboration of legal institutions began to be a continual process. This happens more slowly than one might think. In Athens Solon's laws were written after 600 BC (see pp. 92–93), and the laws of the newly founded Greek city of Marseille (Massilia) were publicly inscribed, very little earlier. The laws of Dreros may date from the 7th century, the laws of Chios from about 575 BC. At the end of the 6th century at Aphrati in Crete the laws were codified by a high official, a scribe and remembrancer, apparently for the first time. Some 7th-century legal fragments do exist, but they are always fragments. No doubt the great Cretan cities inscribed their laws early, but many inscriptions must have perished. It is fascinating that the Marseille constitution seems to have lasted, with few changes, into the Roman period, but its stiff, oligarchic quality may have been preserved by the relatively tough conditions of colonial life and by isolation: economic and juridical power were both inalienably concentrated in the hands of 600 hereditary landholders.

The longest archaic law code we have is that of Gortyn, in southern central Crete. It is inscribed in splendid lettering on a series of fine stone tablets that survived built into the embankment of a water mill, in a channel of the mill stream, where they were discovered in the 19th century. They seem to have supported the fabric of a theater built in the 1st century BC, which must have been raised on the ruins of a law court or council chamber. There are 600 lines of the inscription; its likely date is just after the mid-5th century. The laws themselves are indeed earlier, and the oldest part of them probably dates from the 7th century. They indicate a clear division of classes, the free, those without political rights, the household slave, the serf and the slave. The bonds that linked one group to another, that guaranteed the calm inheritance of land and took the strain of inevitable social changes, were supple

Above Sparta lies near the head of a long river-plain protected by spectacular barriers of mountains. This is Mount Taygetos, between Sparta and Messenia, seen from the Spartan side, which is even richer than Messenia.

Left The code of laws of the Gortynians is one of the best-preserved and longest of early Greek inscriptions. The form of the laws is archaic, not unlike the form of early Biblical laws. But the laws of Gortyn were inscribed in the 5th century BC.

and complex; they had certainly grown organically, rather than being imposed by law. The law distinguishes between certain cases where a judge is bound to decide according to statute and according to witnesses, and all other cases, in which he decides freely.

Tyrants

The active lawgiver is implicit in the wording of the law of Gortyn. He revived in Greece in another form, particularly in the area of the Isthmus, a little before 650 BC. As in Egypt and Lydia, at this time at Corinth outsiders (Kypselos, followed by his son Periander) took over and vigorously controlled the state; the same happened at Megara (Theagenes), Sikyon (Orthagoras, Kleisthenes) and Epidauros (where Periander seized control), and in the late 7th century Kylon nearly took control of Athens by force of arms. Early in the 6th century a public arbitrator was elected at Lesbos, who held office 10 years, and at the same time Solon of Athens as public arbitrator and lawgiver altered aristocratic government and reversed some of its social results. However, Peisistratos and his son subsequently made themselves tyrants, or unconstitutional rulers, of Athens (546–510 BC). Other tyrants imposed themselves in the city-states of the east (Miletos, Ephesos, Samos, Naxos) and west (Akragas, Gela and Syracuse, Himera, Selinus, Rhegion). It is possible that the Spartans avoided a disturbance of the same kind only by imperial success; in the 7th century they distributed new landholdings in the rich agricultural territory of conquered Messenia to the poorer Spartan citizens.

This rash of local tyrannies, which continued into the 5th century, may well have been partly due at least within Greece to the influence of Pheidon, an active and tyrannous king of Argos, probably in the mid-7th century. It indicates also some general social conditions. There was unrest everywhere, the aristocracy was sufficiently powerful and disunited everywhere except Argos to throw up outsiders who could take over the state. The new dynasties caused a conflict of loyalties, and they usually ended badly. Meanwhile they usually increased public wealth; they were lavish and showy patrons, and in this way expected to acquire worldly success and heroic international prestige. Tyrannies arose first in trading cities with small territory. The same pressures, social or economic, which caused these entangled civil quarrels and tough regimes, must have operated at the same time on the colonial movement. It may be too simple to call it land hunger; it was certainly economic competition of some kind, probably of more than one kind. It used to be thought that the new invention of coinage contributed, since for the first time one might pay mercenaries, and social bonds might be disturbed, but coined money came too late to have been quite so influential at this stage. The competition in trade which at last brought money into use in the 6th century may well have been a disturbing factor; as a direct influence it fell first on the rich. It was they who fought civil wars, who founded colonies, who imposed tyrannies. It may be important that the routes of colonization were also the routes of metal hunger, and also that useful metal was already the medium of exchange in the form of iron spits, as obsidian for blades had been in the past, before the first electrum, silver and, later, bronze coins.

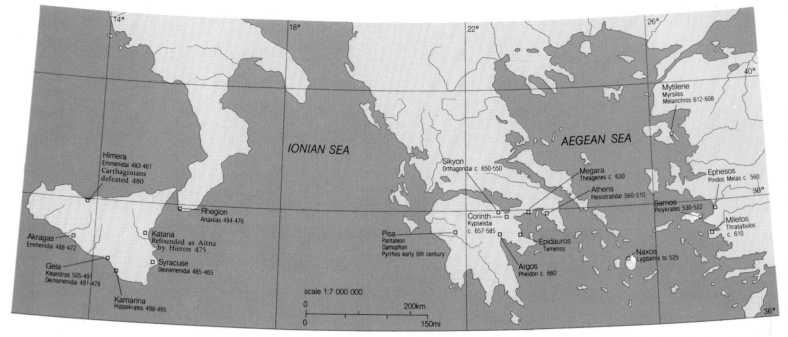

The European context

Iron came into use in northern Europe toward the end of the dark age of the Greeks. It is as well to see this troubled Greek renaissance in a European context, even though most of the influences, after 700 BC, are from Greece and equally from the east on Europe, with almost none from Europe on Greece. The first European long iron swords and iron harness appear at that time. Wealth increased, so did population, and so therefore did fortification. From the 10th century to the 7th the strong places grew in strength and numbers. From the Greek expansion onward, there was even some influence of Greek building techniques, at Heuneburg on the upper Danube for example, where in the 6th century and the 5th they drank the wine of Marseille from imported Greek cups. Were these walled towns not city-states? Does the city-state not arise from similar reasons both in Greece and in the north? Whether this is so or not, in Greece the community of language, and the geographically determined stability of tribal territories, created an advantage.

As for direct eastern influences, Oriental metalwork reached Europe. Down to 500 BC, the metalworkers who entered the Balkans are probably best explained as refugees, but the Scythian penetration of central and even of western Europe is remarkable, and hard to explain without a big migration. The mixture of influences, some of them certainly directly Oriental with no Greek transmission, that produced the material culture of the early Etruscans, sets some difficult problems. Before the 8th century, local styles and local skills were similar, and equally provincial, all over Europe. Greece recovered first, perhaps because it was closer to the east. The bronze bowls that the Greeks so loved, with griffins or sirens or bulls' heads, have their remote origins in Urartu, to the east of Lake Van in modern east Turkey. (Urartu was taken by the Medes in 585 BC.) Those cauldrons have been discovered at Angers, at Auxerre, and at Sainte Colombe, and one stripped of its ornament near Stockholm. But from about 600 BC France, Spain and Scandinavia were being supplied with imitations of

them, made in Britain and Ireland.

Even the early La Tène style in bronzework in the early 5th century, the first version of one of the most idiosyncratic and brilliant of all European styles, is visibly close to Greek, as well as to Oriental models, much closer than the developed La Tène style became. From 700 to 500 BC Europe was more Orientalized than it was Hellenized, but Greek influence continually increased. When Professor Piggott put it that "by about 800 the Mediterranean had become a civilized lake" in contrast to barbarous Europe, one may feel that the paradox was too sharply phrased, but politically, economically and culturally, the Mediterranean was certainly dominant, and within the Mediterranean, Greece. Much of the Greek penetration of Europe, particularly in the west, can be understood in terms of movement toward the sources of metal, in Spain, Brittany, Cornwall and of course in Sardinia, an island of metalworkers.

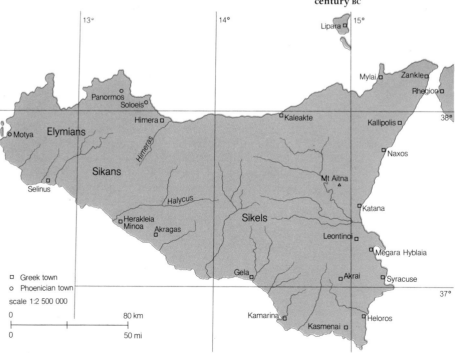

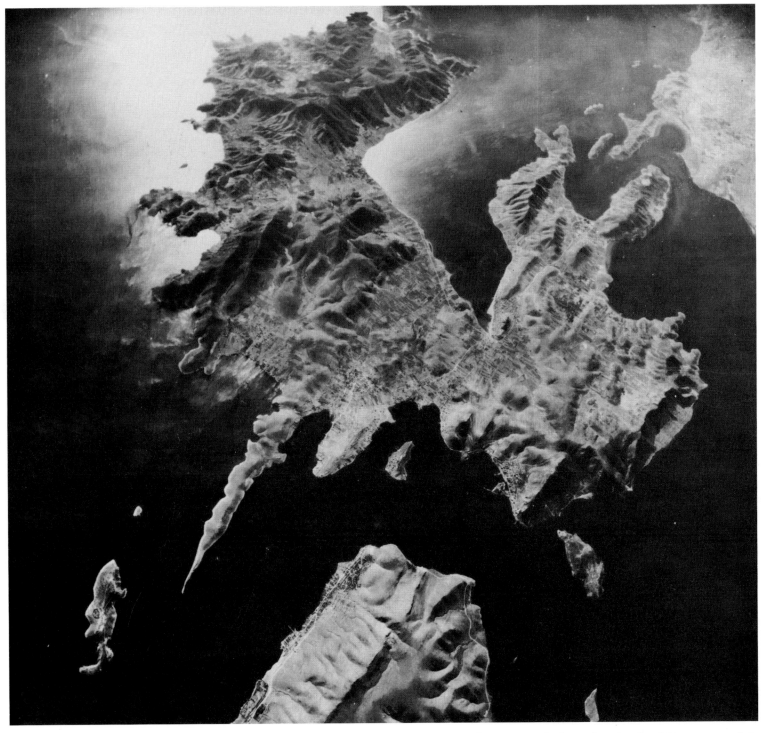

Salamis from the air. The island was first taken from Megara by Athens in the time of Solon.

The rise of Sparta

The archaic age was a period in which not only great families but also peoples conflicted. It has been a common practice to offer a chart of the movements of Greek peoples, in which the theories of Herodotos and Thucydides, the evidence of the relations of dialects, the suggestions of mythology and those of archaeology, are to some degree reconciled. No detailed scheme is quite satisfactory, but the tradition of literary historians does strongly suggest, and the evidence of dialect does confirm, that there had been some redistribution of peoples in Greece, and the end of the process was still going on in historical times. When the Spartans took over Messenia in the 8th and 7th centuries, we have no knowledge of any refugees, but after the third Messenian war, which began at the earthquake of 464 BC, the refugees settled in 455 at Naupaktos, on the north shore of the gulf of Corinth, unapproachable except by sea.

They retained their identity for 100 years, and in 369 BC Messenia was restored. In the dark age there must have been many unrecorded movements of peoples which were at least on a similar scale.

Spartan expansion in the Peloponnese was an arduous policy, in the end successfully executed. The first conquest of Messenia took place between 735 and 715 BC, but in the next generation, in 669 BC, Sparta was defeated at Hysiai in Argolis during a move against Argos, and about 660 Messenia rebelled. It was the mountains southwest of the Argolid and the Messenian mountains, rather than the Isthmus or the sea, which were a natural limit to the Spartans, and the big mountains of the northern Peloponnese and of Arcadia, which lay between them and the gulf of Corinth, were a barrier they never ceased to feel. In the 6th century they reached the east coast of the Peloponnese, and the island of Kythera in the south.

The World of Greek Sport

The Greeks believed vehemently in the value of sport as training, particularly for warfare. Ancient warfare and ancient sport have a lot in common. Success in the great athletic festivals was thought around 500 BC to demonstrate breeding and to add glorious prestige to a family, but later perhaps only to an individual and a state. Greek sport was competitive and frequently bloody, sometimes disgusting and lethal. But its discipline was severe, and breaches of its rules were heavily avenged. In their beginnings the old contests at Olympia had a ritual meaning, but that had been almost completely lost by the 5th century BC. On the other hand, the status of the winner was never higher than in the late 6th and early 5th centuries. A number of stories preserve a popular belief that these men were heroes, half-divine supermen, whose mere statues could work miracles.

Left This boy is tying on a ribbon for his victory, or untying it to dedicate it to some god. He is hollow at the top, to hold the oil that an athlete would use to rub himself before and after exercise.

Below Through this long, arched entrance athletes walked out to their contests in the stadium at Olympia. The names of those who had cheated were recorded nearby on the bases of statues of avenging Zeus, bought with their fines.

Below The starting-line for the foot-races at Olympia (it replaced an archiac starting-line now in the Olympia museum). The stone line is cool under the feet, even on hot days, when the Olympic dust can be painfully hot.

This young man is exercising with stone weights used in a jumping contest. They were very carefully shaped for their use in balancing a jump. A number of these weights, called halteres, have survived, some of them in the Olympia museum.

Greek wrestling was comparatively polite compared with all-in fighting, with its repellent repertory of vicious tricks and its deaths in the ring, or boxing, in which the gloves were like boot-soles and fighting continued when one boxer was down.

Below The origin of Olympic foot-race winners from 700 to 400 BC. Note the gradual enlargement of the Panhellenic sporting world.

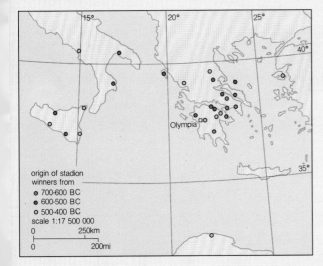

origin of stadion winners from
● 700-600 BC
● 600-500 BC
○ 500-400 BC
scale 1:17 500 000
0   250km
0   200mi

When this statue was made in the 4th century BC, horse-racing was a spectacular and popular part of the Olympic and other festivals, but although it retained its excitement it had lost the grandeur of the 6th century, when it really was the sport of kings, when a horse might be commemorated, even by name for its breeding, but a jockey never. The greatest spectacle of Olympia was probably the chariot-racing at that time. Its starting-mechanism appears to have been a bizarre imitation of the movements of the constellations, the Eagle, the Dolphin and the Horse. This splendid and vigorous bronze statue, very skillfully restored, is in the National Museum at Athens. No other bronze horses have survived so indubitably early, so full of life and action, and so comparatively complete. The little boy jockey is a robustly uninhibited conception, carried along like a leaf in the wind, in effective contrast with the smoothly flowing beast that carries him. This must surely have been a victory monument.

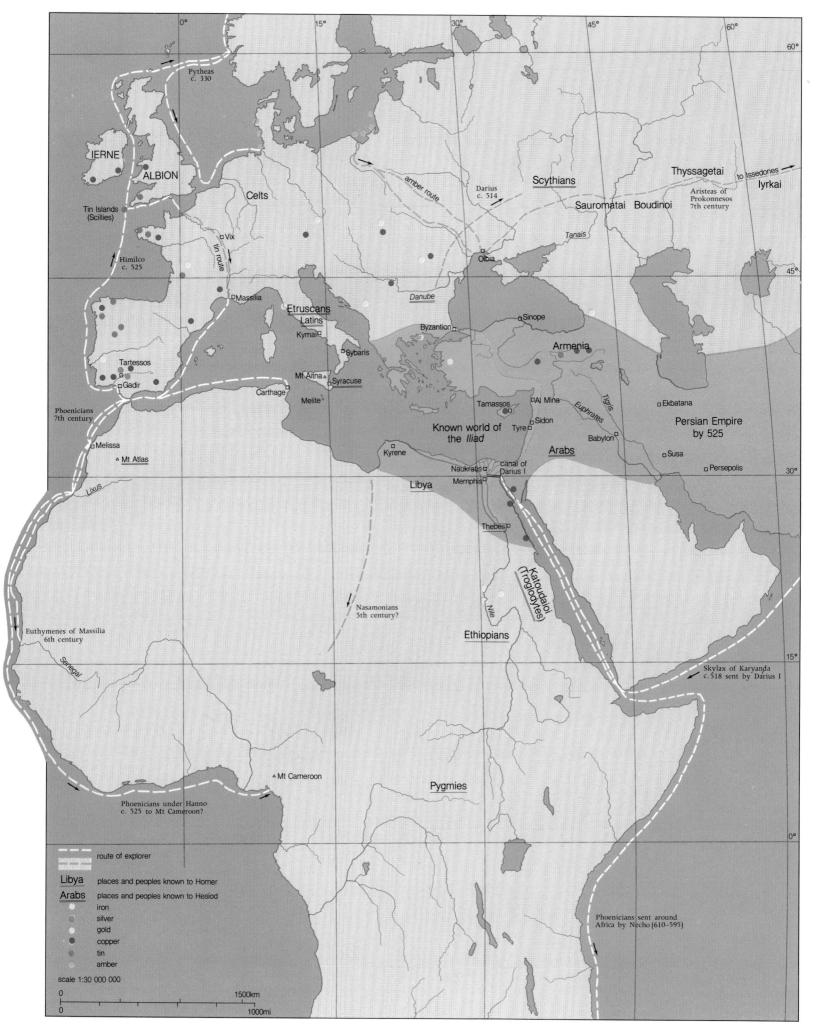

60°

0° 15° 30° 45° 60°

Pytheas
c. 330

IERNE

ALBION

Celts

Scythians

Thyssagetai

to Issedones
Iyrkai

Tin Islands
(Scillies)

amber route

Darius
c. 514

Sauromatai Boudinoi

Aristeas of
Prokonnesos
7th century

Himilco
c. 525

45°

Tanais

□ Vix

Olbia

tin route

Danube

Massilia

Etruscans
Latins

Sinope

Byzantion

Armenia

Kymai □

Mt Aitna △

Sybaris □

Tartessos

□ Syracuse

Mt Aitna △

Melite ○

Ekbatana □

Al Mina

Tamassos

Euphrates

Tigris

Persian Empire
by 525

Carthage

Gadir □

Known world of
the Iliad

Tyre Sidon

Babylon □

Phoenicians
7th century

Arabs

Susa □

Melissa

Kyrene □

Persepolis □

△ Mt Atlas

Naukratis □

canal of
Darius I

30°

Lixus

Libya

Memphis ○

Thebes □

Nasamonians
5th century?

Katoudaioi
(Troglodytes)

Euthymenes of Massilia
6th century

Ethiopians

Skylax of Karyanda
c. 518 sent by Darius I

15°

Senegal

Nile

Mt Cameroon △

Pygmies

0°

Phoenicians under Hanno
c. 525 to Mt Cameroon?

──── route of explorer

Libya   places and peoples known to Homer

Arabs   places and peoples known to Hesiod

○ iron
● silver
○ gold
● copper
● tin
○ amber

scale 1:30 000 000

0 ———————— 1500km

0 ———————— 1000mi

Phoenicians sent around
Africa by Necho (610–595)

By war and a diplomacy which was an extension of war by other means, the Spartans established a dominant position against Argos and a protective alliance with Arcadia. In the second half of the 6th century Spartan armies were active abroad and overseas. They ended tyranny at Sikyon, and so gained an ally on the Corinthian gulf. They menaced Polykrates of Samos off Asia Minor, and expelled Lygdamis of Naxos. They attacked Hippias, son of Peisistratos, and drove him from Athens. By the end of that century, Sparta dominated the Peloponnese in a permanent network of alliances which had become an institution, a formal league of allies with set procedures and assemblies. Only Sparta could summon the Peloponnesian league, and on a majority vote of its members the whole league backed Sparta in arms.

Internally and in social organization, Sparta had to pay a heavy price in military alertness, and in a cruel discipline. From early Spartan society we have a strong impression of vigorous gaiety, both through archaeology and through literature. In the early 6th century Spartan trade abroad, which had been at least noticeable, began to die out, and in Sparta itself the import of luxuries withered, apparently because of the conscious Spartan decision not to use or issue coined money, but to stick to bundles of iron bars or spits. This conservative decision may be thought typical of an imperial society perpetually defending its own purity and strength, but however the terrible disciplines of Spartan life were introduced, by the late 6th century they were fixed. The true Spartans were an elite; the farm work was done by serfs.

There is some analogy with the 19th-century Zulus, and some remote relation to the ethos of an English boys' preparatory school in the full imperial period. But the Spartan system was more exaggerated, more pervasive of every social relationship, and longer-lasting than either of these analogies. It was complete and extreme concentration on producing strong, violent, disciplined, unquestioning and ruthless young men, and more or less similar young women. The Spartans were ruled in battle and in matters of religion by two royal families. Their army was led by a sacred animal; they camped where it sat down. That was quite a common way of choosing the site for a new city: it was not so usual for armies. Sparta was a city without walls; it was considered that the heartland of the Spartans would never be assailed. Religious festivals were much concerned with group initiation; at one of them a boy was flogged unconscious, at another gangs of youths fought one another, unarmed but with no holds barred. The Spartans prided themselves on brute strength, courage and brevity of speech.

The Persian threat

Meanwhile in the east a storm cloud more formidable still was concentrating its energies. It had been moving slowly westward out of central Asia for 1,000 years. The Assyrians who had been so powerful in the 8th century lost their power in the 7th to the Medes, who attacked them from the east, and to the Babylonians. In the early 6th century the Medes took Urartu and threatened Lydia; Lydia survived by dynastic marriage for one active generation, to threaten the Greek cities of Asia Minor, and between 560 and 546 Kroisos of Lydia did conquer

them, all but Miletos. The Lydians were in some ways a Hellenized monarchy; they offered reparation to Greek gods, they consulted Delphi, and they dedicated very rich offerings. It was Kroisos who gave the amazing marble reliefs that encircled the bases of the columns in the temple of Ephesian Artemis. But Kroisos was not destined to survive. At the same time, revolution brought Cyrus the Persian to the throne of the Medes and the Persians. For Kroisos, Delphic advice and a Spartan alliance were ineffective; no help came from Babylon and little if any from Egypt, two powers with an interest in holding Cyrus in check. The Lydians were conquered, Sardis fell, and with it the cities of the coast, about 546 BC. Babylon fell in 539. The Persian empire was now immensely strong, and directly threatening Greece.

It would be possible also to view the events of these years in dramatic terms through Biblical Jewish eyes, or even through Egyptian eyes. The Babylonian captivity lasted from 586 BC until Cyrus took Babylon in 539 BC and the Temple of Solomon was rebuilt by 516. It was contemporary, in fact, with the archaic temple at Delphi but nothing now remains of it. The walls of Jerusalem were not rebuilt until the mid-5th century. Egypt, like other countries, had revived with the collapse of the Assyrian empire, and a Greek penetration of Egypt, as promising perhaps and as interesting as that of Lydia, had taken place at about the same time. Amasis of Egypt, who took power in 569 BC and married a Greek princess from the colony at Kyrene in North Africa, ruled during the heyday of Naukratis, a Greek trading city on Egyptian soil at the mouth of the Nile. But before the end of the century Samos was ravaged by the Persians, Egypt was conquered by them, Cyprus and Kyrene had submitted. On the northern shores of the Mediterranean, through Thrace, the Persians extended their influence toward central Europe.

By the end of the archaic period then, the Assyrians, whose loosened grip had permitted so much to flourish, had been replaced by a single, vast empire in western Asia. The Spartans had to some degree unified the Peloponnese. At the same time the increasingly aggressive and competitive Greek colonies in the west had provoked serious countermeasures from the Phoenicians based on Carthage, and an even more frightening southward thrust from the Etruscans. Rome itself was already a young city; it was beginning to be successful, but not yet on an international scale: the Romans are said to have expelled their last Etruscan king in 510 BC.

Athens

In the 300 years between 800 and 500 BC, the city in Europe that altered in the most startling and interesting way was Athens. It was slow to alter, and at the end of those centuries it was not a world power, except perhaps commercially. The dominance of Athenian pottery in colonial and foreign markets had been established only in the course of the 6th century, and Athenian coinage began to be minted only at that time.

Aegina in the Saronic gulf is not a big island: you can see it clearly from Athens at sunset. Aegina had a coinage, the first in Greece, at least 50 years before the Athenians. The invention was Lydian, and Greek cities in Asia had adopted it by 600 BC. It was also Aegina, and not Athens, which was the only Greek state outside Asia Minor except Lesbos to cooperate with the Greeks of Asia Minor in the foundation of Naukratis. Indeed there were no Athenian colonies at all in this period except for two troublesome and unsuccessful ones in 620 BC, at the approaches to the Black Sea. But Aegina was the commercial rival and the embittered enemy of Samos, at a time when Athens was still inward looking. It is possible that Aegina had in some way blocked the early commercial expansion of the Athenians, even as early as the late 8th century; Herodotos tells us of "an ancient hatred." (Later, in the 5th century, this rivalry was to result in war and, in 459, the defeat of Aegina and its inclusion in the Delian league dominated by Athens.) However, Athens was not without exports, since Athenian as well as Euboean olive jars have been found all over the Mediterranean world, but these presumably were the product of the richest farms. In the 7th century, in the countryside even more than in Athens itself, the landholders were buried with great riches, government was by hereditary oligarchy, and the poor became poorer. The scandal of Kylon and his attempted coup d'etat in the late 7th century was between grandees. In 620 BC Athens adopted a new inscribed code of law, known as Draco's code, in which the only progressive rule was for state trial and punishment of murder, with the consequent abolition of family vendetta.

The reforms of Solon

It is a generation later that we discover the details of the results of the early archaic period in Athens, in the context of the reforms of Solon. Naturally Solon was an aristocrat; he was also a fine poet, as fine in his less ornate way as the Lesbian aristocrats Alkaios and Sappho who were his contemporaries. He was also a traveled man, with experience then or later of Cyprus and Egypt. His contribution was to rescue the Athenian poor from the penalties of debt. All outstanding debt was canceled, and enslavement for debt was abolished. Athenians in exile to avoid slavery, Athenians sold abroad, and of course those enslaved in Attica, became free. Solon seems to have abolished at the same time the dues on certain land, and another type of serf-bondage, by which a laborer became a slave if he failed to provide a certain annual return of corn. At the same time Solon forbade the export of corn, or of any produce except the olive.

In law, Solon introduced the right of appeal. In politics, he removed the criterion of blood for holding authority in the state and substituted graduated criteria of wealth, at one blow removing the unique power of hereditary aristocracy and laying out the battlefield for a political class struggle he failed to foresee. It is important to realize that an intelligent man in the early 6th century could fail to see it. He graded the people into "500-measure" men, riders, rankers and laborers. The rankers were infantry, with an income of 200 measures; riders had 300. The measures were of corn, we do not know precisely how much; they were not large, since it was forbidden to women and children to enter into any contract involving value of more than one measure. (A Spartan soldier's ration was about seven and a half measures a campaigning season.) The difference of 100 a year between rider and

Sparta

The warrior figure found at Sparta (*right*) expresses, as some other Spartan works also do, and as history and literature confirm, an intransigent national spirit, a high value put on strength and courage, and of course on victory.

Sparta was protected not by walls but by its remote situation in the rich valley of the Eurotas among high mountains. But its arts and monuments in the early, archaic period were wonderfully fine.

The Spartans and the Persians were reluctant adversaries, but the military power of Sparta was necessary to the public honor, prestige and influence of the country as chief member of the Peloponnesian league of southern Greek states. It was also inspired by the ambitious and high-handed Spartan attitude to race, and the dominant imperial and economic position of the Spartan elite over territories acquired with the point of the spear. The Spartans were more stylish and brilliant than we used to think, but probably more odious.

The city occupied a large area that included several low hills. In the evening of its power, walls marked the boundary, which was some 10 kilometers long. Little remains of the buildings of Sparta's heyday. At the eastern end of the acropolis was the sanctuary of Athene Chalkioikos, which from the 2nd or 1st centuries BC overlooked the vast new theater, second only to that at Megalopolis in size. On the banks of the Eurotas, at the sanctuary of Artemis Orthia, which dates back to the 10th century BC, Spartan boys were ritually flogged.

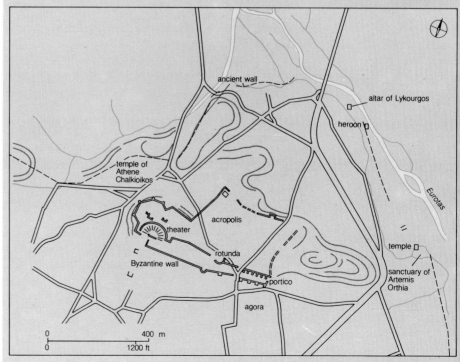

The François vase (c.570 BC) is one of the early masterworks of Greek narrative drawing preserved on pottery. Its scheme is elaborate, its detail fine, its coloring vivid. It is in the Etruscan Museum at Florence, since like many archaic Greek vases it was exported to Italy.

ranker was simply what it cost to keep armor and a horse, which a state officer inspected and certified annually as fit for cavalry service. In the late 5th century one measure cost three drachmas and an agricultural laborer lived on 177 drachmas a year, that is on 59 measures; it would cost nearly twice as much to keep a horse. It has been suggested that Solon used this measure deliberately to tie gentility to landholding, but it is much likelier that the wheat measure was a traditional unit of value. Money was new and confusing; the archaeologists refuse to date Athenian coinage early enough for Solon to have regulated it, though late Athenian historians maintained that he did, and the fragments of his laws mention rewards and fines payable apparently in metal.

The nine governors or chief officials of Athens were chosen from 40 elected candidates who fulfilled the criterion of wealth; the election was from four tribal groups, the names of which existed also in the Ionian cities of Asia Minor, and seem to derive from four cult titles of Zeus. They sound like the ruins of some old system of social grouping, accepted at this time because they existed, but not historically understood; they were never four real tribes, I suppose? The nine chief state officers joined the state council after their year of office. Below this was the general assembly of the people, with a smaller assembly invented by Solon between the two, of 400 elected members, who prepared the agenda for the general assembly.

It was only in the days of Solon that the Athenians captured nearby Salamis; we have some inspiring lines of a speech in verse by Solon that urges Athens to return there to fight, and to wipe out an earlier disgrace. Under Solon, in whatever year exactly Salamis fell, the Athenians had taken an all-important step in national consciousness; scholars as different as Louis Gernet and Sir Maurice Bowra have recognized in the beginnings of democratic justice an articulate social identity, the liberation of a powerful and confident spirit in Athens, a creative breath.

I have said that it is not right to assess a civilized system entirely by its painted pottery; if we did so, we should value the achievements of Corinth more highly than we can. Solon played a part in encouraging this industry at Athens, but the reasons why Athenian pottery ripened to such mastery in the 6th century, utterly overwhelming the Corinthians in the end, may be technical ones. Corinth had received a more direct blast of Oriental influence, and received it earlier. Athenian painters had suddenly to fill huge spaces, and their early designs were small sketches blown up to awkward sizes; in the 6th century they mastered the available spaces as no other painters had done. Were there an unusual number of foreigners working in this art at Athens? Should we think of the effects of constant competition, the organization of workshops, the freedom and abundance of the style, the scope it offered to original genius? In the lifetime of Solon,

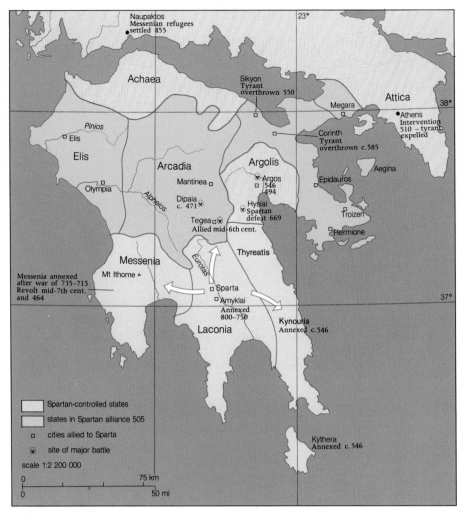

of his contemporary and pupil Kleitias, seem to be created for the weddings of great families.

To concentrate attention on what was developing fastest in the Greek world, and to ignore the more conservative or less successful societies, gives the false impression that history is a linear evolution. In Arcadia, for example, life was quiet, and the energetic young emigrated. A few cities grew from clusters of villages: Tegea from nine, Heraia from nine, Mantinea from five. Athens, after all, had been villages in the dark age, and where later the Roman forum stood was once common ground between two villages. The Arcadian dialect was very old-fashioned, and some of the religious cults of the Arcadian mountains were either unbelievably conservative or very eccentric, or both. But even in Asia Minor there were small oligarchies of land-owners settled on their estates, and the ritual curses of Teos look very ancient indeed compared to the laws of Solon.

It is interesting that Teos had grain hunger in common with Athens. That perhaps was why the first Athenian colonies of the late 7th century looked toward the Black Sea. Wheaten bread was a luxury, and the poor seldom ate it; they lived on various cakes and breads and mashes of mixed grain: barley, millet and so on. It was Solon's law that the official diners who were entertained in the council house at Athens should have barley cakes on normal days and wheaten bread for festivals. We know the wheat production only of certain states, and only for the late 4th century; comparative production may not have altered much over two and a half centuries; if this is so, the list is telling. In 329 BC Attica produced 363,400 measures of barley and only 39,112 of wheat, Salamis 24,525 of barley; in the north Aegean, Imbros 44,200 of wheat and 26,000 of barley and Lemnos 56,750 of wheat, 247,500 of barley. Even mid-Aegean Skyros, with 9,600 measures of wheat, equaled a quarter of the production of Attica. Lemnos produced more wheat than Attica, and more than two-thirds as much barley. Economic historians suggest that Athenian farmers could not compete with cheap wheat from

Spartan expansion in the Peloponnese, 8th–5th centuries BC
After the conquest of Messenia (735–715 BC), grimly maintained against a succession of revolts, Spartan annexation slowed down, but interventions against tyrant dynasties and a system of alliances in the Peloponnese buttressed Sparta's strength.

Athenian workmanship in marble and in bronze must essentially have depended on the patronage of the great; so did the huge early painted vases. The work of Sophilos in the 570s was still adapting Corinthian lessons for an Athenian market, even though some of his work was exported and Athenian painting was beginning to be imitated. Certain of his finest vases, and the one masterpiece

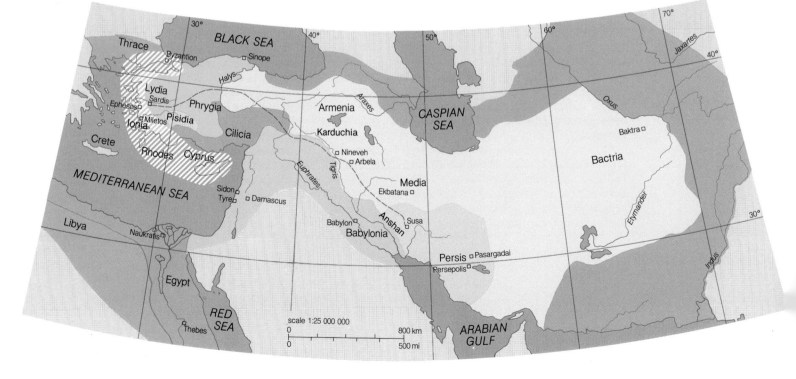

numbers of infantry, and the consequent evolution of mass formations of drilled soldiers, removed the personal basis of power from horsemen, and also from those noble and heroic individuals who had behaved in battle as their fathers had instructed them, and as Homer records (see page 134). The change in tactics became also a social change, and the new infantry became a new and powerful force in Greek politics. At Chalkis in Euboea, the Hippobotai, the horsebreeders, and at Eretria the Hippeis, the riders, began to lose power in the 7th century, though Herodotos suggests that it was a slow process at Chalkis, and as late as 556 BC Eretria gave asylum to Peisistratos in exile. As an Athenian landowner he was a neighbor, his estates being at Brauron, just across the water. In the Middle Ages the French feudal aristocracy of Greece perished by riding its horses in heavy armor into a swamp near Orchomenos and being massacred by Catalans. The end of the equestrian nobility of archaic Greece was less dramatic, and slower, but it was as sure.

abroad; that explanation fits a later date in history, and these statistics after all are late. It is hard to know exactly in what ways the Greek states were interdependent in the early 6th century.

The Peisistratidai and Alkmaionidai

This was an age of great families, of which the Peisistratidai and Alkmaionidai were the greatest, at their best as Pindar praises them, "gentle to townsmen, serviceable to strangers ... may Zeus grant them modesty, and a fortune of sweet delights." But they were mostly doomed, as the same poet also insinuates, to get above themselves; in studying their history one comes to sympathize with the depressing proverbial wisdom that Pindar shared with the Athenian tragic chorus. One of the most famous cases is that of the Alkmaionidai at Athens. In 632 Megakles, a member of this family, was principal magistrate, and when Kylon, an Athenian nobleman who was an Olympic athlete, unusually for an Athenian of that period, and was son-in-law to the tyrant of Megara, attempted to take Athens, Megakles had many of his supporters dragged from sanctuary and murder was committed in a holy place.

A generation later Kylon's supporters contrived to get all the Alkmaionidai banished as being under a curse. But soon afterward Alkmaion, son of Megakles, was in command of the Athenian army, and by 592 he had acquired wealth. He became a diplomatic agent of the Lydians at Delphi, and won the chariot race at Olympia. His son, another Megakles, married the daughter of the tyrant of Sikyon, and his grand-daughter married Peisistratos, tyrant of Athens. That link quickly broke, and there were several more expulsions of the family. But the later members of the same family include Kleisthenes, Perikles and Alkibiades. The last time the curse was invoked was by the Spartans against Perikles, unsuccessfully as it turned out. It was the Alkmaionidai in exile in the late 6th century who built the archaic temple of Apollo at Delphi, the first massive architectural use of marble in mainland Greece. It was the Peisistratidai in power in Athens who began the enormous early temple of Olympian Zeus, designed to rival the new sanctuaries of Samos and of Ephesos.

There are some glimpses to be had of the decline of these great families through the fatal and always unexpected development of technology. The availability of heavy armor and weapons for large

However, the conditions of Solon's day were not quite altered at a stroke. Before the mid-century, Peisistratos had seized the acropolis and was governing Athens. He was Solon's relative, an aristocratic adventurer with international connections, a successful soldier who had taken the port of Megara, and a rich man. His estate at Brauron on the east coast of Attica was close enough to the Athenian mines at Laurion for them to interest him, and later, during one of his spells in exile, he increased his wealth from the silver mines of Pangaion in Thrace. His interest there came also undoubtedly through his neighbors at Eretria on Euboea and their colony at Methone in the north. He installed Lygdamis as tyrant of Naxos, and there he exiled Athenian nobles. As tyrant of Athens he was vigorous and successful abroad, and a strong administrator at home. Roads and public buildings, the circulation of judges to country districts, and a property tax to subsidize the farmers, who by now were back in debt, constitute a policy not hard to understand. It was actively continued by his children. The great Athenian summer festival, the first glorious buildings on the acropolis, and the patronage of artists are their sufficient memorial. Simonides and Anakreon came to Athens, Peisistratos collected the works of Homer. He also brought down mineworkers from the north. Soon after 500 BC the deeper and very much richer veins of Laurion silver and

also the finest marble from Mount Pentelikon near Athens, used in the Parthenon and other 5th-century buildings, began to be exploited.

When the tyranny fell, it fell to an aristocratic opposition and to Spartan intervention. Peisistratos had died and his son Hippias had taken over the state. The assassination of the new tyrant's brother Hipparchos in 514 was carried out by Harmodios and Aristogeiton, two young members of the Gephyraei family, and a year later the Alkmaionidai invaded Attica from Boeotia. The invasion was a tragic failure; it produced nothing but a lamenting verse which was sung in Athens and which has miraculously survived. The small army of exiles died at Leipsydrion, a tiny stone fort in a valley of Mount Parnes, a border garrison post with a view of Athens that they refused to abandon. "Alas, Leipsydrion, betrayer of your companions, what men you have been the death of, good in battle, good by birth, who showed at that time who their fathers were."

Kleisthenes and the unification of Attica

Kleisthenes of the Alkmaionidai was a friend of Delphi, and Delphi brought the Spartans, who under Kleomenes overthrew the last tyrant of Athens. Hippias succeeded or joined his half-brother Thessalos, now a coastal official of the king of Persia, at Sigeion near the Hellespont, in what had once been an Athenian settlement and had only recently been secured by Peisistratos. After a short period of quarreling between great families, Kleisthenes carried through a complete social re-organization late in the 6th century. It was so successful that it becomes difficult now to re-construct the machinery it replaced. The old four clans were allowed to retain some religious functions, the ghost of a social role, but ten new "tribes" were instituted for all political purposes; each tribe was named for a hero as its patron and "ancestor." Apart from one at Salamis, and one at Eleusis, these were all mythological heroes buried in the city of Athens; clearly some attempt was involved to substitute state cults for the heroic ancestors of clans or families venerated in the countryside by small towns whose worship and even whose mem-

The names scratched on broken pottery (*above*) are ostraka, votes cast for the exile (or ostracism) of named individuals in 5th-century Athens, while the bronze disks (*below right*) were used as voting counters in the more ordinary democratic processes of the city.

Below The red-figure drawing conveys some idea of how the Athenians saw their own voting procedure, over which Athene herself presides. She appears to be offering instruction or persuasion. No women vote.

bership the local great family would control. At the same time the towns of the countryside were registered, and each of the three regions of Attica – the coast, the interior and the mountains – whose local rivalry had been a catalyst of trouble for many years, was subdivided into ten; each of the tribes had one division in each of the three regions. There were difficulties and anomalies. We are told the ten heroes were chosen from 100 names submitted to Delphi, and yet a Delphic monument a little later slightly varies the list of ten, under the recognizable pressure of a great Athenian family. But in principle, the new military and political organization that depended on the tribes did its work. It confused any possibility of territorially based baronial conflict; it also sharpened class conflict by setting aside territorial loyalty.

In certain places the boundaries of the new divisions deliberately cut across ancient association. There were four old townships at Marathon bound together by geography and by common religious observance, but one was cut away by Kleisthenes, to be attached to a different tribe, surely in order to leaven a division that had been the homeland of the Peisistratidai. We are not to imagine a new order's influence in daily life, but in elections. Scholars have suggested that other boundaries made the most of any local influence of the Alkmaionidai, but that is perhaps an over-clever argument. The opposition also claimed, surely rightly, that Kleisthenes enrolled new citizens who had no ancient claim to that title. The reforms were not passed without a further struggle, a failed Spartan intervention, an appeal to the curse on the Alkmaionidai, and another

Athenian nobleman occupying the acropolis and withdrawing into exile. By the very end of the 6th century, the system was working.

The ancient council of the Areopagus, consisting by now entirely of former state officers, since its last hereditary members from early in the century must have been dead, was still a supreme judge and constitutional guardian, though its members could be prosecuted personally. A new elected board of ten tribal military commanders had important potential power. The newly registered country towns were given uniform local government. The ten tribes sent 50 members each to the council of 500. It is evident from every one of these provisions that Kleisthenes unified the state. It is also evident, if only from the variety of religious observances still to be found in Attica even in the 2nd century AD, that the Athenian state around 500 BC must have taken some unifying. It was also Kleisthenes who instituted ostracism, the system of voting any one troublesome citizen in a year into exile for ten years. The minimum of total votes (cast in the form of ostraka, potsherds inscribed with the name of a citizen) had to be 6,000, and once it was voted that someone should go, he had to leave within ten days.

The unification of Attica was on a scale smaller than that of the Peloponnesian league and much smaller than that of the Persian empire, which by this time had under Darius I crossed the Hellespont in 512 for an unsuccessful attempt on the freedom of the Scythian nomads. But the changes in Attica were more intricate, and have the fascination of a deliberate and novel attempt to invent an organized society. Its development from this time was head-

The growth of Attica and Athens, 6th century BC
Attica has much rugged land and would never have become rich but for her silver mines and her 5th-century empire. But the Athenians took a special pride in their continuity from Mycenaean times and the fact that they had for centuries been a united people. Like most Greek cities, Athens was intermittently at war with her neighbors from whom she wrested some subject territory. Salamis was won from Megara in Solon's time, and Oropos from the Thebans soon after the Athenian democracy was established in 510.

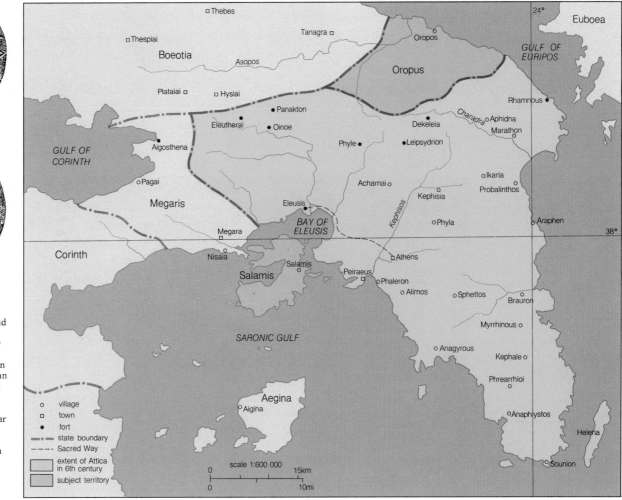

Akragas

Ancient Akragas was a rich and powerful Greek colony on the south coast of Sicily. Its backbone was a long ridge of mountain curving forward at each end to join hands in a low ridge enclosing a vast hollow of land, naturally defended. Akragas was founded about 582 BC from the existing colony of Gela. After a number or tyrannies and a huge agricultural and commercial development in the late 6th century, Akragas became rich enough to challenge and defeat the Carthaginians in 480 BC. Its magnificent ruins are a monument to the triumphant century that followed, when Akragas was one of the largest of Greek cities, with a wealth based on the grain trade. The Carthaginians destroyed it in 406 BC. It was revived later and became a prosperous Roman town, but the mid-5th century could never be brought back.

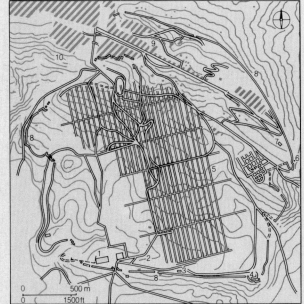

1 temple of Zeus
2 agora
3 temple of Concord
4 temple of Hera
5 ancient road grid
6 rock sanctuary
  of Demeter
7 temple of Demeter
8 walls
9 acropolis
10 necropolis

Right This vast baroque object was part of the facade of the enormous temple of Olympian Zeus, built mostly by slaves after 480 BC. The statues were merely decorative; they were engaged in the walls but carried no real load. They were 7·65 meters high. The temple itself was 112·6 × 56·3 meters, a match for the greatest Greek temples even in Asia.

The temples which top the ridge that forms the southern wall of Akragas are beautifully preserved and rival those of any Greek city. They include the temple of Hera or Juno (*above*) and the temple of Concord (*right*), as they are traditionally called. The temple of Concord was preserved in use as a Christian church. It is thought to have belonged to the Dioskouroi, but Peter and Paul took it over in the 6th century AD. Its porch became a bishop's palace and its side walls were pierced with arches: one of the rare cases where such a late alteration may be thought now an aesthetic improvement.

long. That is partly for economic reasons, partly by the chances of war, partly through the contributions of foreigners, but it is also because the Athenians invented the social basis of democracy. That is why many people are more interested in them than they are for example in the Egyptians, in spite of their wealth, their splendid arts and their impressive monuments. If another reason exists, then it must be the startling literature of the Greeks, though the humanity and rationality that we recognize in their literature belong at least as intimately to their architecture and their democratic experiments as they do to their writings.

In Athens literature flowered late, and so did architecture. By the year 500 BC other Greek centers already had a distinguished record for both. That is particularly true of the eastern Greeks with their magnificent sanctuaries, their thriving cities and their memory of Homer. Even the small colony of Poseidonia in western Italy, which we know by its Roman name as Paestum, could have rivaled Athens in archaic architecture. In the 5th century the rich powers of the Greek west did continue to rival Athens, in some ways successfully, but in the east already at the end of the 6th the Persians had cut off the life of the Greek Levant. It was restored in wealth at a later time, since the Levant until the building of the Suez canal was bound to be wealthy. But the dew was off the thorn, and most of what Greece learned from the east was learned by soon after 500 BC. A great deal was learned in the last generations, and from refugees like Pythagoras of Samos and Xenophanes of Kolophon. In an earlier generation Thales of Miletos, another of these prescientific scientists and prephilosophic philosophers, had proposed a united east Greek state; his pupil or kinsman Anaximander drew a map of the world. The Orientalizing period in Greek art ended with the growth of the Persian empire, but Athens more than any other city inherited the fertility of the eastern Greeks.

Akragas, a Greek colony

Of all the Greek colonies none has a more brilliant history than Akragas in southern Sicily. The Romans called it Agrigentum, and the modern Agrigento, with its shoddily built and unlovely flats, occupies most of the ancient acropolis. The site of Akragas is a vast natural amphitheater with a high semicircular rocky ridge to the north and a smaller barrier of high ground extending southward from the ridge, like two long arms with joined hands, locking in a large area of fertile and protected ground: a crab was one of the crests used on the coinage of the city.

The most spectacular remains of Akragas are the series of temples, several of them well preserved, that stand in line along the southern edge of the ancient city, above the plain and silhouetted against the sky or the sea. It was a huge fortified city, deliberately chosen for its position. Delphi and Olympia grew slowly, Akragas was imposed on nature at one blow. The embellishment of the southern arms of course came later. At first Akragas was a strong natural fortress, looking inward at the provision of its own agricultural needs.

Akragas was founded in 581 BC by a combined party from Rhodes and Gela, a rich trading colony some miles to the southeast. Gela itself was founded

in 688 BC from Rhodes and Crete. The new foundation at Akragas was a deliberately strong colonizing act; colonists came both from Crete and from lesser islands, but the dominant cultural influence was Rhodian, and the policy was that of Gela, which controlled much of the trade of southern Sicily. The first Akragan colonists settled on the northern ridge, but the oldest and most interesting holy place that survives is the rock sanctuary of Demeter the corn goddess (Sicily was an important source of grain for Greece), which is outside the walls, as Demeter's shrines usually were, and older than the walls. There is some evidence from pottery that this was a native Sicilian shrine before the Greeks arrived; it presides over an important watering place.

In the 6th century Greek influence penetrated the innermost native settlements of central Sicily, just as it reached Heuneburg, and the Celtic settlement of Mont Lassois on the upper waters of the river Seine. Akragas reached its dangerous peak of wealth in a later age, when the Sicilian Greeks, under the influence of Syracuse, had a tougher attitude, but the early days were peaceful. The Greeks then were traders, and native cities controlled the upper grazing grounds. The best of the olive crop was sold peacefully to the Phoenicians at Carthage. The Akragantines were despotically ruled, and at the beginning of the 5th century one of their more successful rulers, the tyrant Theron, married his daughter to the powerful ruler of Syracuse. Marriage of the noble outside their own aristocratic clan had become normal in the 7th century. Kimon of Athens was half Thracian; a healthy number of non-Greek names is attested in the great Greek colonial families. But this was a case of dynastic alliance with an imperial aim.

The city of Himera in northern Sicily had been on good terms with the Carthaginians; Theron of Akragas took over Himera in 483, and the exiled ruler called in the Carthaginians. It was Syracuse rather than Akragas which three years later won the battle of Himera, which later proved to be a calamitous victory. The battle produced a fine memorial at Delphi, and a splendid commemorative temple in the plain below the city where the battle took place, but Himera was never rich again, and before the end of the century Carthage had wiped out Himera, and Selinus to the west of Akragas, which was earlier taken by Theron, and finally Akragas itself in 406. There were several restorations of Akragas, even a short Indian summer in the late 4th century, but in the 3rd it became a Carthaginian fortress, and later the Romans took it over from the Carthaginians.

The differences between the Greeks and Carthaginians, and the other aggressive aspects of Greek colonial policy, were exaggerated in retrospect by later Greek historians who had lived through years of conflict. But the two Carthaginian sarcophagi in the Palermo museum, which look at once so un-Greek and so Greek, are a Phoenician type made usually in the Greek island of Paros. The conflicts of Greeks and Carthaginians in Sicily were over trading concessions, and above all over precious metals. There is some resemblance to the wars of the British and French and Spanish in the Americas. Akragas needed peace. It was immensely rich by agriculture and by horse breeding, as well as

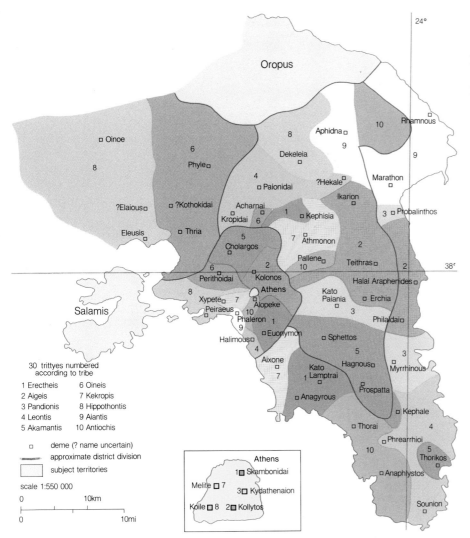

24°

Oropus

□ Oinoe

8

6
Phyle□

□ ?Elaious□

Eleusis
□

Salamis

□ ?Kothokidai

□ Thria

Acharnai
□
Kropidai   6

5
Cholargos□

6
Perithoidai□

8

Xypete□ 7
Peiraeus□
□ 10
Phaleron 1
□
Halimous□

4

Aixone
□

7

□ Anagyrous

8
Aphidna□
9

Dekeleia
□

4
□ Paionidai

?Hekale□

□ Kephisia

1

7 Athmonon
□

Pallene□
10

2 2
Kolonos

Athens
□

Alopeke
□

□ Euonymon

□ Sphettos

5
Hagnous□

Kato
Lamptrai
1

Prospatta
□

10
Rhamnous
□

Ikarion
□

Marathon
□

3 □ Probalinthos

9

2

Teithras□   2   38°

Halai Araphenides□

Kato
Paiania
□   Erchia
□
3
Philadai□

3

Myrrhinous□

□ Kephale

□ Thorai   4

□ Phrearrhioi

10   5
Thorikos
□
□ Anaphlystos

Sounion
□

30 trittyes numbered
according to tribe

1 Erectheis   6 Oineis
2 Aigeis   7 Kekropis
3 Pandionis   8 Hippothontis
4 Leontis   9 Aiantis
5 Akamantis   10 Antiochis

□   deme (? name uncertain)

━━━ approximate district division

▢   subject territories

scale 1:550 000

0   10km

0   10mi

Athens

1□ Skambonidai

Melite □ 7

3□ Kydathenaion

Koile □ 8   2□ Kollytos

**The demes of Attica and
Athens, c. 400 BC**
Herodotos called Kleisthenes the
founder of Athenian democracy.
It is at first sight surprising that
his main achievement was an
elaborate redrawing of the tribal
map of Attica. But it was this that
made democracy possible. The
tyrant dynasty had entrenched
itself because it had exploited
regional conflict. The new map of
Attica united different sections
(*trittyes*) of the regions into ten
new tribes. Men of one tribe now
fought together in the same
regiment; and the Boule (the
Athenian council or parliament)
was reformed on the basis of the
new tribes, 50 from each. Noble
families still exerted great
influence locally and nationally,
but from now on there will
already have been villages
(demes) returning men of no
great wealth to the Boule. The
patchwork of the Athenian tribal
system even outlasted the
democracy and continued into
Roman times. Since a man's tribe
and deme associations were
hereditary, he kept them even if
he moved his residence.

Left The pillars of a vast Doric
temple, built c.500 BC, still
project from the walls and
provide the aisles of the
cathedral of Syracuse.

by trade. Great poets, such as Pindar, and Simonides
of Keos, enjoyed the patronage of Akragas. When an
Akragantine won the Olympian chariot race, he was
escorted into the city by 300 chariots, every one
with a team of white horses. One man in the 5th
century could provide lodgings and a change of
clothes for 500 horsemen. The city of Akragas in an
emergency fed and housed 2,600 refugees. But it
was the battle of Himera, the beginning of cal-
amities, which created the architectural grandeur
one can see today.

The captives became slaves, and there were those
who owned 500 slaves. They built public buildings,
aqueducts, even a sizable artificial lake inside the
city. The temple of Hera and the temple of Concord
crowned the southern aspect. These temples are
wrongly named, but since little evidence exists of
their real ancient names it is better not to quibble.
The temple of Concord survived by being turned
into a church, and is in a better state than perhaps
any other temple in the Greek world. The wall
between the columns of the temple of Concord, with
its perfect and Greek-looking arches, belongs to the
adaptation of the temple as a church in the 6th
century AD. (Its rival for perfect preservation, the
Theseion – another wrong name – at Athens, also
survived as a church. But the strangest and most
moving of all the many adaptations of Greek shrines
by Christians is surely the great cathedral of
Syracuse, the temple of Athene. It gives a longer
sense of continuous history than the scraped and
perfect monument at Agrigento.) There are other
Akragantine examples of Christian adaptations. The
attractive small church of S. Biagio was built by the

Normans on what survived of the temple of
Demeter, just inside the city walls above her rock
sanctuary, to which a precipitous path descends.
Inside modern Agrigento at S. Maria dei Greci, in a
gallery below the church one can visit the bases of
the 5th-century columns of one of Theron's
temples.

The most amazing ruins of Akragas lie to the
south of the modern city, among a complex of
sanctuaries. They are the remnants of the figures of
giants who once stood high up under the entabla-
ture of a huge temple of Olympian Zeus. It was
begun before Himera, probably in the late 6th
century, and was still unfinished when the city fell
in 406. It expresses an unlovely but essential aspect
of archaic Greece, and in its huge proportions and
the difficulties of its construction it recalls the
temple of Olympian Zeus at Athens.

It is very hard not to call this ponderous
construction baroque. It defied space and gravity, it
embodied tricks of technique, it broke away from
the canons of architecture. It had pilasters on its
inner wall to correspond to the engaged Doric
columns of its outer wall. The giants themselves,
alternately bearded and beardless, were a bold
device. Unlike the women who hold up the porch of
the Erechtheion at Athens, these giants were not
doing the work they seemed to do; the real work
was done by iron bars running from column to
column, invisible from the ground. The giants were
not even solid; they were built up with blocks of
stone and then painted and plastered over, as so
many columns were. Monolithic columns are a late
extravagance. In its enormous magnitude, in its
brilliance, its ambitiousness, its lavishness and its
blatant and confident bad taste, this temple embodied a world of which we recognize something
from Pindar and more from the tragic history of the
western Greeks, the world of the grand and self-
elected rulers of rich colonies, an appalling
magnificence.

And yet Akragas, like other Greek cities, was also
a world of sheep and of horses, of excellent vines
and famous olive groves, and Sicily in 600 BC still
had a thriving native population who preserved the
integrity of their customs.

Although the archaic Greek world was a self-
conscious unity of language and civilization, appealing to the same gods and natural laws, eating and
drinking and on the whole living in the same way, it
blew itself apart every so often in armed conflict,
increasingly after 450 BC, and its groups of alliance
or association were still on the whole locally based
in common sanctuaries. Apollo at Delphi seems to
have favored Corinth and Euboea, the earliest
trading powers, good clients of the god. Delos
attracted Athens and the islanders. The 12 Ionian
cities of Asia Minor had their own sanctuary and
their own league. It was common for any Greek
community to shut at least one of its eyes to what
went on elsewhere. Colonization was hazardous,
and by no means always successful. Archilochos,
the first Greek poet after Homer, and the greatest
after him, took part in the colonization of Thasos
from Paros. He has left some sharp phrases about the
unevenness of life, about stormy seas, abandoned
weapons, lost battles, and the wooded crest of the
island of Thasos like a donkey's back, "not good,
not delightful, not lovely."

Greek Coinage

Coins were in origin lumps of precious metal of standardized weight, stamped with designs (and later inscriptions), which identified the issuing authorities. Such coins appeared first in Asia Minor during the 7th century BC and their use spread thence over the Greek world. The earliest coins were minted in electrum, an alloy of gold and silver. From the mid-6th century pure silver came to be preferred; pure gold was not regularly used for coinage before the 4th century. Since coinage was a mark of independence, every city had its own mint: uniform coinages serving wide territories were a development of the Hellenistic age. The photographs show a few characteristic coins minted between c. 600 and 150 BC, and the map shows their provenance. All the coins are shown actual size.

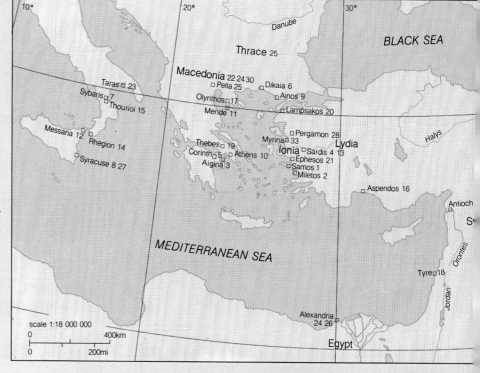

1 Samos, c. 600 BC or earlier, electrum quarter-stater. *Obverse* striated surface. *Reverse* punch mark. A very primitive coin, in a natural gold and silver alloy.

2 Miletos, c. 570 BC, electrum stater. *Obverse* lion. *Reverse* three ornamented punches. These punches, applied separately, may represent the marks of three officals controlling production.

3 Aegina, c. 560 BC, silver didrachm. *Obverse* turtle (connected with cult of Hera). *Reverse* punch mark. The earliest mint of mainland Greece, whose products were widely dispersed in trade by the Aeginetans.

4 Lydia, Kroisos, 560–547 BC, silver half-stater (Sardis). *Obverse* foreparts of lion and bull. *Reverse* two punches. Kroisos was the first to coin in pure gold and silver (cf. nos. 1–2).

5 Corinth, c. 520 BC, silver stater. *Obverse* Pegasus (a figure in local myth). *Reverse* formal punch. From her position on the Isthmus Corinth had political and economic ties to both E and W.

6 Dikaia, c. 520 BC, silver stater. *Obverse* Herakles. *Reverse* square punch. The N Aegean mines supported a number of early mints (cf. nos. 9 and 11).

7 Sybaris, c. 520 BC, silver stater. *Obverse* bull. *Reverse* same design incuse. The bull symbolizes wealth in cattle (cf. no. 15). The incuse technique was peculiar to most contemporary mints in southern Italy.

8 Syracuse, c. 485 BC, silver tetradrachm. *Obverse* chariot, alluding to the international games at Olympia and elsewhere (cf. nos. 12 and 27). *Reverse* Arethousa surrounded by dolphins, recalling the spring on the island where the first Syracusans settled.

9 Ainos, c. 465 BC, silver tetradrachm. *Obverse* Hermes. *Reverse* goat. Like several other cities on the N Aegean coasts (cf. nos. 6 and 11) Ainos produced a handsome coinage from local silver.

10 Athens, c. 440 BC, silver tetradrachm. *Obverse* Athene. *Reverse* owl and olive-branch. This coinage endured with little change from the 6th to the 2nd centuries BC. Local mines ensured an ample supply of silver.

11 Mende, c. 430 BC, silver tetradrachm. *Obverse* Dionysos on ass. *Reverse* vine. These designs allude to the wine for which Mende was famous.

12 Messana, c. 430 BC, silver tetradrachm. *Obverse* racing mule-car. *Reverse* hare and head of Pan. The obverse is derived from Syracuse (cf. no. 8); the hare may allude to speed in racing or to a local cult of Pan.

13 Persia, 5th–4th centuries BC, gold daric. *Obverse* king of Persia. *Reverse* punch. This bi-metallic coinage, initiated by Darius I, c. 510 BC, was modeled on that of Kroisos; Sardis was again a principal mint (cf. no. 4). The designs varied little from reign to reign.

14 Rhegion, c. 390 BC, silver tetradrachm. *Obverse* lion's head. *Reverse* Apollo. Rhegion, like Messana (cf. no. 12), profited from her situation on the straits between Italy and Sicily.

15 Thourioi, c. 390 BC, silver stater. *Obverse* Athene. *Reverse* bull. Thourioi was founded from Athens (hence Athene) in 444 BC on Sybarite territory (hence the bull: cf. no. 7).

16 Aspendos, c. 380 BC, silver stater. *Obverse* two wrestlers. *Reverse* slinger. This illustrates

the spread of coinage into the E Mediterranean (cf. no. 18); this coinage was widely used in southern Anatolia.

17 Chalkidian league, c. 375 BC, silver tetradrachm (mint of Olynthos). *Obverse* Apollo. *Reverse* lyre. On the coinage of this powerful league Philip modeled his own gold and silver coinage (cf. no. 22).

18 Tyre, c. 360 BC, silver shekel. *Obverse* Melqarth riding hippocamp over sea. *Reverse* owl carrying crook and flail (Egyptian emblems of royalty). Another example (cf. no. 16) of the spread of coinage to non-Greek areas; the reverse may owe something to the ubiquitous Athenian tetradrachm (cf. no. 10).

19 Thebes, mid–4th century BC, silver didrachm. *Obverse* Boeotian shield. *Reverse* amphora. The shield was the badge of the Boeotian league. Minted during the period of supremacy won by Epaminondas.

20 Lampsakos, c. 350 BC, gold stater. *Obverse* Zeus. *Reverse* Pegasus. One of the first Greek mints to strike gold coinage year by year; such staters, like the daric (no. 13), provided an international gold currency.

21 Ephesos, c. 350 BC, silver tetradrachm. *Obverse* bee. *Reverse* stag and palm-tree. Both creatures connected with Artemis, whose most famous temple was at Ephesos; under the palm-tree Leto bore Apollo and Artemis on Delos.

22 Macedonia, Philip II, 359–336 BC, gold stater. *Obverse* Apollo. *Reverse* chariot. Apollo was derived from the Chalkidian league (cf. no. 17) which Philip liquidated in 348; the chariot commemorated an Olympic victory. Local gold mines at Philippi ensured regular minting.

23 Taras, c. 330 BC, silver stater. *Obverse* warrior and horse. *Reverse* dolphin-rider. Such designs were long employed by Taras. These coins often used to hire mercenaries to defend Greek cities against the Italian tribes.

24 Macedonia, Alexander the Great, 336–323 BC, silver tetradrachm (Alexandria). *Obverse* Alexander as Herakles. *Reverse* Zeus. Converting captured Persian treasures into coin, Alexander issued a uniform coinage from numerous mints.

25 Thrace, Lysimachos, 322–281 BC, silver tetradrachm (Pella). *Obverse* Alexander the Great. *Reverse* Athene. Lysimachos won Thrace and NW Asia Minor as his share of Alexander's empire; he was also briefly king of Macedonia.

26 Egypt, Ptolemy I, 322–282 BC, silver tetradrachm (Alexandria). *Obverse* Ptolemy wearing aegis. *Reverse* eagle of Zeus on thunderbolt (Ptolemy's personal device). Ptolemy was portrayed with divine attributes like Alexander (cf. no. 24). These designs were retained throughout the dynasty.

27 Syracuse, Philistis, wife of Hieron II, 274–216 BC, silver tetradrachm. *Obverse* Philistis. *Reverse* chariot (cf. no. 8). Under Hieron, an ally of Rome, Syracuse prospered independently for the last time.

28 Pergamon, Attalos I, 241–197 BC, silver tetradrachm. *Obverse* Philetairos (founder of dynasty). *Reverse* Athene. Attalos was a successor in Asia Minor of Lysimachos (no. 25). As with the Ptolemies (cf. no. 26), the founder's portrait was retained throughout the dynasty.

29 Bactria, Antimachos, c. 180 BC, silver tetradrachm. *Obverse* Antimachos. *Reverse* Poseidon. A king unknown but for his coins.

30 Macedonia, Perseus, 178–168 BC, silver tetradrachm. *Obverse* Perseus. *Reverse* eagle on thunderbolt within oak-wreath (referring to Zeus of Dodona). This last king of Macedonia was defeated by Rome at Pydna in 168 BC.

31 Syria, Antiochos IV, 175–164 BC, silver tetradrachm (Antioch). *Obverse* Antiochos IV. *Reverse* Zeus. Antiochos IV attempted to Hellenize the Jews; his aggression against Egypt was checked by Roman intervention.

32 Bactria, Eukratides, c. 170–150 BC, silver tetradrachm. *Obverse* Eukratides, wearing cavalry helmet. *Reverse* the Dioskouroi. This most powerful of Bactrian kings conquered parts of NW India.

33 Myrina, c. 160 BC, silver tetradrachm. *Obverse* Apollo. *Reverse* Apollo within laurel wreath. Some Greek cities were permitted to coin under Roman control.
Note. The reverses of nos. 25–33 are not illustrated.

THE GROWTH OF LITERATURE

In the early 5th century, Greek history takes on a clarity and a detail from written sources, and at the same time it comes to center more and more heavily on Athens. That is not because all the historians were Athenians. Herodotos was from Halikarnassos in Asia Minor and his father had a Carian native name; he himself was an exile, and finally a colonist in the west, but he lived for years by choice in the Athens of Perikles; gossip which is plausible, though it may be unreliable, tells us that Sophokles was his friend. What flowered in Athens in the 5th century had begun elsewhere, and in the past. But it is useful to accept the Athenians at their own valuation, if only because the further we move from Athens in the 5th century, the further backward in time the world seems to be. Far away in Holstein, the Iron Age began only in the 7th century, and so did geometric pottery. In the northwest Peloponnese rocks were still worshiped when Christ was born. The great sages of the 5th century came to Athens, while in earlier generations they were to be found in Miletos, Ephesos and Kolophon in Asia Minor, on Samos and on Syros in the Cyclades. The same was true of epic poetry. It was the fall of Ionia to the Persians in the mid-6th century that shifted the center of intellectual life.

Even after that, the philosophers Protagoras and Demokritos were both brought up in Abdera, an Ionian colony that survived in Thrace, and the western colonies were still giving birth to intellectual movements in the 5th century. But Athens was central.

Dramatic poetry

We think of Aischylos as a purely Athenian writer, and dramatic poetry as a unique Athenian achievement. But choral poetry had an old and a foreign history before the tragic form developed from choral lyrics. In Athenian comedy, a famous old choral lyric could be quoted or adapted; it might be by Alkman, the poet of Sparta. The strange dialect of tragedy, with its Doric coloring in the lyric passages and Ionic in the iambic verses, arises from a mixture of traditions. But even Homer's dialect was mixed, as dialect so often is in heroic narrative poetry that has traveled. Even Athenian Greek was not pure Ionic. But the ritual forms that underlie Athenian tragedy were purely local, even though they had cousins all over Greece.

It was in comedy, not in tragedy, that a separate and non-Athenian tradition seems to have existed. We must assume there were miming dances and carnival farces everywhere: we know of them in many variations and in many places. The Sicilian Epicharmos wrote complete comedies around the beginning of the 5th century, basing them perhaps on the work of an earlier comic writer, Aristoxenes of Selinus, who seems to have inherited the conventions of farce from Megara. We know pitifully little of that tradition. The only comic poet even of the best Athenian generation, some of whose plays we have complete, is Aristophanes. We have almost no Kratinos, and almost no Eupolis, though they were masters that the fine critical intelligence of Horace ranked with Aristophanes, and our own fragmentary knowledge confirms Horace's high opinion. The tradition of Epicharmos at Syracuse lasted into the mid-5th century, as did the works of Sophron, also of Syracuse. Once again, we know just enough about Sophron to grasp his importance; we have no substantial relics of his plays. About 300 BC another Syracusan called Rhinthon left written farces of which we have a few shreds, and only in his case unfortunately, since he was the least interesting of the three, we can fill out our knowledge from a numerous class of south Italian farcical vase paintings.

The Athenians inherited a remarkable repertory of techniques. The Athenian iambic hexameter was already in Solon's use of it unbelievably fluid and strong, with a rhythm that shifted and gathered momentum from line to line like the mature verses of Shakespeare. That is probably because Solon or his predecessors worked it out in actual spoken use, as Shakespeare did. In 1580 the English iambic pentameter was newly invented, or reinvented, yet by 1590 we begin to have the works of Shakespeare.

This head is not a contemporary portrait, but it has been suggested that it may be the head of Herodotos, copied and recopied for those who prized him from generation to generation.

Opposite Top line from left to right:
Herakleitos (c. 540–c. 480 BC), Ephesian philosophizer on universal impermanence, the interrelatedness of all things (notably opposites), on fire as the fundamental element.
Aischylos (c. 525–456 BC), first of the great dramatic poets, was born at Eleusis, fought at Marathon, and died at Gela soon after the staging of his *Oresteia*.
Sokrates (469–399 BC), whose circle included Plato and Xenophon, both of whom recorded in writing much of the man and his philosophy.
Plato (c. 429–347 BC), pupil of Sokrates, and teacher, at the academy he founded at Athens, of Aristotle among others.
Bottom line:
Aristotle (384–322 BC), born in Chalkidike, was a pupil of Plato, was tutor to Alexander, and founded with Theophrastos the Peripatetic School in Athens.
Thucydides (c. 460–c. 400 BC), Athenian naval commander, author of the great *History of the Peloponnesian War*.
Epicurus (c. 341–270 BC), Samos-born Athenian, founder of Epicureanism, the materialist philosophy of qualified hedonism and peace, an influence on Christians.
Zeno (335–263 BC) of Kition in Cyprus, studied at the Athenian academy; philosopher of the stiff upper lip, founder of Stoicism.

Abdera
Protagoras   Demokritos

Athens
Euripides   Plato
Sophokles   Sokrates
Menander   Epicurus
Aristophanes Thucydides
Aischylos   Solon

Askra
Hesiod

Chios
Homer

Ephesos
Hipponax   Kallinos
Herakleitos

Halikarnassos
Herodotos

Kea
Simonides   Bacchylides

Kolophon
Mimnermos   Xenophanes

Megara
Theognis

Miletos
Hekataios   Anaximander
Thales   Anaximenes

Mytilene
Alkaios
Sappho

Paros
Archilochos

Samos
Pythagoras

Sparta
Tyrtaios
Alkman

Stageira
Aristotle

Teos
Anakreon

Thebes
Pindar

Cyprus
Zeno

Poets and philosophers of the Greek world
It is interesting to observe the native cities of poets and of philosophers, and the gradual shifting of the intellectual world toward one center. Pindar the Theban learned his craft in Athens, and sophistry and persuasive rhetoric flourished there.

The development in Greek meters and rhythms may have been as swift, but the period of greatest innovation occurred at least 100 years earlier than the birth of tragedy.

Archilochos of Paros
It is possible to take back further the development in verse rhythms, and also to take back further the splendid comic and invective verses of Hipponax of Ephesos, to the greatest of masters, Archilochos of Paros.

Paros was consecrated to Demeter and was once called Demetrias, and it was the poet's ancestor, perhaps his great-grandfather, Telesikles, who colonized Thasos and brought a priestess of Demeter's mysteries to that island. We know that the Greeks

thought iambic verse took its origin and its traditional subject matter from the impromptu comic invectives and obscenities which were connected with Demeter's mysteries. If it should seem strange to a modern reader that impromptu verses on a popular occasion might have an agile elegance and bite, it will be enough to recall the still-thriving Cretan custom of *mantinades*, which are rhymed couplets sung impromptu, and the custom of the island Zakynthos off the west Peloponnese, where the carnival plays are in iambic verse, and are interrupted by impromptu cross-talk between the actors and the audience, an exchange which always takes place in verse.

Archilochos was writing in the 7th century, and there is no reason to think he was the first iambic

poet, though he may be the first whose work was written down. His father was called Telesikles, like his great-grandfather, but his mother was a slave woman called Enipo, so he was illegitimate, a serious disadvantage under the laws of inheritance and citizen rights of the 7th century. He was a poor man; at one time he went to Thasos, at another he was a mercenary soldier, he had experience of defeats, and he died in battle against Naxos. His antiheroic attitudes, his realism in every aspect of life, and the vigor and variety of his verses have a modernity which is not to be encountered at any later date in Greek poetry, or at least not until Aristophanes in the late 5th century. But the recently discovered love poem by Archilochos has raised his reputation now to what it was in antiquity, second only to Homer's. In this gentle but vivid description of persuading a girl to sleep with him, he speaks directly and at the same time in many changes of tone, and he uses the resources of poetry to the marrow.

Early lyric poets

In the second half of the 7th century, choral lyric poetry was already mature and complex in the work of Alkman, and before the end of it Alkaios and Sappho, the fine craftsmen of individual song, were growing up on the island of Lesbos. Alkman lived and composed in Sparta, but in a happier society than Sparta would know in later generations. He seems to have been born in Sardis, but he was surely a Greek and not a Lydian. For the simple joy in life which is so attractive a feature of archaic Greece, as it is of so many early societies, Alkman has a special place among poets. "Often on the crests of the mountains, whenever the gods enjoy their visible feast days, with a golden bucket, a great pot, of lionesses' milk, with your hands you make a great cheese unbroken for Hermes." In fantasy like this, the gods are very lightly sketched; the familiar human, peasant activity of cheese making is simply transferred to a world of gods, where the buckets are made of gold, and the festivals are on mountain-tops, and the milk comes from lionesses.

Alkman's most famous poem, and the longest fragment we have of his work, was written for an initiation festival of young girls, a nighttime ritual of dancing and singing with strong agricultural overtones. Its liveliness and charm are remarkable enough, but its joking allusiveness suggests an intimacy of atmosphere, a small, local scale of celebration. If a daring conjecture by Professor Huxley is right, as I think it must be, another fragment of Alkman was written for the ritual of a girls' swimming and diving festival. "No longer, sweet-singing lovely-voiced virgins, will my limbs carry me; I wish, I wish I were a *Kerylos*, who flies over the wave's spray with the halcyons, happy at heart, sea-purple sacred bird." The halcyons, in this interpretation, are the Spartan girls, just as they call themselves horses in the poem for the night dance.

The *Kerylos* was a bird that according to legend the halcyons supported in its old age.

The songs of Sappho, and to a lesser extent of Alkaios, express personal emotion in precise circumstances. With an insouciance and a delicate confidence that belong to aristocratic life in all ages, Sappho sings her heart out, playfully and with pleasant formal complexities, though never at the expense of clarity. She tells us the details of her love life, which recall in some measure the passionate crushes of a convent schoolgirl. Archilochos tells us as much perhaps, but without hints and without the full-blooded description of passionate emotions. He does convey passion, and more sharply, in fewer words, but Sappho is more nostalgic, more lingering; she is more a fine than a powerful poet, although she is both.

Mytilene, the chief city of Lesbos, lurched in the lifetime of Sappho and Alkaios from tyranny to tyranny. The brothers of Alkaios were already fighting for Pittakos against a tyrant about 610 BC, and by 606 Alkaios was fighting under Pittakos against Athenian colonists. His great hatred was the next tyrant, Myrsilos, and he went into exile after an unsuccessful attempt to get rid of him. Worse followed; Pittakos abandoned the exiles and joined Myrsilos in power. Alkaios at some point went to Egypt and Sappho to Sicily. Alkaios knew Thrace, and he had dealings with the Lydians. Sappho's family once had land on the mainland of Asia Minor, her brother traded at Naukratis in Egypt; the

brother of Alkaios fought as a mercenary for the king of Babylon. Sappho's girlfriends came from places like Kolophon and Miletos; one vanished into Lydia.

It is hard to call these lives protracted, but they were privileged. Sappho's wedding songs and the political songs of Alkaios were among the substantial attainments of Greek literature in its early flowering. Both poets in most of their songs use a variety of four-line stanza forms, with similar rhythms but very different effects. It is impossible to trace the musical history of these simple-looking forms, or to know to what extent they were popular, a variable folk-art, or to what extent they were first the work of consciously original, individual artists. There is not necessarily much difference. It is clear enough that the Lesbian stanza forms belong to a special and very ancient musical tradition that grew up in that particular dialect; it has been suggested that the same tradition underlies even the hexameter, the epic rhythm. That remains doubtful. We can at least say that a profuse tradition of song rhythm was in flower, and that its use by Sappho and Alkaios was a special development. Their blue blood and their social position to some degree determined their handling of it.

Similar four-line stanzas were in use 100 years later in Athens; many of the political verses of the last aristocrats as well as of the democrats were composed in them. So were invocations to the gods, and since Alkaios also wrote hymns in these stanzas, it is quite possible that hymns were their origin. It may easily be that the 7th-century aristocracy were the first to adapt the stanza forms of traditional singing to political and to very personal uses, and that they were also the first to construct long songs of linked stanzas.

Lyric poetry and work songs existed before Homer, and the highly developed rhythmic sense of the early Greek poets seem to owe more than a little to Asia Minor. The limit of a stanza form is one human breath. The variety of forms, which at least by the 5th century were beginning to mingle, owe everything to the comparative but incomplete isolation of so many islands, and the confluence of so many traditions in Asia Minor. We must not overestimate the personal contributions of the comparatively few poets we happen to know today.

Writing, prose and developments in poetry

The problem is not so much that poetry is early, as that prose is late. Poetry was still disputing the ground of history with prose in the late 6th century, because verse was the traditional device to make memorable. Early written prose still uses many verse devices, not because people spoke like that, though for all we know they may have done, but because they were devices of memory. Written prose had to be invented, and the process was slow.

The written or inscribed verse epitaph or epigram cannot have existed in Greece until the 8th century BC. We have five before 600, and only one before 730; all but one are written in hexameter verse, although in the 6th century the proportion of surviving elegiac to hexameter verses is three to one. The hexameter was the natural verse to use in the beginning because it was the old established traditional verse of epic and of impromptu lamentation. Elegiac verse is a more elaborate eastern version. A lament would be remembered and live in the mouths of later generations. The Gaelic lament for Arthur Leary was composed in the late 18th century but never written down; it was recovered from Kerry fishermen in this century. In the Mani, the central prong of southern Greece, lamentation is impromptu and in verse, although strictly within a given form; the lamentations are remembered word for word for many years.

But, from a superficial point of view at least, all these poets wrote comparatively simply. The technical forms of Greek choral poetry became complex probably under the influence of writing, self-consciously, when it became possible to immortalize difficult and subtle rhythms, and long, wandering sentences, by writing them down. Some of the work of Pindar in performance may easily have been too subtly complex or too polyphonic for many ears to hear; the same, after all, is true of modern orchestral polyphony. The movement was international; Stesichoros of Himera, Ibykos of Rhegion and Anakreon of Teos in the 6th century are unlike each other, but their styles are not regional as the Lesbian style was. Ibykos, rather curiously, went into exile from Italy to avoid becoming a tyrant and worked at

Left Here on a 4th-century red-figure bowl made by Greeks in southern Italy, Pentheus king of Thebes is about to be torn to pieces by the Maenads. This is the subject matter of the *Bacchai* of Euripides, but there are differences of detail as the story is told here, and of course no such scene of violence would be shown on the stage.

Below The scene is apparently the assassination of Klytaimnestra. Drawn on a drinking-vessel now in the Ferrara museum, it conveys perhaps more of vigor than it does of reality, and the story, which takes place among bending olives, overturned tripods and implacable altars, has run a little wild.

The fine team of horses is one of the unchangeable staples of Greek art, from the earliest terracottas to the bronze horses of San Marco in Venice. Here we catch it at the moment of realism, in black-figure with some use of white paint, on a prize amphora. These horses are the pride of some rich nobleman, they are to compete in the races at an international festival, and to win him glory. Pindar praises horses and horse-breeders, but never a jockey, never a charioteer. In this case the driver may be a professional trainer, or just possibly an owner.

the court of Polykrates of Samos; Anakreon, more typically of his birthplace on the coast of Asia Minor, left it when the Persians came, helped to found Abdera in Thrace, worked like Ibykos under Polykrates, and died in Athens. The style in favor at Samos seems to have been love poetry. We are dealing with poets of some social grandeur; to judge from his style, the same seems true of Stesichoros, and it was certainly true of Pindar. He had family connections in several cities; but by the late 500s it seemed natural to learn his art in Athens.

It is at first sight surprising that Greek poetry should be more complicated the more public it is, and simpler the more private it is. Stesichoros and Ibykos composed for public rituals; they celebrated the sacred mythology of all the Greeks; the accent is on boldness, brilliance and dignity. Stesichoros went so far in originality as to invent new episodes, some of which became very popular. The style of these poets is clear and their language striking; it is quite intelligible in spite of its ornament. "Hyperion's son Helios stepped into the golden cauldron, to pass Ocean and to come to the depths of sacred, gloomy night, to his mother and his darling wife and his dear sons; then the son of Zeus on foot entered the grove overshadowed with laurels." These lines of Stesichoros are about Herakles forcing the sun to carry him from the west where he sets to the east where he rises, traveling with him in a gold cauldron across the dark side of the earth.

Even the grandeur and boldness of these themes, which are reflected in the visual arts of the same period, have a long history; they are to be found in the Homeric hymns, and sometimes in the pitifully few fragments that survive of epic poetry after Homer. Only the rhythms are different, and a few aspects of diction and style that depend on the new rhythms: long, flowing sentences sharply ornamented, and richness confused, climax postponed, more than they would be in straight narrative.

In the poetry of Pindar, phrase by phrase the same boldness and clarity prevail, but his style is more rhapsodic, and the patterns he weaves are riskier and even more splendid, more complicated and confusing. "Holy peace where Alpheios breathes again, Green branch of glorious Syracuse, Ortygia, in whom Artemis sleeps, Sister of Delos,

Exekias is perhaps the greatest of Athenian painters on pottery. This serene picture is a miracle of Dionysos. The god was captured by pirates but he turned the crew into dolphins and the mast broke out into vines.

From you the hymn's sweet words set out To lift the strong praise of storm-footed horses For the sake of Zeus of Aitna . . .'' It is not just that one has to know that the nymph Arethousa and Alpheios the Olympic river are runaways who meet to kiss in her spring at Ortygia, the peninsula of Syracuse; it is not the next two phrases, which are perhaps easier to unravel but harder to take; it is the gratuitous, splendid ornament, crushed under its own weight, it is the lack of syntax, it is the overcrowdedness of so much archaic art. But the sentences are intoxicating, and the whole poem profoundly satisfying.

The public grandeur of Pindar and the private brilliance of Sappho are both aristocratic. The contribution of democracy was to come. The poetry of reason was to come. But the objective power of the dramatic poetry of Aischylos arises from the form, from the social situation, from necessary convention of the stage. There is implicit reasoning in Homer, and more directly, though often less powerfully, in many archaic Greek poets. Aischylos is not as novel and progressive as used to be thought; the dramatization of tragic conflict is

bound to make him hit hard, and a long tradition of which we have many glimpses had taught him how to do so. The idea of that conflict, of a rebellion which must fail, of a fall or a curse which must be feared and pitied, was built into the structure of Greek mythological thought long before Homer. To understand the origins of tragedy, it is necessary to presuppose polytheism. ''If the Sun should overstep his mark, the Furies, the servants of Justice, would hunt him down,'' wrote the philosopher Herakleitos, about 500 BC.

It is also necessary to presuppose history. The impact on Athenian consciousness of the city's success, incredible and against all odds, against Persian invasions and Spartan dominance, was so overwhelming that it can hardly be exaggerated. The Athenians took on confidence, deepened their daring, grasped their destiny in their hands. In some sense, by hindsight, we know the confidence was false, and the fate of Athens itself was tragic. But the supreme confidence of the Athenians is justified both by what they inherited from the world, and by what they offered it.

PART FOUR
THE AGE OF PERIKLES

ATHENIAN SOCIETY IN THE 5th CENTURY

Decline of the oligarchs

We may fail to understand the Greeks of earlier centuries because our information is defective; in the 5th most of our failures come from staring too long at well-known information. There are still some gaps in the evidence, though clear patterns can be traced. In the Ionian cities of the Greeks in Asia, after they regained their freedom from the Persians in the 5th century, there were very few public buildings newly or splendidly constructed. Usually it had been one of the functions of aristocrats to display their wealth by such buildings. A lavish public display added to their honor, and therefore also to their power, although power was perhaps secondary to honor in their consciousness. But these were the days of the Athenian alliance of sea-states, including the cities of west Asia Minor, and the islands from Lesbos to Rhodes and most of the Cyclades, who paid a heavy financial tribute to the Athenians. Is that the explanation? Are we to think of poor and democratic city populations that favored Athens, and old oligarchs who retired to their farms and ignored cities in which no generosity would win them a reward?

In Athens itself the 5th century saw a dramatic change in popular morality. Isokrates, who was born in 436 BC, says that in his youth the possession of wealth at Athens was a secure and a socially impressive quality in a man. He refers to a time when the old values of public honor and public shame prevailed. But the action of the state depersonalized the public expenditure of the rich. It was systematized as public duty; it became an entire ramifying system, a sort of supertax, alongside the general tax system. Those who contributed bore a burden, but with little credit. It was the dramatist, not the rich man paying for the presentation, who was applauded. In the 4th century it was common for Athenians to hide their wealth in order to avoid these public impositions. From the 7th century, public display had attracted the ancestors of these rich men; they had built public buildings, commanded their own warships, and sacrificed generously, the meat of course being shared out. In the 4th century they still anxiously insisted in the lawcourts on their generosity to the state, but in later history great generosity was exercised only for the sake of policy by foreign princes, by Pergamon, Macedon, Egypt, Rome, and the wealthiest individuals in the Roman empire. The Athenian-born historian Xenophon in the 4th century BC could no longer understand the ethos of a Sicilian tyrant like Hieron.

Rise of the lower classes

At the same time as this collapse of honorable ambitions in the upper class, the lower class at Athens became for the first time money-minded. In the archaic period the Athenian economy had been essentially a household matter, an elaboration of subsistence economy, with constant exchange be-

tween equals, and with certain communal festivals. But under Perikles in the mid-5th century, the peasants were cut off by war conditions from the earth. The extent to which they lived inside Athens by public doles and payments has perhaps been exaggerated, but that system did exist and there was also (at least for mercenaries) military pay. More importantly, many became small tradesmen, like the sausage seller in Aristophanes. Both their economy and the morality that went with it became money-oriented.

Trade

How far was commercial exchange publicly organized? The corn trade at Athens was publicly regulated, and it was an important part of the city's life, as two-thirds of the city's grain needs had to be met from overseas. The great colonnades built for it in the Peiraeus were one of the monuments of the main harbor. At Olbia, which was one of the centers supplying corn from the Black Sea, and a prosperous city in the 5th century, there were big private houses with storage areas that suggest they must have belonged to merchants. These houses stand closely behind the great public agora, the public business area, and the agora of Olbia is remarkable for the vast size of its public colonnades. Olbia was

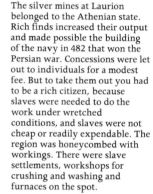

The mines of Laurion
The silver mines at Laurion belonged to the Athenian state. Rich finds increased their output and made possible the building of the navy in 482 that won the Persian war. Concessions were let out to individuals for a modest fee. But to take them out you had to be a rich citizen, because slaves were needed to do the work under wretched conditions, and slaves were not cheap or readily expendable. The region was honeycombed with workings. There were slave settlements, workshops for crushing and washing and furnaces on the spot.

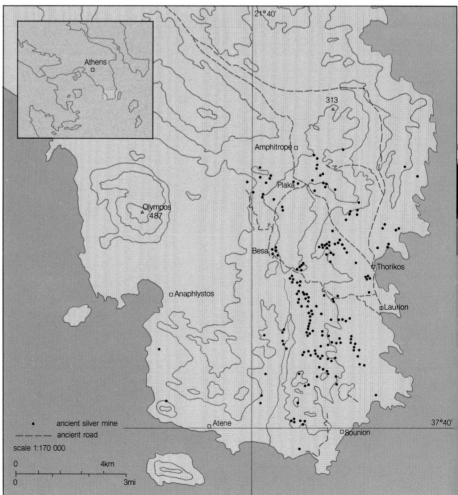

ancient silver mine
ancient road
scale 1:170 000

0   4km
0   3mi

remain the same for long. It was corn starvation and the loss of the fleet that doomed the Athenians at the end of the century. At the other end of the Mediterranean competition for silver and for bronze, sharpened by the hunger for coined money, had disastrous consequences. Even the horse trade inside Greece itself could have experienced severe difficulties, although we do not know that it did so. In Athens some of the horses that the cavalry used, at least in the 4th century and later, came from three different areas of Thessaly, from Macedonia, and from Corinth and Sikyon. Among these, the use of Thessalian horses certainly goes back to the 6th century.

The supply of corn, the breeding of horses, the silver of the coinage and the sacrifices of the gods, must have seemed as secure as anything in nature unless there was a crisis. Mankind was defined as "those who eat the corn of Demeter." Since those who worshiped the Greek gods shared the meat of their sacrifices, the worship constituted Greekness; it is interesting that the Eleusinian definition is wider; can this be the true origin of the universalism that can be detected, as time went on, in the Eleusinian mysteries? But Athenian society in the 5th century was utterly exclusive, for instance of slaves, and of women; wives and daughters of citizens had no more political or legal rights than did slaves. Every Greek city had to do something about the status of foreigners, as their numbers increased and the cities grew, just as it had to do something about bastards and half-breeds. In the 5th century Athens coped with those problems. But slavery was another matter.

Slavery

Chattel slavery, the buying and selling of human beings like a dog or a piece of furniture, is supposed to have entered the Greek world through Chios, but the people of Chios claimed that the slaves they bought and sold were non-Greek. Neither war nor piracy nor even slave raiding could have maintained effectively the systematic slave states of the 5th century without organized trading and organized markets, so the importance of Chios may have been great. In Athens, slaves' nationalities were mixed. Aristotle observes that in any area where slaves were numerous, a racial mixture among them was a useful deterrent against slave revolution. The greatest concentration of slaves was at Laurion in the silver mines, where there were 20,000 to 30,000, nearly the equivalent of the free population of Athens, half that of a really large city of this period like Miletos.

The conditions at Laurion were proverbially nasty, although this was not the only nasty work slaves did. The Athenians had prisoners of war working as slaves at the stone quarries of the Peiraeus foreshore before their own expeditions of the late 5th century reached Sicily, before many Athenians of the last, doomed expedition had died in the quarries of Syracuse. At Laurion the system was one of numerous short-term state leases, quickly exploited. That is probably why the area, as it was left at the end of the Classical times, was such a honeycomb of tiny pits and shafts, holes and galleries, and why what smelting and refining installations have been found have been on so small a scale.

Above right Fragment of an inscription about the sale of slaves, from the center of the city of Athens. Although an Athenian's wealth was to a large extent measured by the number of slaves he possessed, the Syracusans by the 5th century BC were already using slaves on a much vaster scale then Athens.

Below With Greek attitudes to animals we at once seem to be in another, lighter world. These 6th-century animal figurines of terracotta are from Megara Hyblaia on the east coast of Sicily.

an organized, public, commercial enterprise, and it was successful. On the same scale the king of kings, ruler of the Persian empire, traded through his provincial governors or special officials. But at Athens, and probably everywhere else in mainland Greece during the 5th century, trade was more ramshackle.

The system of the corn trade was inherently unstable; conditions were competitive, and did not

Previous page A view of the southeastern aspect of the acropolis at Athens in 1813. The legend refers to the ruins of "Hadrian's temple" (the temple of Olympian Zeus) in the foreground, and between the two halves of the Parthenon, shattered by Turkish cannon, can be seen the mosque that was built some time before 1766.

Athens

Athens has wonderful temples and state buildings, but rather dingy private houses. The acropolis, always the central fortress and principal sanctuary, was enclosed by the 13th century BC by a massive Mycenaean wall. Around 800 BC Athens still comprised a few villages in the shadow of the acropolis. Even at the time of the Persian wars it was hardly a city. The acropolis had its fine architecture, and the Peisistratidai had begun the temple of Olympian Zeus to the southeast, but the agora to the north was little more than one row of buildings, including Kleisthenes' new council chamber.

After the Persian sack of Athens in 480 BC and the Athenian victory at Plataiai came the great period of rebuilding, first under Kimon and then under Perikles. The acropolis maintained its general appearance into Roman times, and today again presents its magnificent Periklean aspect.

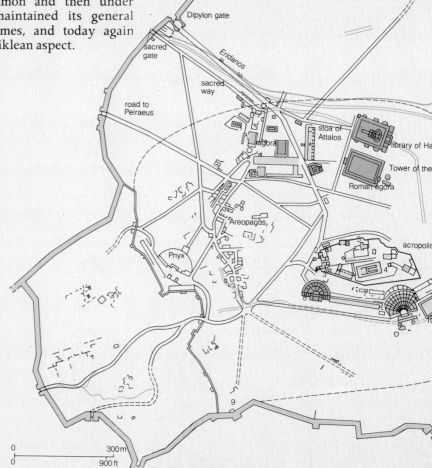

Above left The elegance of the temple of Wingless Victory was a deliberate foil to the grandeur of the Propylaia. It is the last, perfect touch given to the decorations of the acropolis after Perikles' death. It is often thought to be a monument of the Persian wars, built on the site of an old altar of Athene Victory.

Left The theater (or odeion) of Herodes Atticus, of imperial Roman date, was one of the last great public buildings to be built at Athens in ancient times.

Right The stoa of the 4th-century sanctuary of Asklepios.

Archaic

Classical

Hellenistic

Roman

1 Theseion
2 Propylaia
3 temple of Wingless Victory
4 Parthenon
5 Erechtheion
6 theater of Dionysos
7 sanctuary of Asklepios
8 odeion of Herodes Atticus
9 monument of Philopappos
10 odeion of Perikles

aqueduct of
Pisistratos

arch of Hadrian

temple of Olympian Zeus

Opposite, top left The great gate
of Athens toward Eleusis and the
road to Sparta was a massive
piece of engineering, its defenses
strengthened from century to
century. Outside the city,
memorials of the dead (*opposite,
top right*) lined the roads.

Above left The Theseion
(properly, the Hephaisteion) was
the first great building of the
reconstruction following the
Persian wars. It is the most
complete example of a Doric
hexastyle temple.

Above The Propylaia, the state
entrance to the acropolis, was
designed by Mnesikles and built
between 437 and 432 BC.

Above Pheidias' great statue of
the goddess of the Parthenon was
often imitated in smaller models
of no great beauty, like this
Roman 2nd-century miniature.

Above right The octagonal Tower
of the Winds, just outside the
Roman agora, was built in the 1st
century BC by the astronomer
Andronikos of Kyrrhos. It was
sundial, waterclock and
weathervane. The reliefs
represent the eight winds.

The Parthenon (*right*), built in
447–438 BC under Pheidias'
direction, and the temple of Zeus
(*left*) both set out to impress by
their size, weight and richness.
The columns of the Parthenon,
more than usual for a temple of
this kind, do convey strength as
well as incomparable grace.
Olympian Zeus is Hellenistic and
Roman, and so ambitious that it
took centuries to build. The
tyrants planned it about 515 BC,
and after their fall it lay
unfinished until 174 BC, when
Antiochos Epiphanes adopted its
dimensions. Hadrian completed
it. It is curious that the vulgarity
of its size is older than the
Parthenon.

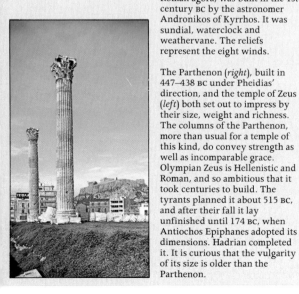

Sculptures of the Parthenon

The Parthenon was designed not merely to honor Athens's city goddess, although it held the finest of all her cult statues, of gold and ivory, some 12 meters high, but also to celebrate Athens's role as leader of Greece against the Persians. The sculptural decoration, most of which was brought by Lord Elgin to London, subtly reflects this double

Above The best-preserved part of the sculptures, the frieze, was also the least conspicuous, set all around the central block of the building, but within its outer colonnade. It depicted a procession culminating in a reception committee of the

assembled Olympian gods and Athenian tribal heroes, and a small group which showed the handing over of the sacred robe given to the goddess's cult statue at her Great Panathenaic festival. The procession is as that for the festival, led by attendants of the

cult (see *opposite*), but the main part was of cavaliers (as here) and chariots, recalling exercises on the processional route which had a distinctly heroic and cult purpose. It is possible that the horsemen were thought of as the Athenians who had died fighting

for Athens and Greece at Marathon, here being heroized in a Panathenaic setting on a building which commemorated success over Persia. Otherwise, it is difficult to justify a subject devoted almost wholly to mortals on a sacred building.

Below The pediment sculpture depicted, at the west, the struggle between Athene and Poseidon for the land of Attica, watched by local gods and heroes, and at the east the birth of Athene watched by the Olympians. The surviving sculptures are few and badly battered, but they give a powerful impression of dignity which is neither static nor unduly otherworldly. The three figures here from the east pediment, long miscalled the Three Fates, are probably Hestia (a matronly figure for the goddess of the hearth) and a languorous Aphrodite reclining in the lap of her mother Dione.

intention. The work was inspired by the statesman and general Perikles, designed by his friend the sculptor Pheidias, and financed from the "surplus" tribute paid by the league of states led by Athens to drive the Persians from Greek soil. This and other Periklean buildings attracted hundreds of craftsmen, masons and sculptors to Athens for the work, yet there is a striking overall unity of style which displays the idealizing and humanist qualities of the Classical period at their best. In their successes over the Persians mortal Athenians seem to have been touched with divinity, and these sculptures glorify both their gods and the heroic character of their people.

Above A slab from the frieze on the south side, near the head of the procession, showing youths leading cattle for the sacrifice. Although we associate Classical art principally with the depiction of the idealized human (male) figure, the artists were also careful observers of the animal world.

Above The metopes were set above the outer colonnade of the temple. On the south the main theme is of youths (Lapiths) fighting the centaurs who had disrupted the marriage feast of their king (the theme also of the west pediment of the temple of Zeus at Olympia). The centaur here, a creature of the wild, wears an animal skin. The expression of strong emotion in the features is not common in Classical sculpture but here there is strong characterization in the brutal mask-like head of the centaur, and in the anguished head of the youth.

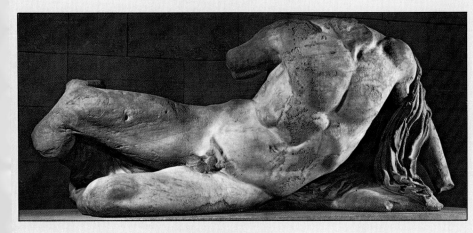

The awkward shape of pediments made reclining figures popular for their corners. From the west pediment there is a figure of an Attic hero (*above*), perhaps a river god. From the east pediment is the god Dionysos (or possibly Herakles) (*right*).

Olynthos

This great city, which dominated the region in the 5th and 4th centuries, stood on the Chalkidic peninsula a little way inland from the sea, commanding the great gulf between modern Saloniki and Mount Olympos. It was at the gate of ancient Macedonia. The Persians took it in 479 BC, and from that time onward it looked east to the cities of Chalkidike and to the Macedonians, becoming around 432 BC the capital of the Chalkidian confederacy. Its alliances with Athens in the 5th century and Sparta in the 4th were for temporary expediency. But in 349 Olynthos bravely combined with Athens against Philip of Macedon, and the next year the Macedonians destroyed Olynthos, with little opposition from the Athenians.

About 100 houses of ancient Olynthos have been more or less excavated, and a whole district of the ancient city surveyed in great detail. The district seems to have been developed as a unity, with continuous rubble foundations for each block of houses. No two houses were exactly alike, so individuals must have taken over, but the general patterns are very similar, and follow rather closely the same ideas that are to be found in Xenophon and in Aristotle.

The houses of Olynthos are the best evidence we have in mainland Greece for developed, late Classical living conditions. The southern court, sheltered in winter, and the northern portico, giving a wall of shade in summer to the principal rooms, represent a traditional formula for comfort. Early Chinese houses blocked up their northern windows for winter at the new fire festival, and there are still traditional village houses in England with no northern window at all. The houses at Olynthos were well adapted to the climate, and acceptable by modern standards. The walls were mudbrick, the bathrooms adequate. The chief rooms or courtyards were floored with magnificent pebble mosaics.

back entrance

0 ———— 5m
0 ———— 15ft

dining room mosaic floor

kitchen

mosaic floor

mosaic floor

anteroom mosaic floor

veranda

cobbled courtyard

storeroom

altar

veranda

porch

Rich and poor

An inscription of ownership from the Laurion mines claims "the ground, the installations, and the *andrapoda*" (the human cattle). Yet a mile or so away, in what is now the same idyllic countryside near Sounion in southern Attica, inland from the fringe of seaside bungalows, there are irises and orchids and anemones and ruins of farm after farm; their honey was famous, it was mentioned in poems. This is one of the best-preserved ancient agricultural landscapes in Greece. It was a proverb in the 4th century BC that one lifetime might compass the appalling contrast between life on a farm and work in the mines. It was a steeper difference than any modern division of wealth and poverty. At Athens, a poor city population accumulated in the second half of the 5th century, but there it was not permanently marked by any contrast of accent or religion. However, the distinction of slave and free was absolute, and few slaves were freed, while war and piracy reduced many to slavery. The difference between wealth and poverty at Athens in the 5th century was a continuous range; few propertied families of the time can be traced more than three generations, and there were no wealthy town houses. Country houses were fortified stone farms, rectangular yards with a corner tower, something like the old farm buildings of the Scottish border.

There are not many regions of Greece thoroughly enough explored to offer a comparison, but the pattern of contrast between town and country is known to be variable: at the colony of Istros (Histria) on the west coast of the Black Sea mudbrick houses clustered outside the city walls; were they native houses? At rich Olynthos in Chalkidike graceful villas grew up outside the city on the extended lines of the same symmetrical grid of roads that existed inside the city; whose houses were they? Were they built on the landholdings, which would be good land close to the city, of the founding families? The egalitarianism of early colonial land division not only ossified into an aristocracy of founding families, but was swiftly disturbed in other ways, even by the natural operation of the laws of inheritance and the equal rights of kinsmen in successive generations.

At Megara Hyblaia in Sicily, which was destroyed in 483 BC, rich and poor were buried in common graveyards until about 550 BC. From that date the rich separated and isolated their tombs in family groups. But even in the early graveyards, three-quarters of the dead died poor. What offerings there were in the graves came in reused oil or wine jars. Of 250 burials, 42 per cent had no offering at all; 13 per cent were bodies simply dumped in the earth. There is a certain poetic justice about the wars that so badly afflicted 5th-century Greece; in wartime the slaves escaped more easily, and slave owners were enslaved more easily. Nikias, the defeated Athenian general of the Sicilian expedition of 415–413, owned 1,000 slaves in the Laurion silver mines, and hired them out to Sosias the Thracian, the number of slaves to be kept at 1,000 by Sosias. It is very likely Sosias was once a slave himself.

Modern analysis of ancient societies has revealed several points of paradox. The Greeks in the 5th century had no state policy on a number of questions we think important.

121

Everyday Life

We know curiously little about everyday life in the ancient world, because the ordinary routines of ordinary people are difficult to trace in great literature and great art. But the evidence we have is sharp and striking, both the literary evidence, from writers like Plato, Aristophanes and Archilochos, and that from physical representations. Sometimes it is only a line from Hesiod about getting a woman, "a bought one, not one you marry, to follow the plow," or a painted tombstone with a lady sacrificing in her garden like a vicar's wife setting out her stall at a bazaar.

It is important to pay some attention to the date of each particular fragment of evidence: there is no period we can reconstruct completely; many things stayed the same for hundreds of years, yet there were differences, and these differences are what we mean by human history. Fish tasted the same for a thousand years, but it was not eaten everywhere or always by everyone, and the trade in pickled fish increased as the cities grew. Not everyone in the dark age of Greece possessed a plow; they cultivated with a mattock. It is an easy question to ask whether the size of fields and individual landholdings increased or decreased, but to simple and essential question like this we know answers only in the broadest outline.

Below In the late 6th century in Boeotia these small terracotta figures representing scenes of daily life were made in some numbers and were commonly placed in tombs. The barber's shop was proverbial in the Classical world, as the forge had been earlier, as the center of gossip. The man carrying the basket is later, but this at least is a scene that can hardly have altered.

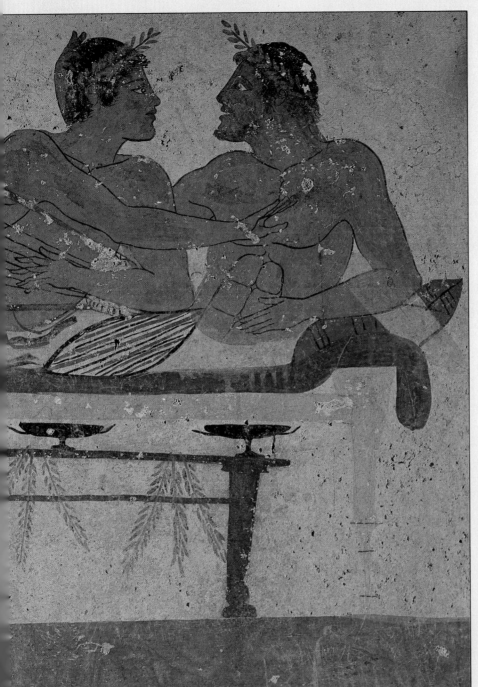

Left This banquet scene, painted with a fresco technique about 480 BC, is from the walls of a sarcophagus from Poseidonia (later Paestum) in south Italy. There are similar scenes in Athenian vase painting. The tradition of these festive dinners was exclusively male except for loose-mannered girls late in the proceedings: hence the homosexuality and benignant irony of this couple. This was the tomb of a young man, and the paintings convey a strong sense of physical pleasure.

Above The gossiping of these painted terracotta women from the British Museum is a permanent feature of Mediterranean life, but this precise observation of it, the mixture of humor, affection, decorative art and realism, belongs to the climax of the late Classical age. The severe lines that made ancient statues even in miniature so impressive have begun here to swirl and to melt, but the process so suits the subject that we are content to put Sophokles behind us, and look forward to Menander.

Above The plow was the most important instrument of human progress in the Greek world, and to judge by its importance in mythology and metaphor, the Greeks knew it.

The precision of the craftsman at work on the last fine ornament of a bronze helmet (*far left*) is well observed. The sharpness is in common between the drawing, the bronzework and the dry exactness of the young human body. This combination of restraint and mystery is typically Classical, but it remembers archaic art. The fish merchant (*left center*) is warmer, more cheerful, less high-powered and typically south Italian, a little post-Classical. The boy carrying furniture (*left*) presumably to furnish a banquet, belongs to the earlier world. There are very restrained erotic overtones, much subtler than the flat words "naked youth carrying a bed."

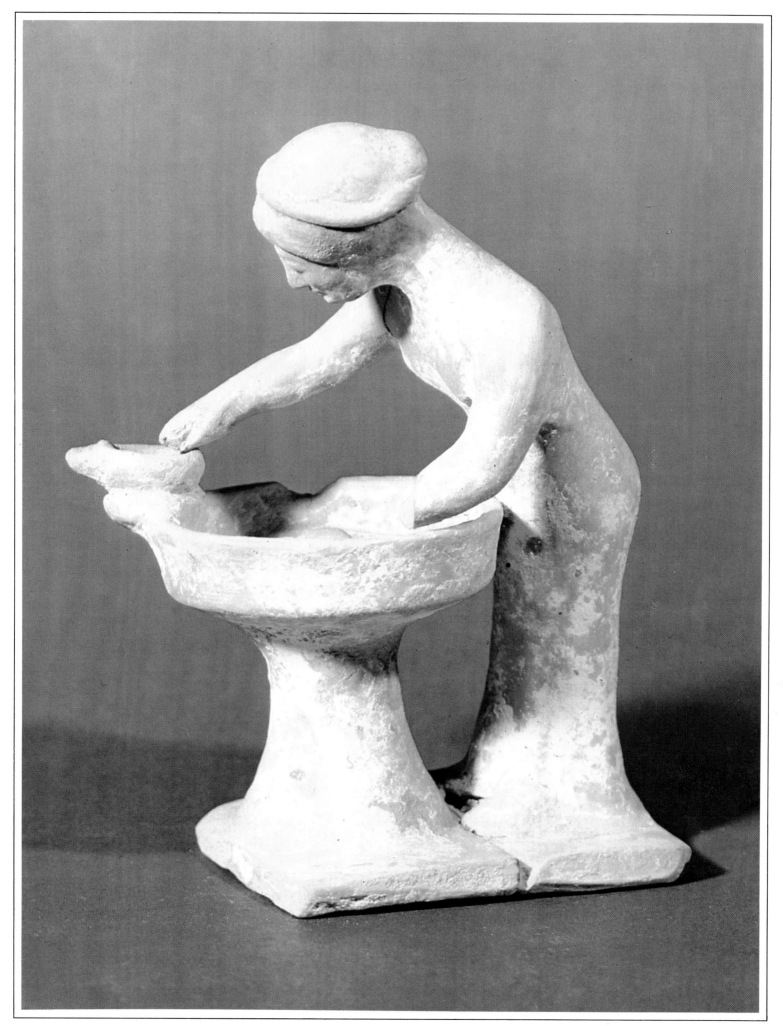

In a sense there was no state, no deliberate, longstanding, self-knowing, self-organizing entity that knew what it was doing and accepted consequences. We are told that the Persian economy could function well only while its wealth was prevented from circulating. It has been said that the Spartan social system was based on war, and yet it threatened to collapse when war broke out. The Athenians prided themselves on the arts of peace, and yet their economy threatened to fall apart under peacetime conditions. The poor were threatened, and not eased, by the increasing reliance on slave labor, which once it was available inevitably penetrated every enterprise. An extreme solution was calmly suggested in a minor work of Xenophon: that the state itself should acquire slaves, just as an individual might do so, in the hope of profiting for ever by their labor; he thought the right proportion might be three slaves to every Athenian citizen.

Religion

Something more, in view of these contrasts and paradoxes, must be said about Greek religion in the 5th century. The system of the gods was apparently unalterable although every element in it was variable. The names of individual gods cover more than one function, and the roles of the gods vary even when their names stay the same. What Zeus does at Elis is partly done by Athene at Athens. In a calendar of festivals inscribed on a rock face in Attica all the celebrations are sacred to Hermes. But what was expected and demanded of the gods, taken together, was the same: rain, bread, wine, physical wealth, healing, oracular wisdom, peace.

Opposite A woman grinding corn in a handmill: 5th-century terracotta figurine in the National Museum, Athens.

Below The riders of the Parthenon frieze are young men of military age riding in the procession to the acropolis on the festival day of Athene. They are the pride of Athens in the pride of life.

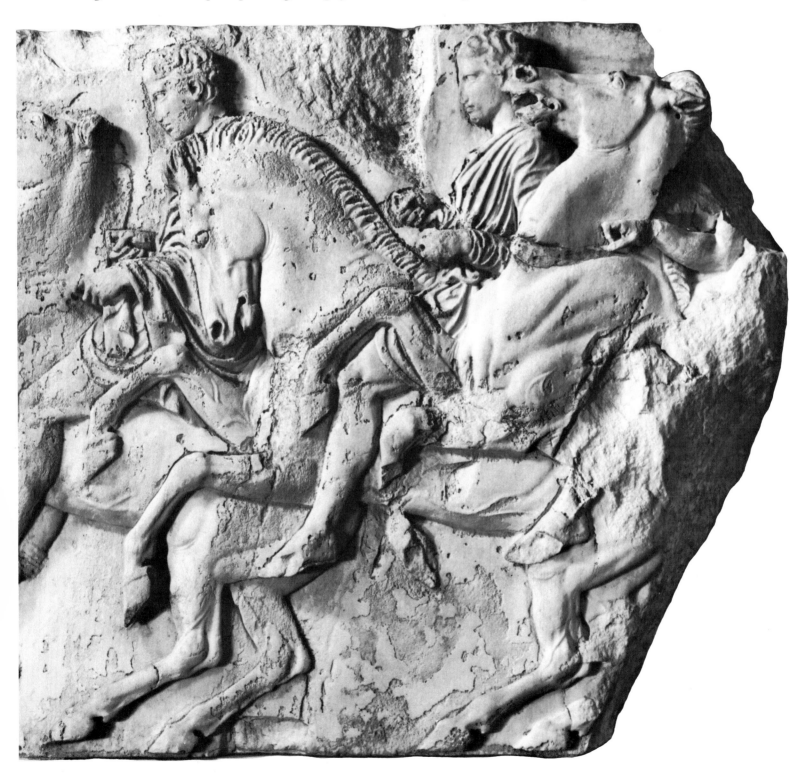

The Classical Moment

The most characteristic quality of Greek 5th-century art is its lively natural geometry. The Greeks saw and expressed natural forms in geometric terms, and geometric forms as if they were growing organisms. The interest in mathematics and the beginnings of science at Athens were a later development than this instinctive geometrizing, but must have helped to shape it in the 5th century. Statues were designed by the use of a network of mathematical proportions. As realism increased, and paradoxes of marble in motion began to be achieved, the old networks were abandoned, but new ones were substituted.

It is useful to observe the strange and marvelous shapes that Greek motifs could take, even at the most stringent moment of Classicism and restraint of form in Athens. Elsewhere, the Greek themes were adapted as vigorously and transformed as creatively as the same or older themes had been by the Greeks themselves in the days of their own innocent eyes. But it was curiously often the spirit of Classical Greek art that traveled, not its mere motifs, so that what might have seemed alien material was transfigured.

The formal palmettes and lotus buds of the 6th century turned out to be capable of endless variation, in marble, in terracotta and in bronze. At their best, in the 5th century, these flowing systems were both free and rigorous; in late antiquity they ran wild.

They were often used, always in a new version, to decorate a building; as in the sober black, tan and vermilion of this version (*top*), one of the architectural ornaments of the workshop of Pheidias at Olympia, where he designed and built the great Zeus for the temple about 430 BC. The golden version (*above*) comes from Brauron in Attica; it is hard to date, but probably belonged to a piece of late 5th-century jewelry. In principle, the design sprouts and twines in gold in the same way as it did in terracotta on Pheidias' workshop, but the difference of effect is substantial.

On this well-executed sarcophagus, found at Sidon and now in the Istanbul museum, Athenian art and the subject matter of the sculptural decorations of the Parthenon have an influence as far away as Asia Minor. The high-pitched shape is said to be Lycian, perhaps in imitation of local roofs, but the polished execution and mythological content are typical of late 5th-century international Greek work.

The sphinx is an old tomb guardian, and the fine cat-like bodies and the heavy smiles of archaic sphinxes preside over some of the earliest Athenian stone memorials. But by 400 BC the realistic and beautiful, almost pretty head, the fully modeled breasts, and the sophisticated animal body have altered the meaning of the sphinx. She is less erotic perhaps, but more sexual. For the remnants of divinity and

mystery, she relies heavily on her wings.

The battling centaurs are in even higher relief. On one end two centaurs fight over a deer; on the other two centaurs batter a Lapith into the earth. The formal origins of the latter may be seen in the centaur and Lapith metopes of the Parthenon, though there are other models in Athens and at the temple of Apollo at Bassai. The technical handling of this sarcophagus is abler than some of the Parthenon work, and one may prefer the centralized and dramatic composition here. But although the composition as a whole is clever it is not masterly. This sarcophagus is fine work, with excellent details, but just slightly mechanical. It was once painted, but the paint is mostly lost.

This astonishing gold piece is one of several helmets decorated with strange embossed eyes, made around 400 BC and found in Romania, this one at Cotofenesti. The eyes have a long history, in Greece as elsewhere. A frieze of eyes ran around the throne room in the palace of Ebla, in prehistoric Syria. Painted eyes decorated the prows of Athenian warships in the 5th century, and have survived here and there in the Mediterranean until modern times. The eyes are not to terrify but to keep away evil. The fantastic beasts that decorate such pieces are no more Greek than the eyes: they are fresh from the same Oriental sources that had fed such hybrids into Greek art and mythology some 200 years earlier.

It is probably a sign of undeveloped traditions of art, however grandiose, that these pieces are visibly a mixture of

undigested influences. The richness of the materials is in a way barbarous, the style and workmanship are wild and, from a Greek point of view, extravagant. It is salutary for Greek historians to see that these luxurious and valued objects, produced so close to the Greeks at this time, have so little Classicism about them. They are not part of the history of Greek art, and scarcely of Greek influence, but they define the borders of Greek consciousness: the Greeks were in contact with these people and some Greeks had seen such treasures. This helmet in a precious metal would probably have impressed the Athenians as much as it impresses us, as splendid and barbarous and formidable.

There is no doubt that Greek art underwent a metamorphosis particularly on the shores of the Black Sea. The formal but relaxed treatment of flower and whirl motifs becomes quite stunning in this golden cap of state found at Ak-Burun in the Crimea. Its creator may well have been Greek, as may its owner – the grave where it was found contained an amphora and a Greek coin. Made probably around 400 BC or soon after, the cap was originally lined with leather. It must stand here for many masterpieces of Greek and half-Greek art in precious material, usually in gold, which have been found in Russia and are now mostly in Russian provincial museums. They are as impressive in design and in line drawing as they are in quantity and in richness, both in ancient and in modern terms of value. It should also be remembered that the same area was in contact with the formalized animal style of art of the steppes, with the textiles of central Asia, and eventually with the silk road to China.

This is part of a wonderfully barbarous piece of ornamental armor that fitted the knee and leg of a Thracian king not long after 380 BC. It was found with more easily datable (and some much more Greek) treasures in the Mogilanska mound at Vratza in Bulgaria.

The wealth of silver and gold speaks for itself. The strange ornaments, the parallel stripes on the woman's head, represent tattooing. Thracian witches who could enchant the moon out of the sky, and the tattooed faces of Thracian women, had been proverbial in Athens in the 5th century. The Athenians appear to have employed Thracian nurses, just as the Normans in England employed Welsh nurses, with a resulting mixture of elements from another folklore into the local tradition. In Thrace, a whole series of rich works of art, far richer than have

survived anywhere among the Greeks, mark the stages of Greek influence. The Athenians, for most of the 5th century, were anti-Persian allies of the Thracians, and some intermarriage took place. In one case, we have a detailed description of the marriage dinner, which was famous for hundreds of years.

The unrestrained decorations arise naturally from the shape of the greave; they were intended in principle to be terrifying, and perhaps magically to turn away evil from the wearer. Faces had begun to appear on the kneecaps of greaves at Olympia in the early 6th century BC, and the spirals and divisions were probably earlier: an Oriental influence, like the griffins on the lower half. This piece is of course far closer to Greek 7th-century taste than it is to the Classical age, but what had withered in

Greece could revive on the borders of the Greek world with uninhibited vigor.

The idea was to decorate and divide up a surface with infinite variations of texture, and at the same time to represent, to impress. The lions trailing like curls from below the ears are flat in conception, and so are each of the other details (although the snakes emerging from snails' shells are in bolder relief). They have some relation to the animal art of the nomads, but the bird on the left and the wing (of a griffin) on the right have a more civilized look. This is not, of course, Greek work, but a native extravaganza on a mixture of themes, some of them Greek.

From the late 5th century onward the burlesque treatment of heroic stories in visual art became quite common, no doubt sometimes under the influence of Athenian comedy, but by no means always.

The introduction of full individualistic realism into art came in the 5th century, as it did in the Renaissance, by way of caricature, and there seem to have been elements of caricature in the work of the subtlest painters of the end of the century, among them Zeuxis of Herakleia, a colony of Taras (Tarentum) in Lucania on the "instep" of Italy.

This vase is from Pisticci, not far from Metapontion, very much from the world of Zeuxis, though hardly characteristic of his better-known paintings, which were of Eros wreathed in roses, of bunches of grapes or of a family of centaurs.

This rougher sketch shows a famous ambush (of Dolon by Odysseus and Diomedes) in the *Iliad*. The trees with their lopped-off branches are probably meant to give an element of perspective as well as formality. The action moves out of the picture toward you as you look at it. The surface is once again as fully covered as it was in the very early Greek vases, but the detail is more ornamental, also more realistic. The animal on the helmet of Diomedes is meant to be just as funny as he is, but this artist cannot avoid bringing everything he touches to life, even a helmet crest, even a garter. His use of the most worn-out conventions, for example, the flying cloak or the lines of the stomach and chest, is notably gleeful.

127

Bassai

Below The *cella*, with its 10 Ionic buttressed half-columns and single central Corinthian column (one of the earliest known). The British stripped the temple of its sculptured decorations; they are now in the British Museum.

The temple of Apollo the Helper stands near a water spring, very high up in the Arcadian mountains. It belonged to the people of Phigaleia, a powerful ancient hilltown not far away across country. It is said to commemorate the turning away of a plague, and the architect is supposed to have been one of the architects of the Parthenon. It is an extremely peculiar monument with a unique ground-plan, a side door for its main entrance, and its north – south orientation. There is something mysterious about this great temple among high mountains, and the weirdness of its atmosphere at night or in winter still recalls some nuances of ancient religion.

The contradictions in the nature of individual gods troubled no one but philosophers; the individual acquired his religious wisdom from tradition and selected from it automatically.

That is why the Athenians were open to such bold conceptions as those of Aristophanes or of Plato's *Symposion*. Theirs were brilliantly inventive and unashamed minds, to whom no god was all-important and who knew of no creed. In their adaptations of existing forms they showed an astonishing power. The craftsmen of the Parthenon frieze must have learned to carve horses from an art preoccupied with heroes and the dead. After the work was complete, a few tombstones appeared, surely by the craftsmen of the Parthenon, which readapted its figures. The tombstone of Sosinos, a smith from Crete who lived and worked in Athens, and the tomb of the cobbler, Xanthippos, who seems to have been a slave, model their portraits on the seated gods of the Parthenon. The crop-headed slavegirl Minno sits spinning on her tombstone like a goddess.

But there is no doubt that Athenian religion had its dark side, which was taken seriously. There were ceremonies of exorcism, and many primitive rituals. Sophokles was more respected in his own century as the servant of a holy snake than he was for his dramatic poetry. Nikias, who delayed military action at Syracuse because of an eclipse of the moon, was not unique in his superstitious anxiety. Before the battle of Salamis in 480, when the Greek fleet decisively defeated the Persians, the Athenians performed human sacrifice, combining their disgusting ritual with a wild barbarity in the execution. There was talk afterwards of miracles, a magic apparition from Eleusis and the omen of a dove, of an owl, of a snake, even of a dog. The Athenians believed that a dead hero rose from the ground to fight for them at Marathon, scene of an earlier famous victory over the invading Persians in 490. Here and there in the countryside Dionysos was ivy or he was the fig tree. Annual processions with transvestite dancers placated this or that god, commemorated this or that initiation. In the ritual of child initiation at Brauron, a little human blood had to flow.

It is against this dark and disoriented aspect of the century that the intellectual pride and confidence of the Athenians are to be measured. The 7th century BC had lesser problems, but the spirited and attractive poetry of Archilochos is equally to be measured against them. The new element in the 5th-century darkness is disorientation, a condition like nervous fatigue, which entails loss of meaning, something close to the *anomie* described by sociologists. The ancient ritual forms of Greek religion, the public and collective rituals which were integral to a whole society and way of life, had lost their force to some degree at the end of the 6th century. They had lost their "natural" context, and many crucial functions had been taken over by the state. The Athenians no longer understood what rituals they were performing (hence the mock rationalism of the sophistic generation of the tragic poet Euripides) and widespread anxiety was the result as well as the cause. It was accompanied at a later stage by an otherwise unaccountable increase in wild and exotic cults, and in private religious and magical indulgence.

THE PERSIAN AND PELOPONNESIAN WARS

The entanglement of the Greeks in the edges of the Persian empire was inevitable, and the Greek cities of Asia Minor were almost all eaten at once. Thrace was at first safer in spite of its neighboring barbarians, and the Black Sea colonies in spite of the Scythians. Since the fall of Kroisos king of Lydia to Cyrus in 546 most of the Greek cities in Asia and all the Lydians had been ruled from Sardis, Phrygia and the Greek cities there from Daskylion, by Persian governors, but each city had a ruler of its own, much like a tyrant. He was independent as long as he paid his taxes and produced his regiment. As a class, these men were not loyal to Persia; they were self-interested local barons.

The Persians invade Thrace

In 512 BC Cyrus' successor Darius invaded Thrace. A floating bridge was built from Asia into Europe by an architect called Mandrokles of Samos, and Greeks among others added their regiments to the vast imperial army. It crossed the Danube on another Greek bridge of boats, and Darius adventured north against the Scythians.

On the tribes of the region he had little effect, nor did he attain the gold mines north of the Danube. Had he done so, he would have controlled the mineral wealth of the earth from central Europe to Afghanistan, where at about this time a Persian governor's palace was built on the upper Oxus, close to the lapis lazuli mines. His communications with his own empire were at one time cut off, and the three Greek cities of Byzantion, Perinthos and Chalkedon rebelled behind him. He retired into Persia, but he left an army in Europe that in the end conquered the coastal states from the mouth of the Black Sea to the Axios west of Chalkidike;

Macedonia acknowledged Persian supremacy. Yet these were not secure conquests; the Scythians retaliated by raiding into Thrace and driving out a Greek ruler the Persians had appointed.

This man was Miltiades of the Chersonese. At the bridge of boats on the Danube, when Darius had crossed, Miltiades made contact with the Scythians, who sensibly proposed he should destroy it. The plan to do so was thwarted by Histiaios of Miletos. Histiaios' reward when the king of kings returned was Myrkinos on the Strymon east of Chalkidike, a fertile agricultural settlement not far inland, poised on the slopes of Mount Pangaion, near the silver mines. The colony was in fact unsuccessful, and so was Amphipolis, a later Athenian colony in the same position. But the prospect was glittering and the Persians soon became envious. Histiaios was recalled into Persia and kept there 12 years. Meanwhile his daughter's husband Aristagoras ruled Miletos under the empire, and it was he who brought Persia finally into direct conflict with mainland Greece.

Aristagoras and the Ionian revolt

An oligarchy of great families, thrown out of Naxos by the population, had appealed to Aristagoras, who was inspired to suggest to Darius a plan to subdue not only Naxos but all the islands and the ancient trading cities of Euboea as well. In 499 an expedition of 200 ships against Naxos achieved nothing in four months, and Aristagoras was suddenly in disgrace, as swiftly as Histiaios had been. His reaction was devastating. He organized a series of rebellions, the tyrants were expelled from every Greek city he could reach, except at Mytilene on Lesbos where one was stoned to death. Aristagoras

The Persian empire in the 5th century BC
The Persian palaces at Persepolis and the royal tombs at Naqsh-i Rustam give lists of the peoples who were subject to the Persian kings. Their representatives are portrayed each in their characteristic clothing and bringing the gifts from their region. Unlike Egyptian and Assyrian representations, the Persian reliefs show the subjects upright and dignified, led by the hand to present their offerings. There is a noble concept of empire here. The names are selective: there were far more tribes and peoples under Persian rule than the ones listed. A different official list, preserved by Herodotos, gives the satrapies organized by Darius and the tribute assessment of each one. We should not expect the list of satrapies to square completely with the list of peoples, and in any case the satrapies were subject to reorganization from time to time.

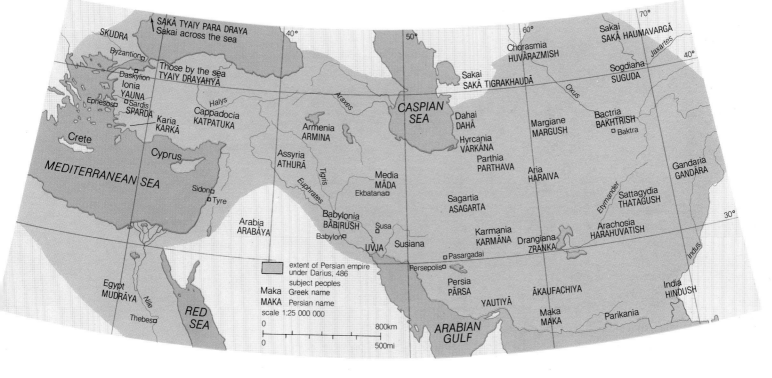

Aegina

The island of Aegina was wealthy and independent until Athens grew strong enough to overwhelm it in the 5th century BC. In the 7th century and the 6th it was a great sea power. It has a number of fascinating archaeological areas and has produced at least one great treasure of gold, dating from the Bronze Age, or so it seems, and buried in an old tomb just outside the sanctuary of Apollo, at the island's modern capital. Aegina's silver coins were the common coinage in much of Greece and circulated widely in the Mediterranean; Aeginetan late archaic sculpture was of international significance. The island lies about halfway between Athens and the Peloponnese. It is mountainous and partly forested.

The most important surviving temple is the sanctuary of Aphaia, a local goddess, which stands on a low hill above the sea. This temple was built in the early 5th century, but the sanctuary had earlier buildings and the cult dates at least from the 7th century BC. The sculptural decorations of the 5th-century building point to an identification of Aphaia with Athene.

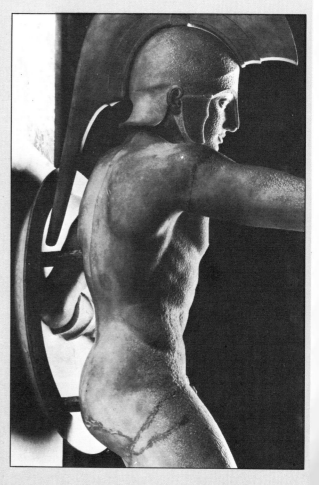

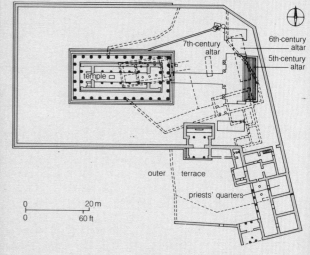

The temple of Aphaia (*left*) is still fine and strong in spite of the theft of its sculptures, now in Munich. Not long ago it was damaged by lightning, but it still looks more idyllic than it would have done in antiquity, when it was a busy place. The sculptures (*above*) have also suffered a transformation, having been retouched by Thorwaldsen in the last century. Still, they are sharply imagined and well-executed figures, and in a less romantic light and in the detailed handling of the stone they have a great deal to teach about the last moments of the archaic age and the severe and experimental beginnings of Classicism.

Top The temple of Artemis at Sardis was built by Greeks in the 3rd–2nd centuries BC. The fluting of the columns was never completed.

Above This late Classical Athenian wine-jug carries a design of battle between a Greek and three Asiatics. There is a similar sense of confidence in the writings of Xenophon, and of Menander. It was first created in the generation of the Persian wars, or more likely in the period that followed them.

himself resigned the tyranny of Miletos, silver coinage was issued by the new democracies on a single standard, an appeal to Sparta failed but appeals to Athens, and to Eretria in Euboea, brought a fleet of 20 warships and a flotilla of five. The Persian empire was slow to act. Aristagoras had burned Sardis, the chief city of Lydia, though without taking the fortress, before the Persians found and defeated him near Ephesos. The tide turned, and he fled to Myrkinos. He thought of moving on to Sardinia, with its mines of silver and iron and its famous bronze industry, as the Phocaeans in c. 540 had moved on via their colonies of Alalia in Corsica and Massilia (Marseille), to found Elea (Elia or Velia) near Paestum, rather than submit to the Persians under Cyrus.

But Aristagoras died in Thrace, and his erstwhile allies in Athens, in a sharp reversal of their anti-Persian policy, elected Hipparchos (not the son of Peisistratos but a Peisistratid) as chief magistrate. At this stage Darius sent Histiaios down from Susa on the three months' journey to the coast, with a commission to put down the rebellion. Histiaios at once changed sides as Aristagoras had done, fled to Chios, got ships from Lesbos, and operated as a pirate out of Byzantion. The Persians caught him and crucified him in 493 BC. Miletos fell, after a sea battle in which the Greek fleet was little more than half the size of the Persian. The Lesbians and the Samians deserted, and only Chios fought effectively. The surviving men of Miletos were removed to the mouth of the Tigris, and all the women and children enslaved. The sanctuary of Apollo at nearby Didyma was burned down. Far away in Athens, the news of what happened at Miletos was heard with an outburst of grief and anger.

The Persians continue their advance
The Persians had already subdued Cyprus and now they proceeded to do the same to the Greeks of Caria,

in southwest Asia Minor. In the north Darius' son-in-law Mardonios moved in 492 BC to restore Persian supremacy in Thrace and Macedonia, and to destroy Eretria and Athens. He fulfilled his substantial purpose and took Thasos on his way, but he lost much of his fleet in a storm off Mount Athos, so Athens and Eretria escaped. In 490 the Persians entered Europe for the third time, with the Athenian exile Hippias, son of Peisistratos, among their staff. This time they sailed straight across the Aegean, conquering island after island as they went. The city of Naxos was burned down, but Delos, the sacred island of Apollo, was spared, as the sanctuary of Miletos probably would have been if policy had been precisely followed. The Persians were not fanatical ideologists or political or religious maniacs. When the local rulers of Greek Asia showed themselves unreliable, the Persians governed through democratic local systems, so long as taxes were paid, and so long as the tribute of ships and men was still forthcoming. The action against Athens was in one sense a baronial civil war, with Hippias son of Peisistratos on one side and Miltiades son of Kimon on the other. The same Miltiades, when tyrant of the Chersonese, had thought of betraying Darius nearly 20 years before at the Danube bridge. When the Scythians pushed him out of the Chersonese, he came back to Athens with the gift of Lemnos and Imbros; he was now a democratic Athenian nobleman and one of the commanders in the field. The sons of Peisistratos had murdered his father.

The battle of Marathon
The invaders burned Eretria after a campaign of seven days, and its people were sold off as slaves. The Persians then landed at Marathon, perhaps on the advice of Hippias, since this was where his father had landed to capture Athens 50 years ago, on a wide marshy plain remote from the city.

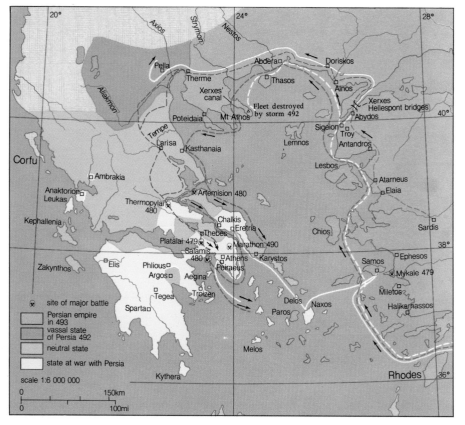

**Persian campaigns from 490 to
479 BC**
From the Persian point of view
the expedition of 490 was a raid
to punish Eretria and Athens for
their share in the Ionian revolt
and to restore the tyrant dynasty
to Athens. The setback at
Marathon led to a massive
campaign which took years to
prepare and to which the whole
dynasty and every province of
the empire were committed. The
fleet could not afford to keep far
from the army; so the canal
across the Athos peninsula was
not only a prestige project but
made strategic sense. An attempt
to stop the Persians at Tempe had
to be abandoned because it could
be bypassed. Thermopylai was
the best place to try a holding
operation: the outflanking route
betrayed to Xerxes has only
recently been rediscovered. The
next land barrier was the
Isthmus, but the Greek victories
at Salamis in 480 and Plataiai in
479 meant that the Persians
never got so far. The way was
now clear for the Greek sea
victory at Mykale (479) which
liberated some part of Ionia. The
pressure was then off mainland
Greece, but the Athenians and
their allies continued the war in
the eastern Mediterranean for
another 30 years.

Athens had already appealed for help to the
Spartans, but it was full moon, a holy time in Sparta,
and no help came. Some 9,000 Athenians, with no
allies except about 1,000 men from Plataiai, faced a
big Persian army alone. The Persians expected to
overwhelm them with arrows and then cut them to
pieces with cavalry. Against all reasonable probability, the Athenians won. They charged on foot at
a fast pace, cut the Persian center away from its
enveloping wings, and turned in against the central
division. The result was a massacre; it ended with
Persians lost in the marsh and slaughtered in the sea
as they ran to their ships. The Athenians lost only
192 men. Their grave-mound still stands. Some
ships were set on fire, but the mass of the fleet of 600
ships sailed on around Sounion to Athens. The same
Athenian army met them again, and they withdrew.
There seems no doubt that someone on land was
signaling with a flashing shield to the ships at sea.
Hippias still had friends.

Memorials in marble and bronze at Marathon and
Delphi can hardly express the Athenian triumph.
There were poems, a famous painting, legends and
written histories. Six hundred and fifty years later,
travelers still believed they heard ghostly noises of
armed men when they crossed the battlefield. Those
who fought at Marathon were known as the "men
of Marathon" for the rest of their lives. At that time
the Athenians undertook the strong and splendid
older Parthenon, which was still unfinished ten
years later, when the Persians came back. These
were also the years of the early development of
tragic poetry (Aischylos was one of those who had
fought at Marathon). In foreign affairs the
Athenians were occupied with the continuing
struggle, slightly more successful now, of their city
against Aegina. It is instructive that in an action in
487 BC, the Athenians still had only 50 ships and
dared not attack Aegina without borrowing another
20 from Corinth.

At home, Athenian politics developed towards
direct democracy. The board of state officers was
now appointed by lot, and since that is no way to
appoint a military commander, authority in war was
given to a board of ten elected generals, one from
each tribe. In 487 Hipparchos the chief magistrate
was exiled, and in 486 Megakles, a nephew of
Kleisthenes, followed him. In 484 it was
Xanthippos, who had married Kleisthenes' niece
and fathered Perikles, who was ostracized. Miltiades, the hero of Marathon, died a disgraced
adventurer. One at a time, the menace of individual
members of these great families was being nullified.
In the same years Themistokles was active. He first
held office before Marathon and was another who
fought there; his family was rich and noble, though

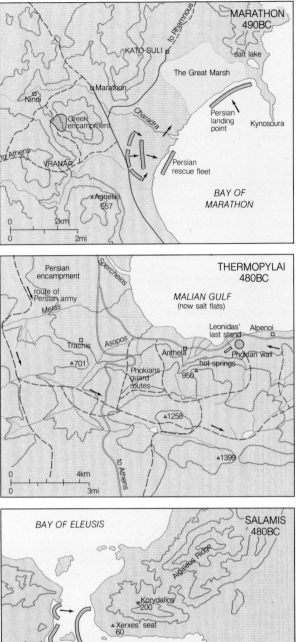

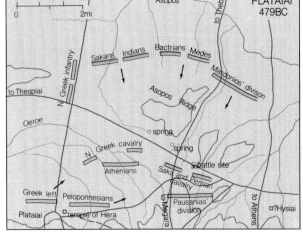

Above When the Persian fleet first attempted to round the headland of Athos they suffered severely in a storm. They are therefore reported to have cut themselves a canal across this narrow neck of land, and passed safely through it.

▭	Greek forces
▬	Persian forces
——	main road (passable by cart)
- - -	track
═══	modern road
VRANA	modern name
Athens	ancient name

he may himself have been a half-member of it; in the end he too died in exile, having been ostracized, as governor of a Greek city in the Persian empire.

It was Themistokles who fortified the Peiraeus, perhaps in imitation of the lagoon harbors of Corinth at Lechaion, but easily surpassing Corinth by the adaptation of rocky natural advantages. In 483 and 482, when the mines of Laurion first vomited silver in quantity from a deep level, he built up a fleet of 200 ships. When the Persians struck again, in 480 BC, Athens was for the first time in its history strong enough to win a victory greater than Marathon. It was Marathon that was remembered as the example, the first turning back of Asia. But the campaign of 480 was a much more serious threat. Darius himself did not live to invade again, although he began preparations. He was distracted by a rebellion in Egypt, and in 486 he died.

The invasion of Xerxes

Xerxes succeeded his father, and by the time Egypt was settled it was 484 BC. Xerxes moved carefully and in massive force. He had a canal cut on the inland side of Athos, to avoid a repetition of the 492 destruction of the Persian fleet, and a bridge built over the Strymon; his army gathered; in 481 he came down to Sardis, and spent the winter there.

Xerxes was a doomed character. When his host at Sardis begged that the oldest of his five conscripted sons be left at home, Xerxes had the lad cut in half and marched his army through the middle. Two great bridges were built for him to join Europe and Asia; when they were blown away in a gale he had the engineers beheaded and the sea itself flogged. In order to get his army across, he had that flogged as well.

The numbers of this enormous host given by the historian Herodotos, who was a young boy at the time, are so colossal it is hard to credit them. The army included Ethiopians in leopard skins with stone-tipped arrows, Persians in coats of mail and trousers, Indians in cotton, central Asians in goat-skins, men armed with clubs, or daggers and lassos, Thracians in fox-fur hats, lancers, swordsmen, archers and persons in "dyed garments and high boots." We are told of more than one and a half million infantry and 80,000 cavalry; the real number of the whole land force was more likely less than 200,000, among whom the elite troops of the Persians numbered 10,000, and the Persian fleet comprised perhaps less than 1,000 ships.

As a flash of lightning at night reveals the shapes of mountains, this invasion reveals something about the communications of the Greeks. The Spartans held a congress at the Isthmus of Corinth, attended by 31 states. Thessaly, most of Boeotia, and the smaller groups of the north stayed at home; they stood in the immediate path of Persia, and had no reason to expect the south would protect them. Argos stayed at home because of the old hatred of Sparta; the Spartans had defeated the Argives severely on their own territory well within memory, and an embassy from the congress was fruitless. So, for various reasons, were the embassies sent to Crete, Corfu and Syracuse. Only Athens and Aegina seem to have been reconciled. But an army of 10,000 Greeks occupied the vale of Tempe, between Thessaly and Macedonia, and a fleet gathered; both these forces were under Spartan command.

The Greek Soldier

There is nothing specially interesting or instructive about the techniques of gut-spilling and throat-slitting in the Greek world. Most wars were unjust, most generals were incompetent, as in more recent history. Weapons were designed as much to inspire terror as to hurt. The capital L for Laconia on the shields of Spartan armies, the nodding crests, the tinkling bells around the shields of one country, the fine-looking but almost useless cavalry of another, were among other things a kind of ballet. Still, it is as well to come to terms with what arms and armor were like, since they were part of everyone's experience of life. The fineness of the design and workmanship of the best bronze armor was meant to express and to generate confidence. At the same time, the edges of the best bronze swords of 5th-century Athens were tipped with steel.

The soldier (*left*), elegant and formidable, lightly but effectively armored, is an 18th-century drawing of a bronze figure, now lost, that was in the Albani collection in Rome. The statue probably came from a south Italian Greek city. (The existence of 12 albums of drawings of this famous collection preserves an exact reflection of what was meant by Classical art and taste in the generation of Winckelmann.) Although this armor is something of an oddity, military dress was indeed often more individual than we think.

In the Classical period the principal weapon of infantry in formation was the long spear, a radically different object from the short throwing spear. The

heads of these spears (*above right*) are real, and sufficiently nasty. Combined with arrows, slings, swords and so on, they constitute a sufficient repertory.

But the essence of Greek infantry tactics was its formations (*right*) and its drill. Battles were between armies, not individuals. In 5th-century Athens soldiers supplied their own arms, and the nobility their own horses. Later, the use of mercenaries, armed and trained and at times hired out in complete regiments, increased greatly. The phalanx, as it was called, of a subgroup of which this drawing (*below*) offers a conjectural picture, was a large mob of drilled men at arms used rather like a battering ram. The first five rows of spear points projected beyond the front rank.

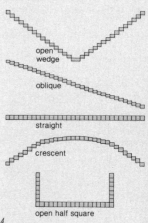

open wedge

oblique

straight

crescent

open half square

The helmet crests of Greek vase paintings were abundant, often weird and wonderful. No doubt they really existed. In Thrace a chieftain rode into battle with an iron bird that flapped its wings on his helmet as he rode.

Kegel

early Corinthian

Illyrian

The variety of Greek helmets is greater than can be shown in a few images, and to some extent is a matter rather of local tradition than of technical evolution. The most popular and successful was the Corinthian style, which was capable of great elegance and maintained its form recognizably from the 8th century (*top right*) to the 6th (*right*) and 5th. The other ancestor of most Greek helmet styles was the "Kegel" (*top left*), which was cumbersome and unpopular and died out soon after 700 BC, though its crest did influence later designs. Its Illyrian derivative (*above*) continued in use until the 5th century.

late Corinthian

Fortifications and War Machines

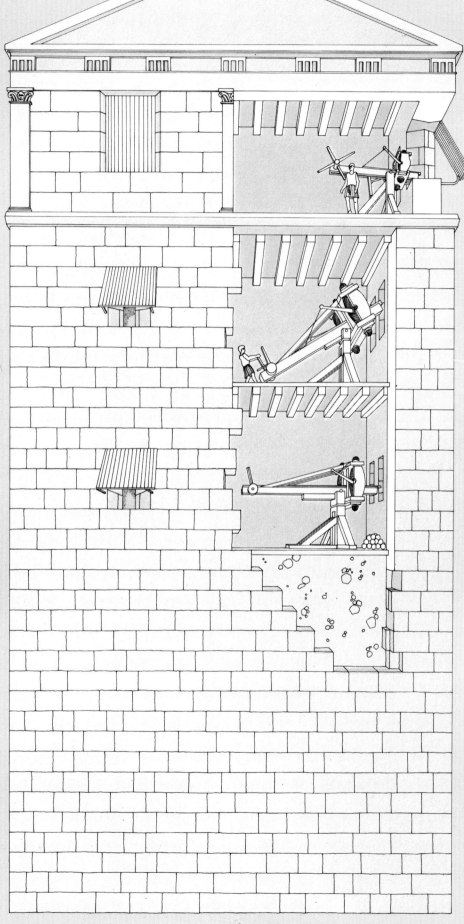

Greek fortresses go back to the Bronze Age and the Mycenaeans; the acropolis of Athens which the Persians took in the 5th century still had Mycenaean defense walls. In the 5th century not only were fortresses and castles walled, but whole cities, and in the case of the long walls of Athens and of the city of Akragas in Sicily, miles and miles of ground. The walls of Rome show Greek influence. The whole Peloponnese was defended by a wall across the Isthmus. The 5th and the 4th centuries saw constant technological progress in the weapons and defenses of war. This progress produced a succession of building styles and devices, and of course of methods of attack. Indeed, it was continuous in spite of setbacks until the invention of the aeroplane made walled towns obsolete.

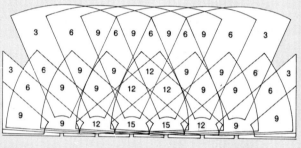

Left Catapults mounted in towers of a long defensive wall (seen here in section) could bring greater density of firing power to bear than we commonly realize. The diagram (*above*) assumes a front of six towers 100 meters apart from each other, with nine catapults in every tower and three more in each outer wall, that is 54 engines over 900 meters. The numbers show how many catapults could bear on any given field.

Right This amazing image of futile ingenuity is a skeletally accurate blueprint of a Hellenistic siege machine. The men are evenly matched on the whole; but nasty, brutish and short as the life of a footsoldier must have been in the *Iliad*, these absurd-looking devices and the enormous stone walls they faced made it nastier and shorter still. To have invented so much and wasted it on war, even to have recognized the power of steam, and yet never to have thought of a railroad train, is an index of human decadence in the Hellenistic age.

Social changes were just as important as technological ones. The fundamental element of war was the individual footsoldier, organized by drill as he had been since the early archaic age. Alexander's soldiers once at a single order reversed direction, formed a tortoise of shields like this one (*right*) with its rear edge to the enemy, and let carts loaded with stones go crashing harmlessly over their heads.

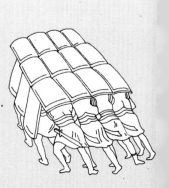

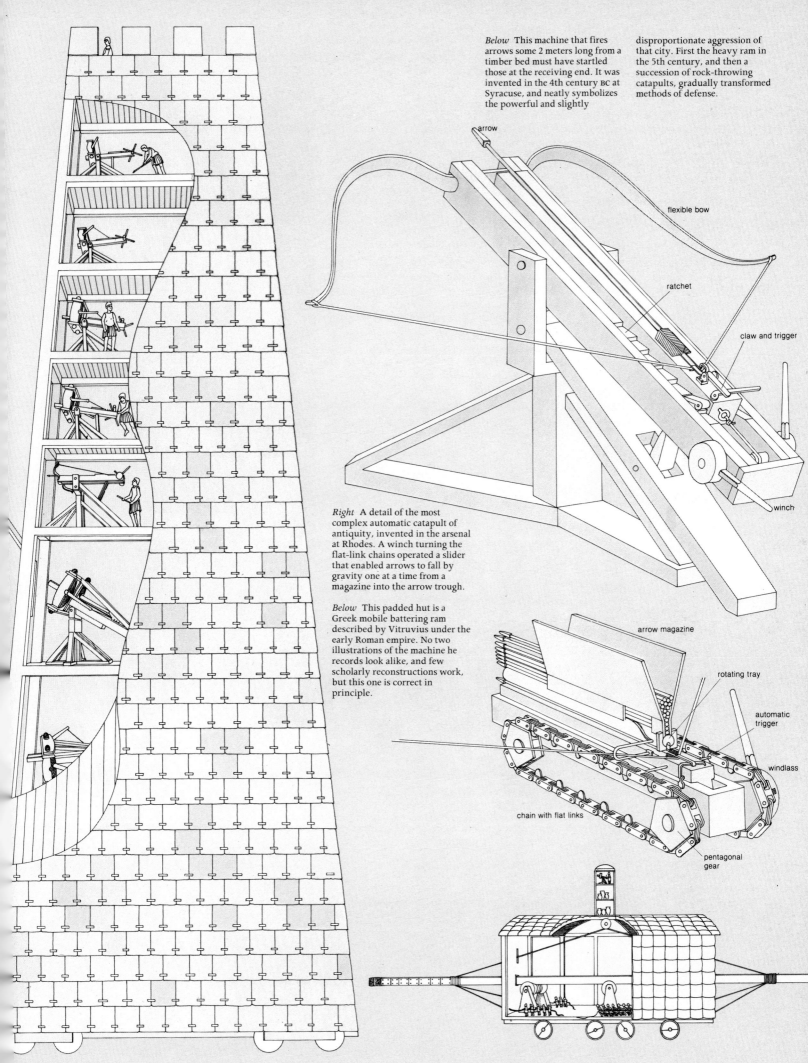

Below This machine that fires arrows some 2 meters long from a timber bed must have startled those at the receiving end. It was invented in the 4th century BC at Syracuse, and neatly symbolizes the powerful and slightly disproportionate aggression of that city. First the heavy ram in the 5th century, and then a succession of rock-throwing catapults, gradually transformed methods of defense.

arrow

flexible bow

ratchet

claw and trigger

winch

Right A detail of the most complex automatic catapult of antiquity, invented in the arsenal at Rhodes. A winch turning the flat-link chains operated a slider that enabled arrows to fall by gravity one at a time from a magazine into the arrow trough.

Below This padded hut is a Greek mobile battering ram described by Vitruvius under the early Roman empire. No two illustrations of the machine he records look alike, and few scholarly reconstructions work, but this one is correct in principle.

arrow magazine

rotating tray

automatic trigger

windlass

chain with flat links

pentagonal gear

Delos

Delos is the central island of the Cyclades, and the central shrine of Apollo in the Aegean. The island was sacred to the god from before the time of Homer, and there is at least some remote possibility of a continuity of religious cult since Mycenaean times. Apollo and Artemis were born on Delos.

In the 7th and the early 6th centuries Delos was controlled by its large neighbor, Naxos, but from that time onward the Athenians were more and more dominant, with a short break at the end of the great war with Sparta. But in 314 Delos became independent, and remained so until 166 BC. Its importance grew as a center of banking and of commerce, and in 166 the Romans made it a free port subject to Athens. It declined in the disturbances of the mid-1st century BC as Roman central power increased.

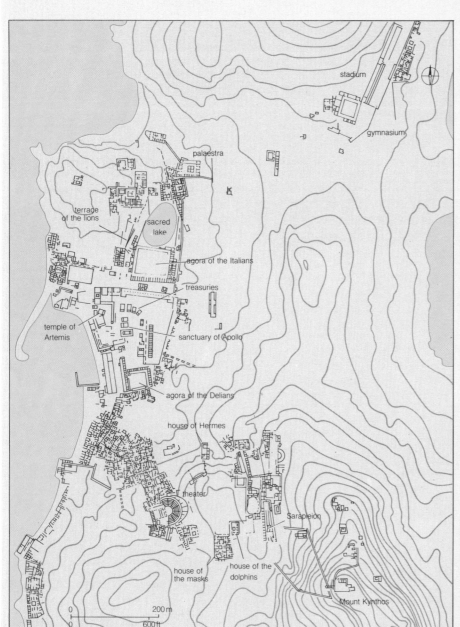

The army at Tempe retreated at once, because it was discovered on the spot that Tempe was only one of several passes, and it was felt that the Thessalians were insecure allies to have behind one's back.

Thermopylai and the plunder of Athens

Seven thousand men under King Leonidas of Sparta took up a new position opposite the north end of Euboea, at the top of a rocky pass above Thermopylai, the Hot Gates. The hot springs the pass is named for are still running, but the landscape has altered utterly; the river Spercheios has silted its estuary, and a coastal plain now carries the main road from north to south Greece where the ancient terrain was impassable. The army of 7,000 would have fallen back further to the Isthmus itself, but the Athenian fleet was now a crucial factor, and Athens must be defended at least symbolically. The main army in the Peloponnese refused to move, excusing itself by a festival of Apollo and by the Olympic festival. Meanwhile, the Athenians prudently evacuated their civilian population to the Peloponnese, retained half their fleet to guard their own coast, and sent half north with the other Greek ships to Artemision on the north coast of Euboea, with a rearguard at the straits opposite Chalkis. The whole Greek fleet had 280 ships. The huge congregation of shipping that the Persians commanded stationed itself opposite, but on a bad shore. A tempest destroyed a large part of it.

At sea, local knowledge and seamanship favored the Greeks. On land, they suffered a disaster. There is seldom really only one route through Greek mountains. The Greeks were outflanked by the Persian elite troops, but they knew it in time, and all but 1,400 men retreated, some Thebans and Thespians, perhaps because their own country was so close, and 300 Spartans. Leonidas and his few men held the western end of the pass against the main body of the Persian army. He died, and two brothers of Xerxes died. After a ferocious and prolonged defense, the last Spartans died surrounded. The spirit in which the Spartans met their fate was one of resolute and insouciant courage, and a certain grim gaiety. "The Spartans," as A. E. Housman put it, "on the sea-wet rock sat down and combed their hair." Their epitaph, almost certainly by the finest laconic poet of that or perhaps any age, Simonides, was simple; in Greek it is simpler still.

> Tell them in Lakedaimon, passer-by,
> That here, obeying their command, we lie.

The Persian army together with the remnants of the fleet hunted the Athenians home. The Greek army mustered at the Isthmus, all but the last Athenians abandoned Athens, the fleet hung in the wind between Athens and Salamis. It took two weeks for the acropolis to fall, the defenders were all murdered and the sanctuaries smashed, burned and plundered. It is the broken and buried remnants of that time that are now the greatest surviving treasures of archaic sculpture, but the harmonious gaiety, the lively delight and the playful or solemn formality of that earlier time were irrecoverably lost. Sanctuaries, except those of Demeter, were not rebuilt for 50 years; they were left in their ruins as a monument of what had been done to the Greeks.

Salamis, Plataiai and the Persian retreat

But it was at Athens that the Persians were checked. By various strokes of cunning and diplomacy, Themistokles provoked a battle at sea, between Salamis and the mainland. It was ferociously bloody, it was a complete victory for the Greeks, and we have an eyewitness account of it by Aischylos. "I saw the Aegean sea blossoming with corpses." "They smashed at men like tunny fish, with broken oars and pieces of timber." Xerxes, with an army of 60,000 men, retired into Asia, and set up headquarters in Sardis. The Persian army then reassembled in Thessaly to besiege fortified cities. Meanwhile, the Greeks were building monuments, settling accounts and distributing loot; it is notable that Themistokles, who had behaved with dashing duplicity, received most nominations for the prize of general, Aegina got the first prize for courage, and Athens the second. The Greeks had won a victory at sea and a moral victory on land; the retreat of those vast Persian hordes for the second time in ten years confirmed that it was worthwhile to continue to resist.

The Persians sent the king of Macedonia, their subject, with an offer to Athens of free and equal alliance; was it the Athenian fleet they wanted, or the silver mines of Laurion, or a safe road to the Isthmus? Athens stayed loyal to Sparta, but as the Persians advanced, the Spartans at first excused themselves with another festival of Apollo, and stayed inside the wall at the Isthmus. Then, at last, fearing what would happen if Athens were to surrender her fleet, Sparta moved, and with the greatest army that had ever emerged from southern into central Greece: 5,000 Spartans, 5,000 tribal soldiers subject to Sparta, and 20,000 serfs, joining an allied army of 8,000 Athenians and the other regional contingents, so that the whole force amounted to a serious number. They met the Persians below Plataiai on the edge of the Theban plains, at the foot of the last hills on the road to Athens and the Peloponnese. The Persian expeditionary force was cut to pieces, their fortified camp was destroyed, their general Mardonios perished, the leading Thebans who were their allies were taken to Corinth and executed.

The loot that was dispersed through Greece was the most magnificent treasure the Greeks had ever seen. The general's scimitar and his silver-footed throne were dedicated on the acropolis of Athens, and the Odeion of Perikles, the first roofed theater in Greece, designed for its acoustics, was an imitation made long afterward of the great audience tent of Xerxes, captured at that battle. At Delphi the memorial of the battle was the massive bronze column of three scaled snakes twisted together, with their three heads spitting outward at the top, and a golden tripod balanced on their noses (see p. 73). The Persian empire had passed its high tide and war moved back inevitably to the eastern Greek cities and the islands. At sea Athens was supreme, and so the form the war took was the expansion of Athenian influence in the east.

At first the Spartan general Pausanias, who had commanded the combined Greek army at Plataiai, pursued the eastern war. He liberated most of Cyprus, a recurring task in Greek history, and the city of Byzantion, but he behaved like a tyrannical and independent warlord of the last generation and

Above The house of Hermes, seen from one of the sanctuaries of foreign gods. Built against the hill, it had three floors and a central courtyard with a colonnade in two tiers, now restored.

The avenue of archaic lions (*left*) is a small part of what was once to be seen on Delos. Statues have been taken from here to Athens, to Venice and further afield. But among such a complicated history these lions recall something essential about Apollo: he was a powerful and terrible god, at Delos as in Asia, and in stone as in poetry.

it is instructive that in the 470s he could not get away with his old-fashioned individualism; he was twice recalled to Sparta, expelled from Sestos and Byzantion (that is, from control of the straits of the Bosphorus) by Athens, and died nastily at Sparta at the hands of the magistrates. The day of his like, and of the likes of Themistokles, was over.

Athens and the Delian league

Already in the early 470s Athens had based on Delos a new alliance or league of cities (the Delian league)

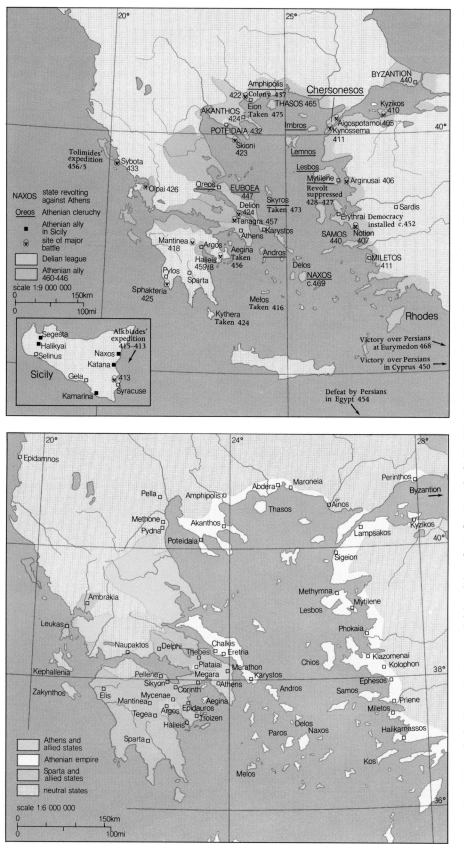

with a common treasury filled by taxation and a common military policy determined more and more by Athens. The increasing domination of the Athenian fleet was a development made possible by the victory at Plataiai.

Step by step, Athens itself became a fortified city, and a great military power. In 475 Eion, the strongest Persian position west of the Hellespont, fell to Kimon son of Miltiades son of Kimon; then the pirate island of Skyros fell. That cleared a route to the timber, the silver and perhaps the gold which were coming out of Thrace. Kimon went on to bring the Lycian and Carian cities of southwest Asia Minor back into the sphere of Greece and to complete the liberation of the Greeks from Persia with a victory by land and sea at once, at the Eurymedon estuary in southern Asia Minor in about 468 BC. When any city seceded from the Delian league, a severe sanction was automatically applied, as if the offense were desertion to the Persians. Karystos in south Euboea was brought into the league by force, the loyalty of Naxos was forcibly renewed, and when Thasos rebelled against Athenian control of a gold mine on the mainland, Thasos was defeated at sea, her fleet confiscated and her city walls pulled down, in 463 BC. Thasos had appealed against Athens to Sparta, but the Spartans were busy murdering their own rebellious serfs.

The seeds of the Peloponnesian war

The next ten years were the hinge of the century. Until that time, the climax of an older world had been playing itself out, but from about 460 BC the consequences of that last act began to emerge in a surprising way. Athens was ascendant, and between 463 and 454 she came close to supremacy. It is always real forces, however improbable or unlooked for, that decide a power struggle. The Persian empire had collapsed against the Greeks in froth and fury. The Phoenicians had suffered in that process, just as in the west the Phoenician colony of Carthage was suffering from aggressive Greek rivalry. The Athenians, driven on by an amazing energy, were asserting a supremacy that no one city could sustain, and even though the sea was theirs, with its commerce, the mines and the green riches of the earth, they could no more finally dominate the eastern Mediterranean than the Spartans could: the Spartans were to the Athenians in the end what the Greeks were to the Persians.

In 464 BC Sparta was bleeding; the Messenians had rebelled, a little force of Spartans had been cut down, and the allies were summoned to besiege Ithome, the ancestral stronghold of Messenia, the true site of which has never been found to this day.

Among others, Kimon of Athens went to help with 4,000 men, but he was insultingly sent home. In 461 Kimon was ostracized. Athens allied herself with Argos, in a diplomatic move against Sparta. Meanwhile, steadily, or rather irreversibly but unsteadily, Athenian democracy increased. From 462, judges at Athens were paid, so the less well off could serve; in 458 the supreme offices were opened to citizens of the third in the hierarchy of classes (see p. 92). In 459 Megara, in the course of a quarrel with Corinth, left the Peloponnesian league and accepted the alliance of Athens. Corinth was provoked in many ways, economically in the western Mediterranean, and closer at home in the gulf of

Perikles, the elected ruler of Athens at the time of its greatest power and the engineer of its magnificence, therefore also perhaps of its downfall.

Left above: The Athenian empire, 460–446 BC
Sparta withdrew from the war against Persia in 478 and an alliance led by Athens was formed in winter 478/7 to continue fighting the Persians. Originally its synod was at Delos. Successive revolts had to be put down and by the mid-century the Athenians had come to speak openly of rule rather than alliance. But Athenian support of local democratic parties resulted in a surprising degree of loyalty even after the Spartans, and then the Persians, could bring force to bear on Athenian-ruled cities. Perikles said it would be dangerous ever to give up the empire; and indeed the lifeline of Athens bringing corn for its swollen population from the Black Sea was only safe as long as Byzantion was tributary and Athenian settlements (cleruchies) were strung along the route.

Left below: Alliances at the beginning of the Peloponnesian war, 431 BC
As in 1914, the Greek world found itself divided by two hostile alliances. In the long term the consequences of the great war of 431–404 were to destroy both.

The battle of Pylos and Sphakteria
A brilliant coup enabled Athens to seize Pylos in 425 after capturing crack Spartan troops previously believed invincible. From now on they maintained a base on Sparta's soft underbelly which could be a focus for Messenian unrest.

The siege of Syracuse
Athens's most ambitious venture ever was the attack on Syracuse, for which she risked more money, men and ships than she could afford. The annexation of Sicily was a glorious prospect but the long siege of Syracuse was mismanaged and ended in utter defeat. Athens was fatally weakened at home, though she held on resiliently for another nine years.

Corinth by the Athenian seizure of Naupaktos from Lokrians. It was at Naupaktos that Athens installed the Messenian exiles. A war followed which was fiercely fought, but of which the details are obscure. At the same time Egypt rebelled against the Persians, and the Athenians were called in to support the rebellion. That war dragged on (456–454), and it ended badly, with the Persians back in control, the Athenians staggering home, and Phoenician ships in the Nile delta defeating an Athenian fleet. But meanwhile Aegina had finally fallen, and in 456 paid its tribute to the Delian league.

In 457 Athenians fought against a Spartan army at Tanagra. The Spartans were now reacting with defensive agression, and had sent an expedition of great size into Boeotia to strengthen Thebes as a counterweight to Athens. About 1,500 Spartans and 10,000 allies fought and won, though not overwhelmingly, against 14,000 Athenians, 1,000 Argives and some allies. Thessalian cavalry also fought, appearing for Athens but changing over to the Spartan side. The battle of Tanagra is a measure of how far things had gone. State confrontation had once been unusual, conflict had been parochial or a matter of family; now it was league against league. In 454 BC, at the time of the failure in Egypt, Athens removed the treasury of the Delian league from the ancient holy island to the city of Athens. By 449 the Athenians ruled as far north as Thermopylai and in the late 450s and early 440s the Athenians adventured further in the Corinthian gulf. It is worth quoting an Athenian inscription that names 177 dead in battle for one tribe in the year 458 BC. "These are they who died in the war, in Cyprus, in Egypt, in Phoenicia, at Halieis, in Aegina, at Megara, in the same year." (Halieis, on the southern tip of the Argolid peninsula had been unsuccessfully attacked by the Athenians.) In these years it seems that close to ten times as many Athenians died every year in battle as had died at Marathon.

A peace of five years was patched up between Athens and Sparta, and a substantial peace of 30 years between Argos and Sparta, from 451 BC. Athenian action against Persia continued, and Kimon, home from exile and reconciled with his younger successor Perikles, campaigned again to relieve Cyprus. He died out there in 449, the last representative of the old anti-Persian and pro-Spartan generation. Perikles, if he must choose between war in the east and war at home, chose war at home, and about 449 BC he negotiated peace with Artaxerxes, the successor to Xerxes. At once, the pressure of the Persian war being lifted, the more ambitious acquisitions of the Delian league began to disintegrate. In 447 Boeotia was lost, then Phokis and Lokris. Megara and Euboea rebelled with Spartan help, Megara successfully, Euboea disastrously. Athens reduced the tribute of her allies, surrendered Achaea, Troizen and the ports of Megara, and obtained a treaty of 30 years with the Peloponnese in 446 BC, just as Argos had done five years before.

Inside the Delian league, Athenian policy was in some ways toughening. In about 450, poor settlers from Athens took over land in Naxos, Andros and perhaps elsewhere. In 447 a strategic settlement in the Chersonese and others in Lemnos and Imbros secured the Black Sea route. It was the cities on that

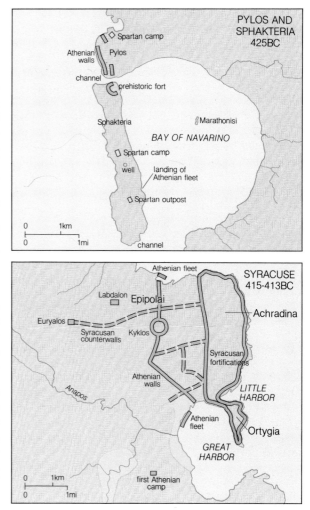

route that were now rich; Lampsakos paid to the league twice as much as Ephesos. These settlers were socially and economically promoted by their landholdings, and paid taxes and military service to Athens.

Athenian coinage was compulsory throughout the league. The Athenian imperial policy, in Thrace and elsewhere, was that of Perikles, whose chief political opponent Thucydides (not the historian, but related by marriage to Kimon) was ostracized in 443. A glorious public building policy also belonged to the 440s. Athens was now well fortified, or as well as so large an area without natural strength could ever be, glorified with works of art, and within limits directly democratic. Money was plentiful, prices were rising. The rich Thracians and the Macedonians still barred the land route north into Europe. But by sea, eastward and westward, the Athenians were active, and although Egypt, the Persians and the Phoenicians still guarded Africa, Athens did trade with North African cities.

Perikles himself sailed to the Black Sea. In 440 there was trouble at Samos, and trouble again at Byzantion. Samos had been in dispute with Miletos, another city of the league; Athens had decided the quarrel, but war broke out. Perikles sailed to Samos with 44 ships, imposed a democracy and installed a garrison. But the oligarchs came home from exile and handed over the garrison to the Persian governor of Sardis. This alarming and escalating conflict ended with a blockade by 200 ships for nine months, a colossal fine, and the destruction of the city walls of Samos.

The Peloponnesian war begins

In the west of Greece the same anxious and competitive policy produced in the end even worse results. A dispute arose between Corfu (Kerkyra) and Corinth much like the one between Athens and Samos, but in this case a third party, Athens, interfered.

After a naval victory over Corinth in 435 BC, Corfu appealed to Athens against the heavy vengeance that might be coming, and in spite of Corinthian diplomatic activity Athens did ally herself with Corfu and came into conflict with Corinth. Then Perikles proposed and carried a decree to exclude Megara, now for 15 years back in the Peloponnesian league, from every port and market that the Athenians controlled. Competitive energy and its inevitable injuriousness, the high-handed imperialism of Athens and her ruthless confidence in democratic governments, had now brought her close to an appalling war. The Spartans were angry, probably frightened, certainly envious, and at least as arrogant as the Athenians.

The Peloponnesian war

Apart from one year of truce between 421 and 420, the war was to last 27 years, from 431 to 404 BC. It ended in the destruction of Athens and in those years Greece had shaken itself to bits. Of course nothing in history is quite as clear-cut as these sentences imply. The conflict had started really by 460, well before the never-completed 30 years' peace, and the Athens of the following century was at least a very powerful ghost. During the course of the war the influence of the Greeks, and particularly the Athenians, in Macedonia and Thrace, in Asia, and in Sicily and Italy, even among the Celtic peoples, even as far south as the Sudan, was still increasing.

In 431 a commando of Thebans attacked Plataiai, which was friendly to Athens; most were captured, and very properly had their throats cut. The Spartans invaded Athenian territory, and most of the population, which was probably something like 300,000, crowded into the city, while the Spartans did what damage they could in the countryside, besieging one little rock fortress, building another. The Athenians behaved with more effective energy. They colonized Aegina, secured some western alliances, set up reserves of money and of ships. The Spartan invasion became an annual fixture, counterbalanced by offensives of the Athenian fleet. The people of Poteidaia on the edge of Macedonia, before they surrendered to Athens, had eaten human flesh. Now the Athenians under siege began to die of plague, and Perikles himself died in 429 BC. Predictably enough, in 428 an island seceded from the league; it was Lesbos, and the Athenian reaction was devastating; the sovereign people's assembly at first proposed a general massacre, but then contented itself with pulling down the walls of Mytilene, and confiscating the fleet and the whole of the land; colonists were appointed, who employed the Lesbians as tenant farmers as the Spartans did their serfs. Just as predictably, at this time the outlying hill-town of Plataiai fell to the Spartans, but Corfu, after prolonged and ghastly convulsions, preserved a democracy.

War continued with increasing violence in subordinate cities throughout the 420s. In 425 the

Miletos

Miletos was perhaps the greatest of the Greek archaic cities of Asia. Its extent was vast, its antiquity venerable, its wealth and influence very great. Monuments survive there from every period of its history, to which the key is its position at the mouth of the river Maiandros.

The Hellenistic theater of Miletos (*below right*) was many times reconstructed, and what is visible is Roman, like the reliefs (*right*). This was the biggest theater in Asia and one of the grandest; it held 15,000. This theater was extended under the late empire. A few Hellenistic features survive in it.

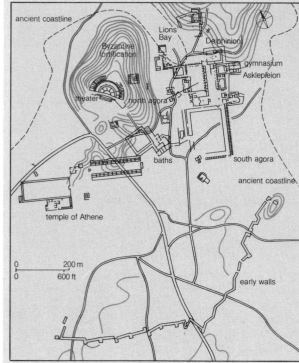

Athenians captured some Spartan soldiers in a daring campaign on the southwest coast of Messenia, in Pylos bay. The monument of that exhilarating and triumphant action survives; it is the Victory of Paionios, dedicated at Olympia by Messenian exiles who had fought at Pylos. Elsewhere the Athenians were not so successful; they failed in Boeotia, and lost Amphipolis, typically of this stage of the war, by neglecting to cover it in time against a brilliant Spartan general, Brasidas. The area of the war was too great to be dominated. Both sides were exhausted, both were losing, neither was winning. After an attempt at truce in 423 BC, which failed in 422 largely because of an attempt by the Athenian general Kleon to retake Amphipolis, in a battle in which both he and Brasidas perished, a treaty of 50 years' peace was agreed in 421 BC. Corinth, Megara and Boeotia were angered by its conditions, and stayed outside the peace. When Athens and Sparta entered into positive alliance, the Peloponnesian league began to break up.

But diplomatic embraces inevitably meant interference. When the league dissolved, Corinth, Mantinea and Elis allied themselves with Argos. In 419 Athens allied herself also with Argos, and with Elis and Mantinea, for 100 years. This new alliance then moved together to attack Epidauros: Sparta supported Epidauros and the war was on again (although it was not formally renewed until 414). Its first great battle was at Mantinea in 418 BC; the Spartans won, and the Athenians temporarily lost all their new-found allies at a stroke. The politics of direct democracy had not had a good effect on the Athenians; they did at this time exile, in the last ostracism at Athens, one of the more offensively demagogic politicians (the original Hyperbolos); but the dangers of the Athenian democracy were expressed in an unprovoked attack on the neutral island of Melos in the south Cyclades, the massacre of all Melians of military age, and the enslavement of the survivors.

The war in Sicily and Athens's surrender

Athens was hellbent on self-destruction. In 416 BC, nothing if not adventurous, the sovereign people entered into the convoluted quarrels of Sicily. The first victim of the enterprise, which he himself sponsored, was Alkibiades, a young nobleman of too much brilliance and unique personal charm.

Alkibiades was a young friend of Sokrates, tricky, as attractive to men as to women, as physically beautiful as he was intellectually formidable. In some sense he embodies the good and the bad of these years, the hope of Athens and the withering of that hope. On the eve of his sailing as a general against Syracuse, he and his close friends were accused, perhaps truthfully, of a drunken and arrogant display, of mocking the mysteries of Demeter and of breaking the erect phalli off the public statues of Hermes. Alkibiades was lucky to escape with his life into an adventurous and treacherous exile. He went to Sparta and his speech to the assembly was instrumental in the decision to send a Spartan force under Gylippos to lead the defense of Syracuse against Athens.

The war in Sicily was a drain and a disaster that no one had imagined. It ended, after a long mismanagement, in 413 BC, with the massacre of

The Victory of Paionios, which stood opposite the great east door of the temple of Zeus at Olympia, high up on its triangular column. Dedicated by Messenian exiles who fought and beat Spartans in the Athenian campaign at Sphakteria in the 420s, it must have been a perpetual embarrassment to the Spartans.

most of the retreating Athenians under the incompetent command of Nikias, when the siege of Syracuse had failed. In written history this catastrophe takes on a tragic and inevitable tone, due perhaps to the formal devices of written prose in the 5th century, which sound through it like a drumbeat. But there is no doubt that this tone echoes the feelings of contemporary Athens.

Athens was sinking. About 20,000 slaves deserted to Dekeleia, a Spartan outpost established in 413 in Attica north of Athens, and the mines at Laurion were shut down the same year since they were insecure. Coinage was in gold, borrowed from temple dedications, and in copper thinly plated with silver. Thracian soldiers were brought to Athens, and sent home again for lack of pay; landing in Boeotia on their way back they slaughtered men, women and children. Athenian allies seceded. Persian provincial governors increased their activity and took some part in the war on the Spartan side. A movement towards oligarchy in Athens began to be discernible, and in 411 BC a council of 400 men took over Athens, and governed it tyrannically for three months, but Sparta was too slow or too vengeful to come to terms, and democracy was restored. Even at this stage, a victory at sea came near to restoring the balance: in 410 it was the Spartans who asked for peace, and Athens who refused. The war was now being fought mostly at sea and in the east. Finally, inevitably, the Athenians lost a naval battle. Their fleet was surprised on shore, and 160 ships were destroyed without serious resistance. This took place in the straits of the Hellespont, near Lampsakos, in 405 BC. Athens lived on for some months under blockade by land and by sea. The Spartan army withdrew in winter, but Athens was starved into surrender. The Athenians were made to pull down their own walls to the music of flutes, they forfeited almost every ship of the fleet, and all foreign possessions. Nominally, Sparta was supreme at the end of the century, as it was at the beginning, but there was no real supremacy.

THE CLASSICAL REVOLUTION

Aischylos fought at Marathon, therefore his grandson was a mature man at the fall of Athens. In historical terms, the 5th century seems to be one part of a single, long process, a swift decline, a steady succession of consequences. In other ways it was a moment of unusual balance, the one moment when the juggler has all his plates in the air. The intellectual serenity and restless curiosity of the best philosophers, poets and historians of those few generations were certainly inherited from an age of greater innocence, but in Athens, where so many streams met, they flourished peculiarly. Polygnotos of Thasos was brought to Athens by Kimon; both the indirect evidence of his influence and the opinion of ancient critics suggest that he was the greatest painter the Greeks ever knew; it is still just possible to trace and to sense the development of the art of painting under his hand. Pheidias was a supreme sculptor; his work was at Ephesos and Olympia as well as his native Athens, but his influence, like that of Polygnotos, was most alive in Athens; he was the designer of the sculptures of the Parthenon.

There is no monopoly of art, even of developed arts; Polykleitos, the greatest and the most influential sculptor in the generation after Pheidias, was born and trained at Argos, and he was not the only important sculptor of his time in the Peloponnese. But we are forced to judge by what we can see; sculpture had achieved an international style. The small 5th-century boy in a strange and coarse-grained island marble effectively contrasted with the smoothness of its Polykleitian shape, which was acquired a few years ago by the Ashmolean Museum at Oxford, must from its technique be by a pupil of Polykleitos and a near contemporary, but it could have been made anywhere in the Greek world. Yet it is Athens where we should concentrate inquiries, if only because, except for Sicily, the more interesting the developments are in other parts of the Greek world, the more on the whole they appear to resemble Athens, while it is only in Athens that we have all the elements together that attract us here and there in other places.

The self-conscious claim Thucydides puts into the mouth of Perikles cannot be quite disregarded, though it must be treated warily. "That the city is in general the school of Greece, and that the men here have each one of them disposed his person to the greatest diversity of actions, and yet with gracefulness and the happiest versatility," is a claim only to power and success, "For we have opened to ourselves by our own courage all seas and lands." The more interesting claim is "For we study good taste, and yet with frugality; and philosophy, and yet without effeminacy." Allowing a little for the four-square style of this translation, the claim is justified and fascinating. It was at Athens, in the mid-century, that restraint, with complete mastery of means, and some austerity of conception, became a keynote of Greek design. The revolution in the arts was to break away from the robust fullness of the archaic style; and the moving simplicity that followed, the brief, delicate balance before the reaction, is what we call Classical. It was engulfed at once in extravagant and baroque styles, it never held the whole field even in its own day, but it marked an important and a recurring ideal.

At Athens the tough and shaggy Herakles, beating up Egyptians by the handful, murdering a whole sky full of birds, wrestling down a lion, and in one local story breaking a boy's skull by mistake with a flick of his finger, gives place to Theseus, a boyish, elegant hero in his youth who becomes a

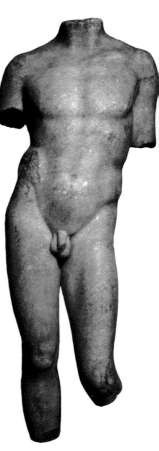

This boy is made of a coarse-grained, island marble which makes a pleasant contrast to his fineness of form. There is no reason to doubt that he was carved in the 5th century, and since he shows the influence of the master Polykleitos, he must have been produced by one of that great man's disciples or apprentices, probably in his lifetime. Now in the Ashmolean Museum, Oxford.

A set of drawings by Douris on an Athenian red-figure cup from Vulci in Etruria (490–480 BC). The deeds of Theseus are shown to rival the deeds of Herakles, the Athenian hero to be the equal of the Dorian demigod. Herakles is a tough, mature man, Theseus is boyish, but he overcomes men.

civilized king. Sometimes the adventures of the two heroes were drawn together. This is not only a change of heroes but a change of styles. It may be that in vase painting too much was sacrificed to it. The splendid decorative power of Exekias and the riotous expressiveness of so many Dionysiac painters would no longer be possible. The concentration of attention, the unity of theme, as if all art had to be seen through a telescope, put a new strain on the meaning of its subject matter. Solemnity, sentimentality and dramatic emotion were the new temptations.

It is curious that the invention of perspective drawing by the Greeks was bound up with the theater, with the art of scene painting. The first wall painting in a private house was commissioned by Alkibiades from a theatrical designer. Just as the stage concentrates attention powerfully on who is to blame, or on what one is to do, so the new conditions of visual art which the Athenian theater to some degree generated threw a dramatic light on the traditional silhouetted figures. The new conventions had an earlier prehistory. The best and nearly the only example we have of archaic or early Classical painting on a flat surface is the tomb of the Diver, the painted slabs of a stone sarcophagus from Poseidonia, the Roman Paestum, on the west coast of Italy. The diving boy was freshly painted when the tomb was closed, on the underside of the slab that covered it.

This is one of very few representations of diving from a height that survive from the ancient world, and it poses a number of questions. Since the rope-marks on the paint show it was freshly painted, the subject was probably commissioned. Was the tomb for a boy who liked to dive? Is the stone diving-board realistic? But none higher than a foot or so has ever been found and no writer refers to one. How does the diver climb up to it? By the palmette and the tree? Why else the two framing trees, or are they part of the water scene here as they are in a vase painting of some swimming girls? There the girls dive from an altar; is the boy diving from a statue pedestal? He is not drawn from life, since the angle of his feet and his raised head are not true; this is a

The diving boy painted on the inside of the lid of a stone tomb from Paestum (c.480 BC). Not only is the subject very unusual, but the technique of painting on flat surfaces has left us few survivals – pots survive because they are fired. This tomb is nearly our only example of early Classical fresco painting. It has an astounding vitality.

Herakles slaughters the murderous water-birds of the Stymphalian Lake. These birds are imagined at the most lavish moment of Athenian black-figure art.

special scene, not an old subject. Paestum was near enough to Cumae, the mysterious caves and the river of Lethe; can this be a boy diving into the water of death, to return somehow to life? Or is it some unknown myth, perhaps about a statue, set by a swimming place, that came to life, as one does in a minor Greek poem 250 years later? The isolation of the boy in mid-air, the fine formal ornaments at the corners, the two bare trees, the bare stone and bare water, create an extraordinary singleness of impression. The banqueting scene around the four inner walls of the sarcophagus compares very well with similar scenes by great masters of vase painting, by Douris and even Euphronios.

The tomb at Paestum was painted quite early in the 5th century, and a tradition of fresco painting on plaster must already have been widely rooted. Paestum was a colony of Sybaris, a little over 100 years old. Sybaris itself has perished with such a reputation for luxury and so little trace that it would be foolish to dogmatize over the style of this unique painted tomb, beyond saying that in its own day it was certainly not unique. We do know that the big change in painting came with Polygnotos, not one of whose works has survived. But the detailed description of his compositions, and the physical evidence of a visual and intellectual earthquake in the work of his contemporaries, do make it profitable to pursue an inquiry. The abandoning of the baseline in drawing, the implication of mighty events in a few dramatic details, the setting of things in space, an ease of movement and a restfulness characterize him as a new kind of narrative painter.

Professor Martin Robertson has written (in his new *History of Greek Art*, published in 1976) with intuition and scrupulous scholarship about this stage of Greek painting. ''On many other vases . . . a figure lays hand to chin, or rests elbow on knee, face on hand. Such gestures are loved at this time, their brooding character according with the taste for stillness and the indirect expression of the action.

The Greek Theater: Aspects of the Drama

Greek dramatic festivals had ancient country origins. The early 5th-century performances were in an empty marketplace with a cart as a background, even in Athens. The theater itself was based on places of political assembly. In this new, grand horseshoe setting the dramatic festival belonged to the new democratic state. The raised stage and the scenery painted in perspective soon followed. Stage machinery and baroque decorations arrived within 100 years.

Above This great bronze votive mask with its empty and horrified eyes and howling mouth is a concentrated and formalized version of the mask a tragic actor would actually wear for performance in the 5th century. It was found in the Peiraeus, where it was stored with other bronzes ready to be shipped out, probably to Rome, when the Peiraeus was destroyed by Sulla in 96 BC.

Left The number of Athenians who attended the early tragedies in the agora is not known, but something close to the whole population must have crowded into the great theater of Dionysos in the late 5th and the 4th century. These tokens seem to be theater tickets. The letters refer to sections of benches.

Left This fine seat was meant for a magistrate or a grand visitor at the Hellenistic theater of Priene, an imitation of the theater at Athens. At Priene the theater was used also for political assembly of the whole people. It was probably the open-air assembly places of an earlier age that bequethed their shape to the earliest purpose-built performing theaters.

Above This lovely little monument was built in 334 BC to celebrate the victory of Lysikrates in theatrical competition. Its popular name is the lighthouse of Demosthenes.

The monument was designed in the late and elaborate style called Corinthian, with a frieze of Dionysos turning the pirates who captured him into dolphins.

Above A composite and imaginary Greek provincial theater, perhaps in the 4th century BC, when architectural elaboration has not yet utterly transformed the stage. Gods speak from the balcony, the chorus parades in the orchestra, or dancing-floor.

Right Comic slaves and servants were favorite figures in Athenian comedy; even Aristophanes, though he expresses some boredom with their routine capers, manipulates them carefully. One can understand their appeal to audiences. There are many comic figurines, often with grotesque masks and padded costumes, very few tragic ones.

The Greek Theater: Checklist

Many of these theaters were built when the Classical moment of the Athenian theater was over. That includes the theater of Athens in its present form. The similarity between the different theaters in different locations reflects the overwhelming prestige and influence of the dramatic art of Athens.

The map and list on this page survey the best-known theaters of the Greek world.

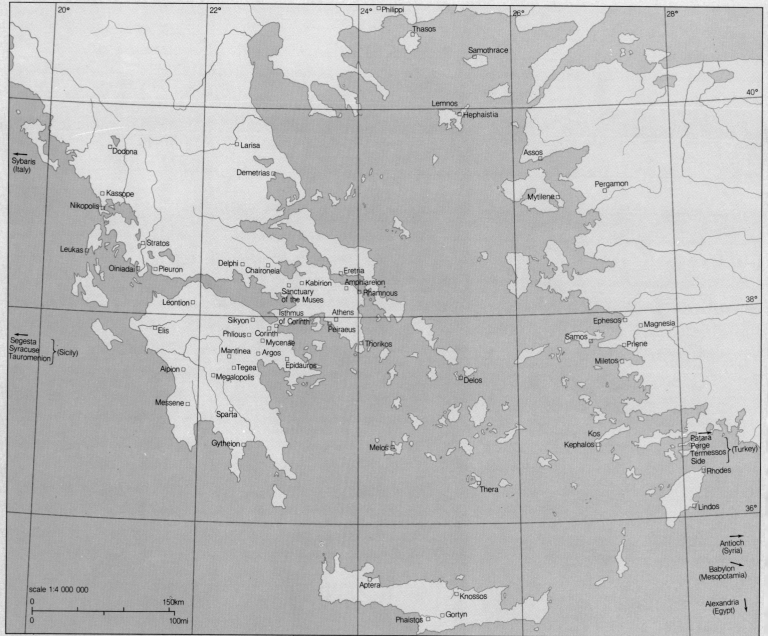

Aipion Atop an acropolis, a small, possibly 3C, theater.

Alexandria Probably begun under Ptolemy I; the reused marble blocks date from the 2C. 12 tiers of seats discovered in 1960.

Amphiareion 4C, one of the most purely Hellenistic in Greece. It seated c.3,000. 5 marble thrones.

Antioch Part of a ?3C theater at the foot of Mt Silpius.

Aptera A small theater (orchestra diam. 18m, cavea 55m). Some seats, a diazoma and part of the proskenion are visible.

Argos Late 4C, one of the finest theaters in Greece, cut into the E

side of the citadel. Orchestra 26m; 81 tiers, seating up to 20,000.

Assos Probably completed first half 3C; incorporated a proskenion, or raised stage, level with the first floor of the skene.

Athens Theater of Dionysos Eleutherios. Site used in the 6C; auditorium in present shape built by Lykourgos c.338–326; modified in Hellenistic and Roman times. 64–78 stone tiers seating c.17,500.

Babylon Dates back probably to a theater built to honor Alexander; unbaked mudbrick construction.

Chaironeia A small theater (14 tiers) cut in, and shaped to, the rock of the acropolis; dedication carved above top tier.

Corinth Cavea laid out in late 5C or early 4C. Apart from the cavea (capacity c.17,500) little survived Roman rebuilding.

Delos Built in 3C to hold some 5,500. Nearby are the mosaics of the House of the Masks.

Delphi One of the best-preserved theaters in Greece, spectacularly sited. 4C, restored 2C and by Romans. Above the orchestra (20m) 35 tiers accommodated some 5,000.

Demetrias Dates from the early 3C. Edge of orchestra, first row of seats, and proskenion foundations have been uncovered.

Dodona Splendidly situated, this early 3C theater with banks of 21, 16 and 21 tiers seated some

14,000. Stone proskenion from late 3C.

Elis Dates from 4C. Spectators sat on a grassy bank or earth steps.

Ephesos Built first half 3C, survives in its Roman form with three levels of 22 tiers, to seat 24,000. Some pre-Roman stage building survives.

Epidauros Best preserved of all Greek theaters, attributed by Pausanias to Polykleitos. The cavea (120m) seats some 14,000 in 34 tiers of the later 4C and 21 2C tiers.

Eretria 4C. A vaulted passage, used perhaps for sudden appearances of personages from the Underworld, leads from the skene to the middle of the orchestra.

Gortyn Greek theater remains at the foot of the acropolis.

Gytheion Some 10 tiers of fine stone seats; an attractive small theater cut into the acropolis.

Isthmus of Corinth Early 4C, its basic Classical character surviving two Roman reconstructions.

Kabirion Recently excavated Hellenistic theater, near the temple of the Kabeiroi.

Kassope A small 4C theater lies by the ruins of a guest house.

Kephalos 4C cavea, with seats of trachyte. In Kardamaina, also in Kos, is another Hellenistic theater.

Knossos One of the oldest in the world (2000–1500 BC), this

Minoan theater has two banks of seats set at right angles.

Kyrene The large Greek theater, in the N side of the acropolis, was converted by the Romans like many others into an arena.

Larissa Late Hellenistic; surviving marble seats bear the names of notables.

Lemnos The Greek theater, in the NE of the island, is late 5C or early 4C; remodeled by the Romans.

Leontion Small 4C theater with several well-preserved tiers.

Leukas Remains of part of a Greek theater in the ancient city.

Lindos Orchestra (5m) and tiers well preserved; this small theater held some 2,000 spectators.

Magnesia ad Meandrum Small 3C theater; skene with 5 rooms and tunnel to orchestra center.

Mantinea Small 4C theater on flat ground. The exterior staircases include fine polygonal stonework.

Megalopolis 4C, largest in Greece. 59 tiers (9 well preserved) seated 17,000–21,000. Fine benches surround the orchestra (30m).

Melos Overlooking the sea, this small late 4C or early 3C theater retains some fine stone tiers.

Messene Small, restored 4C theater; somewhat rectangular cavea plan. Part of a complex of buildings. A second theater remains unexcavated.

Miletos In the large Roman theater the Hellenistic lower stage wall and some benches can be seen.

Mycenae Only a few seats survive of the Hellenistic theater built across the dromos (corridor) to the ancient tomb of Klytaimnestra.

Mytilene Possibly equal to Megalopolis in size; circular orchestra (25m) indicates early date (prob. early 4C); seated 18,000–20,000.

Oiniadai The stone tiers (15 surviving), skene and large orchestra are probably 4C.

Patara The cavea (over 90m across) has an unusually steep gradient.

Peiraeus The great Classical theater is now built over. A small 2C theater survives.

Pergamon The existing steep cavea (early 2C, 80 tiers) seated c.10,000. A road across the back of the orchestra necessitated use of a removable wooden skene.

Perge Greco-Roman, built into a hillside, with seats for c.14,000.

Philippi In the Roman theater, 4C BC circular orchestra and some parodos walls survive.

Phaistos Rectangular, with eight surviving tiers; 2000–1500 BC. Used, like the smaller theater at Knossos, probably for games and rites.

Phlious The visible Roman remains, SW of the acropolis, probably overlie a Greek building.

Pleuron Small, built c.230 BC

against the city walls which, including a tower, served as skene.

Priene One of the best preserved of Hellenistic theaters, late 4C, with slightly later stage building.

Rhamnous Mid-4C, built in a fort-town; rectangular plan. Probably doubled as an assembly area.

Rhodes Small Hellenistic theater, recently reconstructed; rectangular plan, seats c.2,000. The documented main theater has yet to be found.

Samos The as yet uninvestigated ruins of a small Greek theater lie on the slopes of the acropolis.

Samothrace The c.200 BC theater was quarried 1927–37; only the outline remains. Above it stood the Victory of Samothrace statue.

Sanctuary of the Muses Built c.200 BC in a natural hollow at the foot of Mt Helikon. The first tier only was stone, but there were substantial skene buildings.

Segesta Splendidly situated, mid-3C or earlier. The lower rank of 20 tiers survives. Typical Sicilian Hellenistic paraskenia (wings).

Sikyon Cut into the acropolis, early 3C; one of the largest theaters on the Greek mainland; orchestra 20m, cavea c.125m; vaulted entrances to the lower of c.50 tiers; fine front seats.

Sparta Discovered in the 18C by the army of the Russian Orloff as it dug itself into the foot of the acropolis; a large 2C or 1C theater on a fine site marked by numerous inscriptions.

Stratos 4C, still buried on a hill W of the village Surovigli.

Sybaris Excavations have revealed Greek structures below the Roman theater.

Syracuse There was a theater in the 5C. The existing, probably 3C, structure cut into the rock was large (cavea 134m), had monumental stage buildings, and bears many late 3C inscriptions.

Tauromenion Inscribed seats, and masonry walls incorporated in the Roman skene indicate an earlier Greek theater on this splendid site.

Tegea Only part of the 2C retaining wall survives of the 4C theater on which stands a basilica.

Termessos A small well-preserved Hellenistic theater with later additions; 24 tiers.

Thasos 4C; tiers and skene more or less intact.

Thera Among the ruins of Old Thera on a rocky headland is a small Hellenistic theater, reconstructed by the Romans.

Thorikos The 5C theater was gradually enlarged to its existing (4C) strange semielliptical shape, with two ranks of 20 and 11 tiers, orchestra 30 by 15m and a capacity of c.5,000.

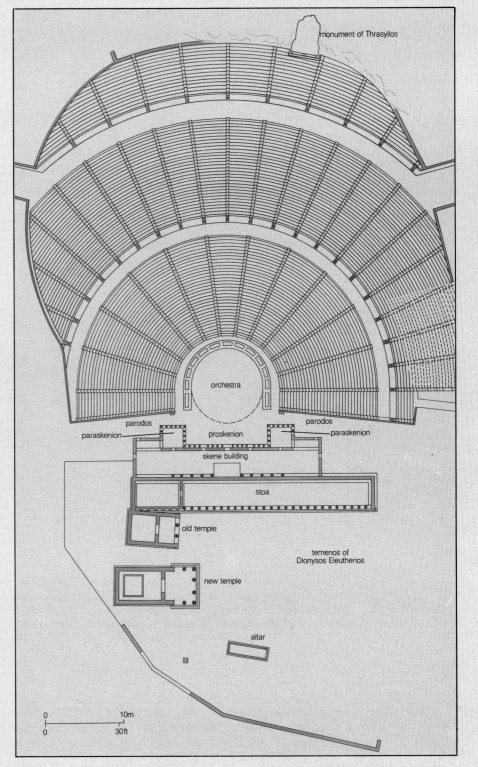

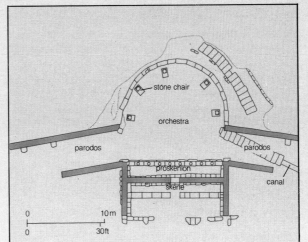

Above The theater of Dionysos Eleutherios, Athens. The actors moved in the 5th century from the agora, where they performed on a cart, to the south side of the acropolis, above the god's sanctuary with its 6th- and 4th-century temples. In Lykourgos' later reconstruction, stone seats replaced the wooden benches on which audiences had drummed their applause, and stone replaced the wooden skene and paraskenia. As theatrical art declined, the stage became more elaborate.

Left At the charming little theater at the Amphiareion, seating just 3,000, the stage is part of the original Hellenistic design.

ADRIATIC SEA

IONIAN SEA

Paestum
Taras
Metapontum
Elea
Hipponion
Kaulonia
Lokroi Epizephyrioi
Segesta
Himera
Sicily
Selinus
Akragas
Syracuse

15° 20°

■ city of which appreciable remains of walls have survived
● fortress of which appreciable remains of walls have survived
□ city of which walls have not survived
○ fortress of which no appreciable remains have survived

scale 1:3 750 000

0
0
200km
150mi

● Doric temple
● Ionic temple
○ Corinthian temple
● theater
○ treasuries
○ stadium
○ gymnasium
○ round building
○ stoa/portico
○ other monument (altar, pillar, gate etc.)

So in contemporary tragedy there is little or no action on the stage. Set speeches magnificently describing events there are; but the actual drama, played out in words between a few characters and a chorus, culminating often in a violent deed offstage, perhaps revealed in a tableau of the slayer and the slain, is surely akin in spirit to the art we have seen some reason to call Polygnotan." The greatest example of it must have been the big wall painting of Odysseus and the Underworld at Delphi, in which tallness created a sense of distance, and a wood between the lower and the upper ground confused the center of the painting. The whole painting was a composition of groups, some of them very strange, but the central group, just below the wood, showed Agamemnon standing with his stick among the greatest heroes, all beardless except the king.

The economy of means, the frugality of Classical art after the first break away from traditional grandeur and vitality, clearly represent a confident and a sophisticated movement. The draperies fall more simply, the inexpressive faces fix themselves as if they were posing for eternity. While sculpture inches forward into a solemn realism, drawing takes on a sculptural quality. This is a more theoretic, a

more self-conscious art. There had, of course, been nothing like it in the history of the world. It was in the 5th century that the Greeks took off finally from their predecessors and contemporaries. Technical books began to be written by artists: Polykleitos on sculpture, Parrhasios on painting, Iktinos on the Parthenon, Agatharchos on wall painting, Sophokles on the tragic chorus.

The reaction to this movement is most apparent in literature, and there it struck first. Herodotos, even though he wrote as late as the early 420s, was still an archaic writer. He balanced his anecdotes, composed his sentences as well as his chapters and whole books, with an apparently intuitive formal sense. Thucydides started to write soon after 431 BC and continued for some 30 years, but his clarity of composition, his conscious restraint as a writer, and the monumental effects at which he aims, place him as purely Classical. This is a mannered style, and Classicism is nothing if not mannered, but the result is an organized clarity of materials and an ease of comprehension. These two close contemporaries belong not only to different generations of writing style but to different worlds, to Halikarnassos overwhelmed by the Persians and to Athens in her

Previous page Dodona, set in the enclosed valley of Tsarkovitsa in the far northwest, was the site of a sanctuary and oracle of Zeus, perhaps the oldest in Greece. The superb theater was built at the time of Pyrrhos of Epirus (297–272 BC). The cavea is partially recessed into the acropolis hill and originally seated over 14,000 spectators. The theater has recently been restored for use in the annual festival of drama.

The Classical Greek world

heyday, to the old Ionian community and the 5th-century Delian league.

Thucydides already lived in the time of the sophists. Their effect on prose style was on the whole retrograde; they regularized into a tinkling, ornamental rhetoric the old-fashioned devices of public speech which had existed before they could be recorded. Speech became an impressive performance which could be taught. This new rhetoric was west Greek, but it was not the only sophistry. They specialized also in the art of argument, frequently of a perverse kind, and sometimes in philosophical positions of radical originality but with little regard for common sense or the morality that goes with it. None of this was quite new, but in the sophistic movement they got out of hand. An arrogance of liberty not chastened by good manners has more than once led to disaster, and so probably it did on this occasion; but in so far as their effect on style, which is after all a kind of manners, a social gesture, was to make it more conscious, they did well. We owe to them to some degree the prose style of Thucydides.

The reaction into wildness and extravagance can be measured in the late plays of Euripides, their powerful and complicated impressionism, the structural brilliance and confusion, the exotic coloring. The best and greatest is surely the *Bacchai*, though underlying that there is almost certainly a lost masterpiece by Aischylos. But in dramatic poetry, the Classical moment is usually said to be Sophokles. If I may be allowed a little honest autobiography, I was taught this at school, and I have been resisting it all my life; I have heard great scholars and careful specialists turn it upside down, and yet as I grow older, it seems within certain limits true. The deadly concentration of arguments, the simplicity of conceptions, and economy of structure are strongest in Sophokles. His material is wild, even appalling, but not extravagant.

Dramatic poetry is completely Athenian, while the sophists and philosophers, except for Sokrates, who was satirical about the others, were foreigners. They were mostly Ionians, Protagoras from Abdera, Prodikos from Keos, and so on. The greatest influence of these traveling sages at Athens was probably in the late 430s. The first plays of Aristophanes were produced in the 420s and later Plato set the date of his *Symposion*, the golden age of Athenian conversation, in 416 BC.

Music in Ancient Greece

The practice and theory of music deeply influenced society at all levels. Cult days, banquets, labor (even so specialized as baking bread or mating horses) had their own tunes and chanteys. The warrior trained at swordplay and the athlete at boxing to the pipes' cheerful burble. Dancing was, as never again in Europe, universal. *Mousikos*, "muse-ish," was in the jargon of Athens synonymous with "refined." The self-controlled man "stepped in rhythm," and the man out of sorts "went off tune" (an allusion to a mishit on the lyre and an error which cost at least one player his reputation with the concertgoers of Alexandria). Goatherds whiled away the weary noon with the flutes of Pan; and even from prisoners of war melody was required in their heaviness. And very nearly all these tunes were taught by example, not by notation, and have therefore perished.

It was to west Asia and their Thracian neighbors that the Greeks owed (a debt they admitted) their instruments and early melodic dialects. What they created with them was a new, durable science and aesthetic of music. In acoustics, for example, the mathematicians made spectacular progress once Pythagoras had demonstrated the numerical basis of consonance. As for psychological insight into the performer, Plato's portrait of the lyre-singer Ion is supreme.

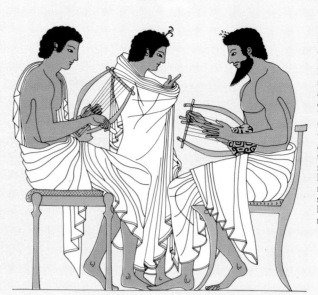

Above "... So also the lyre teacher sees to his pupils' restraint and good behavior. Once they are able to play, he teaches them songs by suitable poets, stringing these into the lesson, and gets the rhythms and tunings into the boys' minds, to make them less wild, and better in tune for effective discourse and action ..."

Below Sociable music – an offering, a party, a war dance.
"This song I love to live and sing; and when I'm dead,/Put my lyre at my feet and my pipes over my head;/Pipe away!"

"He slew and gutted the tortoise with a polished knife ... He cut measures of cane [as *socket-posts*] and fixed them in holes bored through the stonehard *shell*. Round about the shell he skillfully stretched *skin* of an ox, and into this he passed the two *arms*, fitting a *crossbar* to them. When at last he had the lovely toy in his hands, Hermes tested with the *plectrum*, part by part – and a brave din she made! Then the god sang a fine burthen, making it up as he went along, like lads who dare each other at a revel: the tale of a god and a sandaled nymph ...; and even as he sang the one thing, he had the rest in his mind."

Below Greek philosophers put the highest value on theory which in music led to the development of a single-stringed measuring instrument known as the monochord. With this "acoustic potentiometer" Greek mathematicians, notably Pythagoras of Samos in the 6th century BC, were able to calculate and demonstrate the numerical relationships between different pitches. A single string, stretched between two points and spanning a hollow sounding box, when plucked, sounds a note. Dividing this string into two equal parts produces a note an octave higher, at the ratio of two to three produces a fifth, and of three to four an interval of a fourth, and so on. This is more clearly shown in the diagram below where the string is subdivided into 120 equal parts and pitch has been added assuming the open string to be sounding C.

Left "And in the center Apollo, running his plectrum of gold across the seven-voiced lyre, led all manner of melody ..." At the four great international festivals gorgeously costumed soloists and teams shared their virtuosity with a cosmopolitan audience. Song to the ceremonial lyre (*kithara*) was the senior musical contest.

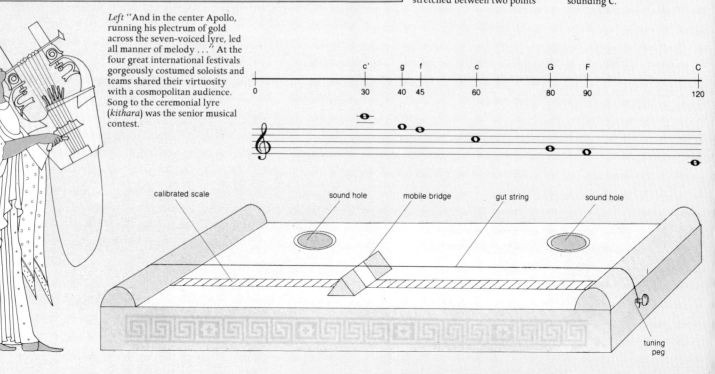

calibrated scale   sound hole   mobile bridge   gut string   sound hole

tuning peg

Right The pipe – made of hardwood or bone – was jointed, cylindrical (as the clarinet), and voiced by a bivalve reed (as the oboe), so that it sounded perhaps not unlike a krummhorn. Multiple boring and the invention of a rotary metal sleeve improved its range and ability to switch from mode to mode (*polyphonia*). The various sizes, from "virginal" up to "sub-bass," together encompassed just over the three octaves which was in practice the field of play.

Above The pipes were not joined. Varying their angle, as one played "with crab fingers," was a subtle art. How the tune was shared out between them is – like so much in ancient Greek music – speculative. This professional is wearing his prize crown and the leather cheek-strap which (like the trumpeter) he used for a heavy session.

Right Trumpeter, in the uniform of a Black Sea archer. The trumpet, capable of two or three notes only, had a good repertoire of signaling rhythms.

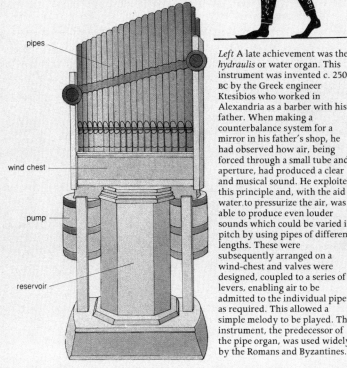

pipes

wind chest

pump

reservoir

Left A late achievement was the *hydraulis* or water organ. This instrument was invented c. 250 BC by the Greek engineer Ktesibios who worked in Alexandria as a barber with his father. When making a counterbalance system for a mirror in his father's shop, he had observed how air, being forced through a small tube and aperture, had produced a clear and musical sound. He exploited this principle and, with the aid of water to pressurize the air, was able to produce even louder sounds which could be varied in pitch by using pipes of different lengths. These were subsequently arranged on a wind-chest and valves were designed, coupled to a series of levers, enabling air to be admitted to the individual pipes as required. This allowed a simple melody to be played. This instrument, the predecessor of the pipe organ, was used widely by the Romans and Byzantines.

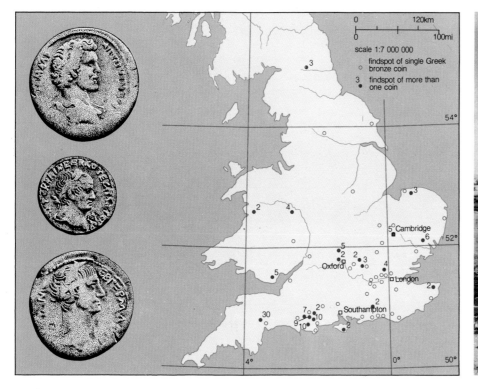

There is no need to take too seriously the kind of accusation that is always made against intellectuals and foreigners after a crisis in the state. It was no more the sophistic influence that brought down the Athenians politically than it was Voltaire who caused the French revolution. When things go well, no one blames the intellectuals, chattering away in their corner, for exactly the same kind of conversation that on other occasions seems to bring down Olympian wrath. Protagoras was prosecuted at Athens, nor was his case unique; the most famous victim was Sokrates. He was condemned because of the dangerous behavior of his pupils, but that was after a coup d'etat, at the end of a lost war, when the Athenians were predictably angry and confused. Whether one approves of the sophists or not, and Sokrates did not, Plato makes them seem rather innocently bad.

It is doubtful whether they genuinely affected belief or disbelief in the gods. The behavior of the Athenians at the end of the century shows hysterical anxiety, but public religion continued without faltering, and private cults increased rather than decreased. In every sanctuary where worship was continuous, so far as I know, small offerings of the late 5th century are even more numerous than those of the early 5th century. The sophisticated dramatic arguments of Euripides by no means suggest atheism, and the Athenian women at Delphi in his *Ion*, who cry out at a statue of "Athene, my own goddess," are likely to be realistic. For poetry of real religious awe, and of many levels, the *Bacchai* has few rivals even in Greek.

The most interesting index to what was going on inside Athens in the 5th century is the career of Aristophanes. The differences between his styles are very great. The first plays are spirited, lyrical and terribly hard-hitting. After 424 the political edge is slightly blunted: in the *Clouds* he mocks Sokrates, in the *Wasps* a mad old man obsessed with the law-courts, and in the *Peace* in 421, in which year peace was a topical subject, he is as lyrical and as vehement as he was in 425, in favor of the farmers,

Above: Findspots of Greek coins in Britain
The coins illustrated, of Antoninus Pius, Trajan and Vespasian, probably reached Britain from the imperial mint at Alexandria in the 2nd century AD.

Below It is suggested that the scene in this Athenian vase painting is taken from the *Antigone* of Sophokles. It is a strange compromise between truth to life and truth to the theater. Antigone is about to be condemned by the tyrant Kreon for attempting the decent funeral of her dead brother. It is an almost invariable rule that such scenes of violence were described in the text of plays but not enacted on the stage.

The Erechtheion is a 5th-century rebuilding of the House of Erechtheus at Athens which Homer mentions. Seen here are the north porch (*above*), the east facade (*right*), the west facade (*below right*) and, from the upper level, the southwest aspect (*bottom right*).

The Erechtheion is built on the site of the Mycenaean palace of Athens and the sacred, original olive tree that grew beside it was probably Mycenaean. Erechtheus was also Poseidon. Here Poseidon and Athene disputed the ownership of Attica; the mark of his trident was visible in the rock. The south porch – held up by stone women or caryatids – is where something sacred, maybe a statue

or its dress, was held up to the people. Inside the main building was a twin temple, of Athene in one room and Poseidon-Erechtheus in the other. The old wooden idol of Athene was kept there. The Romans repaired the Erechtheion after a fire; some of its original marbles were reused for a temple of Rome and Augustus. The Erechtheion looks directly down from the acropolis northwest towards the sacred road to Eleusis.

Far right Gods portrayed on a portion of the east side of the Parthenon frieze.

but now with less fury. By 414, to judge by the *Birds*, the theater has become more spectacular, more musical and more Utopian: the rhythms of choral poetry are subtler than ever before, there are still some sharp remarks, but the plot is amusing, the atmosphere that of a happy never-never land.

The *Frogs* (405) has another brilliantly invented animal chorus, the same rhythmic mastery and lyricism, enough jokes, and for the first time some intellectually penetrating literary criticisms. One would expect the play to be plunged in gloom, since Athens faced defeat, but not at all. It adapts a device of Eupolis from a lost comedy, in which the country towns of Attica send down to the Underworld to bring back a statesman from the dead to save Athens. There are hints of this in Aristophanes, but in his version no one saves anything; what is wanted is only a good tragic poet, Sophokles and Euripides having joined Aischylos among the dead. The chorus of the Eleusinians in the Underworld could hardly be more otherworldly.

The last plays of the Athenian theatrical poets before the fall of the city are Sophokles' *Oedipus at Kolonos*, an intensely moving and religious play, Aristophanes' *Frogs* and Euripides' *Bacchai*. On this evidence, whatever else was in disarray, wit was not, religion was not, and poetry was not. It is of course possible to argue that Aristophanes' *Lysistrata* of 411 BC, a knockabout comedy in which the women of Greece conspire to refuse sex to their lovers until the men agree to peace, shows a healthier political tone.

The public buildings of Athens in the last years of the Peloponnesian war are smaller in scale than the Parthenon, but in delicacy of detail, crispness of conception and subtlety of composition they show no falling off. The Erechtheion was begun in 421 BC and after some interruption its friezes were being carved in 408 and 407. It owes its complicated plan to a whole group or involved knot of elements of ritual: a sacred snake, the twin temple of Poseidon–Erechtheus and Athene, a solemn balcony, and a deep hole in the rock, to name not quite all of them. To make matters worse, in the course of building, a prehistoric tomb was discovered which was identified as the resting place of a legendary king, and allowance had to be made for it. The Erechtheion itself is a triumph, different from every aspect, and yet transforming perfectly from view to view. It is a slender, catlike Ionic masterpiece, both beautiful and brilliantly clever. After the Erechtheion, no Greek temple would again be rebuilt that was not less beautiful than one it replaced.

One can tell something also from the funeral vases called white-ground *lekythoi* that were decorated for their purpose, and used almost nowhere but in Athens and in Athenian colonies in the second half of the 5th century. Hypnos and Thanatos, the twin brethren Sleep and Death, who carried away the body of Sarpedon in the *Iliad* and in the fine red-figure vase painting by Euphronios of c. 500 BC, in New York, carried away the bodies of many Athenian soldiers. Sleep is young and beautiful, but Death is not, and nor is the ferryman Charon, who appears on many of these vases. In the Charon vases only the ferryman and the stern of his boat appear; Hermes guides the dead. Some of the later scenes of this series have a curious ambiguity, and so have the carved tombstones of the same years. Grief is

Above The Northeast wind and the West wind carry away the dead body of a young soldier to his grave.

Far right The goddess Athene stands in sorrow over a monument to the Athenian dead.

expressed, there are scenes of departure, last looks, gestures of mourning, but it is not obvious who has died, the sorrow is ambiguous and universal.

And what had happened to the gods? Their representations had become more and more human. Athene leaning on her spear in mourning at a stone memorial was evidently not drawn from life, but completely convincing as life. The male gods had the bodies of athletes, Aphrodite was sexually attractive, and even Pans and satyrs were elegant nudes, and a great deal less wild than they had been. What had altered? The answer seems to be that in some areas, or among some people, not much had altered except art, and even that less than we think. At the court of Polykrates on Samos, Zeus and Hera were mischievously erotic figures, and the *Iliad* confirms that such a conception of gods was not a new or impossibly shocking idea even in the archaic period. The Zeus of Pheidias had great dignity. The wild Oriental Zagreus (the Cretan god with whom Dionysos was identified) prancing on a bull on a bronze disk from a Cretan cave from centuries earlier was a being in another idiom which had never been Greek at all. The simpler dedications continued conservative throughout the 5th century. Zeus Ktesios was still the name for the household snake, Apollo Aguieus was still a stone post, and Hermes still received wreaths on his perpetual erection. Religious poetry was almost too clever and versatile to be taken seriously, but that proves little: it both was and was not serious, like the conversation at Plato's *Symposion* in 416 BC.

PART FIVE
THE
AGE OF
ALEXANDER

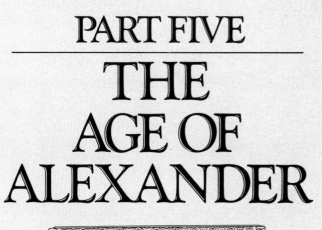

NEW PATTERNS IN LITERATURE AND RELIGION

Archaism in literature

In the 4th century BC archaism had already entered into literature, and into visual art. The great high tide of nostalgia was to come 100 years later, when the 4th-century masters of Athenian prose would be studied like the 5th-century poets. Epic poetry was already in the past in the 5th century; by then Athenian children had to learn special meanings and strange words in order to understand Homer. Homer was still a sort of god, but his poetry seemed to them as remotely ancient or as venerable as his subject matter. Indeed it was at this time he was first classed as the earliest, and curiously as the most reliable, of historians. Already by the end of the 4th century BC the three poets we know today as the great Classical tragedians – Aischylos, Sophokles and Euripides – had been recognized, in the case of the latter two less than a century after their life-times; their works were preserved by the state of Athens as Peisistratos had earlier preserved the *Iliad* and the *Odyssey*. The reemergence of Athenian fleets and Athenian alliances after 400 BC, the rebuilding of the city walls and the recovery of wealth were not able to bring back the 5th century.

Even Thucydides in the late 5th century archaizes as a stylist, but Athens believed old-fashioned language had a greater dignity and poetry than everyday speech, and an ancient critic acutely observed that Thucydides was "political in his wording, versatile in his rhetoric, rough in harmony and swift in meaning." The interest to us of 4th-century archaism is not that innovation then ceased, but that a process can be seen to have begun which was to continue a very long time. Critics were more severe in their devotion to the past than poets or sculptors or architects: Aristotle thought Sophokles the greatest tragedian, Plato went back to Pindar for nourishment; the 4th-century elegiac poets are underestimated to this day, and so is the best of 4th-century sculpture.

Theokritos and pastoral poetry

At the same time we have the strong impression of a more level and (there being no other word so exact) a more bourgeois Athens. The severely beautiful blushed a little deeper into prettiness until it was all but overblown. The Athenian Menander's mild comedy of manners is too tame and too smooth after Aristophanes, but he was more popular than Aristophanes ever had been. Representations of the Gorgon's head had once been terrible, then grotesque, then by the early 5th century partly funny, and now she could be a beautiful woman. The Cyclops had been an antigod, then a terrible monster, then an amusing pantomime creature in Euripides' satyr play *Cyclops*, and now in the early part of the 3rd century he was pathetic and hopelessly in love with a sea nymph: "My sweet honey-apple ... for thee I rear eleven fawns and four bear cubs."

The poet of these lines is Theokritos, a Sicilian Greek who learned the sweet-sour conventions of pastoral poetry from Philetas of the island of Kos, and lived at the Macedonian Greek court of Ptolemy in Alexandria. It is worth noticing that he wrote his poems in dialect. The dialect is Doric, and it is meant to be a peasant speech like the Dorset dialect of William Barnes and like modern Austrian dialect poetry. But Theokritos exaggerates, very likely deliberately; his dialect was never really spoken, or written by anyone but him. It is a deliberate distorting medium, partly a joke, partly a device like stage dress or pastoral scenery. At the same period and also at Alexandria, with the same mixture of realism, traditional verse, and a dialect, in this case Ionic, that never exactly was on sea or land Herodas wrote theatrical pieces, short scenes from common or low life.

Again in the same period, but in quite another mood, someone seems to have created a piece of pastiche clever enough to deceive many scholars, ancient and modern; it pretended to be the poetry of Corinna, a 6th-century Boeotian dialect poetess and rival of Pindar. The attractive fragments that have survived include parts of a hymn for a spring festival and a singing contest between the two mountains Kithairon and Helikon. Unfortunately her spelling and some other linguistic evidence, also perhaps the simplicity of her verse forms, and above all the fact that she is really too charming to be true,

Below The Mistress of the Wild Animals, who is identified with Artemis, is moving already, in this early representation, from severity through the grotesque towards gaiety and charm.

combine to put her in the 3rd century BC. She is not the real Corinna. Taken together, these dialect poets of the 3rd century mark an important development in Greek consciousness of the world: a logical extension of the curiosity of Herodotos, combined with a social curiosity (since Theokritos as well as Herodas drew scenes of common life), and a nostalgia for simplicity, poverty and security, for beliefs no longer shared, emotions no longer felt by intellectuals.

But literature makes tricky evidence. The fundamental obsession of the poetry of Theokritos is love, and his herdboys are only part of a gallery of strange lovers. He sees their lives and feelings with lover's eyes. (It is notable that the pastoral romance *Daphnis and Chloe* written by Longus some 500–600 years later, which is one of the few intense erotic masterpieces of ancient literature, exploits the same conventions in very much the same way.) There is a poem to the syrinx, the shepherd's and goatherd's flute, by a contemporary of Theokritos, Mnasalkes of Sikyon, written perhaps in the mid-3rd century: "Syrinx, what are you doing here with the Seafoam's daughter Aphrodite? Why here away from the shepherd's lip? There are no mountain

ridges here and no ravines, only Eros and desire; the wild Muse lives on the mountain." This mixture of themes is never far away from pastoral poetry, though the themes are often in tension. The style swiftly became international, as all styles did at that time, the patronage and the readership of poetry being no longer regional.

Public ritual

And yet something had certainly altered by the 3rd century BC in the emotions and the beliefs even of quite simple people. Theokritos wrote a poem about a royal festival of Adonis at Alexandria. The worship of Adonis was well known in 5th-century Athens, though its origins were Babylonian and it took its Greek form in Cyprus; Adonis was wounded Thammuz, a dying god of vegetation. We first hear of his worship by Greeks in a fragment of Sappho. In Athens his festival was in April, but at Alexandria in September; there were deeper differences. Theokritos' characters are Syracusan women, and the festival for them is an excited excursion through a huge press of people to see a spectacular tableau of Aphrodite and Adonis feasting together on a couch, in a bower of green branches, and to hear the praises of the god. "Lady Athene, what workmanship! What art! The figures stand and turn so naturally, it's life not weaving! What a brilliant thing is man. And look, how wonderful, lying there in his silver chair with the first whiskers on his cheek, thrice-loved Adonis, beloved even in death!" These are coarse women from the poorer, outlying districts; they despise native Egyptians and their own slave girls, they are terrified of horses, they have a salty, proverbial humor.

Above left Perseus in winged boots beheads the Gorgon. This is a well-preserved piece of mature archaic sculpture from a temple at Selinus, a Greek city on the south coast of Sicily.

Left This Gorgon or Medusa from a hydria found at Tarquinia, made in about 490 BC, and painted perhaps by the Berlin Painter, was executed with enthusiasm and a degree of hilarity.

Above As a terracotta ornament on an Etruscan temple the Gorgon remained fearsome, but even here she was modeled and painted with enjoyment.

Greek Medicine and the Cult of Asklepios

Greek medicine moved on from the traditional wisdom and magic of early societies toward the beginning of scientific medicine in the 5th and 4th centuries BC. In the earliest 5th-century medical writings there are still elements of magic: gastritis is the curse of Apollo because it recalls the liquid droppings of swallows, the birds of the god. But by the time of Aristotle anatomy and solid observation had begun to show their influence.

The early centers of practical medicine were sanctuaries of Asklepios, and the cures effected there were remarkable. They were shrouded in religious mystery, but the cures were not thought to be precisely miraculous. Other gods and heroes could cure, but the spread of the cult of Asklepios suggests a disciplined craft or science and a corpus of knowledge, a method, that could be transmitted. Miracles of course also existed: the toe of Epaminondas of Thebes, which his funeral fire failed to consume, did miracles of healing thereafter wherever it was taken.

The more orthodox cult of Asklepios spread from the island of Kos, the home of the famous Hippokrates, to whom several surviving Greek medical works have been attributed, one or two perhaps justly.

Left This statue of Asklepios from the great sanctuary at Epidauros was made in the Roman period. The kindly old gentleman with the wise and benevolent snake has almost forgotten the wilder and more ambivalent origins of medicine. Still, he is not quite a scientist. Statues of Christ have sometimes owed something to statues of Asklepios. The consort of Asklepios was Health, and her attendant All-Healing. As for the snake, he was the most important person in the sanctuary. It was thought even in the 4th century that, if the snake of Asklepios licked your eyes, he might cure blindness.

Right This enormous leg from a relief in the Athens National Museum is a more than life-size offering of a model of what the god had cured. But a stone relief is more permanent than a model leg, and no doubt it was thought more seemly.

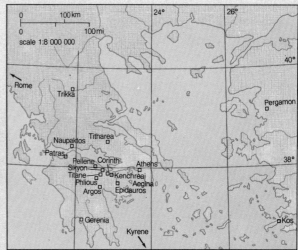

Left This stone relief carving from the Athens National Museum shows a doctor or priest of healing with a nurse or priestess in attendance. He is at work on the patient. Much of the medical work done in the name of Asklepios was done at night; the patients slept, perhaps they were drugged. Although we often know the details of what was cured, an old spear-blade in the cheek for example, we know little of the details of treatment. Patients seem to have believed the god himself came to cure them.

Above This relief, like the other, is a thank-offering for a successful cure. These thank-offerings could take the form of a model of the afflicted part, an ear, a nose, an eye or a genital organ. The same custom has survived around the Mediterranean into modern times. But this relief conveys a more systematic and sober kind of medical practice.

Above left These surgical instruments, now in the British Museum, are Hellenistic in date. Anatomy and surgery progressed greatly in the Hellenistic world, under the leadership of Herophilos of Chalkedon.

Top The principal sanctuaries of Asklepios in the Greek world.

Epidauros

The city of Epidauros lies by the sea, on the Saronic gulf, but some kilometers inland a sanctuary of Asklepios grew up which had an international prestige that was at its height in the 4th century BC. The theater there was thought the most beautiful in the world, even as late as the age of Hadrian, when much grander constructions existed. It was simple and Classical. Games were held at the sanctuary, almost on a level with the greatest international festivals. Its architecture and sculpture were extremely rich, with a certain slight heaviness that marks the end of the Classical high summer. Of the late 5th-century temple of Asklepios itself and of the elaborate tholos, or rotunda, built in the 4th century, only the foundations and some fragments remain, some of them built into churches.

The ancient roads that connected the sanctuary of Asklepios with the coastal city can still be traced, and some distance away stray blocks of finely carved decorated marble from the shrine of the god can still be spotted built into the walls of churches. The sanctuary, or *hieron*, was a place of healing, innocent of history.

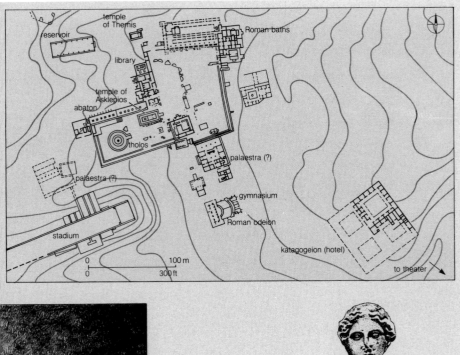

Throughout the passage in which Theokritos recounts the reactions to the tableau, there is no touch of religion. The formal hymn that follows has an elaborate, literary beauty; it has touching lines, and if one were not so lost in admiration at the contrasting rhythms of this whole poem, and its obvious and admirable artifice, one would be much moved by it and perhaps think it religious. Maybe it is, among other things, religious. The festival has an exotic charm but its character is secular, a popular show put on by Ptolemy for the crowd.

Even the sequence of events in the festival is strange. We are lucky enough to be able to deduce from some literary sources and a Fayûm papyrus of about 250 BC something about the cult of Adonis in Egypt. Almost all the evidence coincides to start the festival with the dead Adonis lamented and to go on to his resurrection and ascension a day later. The papyrus seems to suggest a festival day of happy celebration followed by a fast day and finally another expensive day, probably a public or mystical reenactment of the resurrection; that is, the papyrus, which is a daily record of accounts, suggests a three-day festival. The Christian theologians Jerome, and Origen and Cyril of Alexandria were in no doubt that the resurrection followed the death. In Theokritos' poem, Arsinoë, queen of Egypt, begins with the union of Adonis and Aphrodite, goes on to death and lamentation the next day, and then closes the festival. In Athens the festival of Adonis was private and confined to women. Its elements as far as we know them were tiny gardens that sprang up and withered quickly on the tops of houses, and a loud lamentation by the women on a given day.

In Ptolemaic Egypt at least, home of a new Greco-Egyptian culture, a public celebration of romantic love and death, taking place in the royal palace with an expensive display of devotion and enjoyable competitive artistry in the singing, had replaced the private ritual of a dying god who mysteriously came to life. The only coming to life Theokritos mentions is next year's reenactment. His last words are "Goodbye dear Adonis, and welcome again next year." The keynote of the palace festival is its richness. The place is hung with new and magnificent tapestries of Adonis dying in his silver chair, with Aphrodite lamenting. There are bowers of sweet-smelling greenery. The centerpiece in a central bower is a couch of ebony and gold, with legs of ivory, a carving of the eagle carrying off Ganymede. Here figures of Adonis and Aphrodite lie together with a fine display of food in front of them.

The same process was at work on a less generous scale even among the state rituals of Athens. The lavishness of celebration increased, and the crowd increased and diversified. The ritual duties of the young men doing military service increased in their ceremonial quality and lost reality. It was the spectacular parts of public rituals that increased. Not unnaturally, the young men in their fine new cloaks appealed more to the city than the mysterious and ominous private processions that also appeared in the streets. Demosthenes maintained that his enemy Aischines took part, for example, in the rituals of Sabazios, an untamed Phrygian version of Dionysos: he read the holy books while his mother initiated new devotees, he wore a fawnskin at night, he smeared the devout with clay and bran,

Left The theater at the sanctuary of Asklepios dates from the 4th century and is the best-preserved of all Greek theaters. It seats 14,000 and has particularly fine acoustics.

The lady on the horse (*above*) is an *akroterion*, a pinnacle decoration from the roof of the temple of Asklepios. Figures like this took on the nature of the wind: they flew or ran lightly, they had wings, or their clothes billowed around them. They contrasted with the heavy, crisp lines of the temples themselves. This one comes late in the series, about 380 BC. She seems to be rising from the sea; she may be the spirit of a wind.

Ephesos

Ephesos was another of the teeming, mixed Greek cities of the Asian coast. It rivaled Miletos and later Alexandria in importance and size. The ancient local mother goddess was identified with Artemis, and by the Romans with Diana; the Ephesian Artemis was covered in egg-like breasts or breast-like eggs. Her great sanctuary, one of the seven wonders of the world, incorporated 117 columns, each over 18 meters tall. Ephesos was the great city of Roman Asia, and nearly all the remains uncovered are of Roman date. It declined like its predecessors and successors when its river estuary silted up, but it was still important in the Middle Ages: indeed, more magnificent than ever.

Above This statue of Artemis from Ephesos dates from the classicizing and archaizing period of the Roman afterglow, in the 2nd century AD.

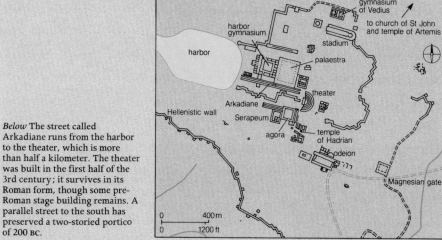

Below The street called Arkadiane runs from the harbor to the theater, which is more than half a kilometer. The theater was built in the first half of the 3rd century; it survives in its Roman form, though some pre-Roman stage building remains. A parallel street to the south has preserved a two-storied portico of 200 BC.

and spent days leading crowds through the streets with snakes in his hands, yelling out *Euoi Saboi* or "Yarroo!" It is easy to see how this sort of thing will have infuriated the intellectuals and the conservatives equally. It was absurd behavior with a touch of the sinister. It is also easy to see how on the edges of society, an increasing area in Athens, it might find converts.

The cult of Asklepios

But the biggest increase in religious cult from the late 5th century onwards was that of a perfectly respectable minor god whose benefits were not invisible: Asklepios god of healing. In many sanctuaries he took over from an existing god or hero, and he never controlled all healing shrines whatsoever. The nymphs healed eye diseases in remote mountain springs, the oracular hero Amphiaraos never ceased to heal at a successful sanctuary on the borders of Attica and Boeotia, and even in the Athenian agora a sanctuary to the unnamed "Healing Hero" stood close to the burial place of Theseus. The cult of Asklepios reached Athens in 420 BC from the Peloponnese, probably by way of Aegina, where Aristophanes sends a character to be healed in his *Wasps* in 422 BC. But there is no doubt that the great parent sanctuary of Epidauros was recognized, since the new festival of the god at

Athens was called the Epidauria. It was usual for any new sanctuary of Asklepios to be formally set up by the arrival of a sacred snake of the god, brought from the mother temple. That is what happened in Athens, and the poet Sophokles entertained the snake until the new hospital was built.

It is hardly too daring to call it a hospital. At Epidauros we have a series of inscriptions of the miracles of Asklepios. It is evident they involve surgery and a serious knowledge of some branches of medicine. At Epidauros, as well as at the many other sanctuaries Epidauros founded, it was the late 5th century that saw the great expansion of the cult and perhaps the 4th that saw its climax. By about 400 BC for Asklepios at Epidauros there was an international festival with athletics, horse races, music and poetry. His new sanctuaries appeared at Kos (where Hippokrates in the 5th century laid the foundations of medical science), Pergamon and Kyrene by the 4th century, and at Rome in 293 BC. At Naupaktos in the 3rd century the diplomatic messenger who was the means of setting up his cult was a woman, Anyte of Tegea, a fine poet. Asklepios acquired sanctuaries at Sikyon, Corinth, Kenchreai, Phlious, Argos, Patras and Pellene in the northern Peloponnese, at Tithorea and Naupaktos in Phokis, and proportionately many more further south. The increase was as much due to a special kind of

These boys are guarding and guiding the sacrificial cattle in the procession of Athene on the marble frieze of the Parthenon. Most of the cattle are quite calm. It is possible that these boys are young herdsmen.

religion as to the organization of medical science. It was a cult for individuals, and the rich paid for it. There are no state treasuries at Epidauros, but its buildings are lavish and decorative.

Oracles and places of healing are often the same, in modern Africa for example as in ancient Greece, and in the 4th century the Greek oracles were already replying to individual questions, even on a small scale. Such questions probably took the form "Herakleidas asks whether to expect a child by his present wife," or "Nikokrateia asks to what god she ought to sacrifice to be rid of her illness." That is partly because each disease was believed to have its own god; Apollo for example was thought to cause and cure enteritis, because the symptoms resembled the droppings of swallows, his sacred birds. Asklepios was ambitious in curing all diseases; in a 4th-century apparition of the god his handmaid was called Panakeia, "All-Healing." The sick would go far to find such a god; we read in the Epidauros inscriptions of a man who had metal in his body for years, after a battle wound, until Asklepios cured him. Asklepios was also unlike the older gods in having no severe, terrible aspect. There is a legend about his being destroyed by the gods for raising a man from the dead. With the coming of Asklepios, divinity was tamed in an important respect.

Private philosophy

The 4th century saw the vast increase of small merchants and shaky commercial enterprises. The hazards of fortune had become extreme; one could rise and fall more easily in the city, and the city itself could rise or fall more easily. It was no longer possible for the Greeks perfectly to comfort themselves with the ancient gods, their proverbial morality, and their 5th-century concern for the state. There was a noticeable increase in religions and philosophies of withdrawal, of individual salvation and peace of mind. The gentle and austere Epicurus was born in Samos in 341 BC and died in Athens in 270; he was by no means extreme among his contemporaries. He studied in Athens in 323, and lived at first in Kolophon in Lesbos and in Lampsakos in the Troad, at the east end of the Hellespont: his closest friends to the end of his life were from Lampsakos and Mytilene on Lesbos, places outside the great power struggles of the Macedonians; his community of disciples included slaves and women.

These movements entailed a new selection of mythology, a different retelling. In the 3rd century in particular, a whole new area of local mythology began to be exploited in Asia Minor. Some of the stories that became popular then were those which eventually appeared in Latin in the *Metamorphoses* of Ovid. The gods were as slippery as fishes, unpredictable, and the disasters of sexuality had infinite permutations. These were tales "to keep a drowsy emperor awake." The intention, at least in the retelling, was no longer very serious. For the serious analysis of experience, for criticism of life, the Greeks turned in the 4th century to philosophers. Serious philosophy and serious poetry were closer together then than they are now, but from the lifetime of Plato onward, there was a slightly literary feel about any engagement in ancient mythology.

Kos

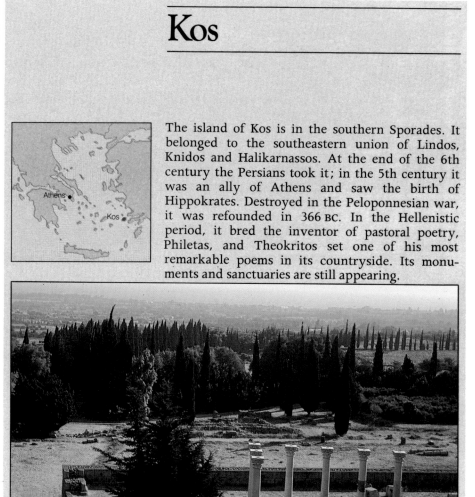

The island of Kos is in the southern Sporades. It belonged to the southeastern union of Lindos, Knidos and Halikarnassos. At the end of the 6th century the Persians took it; in the 5th century it was an ally of Athens and saw the birth of Hippokrates. Destroyed in the Peloponnesian war, it was refounded in 366 BC. In the Hellenistic period, it bred the inventor of pastoral poetry, Philetas, and Theokritos set one of his most remarkable poems in its countryside. Its monuments and sanctuaries are still appearing.

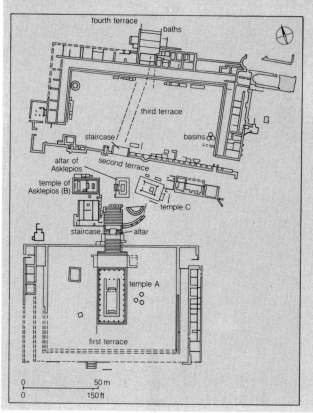

The famous sanctuary of Asklepios, where Greek medicine more or less began, is close to the city of Kos. It was once a sanctuary of Apollo; some time after the death of Hippokrates, in the mid-4th century, building of the temple of Asklepios and its surroundings was undertaken. It contains several 3rd-century features.

The view from the first and highest terrace (*above*), site of the main temple, includes the remains of the great altar and columns of a Roman temple on the second terrace, and on the third terrace the area where the Asklepian festivals were probably held.

THE RISE OF MACEDON

Sparta and Thebes vie for power

At the end of the war between Sparta and Athens the Spartans entered a position of dominance which lasted more or less for one whole generation, from 404 to 371 BC. The course of history after the war, before the 5th century was over, mirrored what had occurred 80 years before. The Spartan hero Lysander, like his predecessors after the Persian wars, flaunted his power in the eastern Mediterranean, had himself venerated at Samos as halfway between a king and a god – setting a precedent that was followed by Alexander – entered into tricky negotiations with the Persians, and was recalled and disgraced. The entanglement with Persia was doomed to be played through again and again until it was settled, impermanently and against all expectation, with the victories of Alexander.

In 401 BC Cyrus the brother of Artaxerxes king of Persia and chief governor of Asia Minor, had decided to attempt the Persian throne. It is significant that he marched inland with a force that included 13,000 Greeks, 10,600 of them heavy infantry. The Greek division was raised by Klearchos, a Spartan official who had been exiled from Byzantion for the atrocities he committed there. These Greeks must have been left over from many military adventures; the record of what happened was written later by an Athenian cavalry-man, a pupil of Sokrates called Xenophon. In the fatal battle, at Cunaxa north of Babylon, Cyrus was killed after personally wounding his brother. Artaxerxes was cured and remained king of kings; his court physician, Ktesias, was another Greek, and wrote his own account of the battle.

Even after the defeat of Cyrus, the Greek division, which was itself undefeated, refused to surrender. Its chief officers were murdered during negotiation, but under Xenophon the Athenian, one of their elected commanders, the Greeks fought their way out of the Persian empire. It would have been an astonishing march even if it had been quite unopposed, but they had also to deal with angry and tough-minded Kurdish mountaineers, and of course with Persian forces. They returned to the Mediterranean by way of the southern shore of the Black Sea, but there they were an embarrassment. The Spartans shipped them to Byzantion and abandoned them; they fought under Seuthes the Thracian in tribal wars; no one could afford to pay them and they were too dangerous to be kindly entertained. The last 6,000 went back into Asia in 399 BC as a Spartan force against the Persian empire. Xenophon spent 20 years in exile, mostly at Skillous in Triphylia, on a high hill in one of the pleasantest countrysides in Greece, just south of Olympia and independent of both Sparta and Athens. He was not back at Athens until the 360s.

The long walls that linked Athens with the Peiraeus, its fortified harbor, made it possible for the city to stand a long siege. Completed in the mid-5th century, they were pulled down at the end of the Peloponnesian war, and then rebuilt by Konon of Athens, with Persian assistance, early in the 4th century.

Alexandria

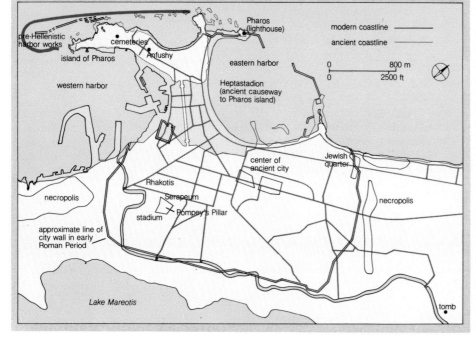

Alexander was buried in the city he founded in Egypt in 332/1 BC, the first of 13 or more of the same name up and down the world. The masterstroke was to join the island of Pharos to the mainland by a mole some 1,500 meters long, creating two fine harbors, back to back. Under the Ptolemies (*left* Ptolemy II, 285–246 BC) Alexandria became for a time commercially and culturally the center of the world. It saw the world's first great library, the first poetry of a new kind and the first great literary scholars. The Romans dealt harshly with it, and the Arabs in the end destroyed it.

The Spartan war with Persia in 400 BC was inevitable in face of Persian threats to Greek cities, but the war was not very successfully or even energetically carried on, and when Konon of Athens, an admiral who had escaped the massacre of the Athenian fleet at Lampsakos in 405 BC, contrived by dealing with Ktesias the court physician to command a Persian fleet, he took Rhodes from the Spartans in 395. A year before, Agesilaos king of Sparta had crossed over into Asia (where he received the news of the loss of Rhodes) with his head full of fiery notions that Alexander would later make real. He had imitated Homer's Agamemnon by beginning with a sacrifice at Aulis on the east coast of Boeotia, but since he stupidly forgot to ask the Thebans for permission, his sacrifice was interrupted by armed men. Agesilaos did well in Phrygia, but Konon ruled the sea, captured an Egyptian grain fleet sailing to the Spartans, and finally annihilated the Spartan naval force off Knidos in 394 BC.

In mainland Greece the Spartans had also provoked fierce resentment. In July of 394 a confederation of their enemies faced them in a bloody but indecisive battle near Corinth. Meanwhile Agesilaos was recalled from Asia, following the death in battle of Lysander in Boeotia. In August, at Koroneia in Boeotia, the Boeotians and Athenians defeated Agesilaos. Sparta was blockaded inside the Peloponnese, at least by sea, as she had been under Perikles, but there she remained indomitable for years of stalemate. Konon, with Persian connivance and Persian money, restored the long Athenian walls and the walls of Peiraeus, and Athens recovered the islands of Lemnos, Imbros, Skyros, Delos and Chios. After the battle of Knidos, the Greek cities of Asia Minor threw out their Spartan governors and the new democracies claimed not Athenian but Persian protection. It is evident that all the Persians could hope for in Europe was a more or less faithful ally, through whom Persia could dominate the other independent peoples. It goes without saying that this position would be tempting

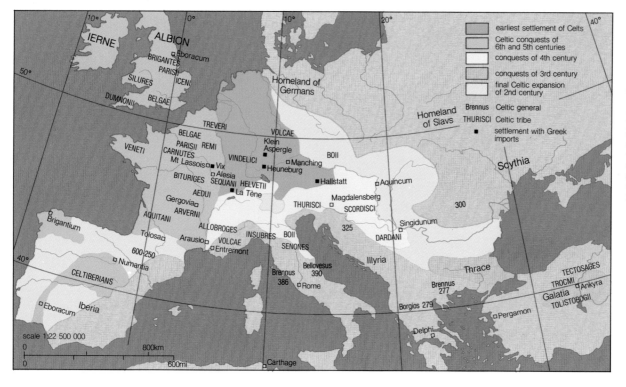

Celtic Europe and invasions
We speak of a Celtic fringe today, but between the 6th and 3rd centuries BC Celtic invasions spread over much of Europe. Rome was invaded by Brennus in 386, and another Brennus reached Delphi in the 3rd century. The Galatians, who settled in the central Anatolian plain in the 3rd century BC, continued into Roman times to speak a Celtic language. Celtic tribal organization, under chieftains of great distinction and wealth, survived Caesar's conquest of Gaul and the imperial conquest of Britain.

to any Greek state in desperate circumstances, but that no Greek ally would be faithful. For the present the sun shone for Athens; in six years she had control of the entrance to the Black Sea.

Another central feature of the power struggle of these years was the availability in vast numbers of mercenary troops. They were not the strayed regulars of Xenophon's army but swiftly moving mountaineers from Crete and the Pindos, better armed than in the past, with longer swords and javelins. In a small action near Corinth in 390 BC, under an Athenian named Iphikrates, they cut to pieces a force of 600 Spartans, and in 388 BC, in an ambush in the mountains of north Greece, under the same commander, they obliterated a Spartan expeditionary army.

All these events foretold the future. Persia was not invincible, nor was Sparta; mercenaries and money and the control of commerce were going to be important; sooner or later wilder Greeks and those on the edge of the world were going to have their say. Meanwhile in 386 BC a general peace was suggested by Persia and agreed to by everyone. Persian diplomatic strength had never been greater, but that may be because communications were easier. Cyprus was now in the Persian sphere of influence, but Evagoras, ruler of Cypriot Salamis, although he paid tribute, continued to do so as an independent sovereign to his dying day, so Persian power was not absolute. The Salamis of Evagoras was utterly Greek. The death of Evagoras, in 374 BC, had its Greek as well as its Oriental aspect; he and his eldest son were both murdered by the same eunuch to revenge his master's exile, each of them being lured away in the hope of the same lady's favors. Evagoras was succeeded by another son, Nikokles, friend and patron of the famous orator Isokrates.

In 382 the Spartans occupied the fortified area of the city of Thebes. It happened by a coincidence of treachery, on the day of a women's festival when no men were on the walls, with the passing nearby of a Spartan army on its way to put down the growing

Left Philip II was lame, but he was a successful soldier and diplomat, who achieved the unification of Greece under his personal authority. His generals contributed greatly to the successes of his son, Alexander the Great.

Below This bronze statuette was modeled under the Roman empire, but it is probably a copy of a much earlier original. It shows Alexander the Great on horseback, and perhaps comes closer in feeling to its subject than most of his portraits.

The march of the ten thousand, 401 BC

When in 401 Cyrus the younger made a bid for the throne against his brother Artaxerxes II, he took with him 10,000 Greek mercenaries, the best soldiers anyone could employ, together with his Asian troops. To begin with he told them they were being taken on a punitive raid against the independent Pisidians. But they were glad to follow him into Babylonia. At the battle of Cunaxa the Greeks won but Cyrus was killed. After a truce the Greek leaders were treacherously killed by the Persians, and the men had to make their way across difficult mountain country to the Black Sea and the Greek cities there, and so back home. The expedition revealed to the Greeks just how weak the Persian empire had become. But Greek states were still bitterly disunited, and Artaxerxes II could use his money to play a decisive role in Greek mainland politics for many years. Persian weakness was not finally shown up until Alexander attacked.

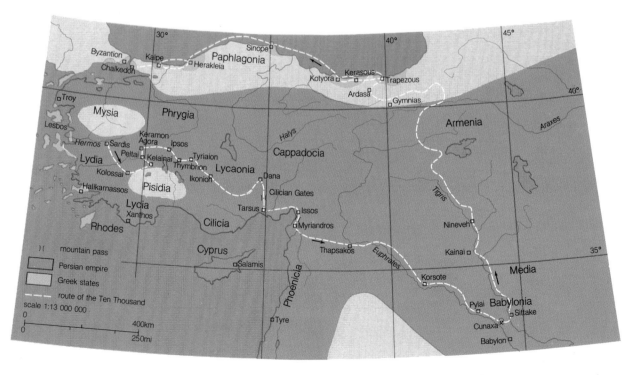

Chalkidic league of cities based on Olynthos in the far north, a league of Greeks that the Macedonians had joined for support against the Illyrian tribes. In Boeotia the Spartans were successful, but several years passed, and King Agesipolis of Sparta had been sent home dead and pickled in honey, before the Spartan action was successful in the north, in 379 BC. The following winter the situation at Thebes was reversed by an exotic stratagem in which armed patriots were disguised as veiled women at a drunken official banquet. A volunteer Athenian army assisted, but it was disowned by Athens; in revenge, a Spartan force struck at the Peiraeus, though unsuccessfully, but that attack was not disowned. As a result in 378 BC Athens allied herself with Thebes in another war against Sparta, and undertook the leadership of a new Athenian league. But the key to the next few years was not Athens, it was the revival of Thebes as a military force, with a spearhead of handpicked athletes who were couples of homosexual lovers. This force, under a modest, intellectual general called Epaminondas, altered history.

Little by little, year by year, the Spartans lost and the Thebans won, always on Boeotian territory. The Athenians utterly defeated the Spartan fleet, which threatened their grain supply, at sea between Naxos and Paros. In 376 an Athenian fleet was active at Corfu (Kerkyra) and Kephallenia, among the Acarnanians and among the Molossians of Epirus in northwest Greece. Within half a lifetime, the Molossian connection was going to be important in a future that no Athenian in the 370s foresaw. In 374 there was an attempt to patch up peace, but the war

smoldered on. Athens found it hard to protect Corfu, an ally too distant; the diplomatic and the military network, and above all the money, were being overstretched. The Athenians blamed their own generals, but it is significant that when the general Timotheos son of Konon was tried, Jason king of Thessalian Pherai and Alketas king of the Molossians came to Athens to swear to his integrity. Corfu was saved and Timotheos was acquitted. In 371 a peace was concluded between the Athenian and Spartan forces in which leagues were dissolved and spheres of influence admitted; Thebes, who refused to dissolve the league of newly liberated Boeotian cities, was left out of the final treaty.

By this time, between Thebes and Macedonians, all Thessaly was controlled by Jason of Pherai. Alketas the Molossian became his vassal, so that Jason's power crossed the Pindos mountains and touched the Adriatic, while on the other side it extended to Macedonia. He was poised to threaten Sparta. In 371 the Spartan army was in action against Thebes; they took the port of Kreusis and 11 Theban ships, and they marched on the city in the great plain. At Leuktra, where the Theban general Epaminondas confronted them, they were crushed: 1,000 of them fell and 400 of these were pure-bred Spartans. When this news spread, Jason of Pherai rushed with cavalry to support the Thebans, but Athens listened in silence. The Spartans withdrew. On his way home, Jason smashed the Spartan fort that controlled Thermopylai. At this time he was building a fleet, and his plan was to act out his new dominance of Delphi at the next festival. But the next year, in 370, he was

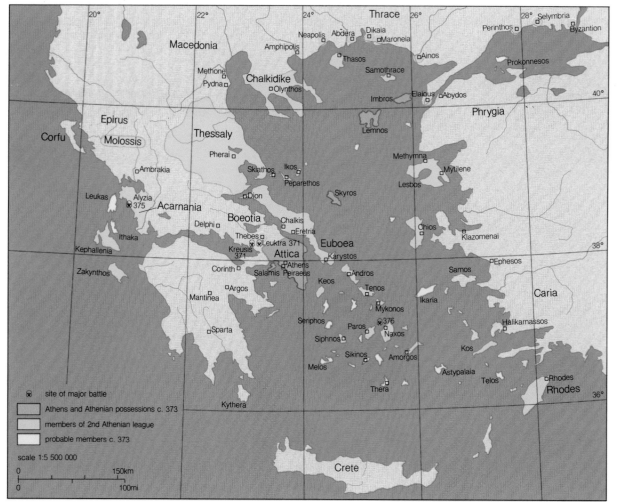

Below This is a coin of Kyrene, a Spartan colony on the coast of North Africa, which was in touch with the desert oracle of Zeus Ammon and had special privileges there. The coin is a tetradrachm.

The second Athenian league, 377–355 BC
The second Athenian league was established in 377 to resist the dominance of Sparta. Persia had now recovered the Asian mainland but not the offshore islands. The second league was a more modest affair than the Delian league. Athens avoided imperialist excesses: there were "contributions" instead of tribute. When the Spartan empire collapsed in 371, and Thebes for a time dominated the mainland, Athens swung round to support Sparta. The lifeline from the Black Sea was restored, but the Athenians struggled in vain to take Amphipolis. After the "social war" of 355 much of the league fell away, and Athens had only a few islands with her when Philip II began to turn Macedonia into a superpower.

The walls of Messene are the fortification of an entire landscape. This refounded and heavily protected walled town was intended as a balance and limit to Spartan power in southern Greece. By liberating Messenia from the Spartans, restoring the Messenian exiles from Naupaktos, and building these vast, modern defenses, the Thebans hoped to restore a situation which had not existed since prehistory. The surviving walls are the best example of a fully developed system of 4th-century stone defenses that we have.

assassinated. The Theban victory at Leuktra and the death of Jason heralded a period of increasing Theban power.

Meanwhile in southern Greece there were appalling civil disorders; the wealthy had control and the less wealthy and the poor had reached the stage of being prepared to beat them to death with cudgels, as they did at Argos. The Peloponnese was seething with discontent. In eastern Arcadia Mantinea was rebuilt, and Tegea expelled the 800 persons who ensured loyalty to the Spartan alliance. The Arcadians' appeal to Athens failed, but an appeal to Thebes prospered; Epaminondas invaded the south. Sparta was in a state of decay, the privileged pure Spartans had declined in numbers and the first attack in human memory on the Spartan homeland discovered few other loyal defenders. Sparta was saved only by its few allies, and by promising freedom to 6,000 of its serfs. Epaminondas refounded Messene as a strong fortified city in the southwestern Peloponnese, to be used against Sparta rather as the French in the Middle Ages used Scotland against the English throne. The magnificent ruins of that refoundation still exist. But Athens hated Thebes worse than she hated Sparta; she now took the Spartan side by formal alliance in 369 BC.

Epaminondas invaded Sparta several times and

the history of the next few years was of a fragmentation of alliances and realliances, as each in turn buckled under the pressures of fear and ambition in the shadow of the conflict between Thebes and Sparta. In 365 Elis went to war with Arcadia, and in 364 they fought a full-scale battle at Olympia that coincided with the Olympic games. Epaminondas died in 362, in victorious pursuit after a battle at Mantinea against Athenians, Spartans and Arcadians. The permanent result of his career was not only the moral defeat of Sparta, but the survival of two energetic cities, designed between them to check any expansion of the Spartans: Megalopolis, the new city formed from the combined populations of many Arcadian mountain towns, and Messene, the capital of a new Messenia. But Theban military energy scarcely survived Epaminondas, any more than the empire of Jason of Pherai survived its lord, or the Syracusan empire in Sicily survived.

Philip of Macedon

In Epirus, Alketas the Molossian was an Athenian ally, so was his eldest son Neoptolemos. The younger son on his father's death disputed his brother's right and ruled jointly with him in his lifetime, but alone after his death. This was Arybbas, who was honored at Athens in the late 340s, in an inscribed decree, which still survives today.

The Royal Tombs of Macedon

The site at Vergina in northern Greece of the Macedonian royal tombs, including the tomb of Philip, father of Alexander the Great, was conjectured correctly by N. G. L. Hammond, and pinpointed and excavated a few years ago by Manolis Andronikos, one of the most brilliant and persistent of Greek archaeologists.

The contents of the tombs are extraordinary, the most glorious treasure any Greek was ever buried with, and somehow much more moving than that phrase might lead one to expect. The tombs themselves were finely decorated and made of marble. They lay under an enormous mound of earth which effectively protected them.

This head belongs to a small portrait statue of Philip of Macedon found in the burial. Its tiny scale (this is an ivory head just over 3 centimeters high) leaves room for little more than the expressive liveliness which is its most obvious quality. It would not be possible to argue from the life story to the face or vice versa, but knowing both, one can see how closely they fit.

Above right The shield cover and the vessels were photographed before they were touched or moved. The vessels are bronze, the diadem is golden. The sponge was still fresh and pliable after 2,300 years. The armor, including the leg guard in the foreground and the greaves which lean against the wall, is also bronze; it is meant for use. So is the gold diadem, but use of a different kind.

Below Another of the five miniature ivory heads found in the burials. It has been argued that it represents Alexander the Great, Phillip's son and successor.

Above The fineley decorated quiver speaks for itself; the greaves, one of which is some 3 centimeters shorter than the other, seem to have been made for a slightly lame man. Philip was lame, so that it seems likely he actually wore them.

Below The silver jug is both wealthy and chaste. It is very pleasing that both the high quality and the restraint of nearly everything in this treasure are so marked.

Left The casket which held the remains of Philip after his cremation was small and its decoration was elegant but rather restrained. It measures 33 by 41 centimeters, but its laden weight was more than 10 kilograms. The star on its lid was the symbol of the Macedonian kings. It can be seen that before they conquered Greece, Greece had penetrated them.

Far left The top of the columned facade of the entrance to the main tombs; under the layers of earth was a frieze of a lion hunt. Even finer paintings have been found in the small tomb facing that of Philip.

Arybbas is honored "since the citizenship and privilege awarded to his father and grandfather are available also to him." The decree ends with the ominous words "that the generals in office shall take care that Arybbas and his sons recover their ancestral realm." The Macedonian kingdom now overshadowed the Molossians and all the other tribes of Epirus. It was by now double-natured, the characteristic result of Athenian influence; the court and the principal cities were Greek and very rich, but the tribal power basis extended far beyond those sophisticated or civilized fringes that the Greeks knew. There is some analogy between the role of the tribal vassals of Macedonia and the rule of a maharaja in India as the British advanced, but the Greeks, unlike the British in India, were not protected by any enormous technological superiority. In 359 BC Philip of Macedon, as regent to the child king of a kingdom under urgent pressure from Paionians and Illyrians to the north and northwest, came to power and organized his army.

Philip was 24 years old. In 358 he had 10,000 men at arms and 600 cavalry, by every account well disciplined; in a murderous battle with Illyrian tribesmen, we are told that he left 7,000 dead. Once Macedonia was under control, Philip pushed eastward at once into Thrace, and it was here that he first ran counter to Athenian interest. He took Amphipolis and the gold mines in 357, and built his own fort to defend his takings. Other conquests in that area followed, and corresponding antagonisms; but by now the Paionians were reduced to vassals, the Illyrians utterly crushed yet again, and the Thracians bought off; in 356 Philip assumed the title of king, and in the same year his son was born. He had married Olympias, the daughter of Neoptolemos the Molossian, the niece of Arybbas and the granddaughter of Alketas; Alexander the Great was the child of that marriage.

In the east at this time, Mausolos of Caria attempted like Jason in Thessaly and Philip in the north to establish an imperial power, and inevitably he clashed with Athens. He was a tributary prince of the Persian empire, and his authority was enormous in reality but undefined in theory. The Greek coastal cities had fallen one by one into his sphere of influence, he annexed Lycia and his appetite extended to the islands. He moved down from his old capital city of Mylasa to Halikarnassos on the sea. In 357 Chios, Kos and Rhodes revolted against Athens; they were ripe to fall into the protective hands of Mausolos. In the resulting campaigns, the alarming possibility began to loom of a full-scale war with Persia. Peace was agreed in 354, but the Athenian empire never recovered. The islands achieved their independence, oligarchies took them over, and Carian garrisons ruled in them. Rhodes appealed against the new tyranny to Athens, without success. Meanwhile in 353 Mausolos died and Caria sank back into its old lethargy. The greatest Greek sculptors of the age worked on his vast monument at Halikarnassos.

In the mid-350s a quarrel over the control of Delphi between Phokis and the council of neighboring states brought war to central Greece. Thebes provoked the conflict, but it spread uncontrollably until it involved Sparta and Athens, each cautiously committed against Thebes, then Thessaly and finally Philip of Macedon. Such opportunities were

Salamis

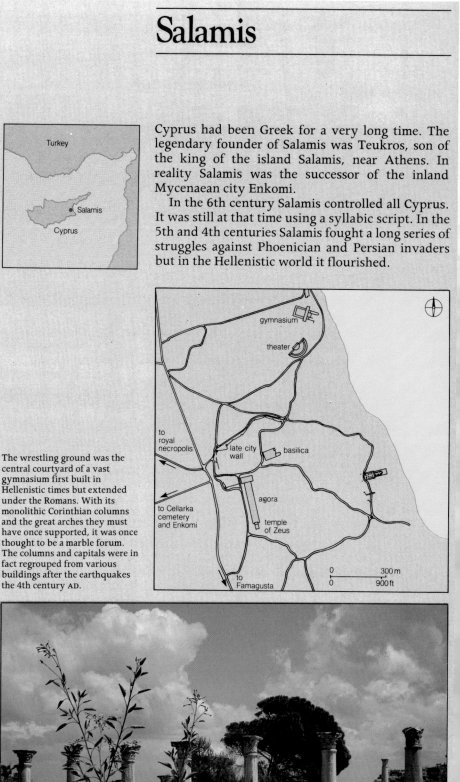

Cyprus had been Greek for a very long time. The legendary founder of Salamis was Teukros, son of the king of the island Salamis, near Athens. In reality Salamis was the successor of the inland Mycenaean city Enkomi.

In the 6th century Salamis controlled all Cyprus. It was still at that time using a syllabic script. In the 5th and 4th centuries Salamis fought a long series of struggles against Phoenician and Persian invaders but in the Hellenistic world it flourished.

The wrestling ground was the central courtyard of a vast gymnasium first built in Hellenistic times but extended under the Romans. With its monolithic Corinthian columns and the great arches they must have once supported, it was once thought to be a marble forum. The columns and capitals were in fact regrouped from various buildings after the earthquakes the 4th century AD.

The expansion of Macedonia
For half a century Macedonia had been an unstable state whose kings murdered each other in quick succession. Strong rule imposed by Philip II, a ruler of genius and utter unscrupulousness, enabled his kingdom to exploit its strong geographical position. Athens was by no means wholly given to appeasement, but she was rarely in time to forestall Philip's annexations and she was no match for Philip's army. The very fact that Macedonia was politically backward proved an advantage when feudal levies profited from superior tactics and discipline. The peace of 346 betwen Athens and Philip led to bitter recriminations among Athenian politicians. But Athens rallied to a last attempt to stop aggression in the war of 340–338. After Philip's victory at Chaironeia he was master of Greece as well as of a vastly extended kingdom, and could now begin to turn his attention to the plan of Asian conquest which his son Alexander carried out. Athenian democracy was left intact for the time being, but the Macedonians did away with it in 322.

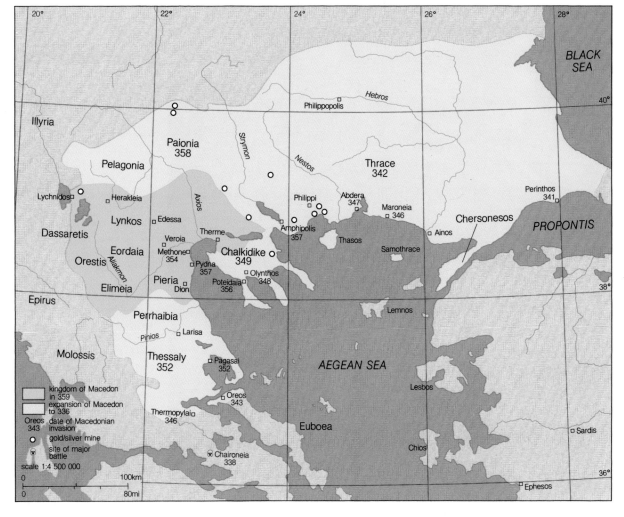

seldom lacking in Greek history but this one was heaven-sent. He took Methone, the last Athenian ally in his track, and moved south. At first he was checked by Phokians in Thessaly, but in 352 he defeated them and moved on. Unable to pass Thermopylai, he attacked Thrace; only his illness saved Thracian Chersonese and the Hellespont.

The panic and horror of Athenian oratory at this time are easy to imagine, but two things about it are surprising, one for better and one for worse. The personal vendettas of the politicians are all but incredible in this time of crisis, yet the lucidity of the political arguments is amazing. They lend an inevitability to events, they are like the long speeches of Athenian tragedy. It is appalling to see to this day so perfectly expressed the fall of all Greece into the hands of Philip. The greatest of these orators, Demosthenes, affirmed that "If Philip dies you will soon raise up a second Philip."

Philip did not die; in 349 he invaded Chalkidike, and in 348 destroyed that peninsula's principal city, Olynthos. In 346, by a treaty sworn at Athens, the Athenians abandoned any claim to Amphipolis, but to the east they kept most of the Chersonese. Meanwhile Philip was busy elsewhere in Thrace, eating up a long meal of fortresses. Once peace was secure, and Phokis isolated from its provisions, Philip came south again. At the games at Delphi in 346 he was president; by controlling Thessaly he acquired membership of the Delphic council. He was now governor of all Thessaly. Kersobleptes of Thrace was his vassal; Messenia, Megalopolis, Elis and Argos, that is those who feared Sparta in the Peloponnese, were his allies. In about 342 BC he

expelled Arybbas the Molossian from Epirus and installed his wife's brother, Alexander. From Epirus, Philip was a close spectator of the Corinthian gulf and the western trade routes; little by little he extended the mountainous kingdom further south.

Athens reacted too late. The whole of Thrace, Macedonia, Thessaly and Epirus constitute a formidable block of territory, and Philip had extended its boundaries; he had founded Philippopolis (now Plovdiv) on the Hebros, and held the western coast of Greece as far south as the Acheron. In 340 the Athenians seduced Byzantion and nearby Perinthos and also reestablished an independent Euboea, where an oligarchy favoring Philip had been in power. Philip attacked Perinthos at once, then Byzantion, but without immediate success. He spent the winter in northeast Thrace, at war with the Scythians on the Danube estuary, and in the following year returned to Greek affairs. Once again the excuse was a quarrel in the Delphic council, this time with the neighboring city of Amphissa. In 338 Philip swept down into central Greece, held Thermopylai, fortified a city in Phokis, and took Amphissa and Naupaktos on the gulf of Corinth. Thebes and Athens, with other less powerful allies, opposed him; in August of that year the allied armies were utterly and finally defeated in a hard-fought battle at Chaironeia in north Boeotia. From now on Philip could dictate his terms to the Greeks. He did so, but they were lenient terms, and in 337 BC he announced a full-scale war of all Greece against Persia.

Also in 337 BC, Philip divorced Olympias to marry

Above This central Italian plate shows one of the Greek war elephants that Alexander's successors brought to the Mediterranean. The battle-castle on the elephant's back appears to be a Greek invention.

Right Alexander wears ram's horns to show his relationship with Zeus Ammon, an oracle in the Libyan desert. The center of the cult was a phallic-looking mummy, twisted up like a banana or a ram's horn, draped in cloths and jewels. As Amun-Re', it became influential in Egypt, and the Greeks adopted it as Zeus.

a Macedonian noblewoman. To placate the Molossians he arranged an incestuous marriage between his daughter Kleopatra, the sister of the great Alexander, and her uncle, brother of Olympias, the vassal king Alexander the Molossian. On the morning of that wedding, as Philip entered the theater of the Macedonian capital Pella, he was murdered with a Celtic knife.

Alexander the Great

At the time of his father's assassination, Alexander the Great was 18 or 19 years old, living in disgrace with his disgraced Molossian mother. His tutor had been the philosopher and scientist, Aristotle, the calmest and the most luminous genius of all antiquity; Alexander was bold, imaginative and violent. At once, in 335 BC, after a year in which he confirmed his succession to his father's dominant role in Greece, he went to war in the Thracian mountains and on the Danube. He showed in his speed and his tactical skill and courage a terrifying brilliance as a soldier; among those who surrendered and entered his alliance on an island in the Danube in the course of that campaign there were Celts. In southern Greece the cities were restless; at a rumor of Alexander's death, Thebes openly rebelled. Within two weeks Alexander had stormed down from Mount Pelion, where he had moved to oppose a threatened invasion from Illyria, and utterly crushed Thebes with a slaughter of 6,000 and an almost universal enslavement of the survivors, including women and children. Athens sent him congratulations.

Alexander invaded the Persian empire in 334, though an army under one of Philip's former generals had gone before him in 335. Alexander crossed over into Asia in the north, performed religious duties at Troy, where he made it clear he was in some sense reenacting the famous poetry, and at once smashed a huge Persian army on the river Granikos not far inland. He sent the mass of the spoils to his mother, the Greek prisoners he took as slaves to Macedonia, and he sent 300 suits of Persian armor to Athens. In Asia Minor he retained the Persian title of satrap for the Macedonian governor he appointed, forbade plunder, and left tributes and taxes at their old level; it was evident that he intended to rule this land on a permanent basis. His admiration for Persian institutions may well have derived from the comparative studies that Aristotle made of the institutions of states, both Greek and barbarian. Alexander refounded Troy and liberated Sardis, the old royal city of the Lydians. Everywhere he made plain his serious intention to govern. At Ephesos he restored democracy but forbade reprisals, and this was the beginning of a triumphant series of liberations and restorations of the old Greek cities. By a serious if allegorical flattery, something stronger than a metaphor, Alexander began to be worshiped as a god.

He was checked at Miletos, but not for long; the city fell to him in spite of overwhelming Persian strength at sea. Alexander's reaction was to disband his own inadequate fleet, and to occupy every fortified harbor in the Levant. The story of the next two years is monotonously triumphant. In October 333 BC Alexander encountered the king of kings, Darius III. The Persians had advanced slowly to the sea but the speed of Alexander was so great that the

Above It is uncertain whether this skeptical and melancholy philosopher is a portrait of an individual, or simply an imagined type. He is certainly very fully imagined. He may easily be the philosopher Bion.

Top right These heads were drawn on local limestone at the Persian palace of Persepolis. They are certainly the work of an archaic Greek artist.

Overleaf The inner east wall (4th century BC) of the fortified city of Aigosthena situated at the easternmost point of the gulf of Corinth. The inner wall defending the acropolis and the wall encircling the whole city, both provided with towers, are among the best examples of Greek military architecture.

first they saw of him was the Macedonian sick at Issos on the coast of southeast Asia Minor; the Persians were already some miles in the rear of Alexander's army. Darius cut off the hands of the sick, and this news reached Alexander. Weary and soaked by storms, his army made a last forced march, and the next morning attacked the Persians with surprise on their side in a narrow coastal plain. He won as before; the slaughter of Persians was appalling and Darius fled. If the recorded number of Persian dead is the truth, then more soldiers died at Issos than were ever again lost in one day until the first day of the battle of the Somme, 110,000. There were 4,000 Macedonian wounded, though we are told only of 302 dead. Alexander's loot included the royal tent of Persia, and its treasures; his captives included the queen, whom he treated with courtesy and generosity, and a Persian noblewoman of 30,

twice already married to Greeks; he took her for five years as his mistress.

He moved next against Syria, Phoenicia and the city of Tyre, which fell to him after eight months of resistance in 332 BC; 8,000 Tyrians were killed and 30,000 enslaved. After Tyre, Gaza fell, and after Gaza, Egypt. After the battle at Issos he had founded a city named after himself, now called Alexandretta; at the mouth of the Nile he founded the great Alexandria. At Memphis on the Nile Alexander celebrated Greek games, sacrificed to Egyptian gods, and was proclaimed as king of Egypt. He then visited the ancient oracle of Amun, whom the Greeks called Zeus Ammon, in the Libyan desert. The pilgrimage was and still is dramatic and dangerous, over rocks and desert passes of the utmost strangeness and grandeur. Alexander never revealed his questions, only that the god satisfied him. His soldiers thought later that he must have asked whether he would rule the world, and whether he had punished all his father's murderers. The oracle may also have confirmed his suspicion that Zeus was literally his true father.

Now Alexander plunged into Asia with 400,000 infantry and 7,000 cavalry, crossed the Euphrates in 331 BC and then the Tigris with his usual swift assurance, and at Gaugamela fought a second battle with Darius. The Persian army included elephants, scythe-wheeled chariots, the cavalry of the central Asian steppes, Persians, Babylonians, Afghans and Indians. The battle was long and complicated, but Alexander won it, Darius fled, Babylon surrendered, and Alexander was rewarded with Susa, City of Lilies, the ancient capital of Elam and the palace of the old Persian kings. Effectively, the Persian empire had all but fallen, and by a strong symbolism it was here that he discovered the old statues of the tyrant-slayers, Harmodios and Aristogeiton, looted from Athens 150 years before; he sent them home. He and his army pressed into the Persian heartland toward Persepolis, as conquerors and as explorers. His worst task was the storming of the Persian Gates in 330 BC, a narrow and steep pass terribly heavily defended; he found a precipitous track that led behind it, as the Persians had done at Thermopylai, and utterly destroyed the powerful force that masked Persepolis.

The treasure of Persepolis can hardly be exaggerated; it was carefully carried away on muleback and camelback as if by an army of ants; some time later Alexander and his troops ran riot in the palace, and most of it was burned. There are still in Persian museums objects of luxury deliberately smashed which recall the puritanic anger or the debauched

arrogance of that night. Darius did not surrender. Alexander followed him back north to Ekbatana, capital of Media, then on by what is now Tehran and further east. But Darius was made hostage on the road by his kinsman the satrap of Bactria. By riding day and night Alexander overtook him at last; he found him wounded to death by his own courtiers. Some of them continued in resistance and in flight, but one by one they were hunted down, in campaigns of extraordinary hardship and courage.

Many died. The Greeks who had enlisted only to fight Persia were sent home with treasures. New levies came out, but slowly. Alexander adopted some Persian customs, respected his new subjects, married a Persian noblewoman, Roxane (in 327 BC), and set his ambition on all central Asia and all India. It was as if he and his diminishing army might consume themselves in the unknown east, on an endless journey of conquest and exploration. During his conquest of the Punjab, Alexander was badly wounded at the assault of Multan, which he led personally. The troops never failed to respond to him, except that in India they refused to advance through desert country from the Indus basin to the Ganges; on the way home by way of the Indus delta and Gedrosia very many died in a desert. Alexander murdered one old general in a drunken quarrel, and executed another for treason. He had pushed his army to the limits of possibility but those limits were astounding.

At the end of 330 BC Alexander had been on the northern edges of Afghanistan, the mountains and the Oxus (Amu-Darya) plains were his by 327, he had crossed the Indus in 326, and now returned to Babylon, where in 323 BC he died, it seems of exhaustion, of fever and of drink. His last plans had been for the amalgamation of cities, for the unification of Greece and Persia, and for a western campaign beyond Sicily, with a fleet of 1,000 ships. He was 32 years old. The brilliant dash and courageous violence of his career perished with him, but it is a mark of his ruthlessness with his enemies that no native people rebelled for a generation, and a mark of his simplicity, of his foresight, and of the objective situation of Asia as he left it, that history never quite covered over the achievement. From Gibraltar to what is now western China, there was intellectually one world, a Greek world that lasted for centuries.

The over-extension of political power

The political unity of Greece, imposed with such difficulty, was by no means so secure. An alliance of Greek cities was in open rebellion by 323 BC with an army that included 8,000 of Alexander's old mercenaries. Antipater, the general commanding for the Macedonians, spent the winter besieged in Lamia, a coastal city that controlled the chief route between Thessaly and the south. But in 322 BC a victory at Krannon in central Thessaly that was neither bloody nor overwhelming was sufficient to restore Macedonian supremacy. Demosthenes committed suicide; democracy at Athens was restricted to the middle and upper classes, and a Macedonian garrison was installed. When Hyperides had spoken the funeral speech for the Athenian dead that year, he praised them in terms that implicitly acknowledged the supreme myth of Alexander. They would be welcomed in the Underworld, he said, by those demigods and heroes that had fought against Troy, and against Persia.

In these few years Greece itself had exhausted much of its political power. At Athens, amid continuing quarrels, protests and refinements, the schools of the great philosophers preserved the city's position as capital of the intellectual world. But the expansion of its own world had dwarfed it. In the east in the next century a flood of Parthian nomads, future rulers of Persia, would cut off the easternmost Macedonian provinces; but there the isolated Macedonians would survive as kings for generations. The new Indian kingdom of Chandragupta would bite at the southern frontiers in the east; he would have his way on payment of 500 elephants. In the west Alexander the Molossian, brother-in-law to the great Alexander, had already died fighting a campaign of his own in southern Italy; Pyrrhos of Epirus, who first became king as a boy in 307 BC, would be the first Greek to fight against Rome. No mainland Greek city had the physical resources to compete in such a world. Any of the great Macedonian generals who now disputed the world, supplied from the treasury of Persia, could hire mercenaries on a scale no single city could match. Elephants, carrying the new battle castles invented for them by the Greeks, passed from king to king by treaty and by inheritance; Pyrrhos took them to Italy; Athens had philosophers but no elephants.

The disputing Macedonian generals produced chaos on a world scale. The two natural commanders were Perdikkas in Asia, who had possession of Alexander's posthumous child, and Antipater in Europe, the last surviving general of Philip. The crown of Macedonia was settled jointly on a half-witted half-brother of Alexander and on the baby. The other generals were local lords: Ptolemy in Egypt, Antigonos in Phrygia, Seleukos in Babylon and Lysimachos in Thrace. Perdikkas was crushed first, killed in 321 BC by his own men as he tried to invade Egypt, and Antipater died in 319 BC. Antipater's son Kassandros murdered the half-wit, also Alexander's mother, and finally his son, who was lucky perhaps to reach the age of 13: Kassandros himself died in 298 BC. Meanwhile Antigonos and his son Demetrios were active in Greece; their power was at its height from 307 to 303 BC but the next year Antigonos died in battle against Seleukos and his elephants. Demetrios survived in good and bad luck until 285 BC, when he was forced to surrender to Seleukos, and drank himself to death in two years.

The only direct successor of Alexander to die in bed was Ptolemy. Demetrios had married a daughter of the old Antipater, and their son, Antigonos Gonatas, became in his day the ruler of a new Macedonia. Ptolemy had married another of Antipater's daughters, and his son by her, Ptolemy the Thunderbolt, at the height of the power of Seleukos, killed that old warlord in 280 BC. But Ptolemy the Thunderbolt never ruled Egypt; his father had thrown out his mother and left Egypt to a bastard son, the Ptolemy who was the patron of the last Greek poets. Ptolemy the Thunderbolt was active mostly in the north; he died in the great raid of the Celts into Greece under Brennus in 279 BC, the year Pyrrhos of Epirus was marshaling his elephants for the invasion of Italy.

THE ALEXANDRIAN EXPANSION

Consequences of the Persian conquest

In a very few generations, the power structure of the world had altered utterly and irreversibly. When the dust had settled after Alexander's explosive career, 50 years or so after his death, the Greeks had become inevitably conscious of remote peoples and traditions. Nomads in central Asia and on the borders of China, and the untouched peoples of the north and west, came into steadily increasing contact with the Mediterranean centers. In the 2nd century BC we know that an Alexandrian merchant ship of awkward size was wrecked off Anglesey as it rounded the northwest corner of Wales. In Alexandria at that time scientists had already begun to compute the magnitude of the earth.

But the economic consequences of the conquest of Persia were disastrous. Money had not existed for very long, and no one understood that this easy and elegant means of exchange had laws of its own, almost a life of its own. With money, any rich individual, for example one of Alexander's generals or the ruler of a barbarous territory, could buy himself a huge mercenary army. Mercenaries existed after Alexander's campaigns in vast numbers. We have the evidence of petitions inscribed in stone that the farming patterns of the Greek islands altered. It was now that huge herds protected by armed retainers overran what had been agricultural land.

The supply of money had increased colossally because, by the old-fashioned and insouciant kingly generosity of Alexander, the entire hoarded treasure of the Persian empire, which in the past had not circulated, was simply given away, and it flooded the Greek world. We know from the rents of certain farms owned by the sanctuary of Delos, and from records of the wages of mercenary soldiers, that the resulting inflation of values was very sharp indeed. In another important development at the same time, the great national sanctuaries of the gods, which had always been willing to lend from their treasuries to the state in time of emergency, now began to function as merchant banks to the general public. There were even land investment banks. The results in terms of inflation and social disturbance were far-reaching. Class war amounting sometimes to civil war smoldered all over Greece, but it was never the democrats or the municipal socialists who triumphed, or not for long. Rebellions of slaves ended terribly for the rebels. Piracy began again, and as time went on became a worse plague than it had ever been.

Yet, at the height of all these upheavals, at the height of the increase of knowledge and speculation, when the overland silk route with China was open and Alexandrian ships were navigating as far as Britain and Southeast Asia, the Delphic oracle was asked who was the happiest man in the world, and it named an obscure farmer living on a smallholding not very far inland in the Peloponnese, who seldom left his own farm and had never seen the sea. There is something of the sense of this reply in Epicurean philosophy, and even in Stoicism: it had become clear that to be sane and happy in the new age one must limit one's desires and one's fears.

Nevertheless, on a wider scale the destructive process was inevitable. The future already belonged to rich farmers and rich merchants organized in the richest and most powerful community. Such a community would have to expand or perish; it would become a great empire.

Hellenistic baroque was at its most exotic in the temples and tombs cut into the sandstone of Petra, ancient capital of the kingdom of Nabataea, in present-day southern Jordan. Petra was for centuries the center of a vast caravan trade. The Khazné or treasury (*right*) is more than 40 meters high, with a vast interior on a cruciform plan. The building may have been built as a mausoleum for one of the Nabataean kings.

The campaigns of Alexander, 334–323 BC
No European has ever repeated Alexander's conquests. Julius Caesar and Trajan hoped to emulate him but never got nearly as far. His legend was perpetuated throughout the Middle Ages and later portrayed in countless pictures and tapestries. The true story of his conquests comprises rather more atrocity than chivalry. It took one battle, that of Granikos in 334, to enable him to range freely over Asia Minor, reestablishing democracies in Greek cities. Resistance at Issos by the Persian army in 333 was more easily overcome than the stubborn defense of Tyre, but in Egypt, where Persian rule was hated, Alexander was welcomed. Here the oracle of Ammon told him of his divine ancestry. The great battle of Gaugamela (331) put an end to the Achaemenid dynasty. Persepolis was burned, but there was valiant resistance to be overcome in what is now Afghanistan. Alexander's conquests extended beyond Samarkand (Marakanda) and included the Punjab. He would have gone further if his army had been prepared to follow him. His death in Babylon in 323 soon resulted in the partition of his empire among warring generals.

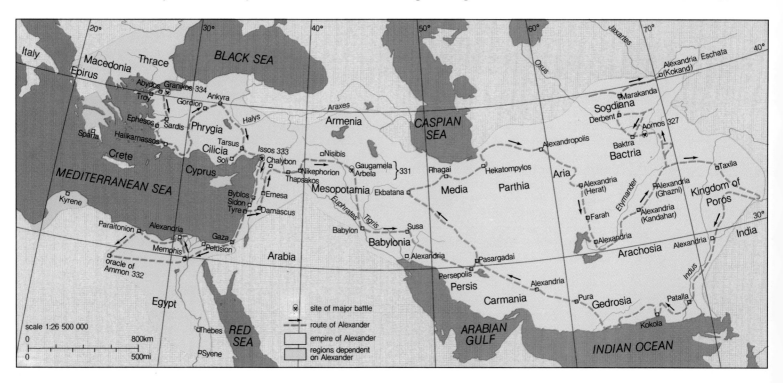

The Development of Vase Painting

The prime interest in the study of Greek vases is their decoration rather than their shapes, and the way in which their figure decoration in particular develops in step with advances in other arts. The earliest Iron Age vases (10th–9th centuries) carry abstract patterns still and only with the fully geometric style (8th century) do figures appear, in a very stylized form. Near Eastern arts introduced the animal frieze as a major decorative element and inspired the "black-figure" technique, where the figures are in silhouette with incised detail and little added color. The finest vases are Athenian but Corinth led and there are regional schools. In about 530 BC Athens invented the red-figure technique, where the figures are reserved in a black ground and detail is painted in. The effect is far more realistic and the white-ground vases display a technique inspired by the appearance of Classical murals. In the second half of the 5th century emigrant artists started important schools in south Italy and Sicily, where there was vigorous production on through the 4th century. After this the red-figure style died out and in Hellenistic Greece painted vase-decoration was uncommon and unimportant.

Far left, top A protogeometric vase (10th century) with purely abstract patterns which derive from a Mycenaean tradition.

Far left, center An Athenian jug (8th century) with the full repertory of formal geometric decoration – zigzags, meanders etc.

Far left, bottom A Protocorinthian vase (7th century) decorated in the Orientalizing style, showing the new, incising black-figure technique. The east introduced new fauna for animal friezes – lions and the two-bodied panther-bird in the lower frieze.

Left, center An Athenian black-figure cup of c. 550 BC. Herakles' exploits are a common subject for these vases: here he is wrestling with the sea deity Triton; in the outer frieze is a dance of sea nymphs.

Top left An Athenian black-figure hydria (water jug) of c. 510 BC showing three girls fetching water from a fountain house. Their flesh is painted white – the usual convention for women in black-figure.

Top right A Spartan cup of c. 550 BC. At the left Atlas in supporting the heavens. Prometheus is tethered to a pillar while Zeus' eagle tears at his liver – a daily punishment. Sparta's austere image in Greek history is belied by the vigor and imagination of her archaic art.

Above left An Athenian red-figure hydria (compare the one above – the shape has two lifting handles, one pouring handle) by an early 5th-century master known as the Berlin Painter. The god Apollo travels over the sea on a winged tripod-cauldron – a vessel associated with his sanctuary and oracle at Delphi.

Left An Athenian cup of c. 460 BC. The seated Aphrodite is accompanied by two Eroses, on a white ground. The technique allows freer use of color.

Above A kalyx-krater (wine-mixing bowl) painted by Asteas at Paestum in Italy c. 350 BC. A young Dionysos, two comic actors (*phlyakes*) in masks and padded costumes, and two actors dressed as women (in the windows) watch the performance of a naked girl acrobat on a stage.

The following labels appear on the map:

20° · 40° · 60° · 80° · 100°

Byzantion · TASHKENT · summer caravan route · TURFAN · Great Wall · northern route · ANHSI · TUNHUANG · KOKAND · Trapezous · Armenia · Marakanda · KASHGAR · Margiana · Stone Tower · YARKAND · southern route · Baktra · LANCHOW · Athens · Antioch · Dura Europos · Hekatompylos · Rhagai · KHOTAN · FENGSIANG · Rome · Tyre · Palmyra · Damascus · Ekbatana · Seleukeia · Persia · Taxila · Sinae Metro · Alexandria · Arsinoë · Petra · Apologos · Charax · Sakai · Mathura · China · Sera Metropolis · Aelana · Egypt · Gerrha · Barbarikon · Ganges · Yangtze · Koptos · Leuke Kome · Ommana · Ozene · Port of Ganges · Berenike · Barygaza · Kalinga · Andhra · ?Cattigara · The Incense Road · Arabia · Paithana · Napata · Ptolemais · Sabaeans and Himyarites · ?Tagara · Meroë · Frankincense Coast · Messalia · Kyneion · Adulis · Axum · Muza · Cana · Naura · Poduka · Kerobotra · Eudaimon Arabia · Aromata · Muziris (temple of Augustus) · Camara · Avalites · Cinnamon Coast · Pandion's Kingdom · Borama · Opone · Nelcynda · Taprobane · pepper route · Sarapion · Azania · Nikon · outrigger canoes to Rhapta via Madagascar · Rhapta (controlled by Arabians)

Axum — capital of kingdom · KHOTAN — modern name · Ozene — ancient name · important trade route · silk route · cinnamon route · scale 1:50 000 000

The silk and spice routes
Rome claimed to rule all the inhabited world, but it was no secret that vast areas lay outside her dominions. In the first few centuries AD merchantmen were plying between Egypt and India. Pepper came from southern India. Cinnamon was imported from the Somali coast, though it came from much further away – from Indonesia by outrigger canoe to Madagascar and up the coast of Africa. Overland caravans carried silk through the central Asian passes from China to the Greco-Roman world. In the 2nd century AD the world map of Ptolemy showed East Africa, India, Ceylon and Malaya. It may have been an Alexandrian who discovered that the monsoon winds could take sailing ships from Aden straight across the ocean to India.

That the new empire was to be Roman, not Greek, is immaterial; the civilized world except for China and perhaps India was imprinted, or to use a more precise metaphor impregnated, with Hellenic life. The Ptolemies in Egypt and the great Greek dynasties in Asia brought to their kingdoms the Greek language and many Greek ways of doing things. Athens became a place of cultural pilgrimage, and its literature became not only dominant but the accepted model of purity and power of language in Latin as well as in Greek.

Alexandrian scholarship
One of the important means by which this happened was the growth of scholarly, critical literature, the commentaries on the classics by the Alexandrian scholars. It was only in the late 4th century BC that Athens collected an official text of the three great 5th-century tragedians, and stored them in the public record office. In the 3rd century at Alexandria the Ptolemies created a vast, probably in most sections a complete library of Greek literature, and supported a community of poets and scholars like the priests of a temple to work in it. Antiquarian critics and theoretic writings had existed since the late 5th century, and Plato and Aristotle had engendered a climate of intellectual and bookish seriousness that was new in the world, new at least in being a general climate, and more than a stray fit of scholarly temperament, just as the Alexandrian library was new in being a full, cataloged library, not a chance or individual collection of books like Aristotle's own library.

Literary scholarship itself was summoned into existence, as Pfeiffer has so brilliantly argued, for the same reason then as it was at its reincarnation in the Italian Renaissance, by the needs of poets, though in three or four generations it had passed through the later stage of massive contributions and thrilling tasks and become something dustier, a scholarship of scholarship, a compilation of compilations, rather like second-rate literary scholarship today. The Romans were overawed both by Alexandrian scholarship, for better and worse, and by Alexandrian poetry. The poetry was spare, educated, sometimes horribly allusive, but also passionate and ironic. For the sake of freshness and freedom it often dealt with obscure or provincial mythology, and with every variety of human love. One of its last products was the prose romance, the adventurous story of destined or doomed lovers told with pathos and with grace.

Hellenistic baroque
The same kind of royal patronage produced an architecture which, like the literature, extended into the Roman period, and like the activities of the Alexandrian library, combined an impressive novelty in the rehandling or recombining of traditional forms at one moment with toppling grandeur, and at another with a sense of luxurious private pleasure that even the Minoans could hardly or seldom equal. There is a further analogy with literature, since the victory of this glorious and heavy style produced a reaction of neoclassicism, a preference for simpler, purer forms from the 5th century or the 4th, embodied in some of the best surviving Roman buildings, and even in the physical removal and reerection of remote but admirable temples in more luxurious and popular urban settings; in the same way the Augustan poets went back beyond the Alexandrians for pure and simple formal models, but in both cases both the styles continued to exist side by side.

The full blossoming of Greek baroque architecture is best preserved for us, in a fantastical version of itself that says a great deal about what its aesthetic attractions were thought to be, in the wall paintings of Pompeii. The paintings confirm our normal instinct that the most attractive buildings were not always the grandest. There is a fresco of a sacred tree framed by columns, in which a knotted pine seems to have grown right through the stonework of what was perhaps a temple gate. In the foreground there are small altars and a friendly-looking statue, with columned buildings lightly sketched in the background. This could almost be an 18th-century sketch, almost a piece of Chinoiserie. It is lightly executed, with the momentary quality that can give life to monuments and ruins. The view is informal; there is something ironic and pathetic about it; this is not a grand religious ceremony, but an everyday piety of the Greeks of southern Italy in their long and on the whole happy decline.

The most exotic survival of developed Hellenistic architecture is in the temples and tombs at Petra, in present-day south Jordan. Petra was an important point on the caravan routes for the spice trade, a rich oasis isolated by the desert, but in constant touch with the coast of Palestine. This was the home country of what Propertius in the early Roman empire called "the Arabian shepherd rich in smells." For civic grandeur, the finest surviving monument may perhaps be the monumental gateway to the south market at Miletos, which now stands nearly intact, but emasculated through its transferral to a museum in Berlin. The most luxurious buildings are baths and palaces, for instance the palace of Herod at Massadah. There are inventive details everywhere. At Ay Khanoum on the Oxus (Amu-Darya), soon after Alexander's death, Corinthian capitals too finely carved to carry weight must have seemed to float high up in the air, with the stone beams resting slightly above them on an invisible extension of the pillars themselves; theaters and water springs grew heavy ornamental facades, subtly contrived for the contrast of light and shadow on the surfaces; the colored marbles of Rhodes appeared at Olympia.

Time, which has ruined so many massive constructions, has isolated fragments, and the detail of fragments is often more attractive to us than the grandiose complete designs could ever have been. In the great buildings of Jerash in Syria (now in Jordan) in the 2nd century AD, the curve of a stone shell or the thin dolphin decorations on a drain could still speak even then of Greek values that we also share. William Pars, the friend and drawing master of William Blake, drew a much earlier tomb which still stands at Mylasa, an inland city of Asia Minor, which speaks as directly to us as it would have done to those who built it. The monument of Lysikrates at Athens in the 4th century, with its feather-like or cream-like roof ornament, was already rather baroque, but that and the tomb at Mylasa were too early for the lavish and dizzy inventiveness, the torturing of surfaces and the turning of things inside out, that defined the developed style. The difference was made by money and by slaves. Architecture may not be created by its individual patrons, but it is certainly deeply influenced by the pressure of one kind of patronage rather than another.

The Greek baroque style was worked out in Alexandria. There can be no doubt that its originators were very conscious of the monumental buildings from a much earlier period that already existed in Egypt, though the details of influence and reaction remain obscure, some of the most interesting, apparently early, baroque buildings being difficult to date. To make things more complicated, the mass of the surviving evidence comes not from Alexandria itself, but from lesser cities known to be under its influence: from Petra, and from buildings

On this elegant but somewhat elaborately shaped pot from Centuripe in Sicily, the warmth and charm of color and decoration have become an end in themselves. The taste of the Greeks has softened greatly since the 6th century BC.

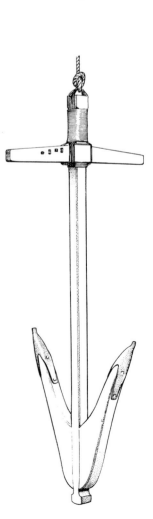

Below An anchor retrieved from the remains of an Alexandrian merchant ship wrecked off Anglesey, north Wales, in the 2nd century BC. Already before 300 BC Pytheas of Massilia had circumnavigated Britain, one of the sources of tin beyond the straits of Gibraltar.

like the Palazzo delle Colonne at Ptolemais in Cyrenaica, 50 kilometers west of Kyrene. In both cases the dates are uncertain, but the vigor of the Alexandrian influence is beyond doubt. The style rapidly became international, and since variety and bold impression were essential elements in it, the adaptations and the cross-influences are almost impossible to chart, particularly under the Roman empire. One of the cleverest of Greek baroque buildings was the temple of Fortune at Praeneste in Italy, while already in the 2nd century BC a Roman architect was employed by the city of Athens, for the vast new baroque temple of Zeus. Elsewhere things were even more complicated. There was no longer a Greek world, only a world.

In that world victory belonged to colossal forces. It was not only the independent cities, but the lesser dynastic powers that were doomed. In the 3rd century BC the new kingdoms altered their frontiers on an imperial scale. Thrace, the kingdom of Lysimachos, was swallowed up. The new kingdom of Pergamon in Asia Minor came into existence. Pergamon was rich, powerful and influential even in the arts, just as Alexandria was. The art of gardening, of the pleasure garden, of which we would know so little were it not for a few wall paintings of the Roman period, developed at Pergamon. Parchment derives its name through Latin from Pergamon. The 2nd-century baroque ornamental sculptures of the altar of Zeus at Pergamon, with their huge, convoluted forms, their super-strength and their shining texture, nauseating as they may be to a classic taste, add a new dimension and an almost new direction to the history of Greek art. There was no lack of *brio* in the Hellenistic kingdoms, or of technical skill.

Pergamon

From 282 to 133 BC, under the Attalid dynasty, Pergamon was a wealthy and formidable imperial power. It gave its name to parchment, the alternative to papyrus, its library was second only to Alexandria's, it bred a new and spectacular school of baroque sculpture; it defeated the Celts and saw them settled in Galatia, held off the Macedonians and kept the Romans friendly; it nourished the beginnings of the art of gardening. The sanctuary of Asklepios, a private foundation in 400 BC, became under Hadrian a "wonder of the world."

Some of the sculptures of the great altar of Pergamon (right), now almost all in Berlin. They are on a vast scale, heavy and muscular and glittering. Spectacular in its finish, and fascinating in its detail, this is the grandest monument of the 2nd century BC. Pergamon was built on terraces on steep mountainsides in a harmonious design of contrasting fine architecture and open spaces. Like much of the civic building, the theater (below) was built by Eumenes II in the early 2nd century.

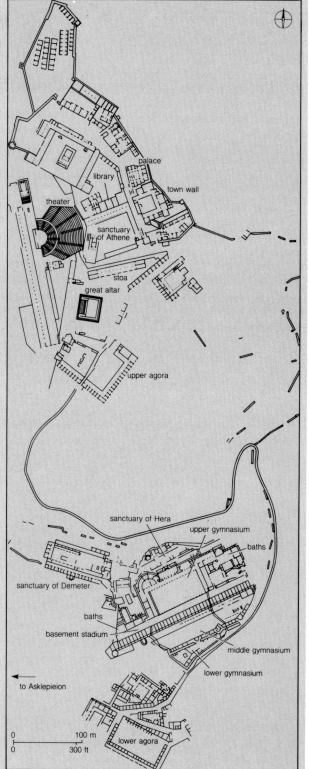

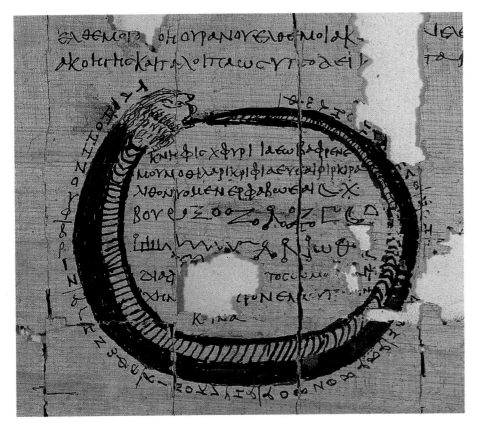

This hieratic but still imaginably real snake is an illustration from a magical text written on papyrus which has been preserved from the lost world of the Greeks.

Commanders and mercenaries

The deadening process that slowly unfolded was a direct result or a further development of conditions after Alexander, but it took place only under the long pressure of forces at that time newly let loose. Mercenary soldiers, for example, did not become a regular, well-organized resource equally available to all great powers until the 3rd century. At first the disloyalties and jealousies of corps commanders who shifted their entire force from king to king seriously disturbed what balance existed in the world. These independent minor commanders were unsuccessful in the end, and they were squeezed out of existence. The role of the Greek armies of the new kings in the 3rd century was colonial, and in Egypt, in Asia Minor and in Mesopotamia, they held land in the new territories, their cities were cantonments outside the native cities, and the lease of land to Greeks might even need to be renewed by the monarch from father to son.

Of course there were also special corps of full-time professional soldiers, archers from the Cretan mountains, or broad-sworded Thracians for example. Their recruitment continued into the Roman army. The Macedonians did not scorn to use barbarian mercenaries. There was also an important distinction among the land-holding reserve army; they were by no means all citizens, for citizen rights were owned only by those whose cantonments were created official cities by decree. By this time, every city in Greece depended as heavily as the rawest military settlement in Asia on the generosity of monarchs. The buildings of the kings of Pergamon at Athens, and the innumerable decrees of gratitude of the Athenian state, illustrate this dramatically.

Changes of taste

Individual citizens might aspire to a ride on the wheel of fortune. A poverty-stricken fisherman in a poem by Theokritos dreamed of a golden fish, though one knows he will never be rich. A peasant might dig up a treasure buried in a field, or a treasure might be washed ashore; theatrical audiences were pleased with plots like that. But most people got on with life without looking for any enormous reversals. There was a middle class. Much of its taste was cloying and hideous, some of it appealing. Vases began to be made, at Centuripe in Sicily and in Alexandria, smothered in ornamental colors and shaped too elaborately. A particularly offensive pinkish purple or magenta came into vogue; it was used on vases, often with disastrous effect. Later, probably in Sicily or southern Italy, from the late 2nd century to the time of Christ, this color was employed on small terracotta figurines that incorporated flasks or fillers for the lamp oil that was used in every house. Some of the figures are charming, most of them are humorous to some degree.

Masterpieces often tell us less about social history, though they deserve notice. But the last masterpieces of Greek vase painting belong to the late 4th century; the last master is probably the Lipari Painter, whose works are found only on his own remote island and on the coasts around it; none of them traveled further away than Naples. The women sit loosely and easily in his drawings; the drawing is sharp and free. He favors a cool light blue paint with a creamy white and realistic flesh colors. The contrast with his traditional black background is fine and cool, and the women themselves seem intent on keeping cool. The magenta vases from Centuripe, and some sepulchral monuments in the Cairo museum that express the same bourgeois velleity for luxury, are much warmer, more fantastical and less fine.

Not that nothing fine existed in the world. This was the age of illustrated manuscripts. We have few early examples, but their existence and nature can be traced through many copies. We know of medical and surgical texts carefully illustrated, of a poem about snakes with realistic colored drawings of each species, and even of entire epic poems illustrated between the lines with a cartoon version of the action. Some of the drawing must have been very fine, and it was certainly popular. It traveled where the language of the verses was no longer understood, and an early Buddhist sculptor in Gandhara, in what is now Pakistan, copied in stone a scene from a sub-Homeric epic showing the wooden horse at the fall of Troy; he used it as a miracle of the Buddha. A silver cup from Tibet of the finest post-Greek workmanship has a scene on it which began life as an illustration to Euripides.

Elsewhere in the east the Greeks adapted in various degrees to native life. We know for example of a Greek making an offering to the Buddha. Someone translated the Buddhist rules of life of the Indian king Asoka into excellent philosophic Greek; more than one copy of the translation has been found. The goddess of Baktra (Balkh), capital of Bactria, was Anahita, the great water goddess of the Oxus, whose cloak was made of beaver skins: she was worshiped in a confused cult as Artemis. The Greek sense of identity was persistent, even when their institutions and almost their language were lost.

What survived was due to the scholarly revivals of impassioned antiquarians, or to the patronage of

Ay Khanoum

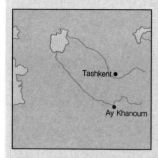

Ay Khanoum is an isolated Greek city, perhaps once named Alexandria, on the borders of Russia and Afghanistan, not many miles from China. Its Hellenistic palace, once a great grove of columns, seems to stand on the site of a Persian palace. At Ay Khanoum the Kokcha, which flows from the lapis lazuli mines and the high pass into India, runs down to the Oxus. This is the only purely Greek city ever excavated in Afghanistan. It was discovered by chance, by the king of Afghanistan on a shooting expedition. It is a well-defended city, with a gymnasium, a temple, and inscriptions in Greek. Alexander himself never came quite so far north-east, but this city is his signature.

The silver disk from the temple (*below*) shows an Oriental goddess, Kybele, in completely Hellenized form, with an Oriental priest at a fire-altar, and a god in the sky, a remarkable blend of religious ideas.

This fine old head (*left*) came from a Herm, a tall stone block with a head on it. In this case it had a portrait head and the cloaked upper body of an official, but not the genitalia of an ancestral god, as it would have had in 5th-century Athens. It was found in the outer room of the hero shrine of the founder at Ay Khanoum.

Below: The palaestra at Ay Khanoum.

This large fragment of foot from the temple suggests the religious cult of a ruler. If the statue was in keeping with the luxury of the palace, it must have been splendid.

Right This is a page of a fine book written out for the daughter of a Roman emperor. It represents the high point of ancient Greek flower painting. The book is the *De Materia Medica* of Dioskorides. It was brought back from Constantinople in the 16th century by Augier de Bousbecque.

A miniature sculpture of a war elephant in action.

the new rich, who found it useful or ornamental. The most physically beautiful of all surviving ancient books is one that contains a collection of botanical drawings made for Flavia Anicia, the daughter of a Roman emperor at the time of the decadence of the empire. It was bought in Constantinople by a diplomat of the Holy Roman Empire in the 16th century and is still in Vienna. (The same scholarly traveler introduced the lilac, the tulip and the flowering horse chestnut to Europe.) The illustrations of this book, part of the *De Materia Medica* of Dioskorides, a Greek physician in the army of Rome in the 1st century AD, seem to be taken directly from life. They, or botanical drawings like them, were copied and recopied in the Middle Ages, more and more formally, more and more unrecognizably. But the Vienna codex of Dioskorides is the last point of a long and rich tradition. In it we have access to the best work of the Greeks under centuries of non-Greek patronage.

Ay Khanoum

The only completely Greek archaeological site ever to have been excavated east of Persia is Ay Khanoum, on the borders of Russia and Afghanistan. Alexander's men fortified it. It was identified through a Corinthian capital found by the king of Afghanistan some 20 years ago on a hunting trip. When it fell to the nomadic peoples who overwhelmed Greek Bactria, Ay Khanoum was abandoned and never rebuilt. The forest of columns was felled with axes, like a real forest of trees, and the place was never used again, except centuries after as a polo ground. But the acropolis still has the name, the Hill of the Lady; it is not at all impossible that in that name the goddess of the place is remembered. Ay Khanoum was a small city with a huge palace and strong defenses; it was almost certainly Persian before it was Greek, since at least one Persian column base has been found there.

The palace stands on the spit of ground where the river Kokcha flows into the Oxus or Amu-Darya, at the only point on the Oxus for miles in either direction where the river is too deep to ford. This is a defensive position. The river Kokcha runs down from high mountains on the Afghan side, from the

only lapis lazuli mines in what was then the known world. It seems likely that the function of this satrap's palace, and of the Greek city that followed it, was to tax or to control the extraction of lapis lazuli. In the same mountains it is still very easy to find Balas rubies, fine gem stones of a deep pink that splinter too easily, and also rock crystal. Ay Khanoum is not very far from the route of nomadic shepherds, who until modern times crossed the whole of Afghanistan, from Pakistan and the Indus valley, through the mountains and across the Oxus into Russia, twice in every year. More important still, Ay Khanoum was extremely close to the silk road between the eastern Mediterranean and China.

The Greeks at Ay Khanoum made some interesting concessions to local religion. A plaque from the ruins of the temple presents the goddess Kybele. The plaque is a disk, finely made in repoussé silver. Two discreetly dancing lions are pulling a chariot across a mountainous landscape toward a purely Persian altar of seven steps, which faces her. A priest in a long robe and a conical hat sacrifices. Behind the chariot comes a Persian priest holding an umbrella over the head of the Greek goddess, who faces outward from the disk. She rides in the chariot, which is driven by a Greek girl. A star, a crescent moon, and the head of a young Greek sun god with 13 rays sprouting from him survey the mysterious scene. We know that Kybele was originally a regional mother goddess adopted by the Greeks in Asia Minor. She was worshiped in Greece itself only by guilds of foreigners, never publicly until the Roman empire, but she was the Asian goddess the Greeks knew best in the 3rd century BC.

The temple was rebuilt. At first its outer walls had a series of recessed square niches, each one receding in a series of three diminishing frames, one inside the other. This was a style of some elegance, popular in the Persian empire. At the rebuilding the walls were smothered over in massive claybrick, with some use of stucco and white paint. A carbonized wooden Ionic capital has been recovered almost complete. The principal cult statue was of great size, and the marble foot which remains of it is that of a male figure wearing sandals which bear the emblem of a thunderbolt: Zeus therefore, or a king indentified with Zeus. Elsewhere in the city was a hero shrine, with two brick graves and two sarcophagi, a small chapel with a pair of columns at its entrance, several times rebuilt, and standing on a mound, perhaps the grave mound of the founder of the city, whose name was Kineas.

Like every proper Greek city, Ay Khanoum had its enclosed palaestra, a sports ground or a training ground. It has yielded a fine Greek marble head of the aging Herakles. But the most quintessentially Greek find of all is an inscription from near the hero shrine. It is written in competent Greek verse and inscribed in lettering of before 250 BC. It records that Klearchos, whom we have met as a pupil of Aristotle, has copied out the precepts of the famous men of ancient times, which he saw at Delphi, and has inscribed them here, in the sanctuary of Kineas. Only one of the Delphic maxims has survived, because a second stone has perished: this was an inscription to encourage the isolated Greeks of Ay Khanoum to the various virtues proper to the different ages of human life. The same advice from Delphi was inscribed at Miletopolis in Anatolia.

THE ROMAN CONQUEST

The Roman expansion in the west

The dynasties that Alexander's noblemen founded had squeezed smaller powers almost out of existence, though not one of the warlords could reunite the Macedonian empire as Alexander had left it. Nor had Alexander lived to carry out his projected campaign in the west, so that many untidy and independent relics of earlier ages still survived there until their day came. Rome in the 3rd century BC was a powerful city near the rich western Italian coast, and it had already conquered more civilized places. The 4th-century Gaulish invasion, which in Asia Minor ended with the Celtic settlement of Galatia in the 3rd century, had swept down Italy. In the aftermath of the sack of Rome (390 BC) the Romans had in 378 constructed a massive city wall. They had challenged the Etruscans to the north, utterly destroying Veii (396 BC), and they now dominated the nearby rival city of Caere whose wealth, like that of Rome, owed its origins to success as a free, open-market city.

From a military point of view, Roman power had rested from the 5th century on a league of the cities of Latium to the south, much like any Greek league of the same period. But the Romans outgrew their league, as Greek cities did, and one by one, with the ruthlessness of a new age, the Romans swallowed up their rivals. Neither Capua nor Praeneste, the second city of all Italy and the home city of the great goddess of Fortune (better perhaps translated Providence) whom the Romans had adopted from Praeneste, could hold out against this 4th-century expansion. The Romans were now in Etruria to the north and in Campania beyond Latium to the south. Roman colonies established in the 4th century stood their ground in the 3rd at Cales near Capua, and on the coast at Ostia by the mouth of the Tiber, and further south at Antium (Anzio), and at Terracina. By 218 BC there were 12 Roman colonial cities on the Italian coast, and more than as many again at river crossings, in the approaches to mountain passes and where big roads crossed. Between 343 and 263 BC some 60,000 new Roman landholdings were established, covering something like 130,000 square kilometers. The results of this creeping, methodical advance were to last longer than Alexander's adventurous sweep.

Of course, this kind of expansion produced war, and victorious war in turn produced further expansions. By 290 BC the Romans had mastered the formidable Samnites of the Apennine mountains. By the end of that century they had annexed Sardinia, Corsica and Sicily, and the vast riches of the Po valley. Their army consisted of two legions, developments of the Greek phalanx, but subdivided each into 30 smaller units, disciplined, sinuous and adaptable. In the course of the 3rd century, they had dealt effectively with the dashing campaign (280–275 BC) of Pyrrhos of Epirus, the Molossian king who had been called in to assist Tarentum against Rome. All Italy now belonged to Rome by irreversible alliance or by conquest. Since they now dominated the Greek cities of southern Italy, the Romans cheerfully took over the Greeks' long-standing quarrel with Carthage. The ensuing war, at sea, in Sicily and in North Africa, drew them into the center of the huge Carthaginian sphere of influence, on the edges of which they had always lived. In the first Carthaginian (Punic) war of 264–241 BC, they fought the biggest naval battles the Mediterranean had ever seen, with appalling losses on both sides. (The best of the Carthaginian commanders, Xanthippos, was a Spartan mercenary captain.)

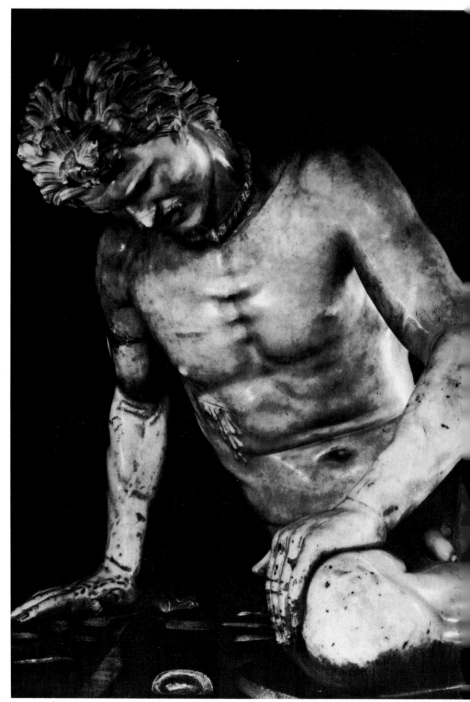

Corinth

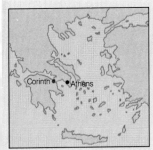

Corinth was one of the grandest and wealthiest cities of mainland Greece. With ports on both sides of the Isthmus, it was a great merchant city and an early colonial power. Its fortress was an almost impregnable rock, its land rich, its visual art, which absorbed many Oriental images, was magnificent. The Romans destroyed (146 BC) and refounded (44 BC) Corinth, which became capital of Achaea.

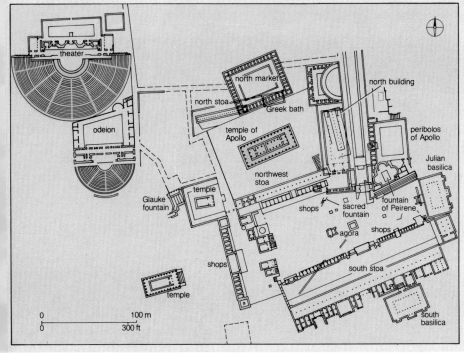

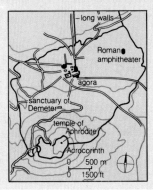

The temple of Apollo is one of the oldest in Greece. It stands on a small hill with a complicated archaeological history. Here fragments of painted wall-plaster have been found using the patterns of the age of geometric art in color. The temple dates from the mid-6th century, its predecessor from the 7th. The surviving monolithic limestone Doric columns are all that is left of a rectangle of six at the front and back and 15 along the sides. The fortress, or Acrocorinth, rears in the distance.

Left To commemorate the turning back of the Gaulish invasion and the settlement of the Celts in Galatia, the king of Pergamon filled his city with glittering statues like this one, in which brilliant finish combined with horrific realism. It was a new style of art.

Another invasion of Gauls, justly infuriated at Roman policies of massacre and expulsion, brought an army of 70,000 men halfway down Italy; in 225 BC it was annihilated at Telamon. In 237 BC Hamilcar Barca, an old general of the first war, had set out to colonize Spain. He founded what is now Alicante on the coast, and the inland territories he acquired, with their mineral wealth, made him a powerful figure. The son-in-law who succeeded him moved further south, where he founded Cartagena. At the same time he advanced his frontiers to the Ebro, more than halfway across Spain. He in turn died by murder in 221 BC, and the enormous basis of his power passed to Hannibal, the son of Hamilcar, who for the rest of that century fought the Romans (second Carthaginian war, 218–201 BC). The course of the war was dramatic, but by 205 the Roman general Scipio had taken Spain and successfully invaded Africa. Carthaginian power was destroyed, and Rome was now as formidable, as wealthy and nearly as far-ranging as any of the kingdoms of Alexander's successors.

First Macedonian war

In the course of their first Carthaginian war, the Romans had already set foot on the eastern coast of the Adriatic. To close the Adriatic to Carthage they had established Brundisium (Brindisi), a powerful and fortified colony on a wonderful natural harbor, and in doing so provoked attacks on Adriatic shipping by the Illyrians of what is now the coast of Yugoslavia. So the Romans sent an expedition and established a protectorate on the Illyrian coast. That could not possibly be the end of the affair. In 220 BC a local adventurer from that coast, Demetrios of Pharos, began to trouble Rome. Naturally the Romans in the end drove him out, and equally naturally, Demetrios appealed to the nearest great power in Greece, to the Macedonian court, to King Philip V. The king, of course, disliked and resented Roman expansion on the east coast of the Adriatic; he took the obvious step of an alliance with Hannibal, then (in 215 BC) at the height of his success. The Romans controlled the sea, and as the Athenians would have done 250 years earlier, they sent ships and landed men in Greece to make what trouble they could. In 205 BC, toward the end of the second Carthaginian war, Philip played another logical move in his losing game. By making peace with Rome, he alienated his new-found allies in Achaea without conciliating the vengeful Romans.

Before the Roman incursion, however, the Macedonians were already in trouble in Greece. By 228 BC the Achaean league of cities, the most important power in the Peloponnese, based in the north and center of the peninsula, had expelled the Macedonians from the huge fortress of Corinth, from Sikyon, Argos, Arcadia, Megara and Aegina. That glorious moment passed quickly; the Achaean league was a threat to Sparta, and in the 220s the Spartans had come close to utterly annihilating it: the league in despair called in their old enemies, the Macedonians, and Sparta and Corinth fell.

During their first war in Greece, the Romans temporarily secured their first active allies in Greece itself. The Aetolian league, a loose confederacy of the cities of central Greece on the northwestern side of the gulf of Corinth, had been an organized federal power since the 4th century. In the 3rd it extended its control to include Delphi itself, and through Delphi to a powerful influence in the wider league of Greek cities that claimed responsibility for Delphi, the Amphictionic league. If Philip V could not now protect them against Roman interference, then they must protect themselves; in 211 BC, therefore, they entered the Roman alliance against the Macedonians, but they were forced to a separate peace with Philip after the Romans' withdrawal.

Now Philip turned to the east. He negotiated an alliance with the king of Syria, Antiochos the Great, the great-great-grandson of Seleukos, satrap of Babylon under Alexander. Under Antiochos the Great, Syria was perhaps the strongest kingdom in the Greek world, powerful in the east as Rome was in the west. The Parthians were its tributaries and the king of Bactria reigned by license of Antiochos.

In 203 BC, in another of the almost continuous dinosaur wars of the great powers, Philip combined with Antiochos to menace the Egypt of the Ptolomies. Smaller powers were seriously alarmed, and Rhodes and the stronger Pergamon rushed into the arms of Rome; at the same time they went to war with Philip of Macedonia. The Romans, whose diplomatic intelligence was by no means perfect, and whose suspicions were correspondingly great, moved against Philip. It is interesting that this war was the policy not of the Roman people, who at first refused to fight it, but of the Senate, whose interests were financially international. There was already in the 3rd century BC a solid and rich Italian presence at Delos, by then one of the greatest business centers in the Mediterranean. The Roman ultimatum to Philip was in direct line with the existing policy of protective interference; Philip must pay indemnities to Pergamon and to Rhodes, and he must never again undertake military action against any Greek state.

Second Macedonian war

The inevitable war began in 200 BC. The Roman plan was to set free the Greek cities as Roman protectorates, as a frontier power against Alexander's successors. The Aetolian cities joined the Romans in 198 BC and Athens welcomed in Attalos of Pergamon; the Achaean cities at once reverted to their old anti-Macedonian policy. The war was exhausting; Philip had already lost most of his naval power in his war with Rhodes and Pergamon, and in 197 BC he could muster only 26,000 men, and even so many only by enrolling boys and old men. The young Roman commander Flamininus with his Aetolian Greek allies defeated that army utterly at Kynoskephalai in Thessaly.

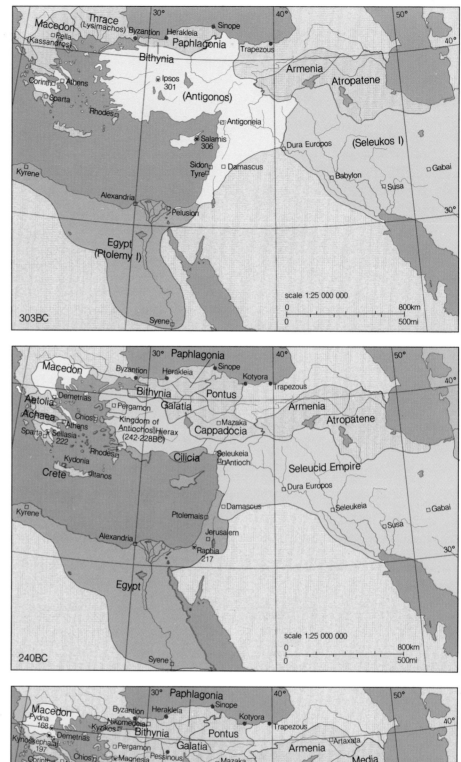

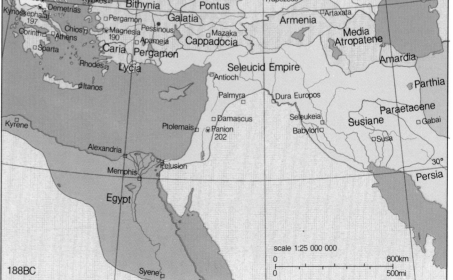

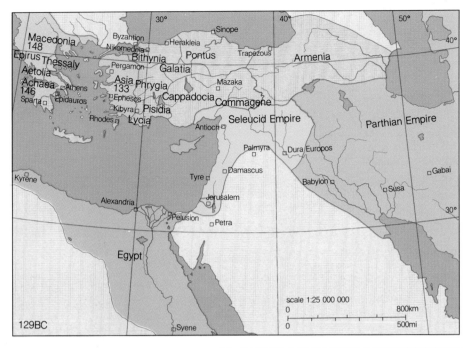

That did not, of course, make the Greeks masters of the situation. Philip was made to surrender what remained of his fleet, all his Asian cities, and certain strategic fortified cities in Greece, including Corinth; he had also to pay an indemnity, but by the terms of the treaty he became an ally of the Romans: the Aetolians gained little or nothing. In 196 BC at the Isthmian games Flamininus proclaimed the nominal freedom of Greece, and many of the principal cities of the Peloponnese, including those of the Achaean league, became Roman allies. There were monuments and dedications, some of which survive. This was the beginning of the heavy stone breathing by Romans down the necks of Greeks at Olympia that lasted for centuries.

The Romans as a protecting power had now to try to settle the deep and furious resentments of the Greek states, the legacy of centuries, particularly of the last. The Macedonians had ceded Argos to Sparta as a diplomatic move in the war with Rome; Sparta had kept Argos and then successfully negotiated a Roman alliance. Flamininus restored Argos to the Achaean league. Sparta revolted with an army of 15,000 men, so Flamininus, summoning all his Greeks, immediately invaded with 50,000. Sparta was not annexed, but it was crushed.

Rome defeats Antiochos of Syria

The Romans had now to play the other role of a protecting power; they had to protect the new frontiers. Antiochos the Great had taken in 197 BC the whole coast of Asia Minor, including some of the kingdom of Pergamon; he was now chewing his way westward along the coast of Thrace. But Rome negotiated with Antiochos for three years, and in 194 BC the Roman army left Greece.

In 193 BC Antiochos married his daughter to Ptolemy V of Egypt. The northern states of Greek Asia were his allies and Hannibal in exile was a refugee prince in his court. Antiochos' relations with Rome were bad, but without a state of war. At this point the Aetolians invited him into mainland Greece, with a promise of alliance with Philip and with Sparta. In an atmosphere of mutual promises trouble broke out at once, and old scores were settled. The Aetolians went to war, and the Achaeans extended their league to include Elis and Sparta and Messenia. Antiochos entered mainland Greece with a small army, but no general rising around him followed, and the Romans were now bound to intervene again in Greece. In 191 BC they destroyed his army at Thermopylai; Antiochos escaped almost alone. The next year the Romans under the Scipio brothers Africanus and Lucius recovered Thrace and for the first time marched on Asia. The Aetolians secured a truce with Rome.

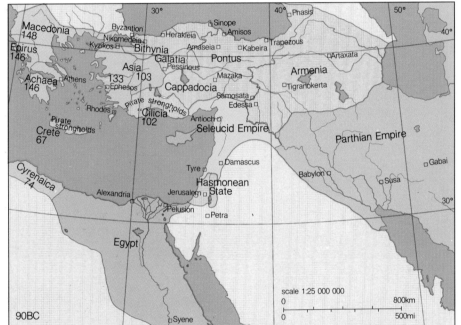

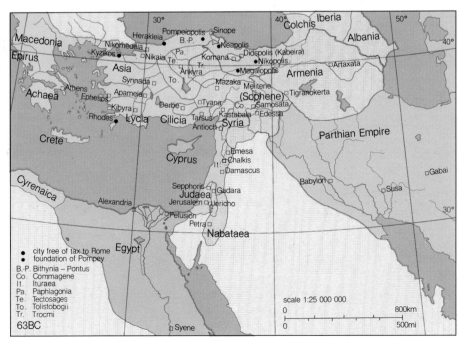

Seleucid territory

Ptolemaic territory

Antigonid territory

Roman empire

Parthian empire

independent kingdom

city-state

site of major battle

The successor kingdoms
If Alexander had lived and established a dynasty, his empire might well have held together for centuries, for it is remarkable that, though Macedonian generals fought over it and successively partitioned it between themselves, there was hardly any native revolt. In Asia Minor small kingdoms asserted themselves in which Greek and Oriental elements fused in various ways.

Paestum

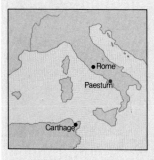

Poseidonia, later called Paestum, was founded in the mid-7th century BC by the existing Greek colony of Sybaris further south. It lies below Naples on the coast of Italy. Its defensive wall was about 5 meters thick and nearly 5,000 long. By a whim of the sea which destroyed it and then retired from it, this city has the best-preserved archaic temples anywhere in the Greek world. At the end of the 5th century it was taken over by the local Lucanians, and in the 3rd it fell to Rome. We know that the Greeks in the Lucanian period lamented the decay of their way of life, but they did produce a fine style of painting.

The temples survived the Middle Ages knee-deep in sea-water. The two big temples were probably both dedicated to Hera, goddess of fertility.

The mid-5th-century "temple of Neptune" (*right*), and the "temple of Hera," some 100 years older, both stand in Hera's special sanctuary; the small dedications that have been found are much the same.

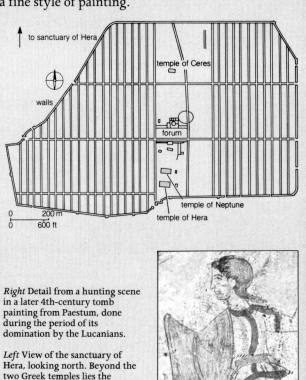

Right Detail from a hunting scene in a later 4th-century tomb painting from Paestum, done during the period of its domination by the Lucanians.

Left View of the sanctuary of Hera, looking north. Beyond the two Greek temples lies the central "forum" (and agora) area with a Roman temple of peace and beyond that a third Greek temple, the so-called temple of Ceres, in fact a 6th-century temple of Athene.

The combined fleets of Rome, Rhodes and Pergamon, in a series of difficult naval battles in the Aegean, in the end destroyed the enemy fleet. Roman naval power was a product of the first Carthaginian war; it is important to keep one's eye on the significance of naval power in the dominance of first the Athenians, then the Macedonian kings, then the Carthaginians, then the Romans. It might not decide the conquest of the world, but it decided the control of much of it.

A successful Roman land campaign in northwest Asia followed at once. Aetolia was punished, but not annihilated. By the treaty of Apamea in Phrygia in 188 BC, one year after his defeat on land at Magnesia ad Sipylum in Lydia, Antiochos lost most of Asia Minor, his ships, his elephants, and a large sum of money. Hannibal escaped inland. By

overstepping its Greek protectorates, Rome had become in substance the governing power of mainland Greece, the Mediterranean was a Roman sea, and small quarrel after small quarrel was decided by Roman commissioners. In the Peloponnese the war between Sparta and the Achaean league blazed up again, until in 181 BC the Romans restored the integrity and the traditional institutions of Sparta. What was restored was not the life of an earlier age, but a new, backward-looking Sparta, not without atavistic exaggerations. The ritual flogging of boys on the altar of Artemis became a show for Roman tourists.

Third Macedonian war
Not everyone was pleased with Roman government, and not everyone was quite impotent against it.

A coin of Hannibal. At the end of the 3rd century BC Hannibal invaded Italy from the north with elephants. Although the Greeks and the Carthaginians had fought bitterly in Sicily, Carthage and the Greek cities of the east and Athens and Rome were all part of one world by 200 BC.

The personal portrait of Antiochos III (242–187 BC) on his coinage suggests a high degree of civilization. He was successful in the east as a young man, but the Romans broke him, and when he died his rambling, enormous kingdom was cut off from the sea.

Before it fell asleep from exhaustion, the Romans were going to have to reduce Greece more thoroughly. Philip V died (in 179 BC) plotting against Rome. His plan was to back an alliance of Celtic tribes on the lower Danube to invade and conquer Italy while he himself conquered Greece. His son Perseus made friends with the Rhodians, married the daughter of the successor to Antiochos, and found allies in Aetolia. The poorer, the democratic and libertarian party in every Greek city looked to Perseus, since it could now look nowhere else. Eumenes king of Pergamon appealed to Rome to destroy him, and when on his way home he was nearly assassinated, Perseus was blamed, and Rome acted. Rome declared war in 171 BC, and in three years' time a Roman and allied army of 100,000 was in Greece. Perseus had less than half that number; his allies were Thracians and Illyrians and tribesmen from Epirus; he failed to get help from the lower Danube because he could not afford to pay for it. In 168 BC at Pydna his army was massacred, and he died in a Roman prison. There were no more Macedonian kings of great significance, and Macedonia was divided into four republics.

After the battle of Pydna Rhodes was stripped, Delos handed over to Athens as a free port and recolonized, the Aetolian league dismembered, Pergamon itself deliberately weakened and insulted, and in Epirus so many were sold as slaves that their price was minimal and the countryside depopulated. When a new Antiochos of Syria (the fifth) successfully invaded Egypt in 169–168 BC, the Romans were already so strong that they simply told him to go away, and he went away.

197

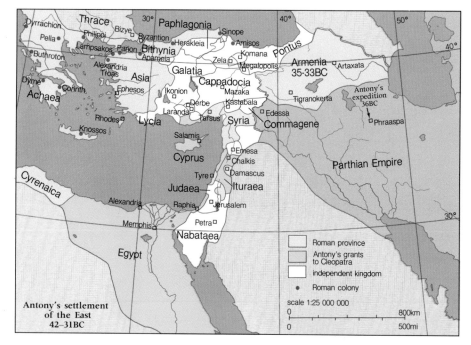

Antony's settlement
of the East
42–31BC

	Roman province
	Antony's grants to Cleopatra
	independent kingdom
•	Roman colony

scale 1:25 000 000

0 — 800km
0 — 500mi

The settlements of Mark Antony and (below) final annexations by Rome

The destruction of Corinth

The final catastrophe for the Greeks was in the forties of the 2nd century BC. It is easier to understand in terms of Roman than of Greek history; Roman government had become heavy-handed, but it was ruthlessly successful: in Spain, where final and crushing victory was deferred until 133 BC, in Africa, where the city of Carthage was forced into a local war in 150 BC before it was utterly destroyed by the Romans in 146, and in Greece. In 150 BC the survivors of the 1,000 Achaean hostages to Rome were sent home; a new quarrel with the Spartans, who chose to leave the Achaean league, was settled by Rome in favor of Sparta, and in the resulting climate of furious resentment Roman envoys were attacked at Corinth, now chief city of the Achaean league. A Roman army advanced at once from Macedonia, fresh from a short campaign against a pretender to the throne; a pitiful attempt at opposition was easily swept aside. The consul Mummius took over command and assembled his army at Corinth in 146 BC. The Greeks, combining rashness with weakness, were utterly defeated; the mighty fortress was scarcely defended.

The Romans ruined every city that had resisted them. Most of the Corinthians were massacred, and the rest sold as slaves, including women, children, and those who were already slaves but had been set free to join in the war. The city was utterly annihilated. Local government by property qualification was established all over Greece, and local democracy abolished. Taxes were imposed on the Greeks, the rich were forbidden to acquire property outside Greece, and all the leagues of cities were finally disbanded. There were fines and indemnities. Macedonia was made a province of Rome, and Achaea was attached to it. The history of Greece became the history of a province of the Roman empire, and then of the Byzantine empire, and then of the Turkish empire. It was to be nearly 2,000 years before Greece was politically independent, but it is astonishing to what a degree during those years national consciousness persisted, still more so how greatly the Greeks contributed to what we value in the history of the human race.

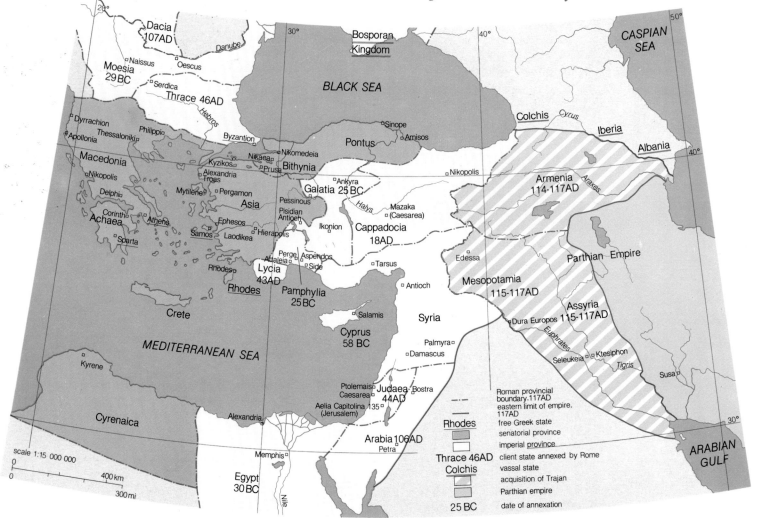

	Roman provincial boundary.117AD
	eastern limit of empire, 117AD
Rhodes	free Greek state
	senatorial province
	imperial province
Thrace 46AD	client state annexed by Rome
Colchis	vassal state
	acquisition of Trajan
	Parthian empire
25 BC	date of annexation

scale 1:15 000 000

0 — 400 km
0 — 300mi

PART SIX
THE FATE OF HELLENISM

THE CLASSICAL IMPACT OF HELLENISM

The influence of the Greeks, the slow soaking of more and more of the world in their arts, their sciences, experience, language and norms of decency, even sometimes in their religion, by no means ceased at the establishment of the Roman province of Macedonia and its subdivision of Achaea (later a province in its own right). The persistence of Greek forms even in the remotest east is almost incredible, but in the shapes of pottery made until yesterday in Swat, in the pillars of wooden architecture still standing in Afghanistan, in elements of Buddhist art, even in the new realism of certain figurines as far afield as China, Greek influence is certainly present. Athenian tragedy and the poems of Homer were known in India, and in Egypt Aristophanes was still acted in the 5th century AD. These examples represent an inevitable diffusion. The place to look for depth of penetration is closer to Athens, and unlike these stray cases it is very well documented; it is the city of Rome. Veii, until it fell in 396 BC, had been more Hellenized than Rome, and so had the whole of Etruria and most of southern Italy. The Romans emerge into history fighting; civilization comes to them late.

Early Latin writers

At the celebration in 240 BC, after their first victorious Carthaginian war, the Romans held public athletic contests, and a version of 5th-century Athenian tragedy was produced for the first time at Rome, in Latin. It was written by Livius Andronicus, a half-Greek ex-prisoner of war from Tarentum, who also translated Homer somewhat awkwardly into Latin verse modeled on Greek verse. The rhythms of Greek poetry did not take at all easily to the Latin language; indeed, the first rhythmically perfect Latin verses, the first verses as free-seeming, as elegant and pliably strong as the best of 3rd-century Greek verse, were written by the generation that saw the fall of the Roman republic some 200 years later. But given this limitation, the Romans already had wonderful poets in Greek rhythms in the 2nd century BC, and their own prose, by rubbing constantly against Greek models, refined itself at the same speed as their poetry, ending in the luxurious abundance of Cicero, just before freedom of speech was lost to them and mannerism set in.

Naevius, one of the greatest of all Roman poets, but sadly ill preserved, was from Capua; he knew the Greeks and wrote tragedy, comedy and some moving elegiac verses. His epic account of the Carthaginian war, in which he fought, was written in an old Latin meter, not in Greek hexameters, but the shadow of Homer nourished it. Naevius died in 201 BC. Ennius, who died 32 years later, chose a Latin adaptation of Greek hexameters, and in many ways he imitated the Alexandrian Greeks as well as their mightier predecessors more slavishly than Naevius. His fragmentary writings are still readable, still awkwardly strong, but less powerful than on the basis of rather fewer fragments we conceive Naevius to be. Lucilius, the first great Roman satirist, was an educated Roman nobleman of the

Above Whatever was best and deepest in the Roman world was deeply penetrated by Greece. This Apollo (c. 500 BC) could almost have graced a sanctuary in 5th-century Attica, but he comes from Veii, a town that the Romans destroyed, in central Italy.

Left Terracottas of two gladiators condemned to kill or be killed for the pleasure of a Roman mob. The depravity of Roman taste extended from life into art.

late 2nd century BC to whom much that was Greek came naturally. He was of course hardly out of touch with his own society nor with the power of its language, but in him Greek feeling entered very deeply. He wrote sometimes in Greek rhythm, sometimes not, he mixed Greek words into his Latin sentences and his philosophy was Greek.

We know much more about Plautus; he was an Umbrian who died about 184 BC. His Latin comedies are brilliant adaptations of 4th-century Greek originals, written in fine, springing Latin with powerful injections of his own society, his own experience, and his own, very Roman jokes. He remarks in a prologue that he "puts this play into barbarous language," and discusses the problems of adaptation with ironic good humor. He is both serious and ironic in his treatment of the smoother-flowing subject matter of his original; in him what is Greek and what is Roman are interpenetrated, and something new has been created that the world had never seen before.

In the adaptations made by the comic poet Terence in the republican age from similar originals Greek elegance is supreme. One would hardly know that translation was involved. The much later fragments of the mime-writer Laberius confirm the fluency and precision of language that the Roman stage commanded in the end. But Terence was not only as elegant as a freely moving ballet dancer or a calligrapher in his verses; he was also exquisitely faithful to the Greekness of his originals. Terence was a slave from North Africa, born about 190 BC. He slipped out of life, having been granted his freedom, at the age of 30, and is said to have died poor in the Peloponnese, no one knows when, beside the Stymphalian Lake in the mountains inland from Corinth. It is reasonable to assume that the finest of all adapters into Latin had gone back to a language, and perhaps to places, that meant more to him.

Perhaps at first whatever was Greek was a fine ornament, like the loot of a city, but early in the course of the 2nd century came what a Roman poet called "the Muse's wing-footed descent on the savage people of Romulus." Literature is a useful index, because it involves philosophy and many intimate elements of a tradition and a society; it involves what the Romans called *humanitas*. The measure of the importance of the Greeks is that *humanitas* is a Greek idea, one which came slowly into existence in the world of ideas, in the course of the painful, particular history of the Greeks. Of that history the Roman writers of the late republic and the Augustan period are a continuation. They would have been the first to admit it.

Sculpture

One of the most striking of all the late achievements of the Greeks is the perfection of portrait sculpture. There is no doubt about its Greek origins; one need look only at the magnificent silver coinage of Greek Bactria. A portrait head in marble exists in the Villa Albani at Rome which is a later copy of a 3rd-century original; it shows exactly one of those familiar Bactrian Greek faces, even to the hat (broken unfortunately in the copy, and half-restored). There are other Greek examples from the same period. But the late republican portrait heads of the Romans have exactly the same quality. They

Priene

Priene was an early Ionian city on the Asian coast, but never so grand or successful as Miletos, its neighbor. In the 4th century it transferred bodily to its own harbor town, which is the Priene we know today. Alexander built a temple of Athene there. But its river silted, and Priene is now 12 or 13 kilometers from the sea. The site is spectacular, on the brow of a great cliff and at its foot. It had fine private houses and magnificent public buildings.

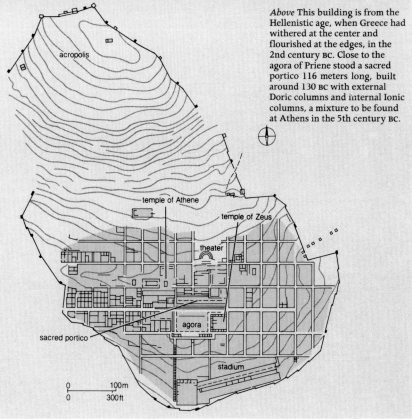

Above This building is from the Hellenistic age, when Greece had withered at the center and flourished at the edges, in the 2nd century BC. Close to the agora of Priene stood a sacred portico 116 meters long, built around 130 BC with external Doric columns and internal Ionic columns, a mixture to be found at Athens in the 5th century BC.

are formidable faces, unashamed of their warts. What went to the making of such heads? The wax masks of the faces of noble Roman ancestors, perhaps? It is a question as far-reaching as what went to the making of Athenian comedy in the youth of Aristophanes; the answers are not at all simple. There is something deeper than self-confidence about them, and at the same time an aggression, a scarred physical toughness, which speak of the cost of survival. They are the faces one might rely on to rule Bactria, or to rule Rome. Anguish was reserved for the faces of philosophers, complacency for town councillors, childishness for children.

Where the Romans were most penetrated by the Greeks, they were most liberated, and most Roman. On the Campus Martius in Rome, the Altar of Peace of the Emperor Augustus dedicated in 9 BC owed its formal origins to the Altar of Pity, the later, popular name for the altar of the 12 gods in the center of Athens. Everything about it is adaptation: Mother Earth has become Italy; Aeneas (one of the heroes of Troy in the *Iliad* but now also considered the ancestor and founder of Rome) is an Athenian elder from the Parthenon frieze; the Roman ceremonies in marble echo the marble representations of Athenian ceremonies. A crowded and grave procession of Roman families with their children, with a long line of magistrates, senators and priests, files its way along one outside wall of the enclosure of the altar, while the imperial family, Augustus himself and the consuls make their way in the same direction along the opposite outside wall. The goddess Rome and the goddess Italy occupy the east wall behind them, and Mars, whom the Romans identified with the Greek god Ares, and Aeneas the west wall ahead of them. The moment that the processional friezes represent is not the climax of the ceremony, which took place in 13 BC, but a moment of calm just before the climax. It owes something to the rather still figures at the head of the procession on the east end of the Parthenon frieze. The atmosphere is serene and reverent, but a few human touches do service for the extraordinary, almost wild liveliness of parts of the Parthenon frieze. Someone is being reproved for talking, a child wants to be picked up. There are a number of characteristic details of late Greek art, but the entire work has a compelling gravity it would be hard to parallel at this date outside a Roman context. Yet it is certainly Greek work, probably Asiatic Greek. The relief carvings on the enclosure of the Altar of Pity at Athens were carved in the late 5th century; they were impressively imitated more than once in the 2nd and 1st centuries BC. But the Altar of Peace is not just a copy; although it includes adaptations from Greek work, it is profoundly original, a new creation.

The Augustan poets

In the literature of the full Augustan period, it is sometimes almost as if Greeks were writing in Latin. The *Eclogues* of Vergil are steeped in a wide variety of late Greek poetry. When his shepherds sing in competition, they sing perfect Latin examples of several types of epigram well known to us from the 10th-century *Greek Anthology*, a collection of short poems that spans over 1,500 years of writing. In the *Aeneid*, Vergil is conscious not only of Homer,

but of Alexandrian scholarly criticism of Homer. Sometimes he accepts it, and alters his own poetry by its rules, at other times one can see him making a point against it. Some of his adaptations are failures, but even in his mistakes, Vergil was Hellenized to his finger tips. He died on his way back from Greece in 19 BC, where the Appian Way falls into the sea at Brindisi. No one will ever pass through Brindisi again who understands as much as Vergil did about Greek literature.

Humanly perhaps the deepest and the greatest of all Roman poets is Horace. He was also the most unregenerate Italian of the Roman writers of the Augustan age. Perhaps for that reason, the boldness of his handling of Greek models was beyond anyone else's. Except as a moralist he had no followers for hundreds of years. But in his own work, and against every law of probability, he revived (and in the end it was Horace who transmitted to Europe) the Greek art of lyric poetry: Ronsard knew no better model. Even in his moral, conversational, satiric poems he himself pointed to Greek examples. Where he differed from his contemporaries was in a preference, based on his personal scholarship, for very early models, Archilochos, Alkaios and Sappho among them, although there are late Greek elements in his poetry, as there were bound to be, since in his lifetime they were part of the air that Roman writers breathed. His freedom in his own skin, his concentrated power of phrasing, his shifts of tone and his persona as a moral poet owe everything to the Greeks, and a little maybe to Hellenized Latin. He tells us so when he speaks of his own education, the end of which was in Athens. His advice to young writers was "read the Greeks at night, and read the Greeks in the day." There were other scholars and other poets, after all, but the moral poetry of Horace, which includes many of his lyrics, would not have been possible without an ingrained and certain sense of his own liberty. He valued that sense and fought for it, even against his patron Maecenas, and even against the emperor. He was the son of a liberated slave who became a provincial auctioneer in southern Italy. In the civil war he fought as an officer under Brutus, on the losing

The Ara Pacis was the monument that Augustus built at Rome to commemorate his peace. It combines Greek and Roman elements as subtly and brilliantly as the poems of Horace or Vergil. The Ara Pacis is almost perfectly preserved.

This tough and experienced face was that of a Greek king who held Bactria against the central Asian nomads, and commanded the trade route to China.

An example of the silver coinage of the Greek kingdom of Bactria, which combined what is now Afghanistan with part of southern Russia.

libertarian side. As the world then was, only the subsequent patronage of Maecenas and of Augustus, which he won through Vergil and on his merits, could give him the liberty and security and the sense of mission which were necessary to great poetry. It is a curious irony that Augustus wanted poets, and Maecenas loved poetry, only because Greek literature existed.

The most obvious Greek element in the soul of Horace's poetry is the powerful drug of philosophy, not of metaphysics or of a dogmatic system but of an articulate and rationalized human wisdom which had been argued for many generations. When he packs his books for a journey, the Plato he is going to read is not the philosopher but a comic poet of the same name. But the seriousness of philosophy depended for his generation on written books, on the convincing seriousness of Plato and on Aristotle's critical descriptions of human behavior. There was also a more recent tradition of street-corner philosophy, almost of street-corner sermons, by later and lesser philosophers, full of biting common sense; we have little left of that tradition, but what we have is extremely close to the conversational poems of Horace. Horace himself claimed as a spiritual ancestor Bion of Olbia. Bion lived from about 325 to 255 BC, through the worst disturbances that followed Alexander's death; his father was a freed slave, his mother a whore, and he in his turn was sold into slavery and lived to be set free. He studied under Aristotle's pupils as well as under Plato's, and also under hedonists and the so-called Cynics, whose invective against the established world had so strong an influence, almost in Horace's generation, on Jewish and early Christian invective against the pagan gods. Horace's satire is gentler than theirs, but still terribly strong.

The most complete literary statements we have of a philosophic position in this period were written in Latin. Some of the philosophical works of Cicero are inadequate; his reflections on duty for example are almost wholly concerned with manners and propriety, and he is too consciously civilized, but the old gentleman had a sharp mind, and the structure of his beliefs is at least dramatically convincing; one can understand what he did believe, and why. In the 1st century BC in which he wrote, when republican manners and republican public life were closing down even in Rome, what Cicero has to say is often moving. But the most surprising example of a complete philosophy is the long Latin poem by Lucretius, who died about 55 BC. In *On the Nature of Things* Roman verse is just in its early flower, and the philosophy, which is Epicurean, derives from the Athenian schoolmaster's son who lived when Bion of Olbia did.

The theory of liberal arts, and of philosophy as one of them, and as the crown of life, is pathetically vulnerable. Liberal, in this Roman sense, meant suitable as an occupation for someone not a slave or a tradesman, therefore in practice (if not in theory) for a slave-owner. As for the disinterested freedom of this privileged class, Cicero's friend Atticus owned most of the grazing in Epirus, and in Cyprus Horace's friend Brutus was getting 48 per cent, not without violence, on money he had loaned. As for the nature of Roman philosophy, to propose that the consideration of the nature of the soul and of its immortality, the existence of an absolute, and the

rules of propriety (is it proper to dance in public?) are fit occupations only for a slave-owning class, is to use an argument that may be turned against one's class and one's subject. Gramsci remarked that the three forms of human wisdom are philosophy, which is reason, and religion and common sense, and that religion is disjointed fragments of common sense. By philosophy, he says, we overcome religion and common sense. In this modern definition, Lucretius was a philosopher, and Horace a religious poet. Horace was both more deeply Roman and more deeply Greek than Lucretius. He cultivated his garden, as Epicurus did, he had Stoicism in his bones, and he worked in the field beside his own serfs.

The world in the late 1st century BC was in many ways still the Alexandrian world. All over the Mediterranean, and in places as far afield as the silk road to China, Greek manners and Greek architecture and the Greek language existed. In Rome it was Augustus who first exploited the marble quarries of Italy, and the imperial Romans came to use ornamental colored stone from all over the world; but Athenian marble and Athenian workmanship did not lose all their prestige, although they did lose their monopoly of it. When the Altar of Peace was built they still had most of that. As late as 331 AD, for a dazzling inlay of colored marble, the consul Junius Bassus still chose a copy of a Greek painting of the 4th century BC, Hylas and the nymphs.

Jewish literature
One area where we do know something about Greek penetration, and where the literature is well preserved both in the native language and in Greek, is the expanding world of the Jews. In the centuries before Christ there was a huge Greek influence and physical presence; there was a Roman physical presence from 63 BC but no profound Roman influence. Judaea was part of the Greek east, and the last historical books of the Old Testament were composed in Greek, as were the works of Philo (c. 30 BC–c. 45 AD) on religious philosophy. Josephus, one of the Jewish leaders at the time of the revolt of the Jews under Nero, wrote most of his histories in Greek, not Aramaic. Jewish settlements in Asia, in Greece and in Alexandria, the center of Hellenistic Judaic literature where the Greek Septuagint translation of the Bible was made, retained their identity and their religion; but they came to speak Greek, politically their existence was tenuous, and it is clear enough from many kinds of evidence, in spite of the later closing in of their traditions and the mistrust of foreign influence that followed the Roman destruction of the Jewish state in the 1st century AD, that they absorbed from the Greeks before the birth of Christ more than the Greeks absorbed from them. Even the Alexandrian Acts of the Jewish Martyrs recall Euripides, and the Jewish art of Palestine in the time of Christ, including its symbolism, is Greek in origin and form. Even the roots of the Book of Revelations, the Apocalypse of John, are entwined among those of other strange documents written in Greek Asia. Heaven at least is not Greek, but according to John it contains Greek architecture, and in the earliest Christian paintings it has something in common with the ideal pastoral landscapes of Theokritos, the Sicilian-Greek poet who lived in Kos and Alexandria in the 3rd century.

POST-CLASSICAL REVIVALS

For close on 2,000 years Greece lost its political independence; but the Greeks did not cease to exist. Greece itself was still a shrine of sentimental cultural pilgrimages, favored by the fastidious as a place to live, frequented by scholars and philosophers, looted by emperors. Athens became a university town. Augustus had trouble with the Athenians, but they soon settled. The last battle in which the Greek east might possibly have revived its independence was the battle of Actium (31 BC), where Antony and Cleopatra were defeated by the fleet of Octavian (Augustus). Aktion is a headland guarding the entrance to the Ambracian gulf in northwest Greece, but we know the word in its Latin form.

The Romans in Greece

Antony was "a Roman by a Roman valiantly vanquished." On the night before Actium one of the bad omens recorded is that his statue and Cleopatra's crashed down from their pedestal at the entrance to the Athenian acropolis. One may well wonder who put them there and how they came to fall. The column still stands; it had been built for a Hellenized prince, and after Actium it was reused for another Roman. The worst looting of Greece was for a huge series of interconnected squares and colonnades that spread over central Rome. Some of what went was not much loss; in a little temple in the gardens which Julius Caesar left to the Roman people, he kept what must have been the tusks of a mammoth, taken from Arcadia where they were believed to be the gigantic tusks of the mythical Kalydonian boar hunted by Herakles and Theseus among others. The people of Pallantion in Arcadia were especially favored because the Romans believed their own ancestors were Arcadian, and that the Palatine hill at Rome took its name from Pallantion.

Some of the looting was more serious. The four horses of San Marco in Venice come from the capture of Constantinople by the Crusaders in 1204 AD, but they had already traveled east, probably from the immense treasury of art that Nero looted from Greek sanctuaries. The Peiraeus was destroyed by one Roman general and rebuilt by another; in the ashes of the Roman burning, which are still easy to identify not far below street level, some wonderful Classical bronze statues have been found which must have been in store in what was called the Long Colonnade of the Peiraeus, awaiting shipment probably to Rome at the time of the fire. The Romans genuinely loved what they looted. In the 1st century BC the rich Hellenophile Titus Pomponius Atticus had an ancient temple of the Graces in his gardens by the Ilissos, between Athens and the sea. Famous temples from the countryside were reerected block by block in central Athens, including the temple of Ares from Acharnai, which was rededicated to Gaius Caesar, the young heir of Augustus, as commander of the youth of the empire and a second Ares, a new god of war.

In Athens, as elsewhere, the Romans dedicated new buildings and constructed aqueducts for the urban populations on whom they depended. The climax of Roman building was in the 2nd century AD, under Hadrian. At that time a Romanized Greek and a Hellenized Roman must have been hard to tell apart. The Romans were in Crete, where they still recruited soldiers, in Athens, in the north and in rich farms all over the Peloponnese, few of which have been excavated. We know, from the lives of Herod of Athens, of the entrepreneurs of the Spartan green marble quarries, and of Roman writers like Aulus Gellius, that official and literary worlds overlapped. There was a curious similarity of taste between the literary critics of Latin and of

The four horses of San Marco in Venice. There are some technical reasons for suggesting they may be Roman copies of Greek work, but the arguments are insecure, and the magnificent and restrained workmanship of these horses creates a strong probability that they are original Greek works of the 4th century BC.

Below The Roman emperor Hadrian, the philhellene who in Greece adopted the title "Olympian."

Bottom White marble statue of Antinous, the Asian Greek favorite of Hadrian.

Right What is left of the temple of Olympian Zeus at Athens is a very slight proportion of the enormous object which Hadrian completed. Its principal interest must always have been its overwhelming size, but it has also a certain grace, at least as we see it today.

Greek originals, and the Romans have left many traces in that vast anthology of anthologies of short Greek poems known to us as the *Greek* or *Palatine Anthology*. Hadrian himself had an antiquarian and comprehensive taste for all the arts he could recognize in the Roman empire, and the statues in his gardens at Tivoli near Rome were a sort of museum of provincial and worldwide curiosities.

But Hadrian's passion was Greek. He was in love with a youth called Antinous, a Greek from Asia Minor, who was drowned by accident in the Nile in 130 AD. Hadrian commissioned more statues of Antinous, in a variety of classic poses, in white marble, than would seem credible if so many did not still survive, 17 of them in Ostia alone. He was a boy athlete, a boy philosopher, a naked god; some of these statues were remarkable works of art, though on the whole, given the slightly plump or over-blown conventions of the period, he looks better with his clothes on. Games and prizes were instituted in his honor, and a Greek city (Antinoupolis) east of the Nile on a new road to the Red Sea was founded in his name. It was decreed he should be worshiped as a god.

It may be an important condition of Hadrian's infatuation with Greek culture that his father was called the African and his mother was from Cadiz. He came to the throne as a general, and as the adopted son of the general and emperor Trajan. It was Hadrian who dedicated the vast temple of Olympian Zeus at Athens, which had taken so many generations to build. He adopted in Greece the title of Olympian, and further east that of Zeus, no less, "the new Panhellenic Zeus." An element of practical reasoning, as well as imperial pretension and exaggerated philhellenism, went into the adoption of that title in the east. All that the Romans hoped to build on in Asia really was Greek, and to call oneself the god of all the Greeks was to claim more than local divinity. On a lesser scale, but by the same logic, the proper title of the kings of Greece down to modern times has been king of the Greeks; an inclusive title may have practical uses.

But in Greece and in Asia Minor at least, the tradition of Roman imperial Greek sculpture and architecture did not begin with Hadrian or end with him. There is a head of Trajan in Ankara which reflects the style and gravity of the Romans on the Altar of Peace of Augustus, but there is perhaps something freer about it, something more rugged about the mouth, something in common with the Greek rulers of Bactria. Hadrian's own face in the copies that survive is more interesting, but less impressive. The 3rd-century face of Emperor Caracalla from Corinth is that of a dangerous lunatic, and the representation of his father

Septimius Severus, mother-naked as Father Mars, from the Salamis aqueduct, is as ridiculous for all its classic proportions as the naked bronzes of Napoleon. But the strongest contributions of the Romans in Greek mood to the Greek world were not their own portraits. On the east coast of the Peloponnese, the ruined colossus which is what remains of a Roman lighthouse atop an island at the harbor of Prasiai (now called Porto Raphti, Tailor's Harbor, after a local name for the statue) must once have been part of a splendid landmark. The buildings of Herodes Atticus have a certain subtlety and some degree of boldness.

The Greeks and Constantinople

In 330, when Constantine refounded Byzantion (with the name Constantinople) at the gates of Asia and Europe, as the second capital city of the Roman empire, the Greek world reemerged with at least its language intact, and with a freshness of talent one would hardly have expected. There is an important and real sense in which the Roman empire never fell until the 15th century AD when in 1453 Constantinople yielded to the Turks; but in a more important sense what survived the collapse of the west and the tribal invasions was a Greek empire. The architects of Hagia Sophia (built 532–37) did not just happen to be Greeks; their scientific knowledge, their aesthetic brilliance and their courageous originality are qualities that we recognize in this meeting of Rome, Greece and the Hellenized east. The history of Greek architecture and of mathematics was continuous down to the Byzantine or Eastern Roman Empire.

This was a different world from that of Perikles and Pheidias, not only because it was imperial and immense, not exactly because it was Christian, but above all because Asia penetrated the Greeks as Greece penetrated the Romans. Paul the Silentiary, a chief usher in the court of Justinian who died about 575 AD, wrote in splendid Greek verse a description more than 1,000 lines long of Hagia Sophia, "Yield to me you Fames," he says, "daughters of the Roman Capitol; our king has overjumped that wonder." There is a great deal about Rome and a little about Egypt, but it is when he comes to dwell on the colors and textures of the stones in the great church that his poem is at its best. His feeling for the glorious mingling of so much uninhibited and rare marble is too direct and unabashed to be called exotic. The poem belongs to a well-known type, which in its remote origins goes back to Homer. There is a similar poem over 700 lines long about an allegorized picture of the universe in the winter baths at Gaza, written by a local poet. But Paul the Silentiary's poem has the crispness and freshness, as well as (inevitably) some of the limitations, of Byzantine art.

It would be hard to exaggerate the degree to which the living roots of Byzantine arts, the way in which the Byzantine Greeks saw reality, were embedded in the Alexandrian age. The art of mosaic began when patterns and fantasies of Egyptian colored glass drove out shell-encrusted grottoes in the reign of Tiberius. It was always exotic even when in cheap versions it became commonplace. Saint and emperor no longer look at all Roman; they look like Greeks, even at times like particular figures from Greek art, surviving in an Asian atmosphere.

O sages, standing in Gold's holy fire,
as in the gold mosaic of a wall.

The seriousness, the quality of the seriousness, has altered again, and yet that also has familiar roots. The suffering on these faces is not really otherworldly, it is the suffering of their kind of world, compounded of the anguish of Hellenized philosophers and their seriousness and the sufferings of slaves and peasants, which hardly altered from the 3rd century BC to the 20th AD, in Greek lands, because with or without Christianity, its social and economic causes remained the same. Not long ago a head of Homer made of colored glass was recovered at Kenchreai, the eastern port of Corinth, from a little temple of Isis that a shallow sea now covers. This panel and others had come from Egypt in about 370 AD, but the temple was destroyed by earthquake before they could be installed. They were found still crated. The head of Homer is like a Byzantine head of Christ. The Byzantine face of Christ is often terrible; can it be that its formal origins were in such portraits of Homer? Is the tragic sadness of the condemning Christ at Daphne a projection of the *Iliad*?

No doubt that is a wild and an unanswerable question, or perhaps the true answer would be so qualified by a more refined and detailed art criticism that it would no longer seem striking. There is very little striking to be known about the Greeks in mainland Greece between the earthquake at

Above Mistra, the city of monasteries near Sparta, where Cyriaco of Ancona visited the scholar Gemisthos Plethon in the 15th century and (*above right*) Cyriaco's copy of Strabo's *Geographia*, with the marginal annotations made for him by his friend the scribe Agallianos.

Opposite top The head of Homer painted on glass for a panel to decorate the temple of Isis at Kenchreai, the port of Corinth. Its suggestive likeness to Byzantine heads of Christ repays consideration; the imaginary head of Christ probably really is an adaptation of the most serious of all imagined heads in the Greek repertory, that of the poet of the *Iliad*.

Center Head of the Roman emperor Caracalla, 3rd century, from Corinth.

Bottom Head of emperor Septimius Severus, Caracalla's father, from the aqueduct at Salamis.

Kenchreai and the Renaissance. Vikings who crossed Russia to fight in the imperial bodyguard of Byzantion, against other Norse armies invading Sicily from the west, left runic carvings on a Greek marble lion at the Peiraeus. Greece itself was invaded in the 4th to 9th centuries by Vizigoths, Huns, Avars, Slavs and Bulgars. The Macedonian dynasty of Byzantine emperors (867–1025) was followed by the attacks of the Seljuk Turks from the east and the Normans from the west, and by interventions into the Byzantine world by the forces of the Crusades from the 11th to the 13th century. The French built castles, and a Cistercian monastery arose beside Stymphalos in northeast Arcadia, where Terence had died and Herakles had persecuted the birds. Italian princes built their palace in the existing buildings of the Athenian acropolis. The Ottoman Turks took Athens in 1458, five years after Constantinople. The Parthenon, then a church, became a mosque. It still has a charming painting of the Annunciation high up on the west wall, faint but traceable, and a Latin epitaph in black Gothic script, almost vanished.

The rediscovery of ancient Greece

The Renaissance came to Greece not from the west but from the east, with the last Byzantine princes, who held out for years in the castles of the Peloponnese. The Venetians held other parts of Greece, and a number of islands. There is still a letter in the Venetian state archives requesting permission for three English galleys full of marmalade to proceed homeward from Crete. But in the 15th century Gemistos Plethon, an intellectual of strong capacities born and trained at Constantinople, a scholar and a philosopher, had founded a society of humanists at Mistra, in a city of monasteries near the ruins of ancient Sparta. It was by visiting him that the Italian Cyriaco of Ancona, whose scholarly curiosity was passionate although his scholarly attainments were patchy and compared to those of Gemistos unsystematic, brought back to the west the first knowledge of the archaeological riches of Greece.

We have Cyriaco's manuscript of the Augustan geographer Strabo. If it were Pausanias, whose descriptions are so much fuller and more useful, we should be better off; but the manuscript was copied for him at Constantinople, where the study of Strabo had already revived, and the study of Pausanias never began. It is noticeable that some of the identifications of ancient with modern place-names written into the margins for him by his distinguished friend and scribe, Agallianos, are incorrect. From the east Cyriaco took his book by way of Mistra, where he copied out a missing page of the text. From the moment that he stayed with Gemistos Plethon, all his identifications are correct, and some of them were difficult to make. He visited and correctly identified site after site, often noting down inscriptions. This was Byzantine knowledge before it was Italian. Almost the same list of identifications survives in the margins of manuscripts of Ptolemy, and in one case as a separate short work, printed fortunately together with the works of Gemistos Plethon in the 16th century by a Hungarian adventurer at Amsterdam before that stray page was lost. But when Cyriaco stayed with Italian princes still ruling in northern Greece, he identified nearly all his ruins wrongly.

Now the Turks controlled almost all of the eastern and southern Mediterranean, and the reawakening of Greece was slow. A French embassy in the 17th century recorded more sculpture on the Parthenon than survives. The center of the temple was destroyed soon afterward in 1687 by an explosion in a battle between Turks and Venetians; the fatal shot was fired by a German officer of artillery. The Venetians made matters worse in an unsuccessful attempt to detach the pedimental sculptures by lowering them with ropes which snapped. The Turks returned, a smaller mosque was built in the ruins and the stones of this and of numerous other buildings began to be destroyed, sold or given away. The agent to Lord Elgin took whatever of the Parthenon he was technically capable of removing, in the first years of the 19th century.

Greece beyond Greece

The influence of the Greeks includes some bizarre adaptations of the dismembered elements of their buildings and styles. The adaptation usually says more about its own age than about the ancient world, but not every adaptation was without merit. Sometimes a new creation arose from it. Creative misunderstanding has often been more valuable than stiff imitation.

In the late Renaissance Greek themes and styles were adapted, usually through Roman interpretations, and medieval legends had an influence. The first westerners to live in Turkish Athens believed that what is now called the theater of Herodes Atticus was the school of Sokrates. Raphael's *School of Athens* in the Vatican (*above*) is a beautiful, monumental dream which owes almost nothing at all to Greek reality. Even philosophy was only a beautiful idea to him. At the Villa Rotunda, by Palladio (*far left*), an archaeological analyst of great genius has made the bones of Greek principle that underlay Roman architecture live. At Osterley House in the 18th century (*left*) the most elegant of classic themes served as restrained ornaments for a banker's house near London. Here Greece is etiolated. Only the door and the grate retain a certain vigor.

Sometimes the old motifs sprouted very wildly. The elaborate tripod from Florence of the imperial period (*below*) is a deliberate piece of virtuosity, an expression of wealth, refined skill, absolute confidence and dandyism. As a lamp, it must undoubtedly have been dramatic.

The Wedgwood pot (*below left*), made in about 1790, departs equally far from its remote originals, and this also is a deliberate piece of virtuosity and elegance; but something new is being born. Its design is more attractive than its detail. The tomb of Makriyannis at Athens (*bottom left*) commemorates a peasant general of the war of independence, a man of extraordinary integrity and a kind of moral genius. His face late in life was that of a starved wolf, and his sufferings under the monarchy intolerable. I find this monument both touching and moving. The neoclassic University of Athens (*left*) is imposing, but less interesting, too blandly academic.

Neoclassic sculpture, based traditionally on Roman copies of Greek works, includes some fearful productions as well as some fine work. The piece *above* is by John Gibson. The graceless improbability of the youth with the dog extends to his nudity, to his anatomy, to the treestump that holds him up, and of course to the delicate leaf that contains his virile member. The dog alone would be unpleasant but realistic. By contrast there is something admirable about the fireman of 1883 in a Greek type of helmet (*top right*), adapted I suppose from a neoclassic cavalry helmet.

The Greek influences in modern art are numerous and multiform.

In the ballet, neoclassicism was an early fashion, but Nijinsky in his version of the Faun in 1912 (*above right*) introduced a style much more profoundly penetrated with Greekness, and in which Greek elements were forcefully understood. It was a kind of new creation, a true rediscovery of what generations had failed to recognize. It owed a great deal to the rather new study of Greek vases. Picasso, who lived for years in the same visual and intellectual world as Nijinsky, adapted themes voraciously from absolutely anywhere, but his sense of Greek myth was always particularly powerful (*right*), and at times a lively Greek ghost haunted his drawing.

Above This battered stone lady is one of the caryatids from a late marble screen at Eleusis, brought home to Cambridge by Clarke. She suffered shipwreck off the Sussex coast, but she survived even that indignity and now lives in the Cambridge Archaeological Museum.

Above right At the end of the 17th century the Venetians took the acropolis of Athens from the Turks and held it for a short time. A German gunner with one unlucky hit exploded the gunpowder the Turks were storing in the Parthenon. Until then the Parthenon was well preserved.

After independence

By the 1800s serious archaeological exploration had begun (see Part One) and the freedom of Greece, utterly unexpected by everyone but the Greeks, was in sight (the European powers recognized Greek independence in 1832). We have noticed that when the peasants at Delphi observed foreigners scrabbling among the ancient marbles, they imagined this was a race called Milordi, the descendants of the ancient worshipers of idols, coming back now to worship the same stones. But poor and simple Greeks did respect their marble inheritance. They were horrified by Elgin, even at the time, and more so by his contemporary Edward Clarke, who removed a statue from Eleusis which they believed was responsible for the earth's fertility. They prophesied shipwreck, and it happened, off Beachy Head; but Clarke survived, and the statue is in Cambridge, in the Archaeological Museum; it cannot be properly studied or photographed without scaffolding. The peasant captain Makriyannis during the war of independence seriously upbraided one of his Greeks for selling ancient sculpture to foreigners. There was, admittedly, a plan of the first Greek parliament to restore the Parthenon in what would have been the style of the 1820s; there was even a plan to convert it into a royal palace; happily, money ran out.

It was not easy 160 years ago to define a Greek. Had the plan which ended in the open war of independence not failed in many places, it would have produced a Christian insurrection of the entire Balkans. When the war ended, the Duke of Wellington wanted the new state limited to the Peloponnese. As late as the Crimean war, most of Crete spoke Turkish just as most of Cyprus spoke Greek. The language had not died out, but it was consciously revived in the late 18th century in many villages, and revived in a missionary spirit.

In all this time Greek communities of Asia Minor played an important part. Already before independence the Greeks were expanding. They were strong, and still exist, in southern Russia. In Egypt in the 19th century they ran the vast cotton industry and the tobacco industry until they were broken by the British. The area of Cairo called Garden City was largely built for them. When Rimbaud left France he worked in Cyprus with Greeks on a building site, and when he reached Harar in Ethiopia, he lived there among the Greeks. It is astonishing how far the Greeks, without establishing a single colony, spread in 19th-century Africa. There were, and perhaps still are, sponge-diving villages in the United States where the signposts are still in Greek as well as English.

The modern history of Greece as an independent nation has been plagued by poverty until almost yesterday, by the terrible and still-unfinished story of struggles with Turkey, and by constant foreign interference. The west has played a part curiously close to Roman policy, and the Turks are not the first Asiatic power against which the Greeks have defined themselves. Physically, Athens has expanded to a terrifying size, too quickly for its center and in a bad period of architecture. Its most distinguished modern buildings are neoclassic, in the Bavarian taste, or else the gift and monument of rich Greeks from the provinces or from Egypt, as they might have been in the late 4th century. The arts however are in no way nostalgic, although things made for tourists are another matter.

LANGUAGE:THE PRINCIPAL INHERITANCE

What there was to hold on to in the long foreign domination was the Greek language, which has survived in continuous use 4,000 years. At no time has so much of so great a merit and so permanent an interest to human beings been written in so many styles in one language as in the heyday of the Athenians. That reflects a potent disturbance that can equally well be traced in other ways; it was a result of freedom and of a victorious confidence, but not a result of great power; and political impotence altered without destroying the possibilities of what we now call literature. It is hard to pick on any later generation when nothing at all one would now wish to read was written in Greek. Of course as the world mingled, literature also mingled. The neoclassic Greek writing of the Roman empire is fine and delightful; one can still read Lucian (2nd century AD) for pleasure and much of Plutarch (died c. 120) for pleasure and profit, particularly Plutarch adapted by Shakespeare, but these late Greeks covet only a limited excellence, and Shakespeare went beyond such writers without fully understanding them.

Holy books

The only writings in Greek written under the Romans that are as valuable to us as Homeric poetry, that contribute as greatly as he does to our wisdom and our delight, and that move us as much by their compassion, are also as mixed in their origins as Shakespeare is. The Gospels are also a holy book, but that is another matter. As Greek writings, on whatever traditional wisdom of this world or the next they draw, in their salt simplicity, in their

"The first battle of Athens," from a series illustrating the war of independence by a Greek peasant painter, presented to Queen Victoria. From a contemporary print. The Turkish garrison surrendered to the Greeks in 1822 but reoccupied the acropolis from 1827 to the end of the war in 1833. The results of the 1667 explosion in the Parthenon can be seen and also the fortifications strengthened against the use of cannon.

directness and courage, in their strange and lasting resonance, they can be considered as books among other books. They need more learned interpretation than they have ever had, but they are too important and too subtle to be left to the theologians. The hands of historians are at least more delicate. One of the winning qualities of these documents is that they translate almost perfectly into simple and moving language, wherever the local literature is not too elaborate to tolerate them. Luther's German version or the English Geneva Bible of 1560 and the Authorized Version of 1611 convey clearly what the original quality is.

There is certainly something moving about the end of the *Golden Ass* of the Latin writer Apuleius; it has a gravity and purity. But his style is so besprigged with flowers, his cadences are so fine and artificial, even his hunger for purity and illumination sits so oddly on the rest of his book and on its Greek origins, that only the thin shadow of the goddess Isis emerges, and we are left merely wondering about that apparently compelling cult. The *Poimandres*, the first treatise of the Corpus Hermeticum, is an Egyptian mystical work written in Greek. It belongs with a library of such works now recovered from the sands, a library more extensive than the already considerable Corpus Hermeticum. They express at their best a personal, mystical religion. *Poimandres* is still I believe the purest or most moving. They all lack the concrete, precise quality of the Gospels; they lack the directness, the simple seriousness, the wandering narrative impulse, the fatal climax. They are simply not as interesting.

The same and worse can be said of the Gospel of Thomas, and of the whole burgeoning mass of apocryphal writings that continued to be produced in Greek in the Middle Ages. These are wild, undirected, sometimes absurd. Medieval Alexander romances are better written. If I may intrude a note of autobiography, I once came across a new, deviant, and it seemed unpublished version of one of these Greek works, in the library of the Monastery of St John at Patmos. Being all too easily excited by such a discovery, I transcribed it from what I recollect as a paper manuscript of the 14th century; but it has never seemed worth the labor of publishing. These works represent an appalling decadence; yet the Gospels are still as powerful and as fresh and as invigorating as when they were written. Paul is patchier as a writer, and either contrary opinion or reverence intrudes into the assessment of his fluently barbarous Greek. One would not like to lose a line, and there are wonderful passages; he says what Greek might have seemed incapable of saying, though that is a verdict that the Greek Fathers of the Church have reversed, perhaps unfortunately. He is certainly less interesting than Homer, regret that as one may. The Gospels are alone.

But the witness of Paul to the quality of life in the Greek world of his day is fascinating. It is not only a matter of the great cities where he traveled, and of their interconnection, but also of the social organization of Hellenized Jews, and of the smaller Christian communities which were an offshoot of them. Every religious group had a social basis, just as it had in Classical Greek cities. The interconnection of guild with guild and community with community was loose-looking, but strong, and Christianity was by no means the only religion to spread in the same way, as certain flowers colonize the cuttings of railways or the ruins of buildings. The religion of the Oriental, half-Hellenized god Mithras spread at the same time as Christianity, largely through the Roman army. The victory of these universal religions was by no means immediate, although they were almost indestructible. Parts of Europe were still pagan in the 9th and 10th centuries AD, and the most intensely serious religious developments took place on the remote edges of the Hellenized world, in the Egyptian desert, in Irish and Northumbrian monasticism, and in northern Indian Buddhism.

Philosophers and poets

Until the collapse of Classical civilization, the Greeks had something intellectually serious to contribute both inside and outside Christianity. In the religious philosophy of Plato, the local basis of the Greek gods was already quite unimportant, and under the Romans the world was sufficiently visibly one place to make the victory of personal and universal religion inevitable. The greatest of all Greek religious philosophers, Plotinus, lived in the 3rd century AD. He was born in Egypt, his name was Roman and his language Greek. He taught in Rome, visited Persia and died in Campania. The metaphysical system he invented was intolerably complex and paradoxical, as most metaphysical systems are, but his writings are also most moving, and utterly original in their tone, which still speaks directly to certain temperaments to this day. His writings were edited in the early 4th century AD by a visionary but much less original pupil, Pophyry, a Greek-speaking Syrian from Palestine who had studied in Athens.

Nor did Greek poetry cease to be written. One of the greatest of all Christian medieval poets, the greatest in fact apart from Dante and Villon, was a Greek hymn writer, Romanos, who wrote in the 6th century AD. He was born in Syria, probably at Emesa (now Homs), probably to Jewish parents. He was a deacon in Beirut until he moved to Constantinople, was famous in that city, but never held any great official position. His work is very close to the Christian poetry written a little earlier in Syriac, the language of Christian Jews and of the powerful Jewish tradition in Christianity which had still not quite ceased to exist. There are dramatic and compassionate qualities in his work which go far back in Greek literary tradition, but Homer and Plato were no more than names to him, and hostile names. The richness and intensity of his work are of a quite new kind; they are a new force in Greek poetry.

Yet Mousaios, who wrote *Hero and Leander*, was his contemporary, and Ausonius, the last Classical poet in Latin, had already been dead for 100 years. The Greeks in fact had emerged from Roman domination with an empire of their own, governed by Greeks in Greek, with all the wealth and flair, and all the inherited weaknesses of the age of Alexander's successors. As a political unity the Byzantine empire was ungovernable, but as a social reality it survived and revived many times, simply because the Greeks refused to give up their identity, either as Christians or as Greeks.

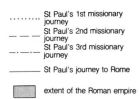

St Paul's 1st missionary journey

St Paul's 2nd missionary journey

St Paul's 3rd missionary journey

St Paul's journey to Rome

extent of the Roman empire

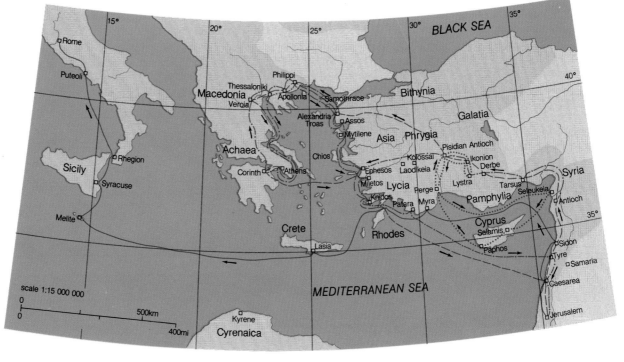

The travels of St Paul, 46–62 AD
Paul, a Roman citizen from Tarsus, had had a rabbinical education at Jerusalem but spoke fluent Greek. His missionary journeys were based on Antioch, where men first called themselves Christians. From here he traveled to the cities of Asia Minor where there were flourishing Jewish communities and where his preaching could begin in the local synagogues. It was at Pisidian Antioch that non-Jews first took an interest, whereas a good number of the local Jews opposed him. From now on Paul's mission was to non-Jews as much as to Jews, though he repeatedly returned to Jerusalem for the Jewish festivals. It was a further development when he felt the call to bring the Gospel into Europe. At Athens he spoke on the Areopagus instead of in a synagogue, and tried to do so in terms suitable to a Greek university town. His hearers were polite but unimpressed. His major effort was concentrated in a two-year stay at Ephesos. Thanks to him Asia Minor, where Christianity has been almost eliminated today, was for centuries the region where it flourished most strongly. Arrested in Jerusalem by an army officer to save him from mob violence, he was kept in captivity by the governor of Judaea for two years before his appeal to the emperor took him to his final destination at Rome. Here he continued to teach and send letters to Christians in Greece and Asia Minor until his execution.

Modern writers

In 1453, when the last of the old Greek historians rode around the walls of Constantinople with the last emperor a few hours before the city fell to the Turks, and in full consciousness of that inevitable event, he thought of the whole weight of Greece and of Rome as too heavy a burden for one man's shoulders.

This historian was George Phrantzes; he wrote in old age, as a monk in Corfu, where sculpture of the 6th century BC lay in the fields. We know that on the night on which the city fell Cyriaco of Ancona was reading from Livy to the sultan in his tent below the walls. But it was not of course the whole of Greece and Rome that fell on one night, and the sultan is not remembered like Livy's heroes. Greek in verse and in prose persisted. The *Erotokritos*, the Cretan national poem, was written around the turn of the 16th and 17th centuries. It is a romance under heavy Venetian influence, but in its verse, in its dialect and spirit, is purely Cretan Greek. Until the present generation, Cretan shepherds knew it by heart and sang it in the mountains. In prose, at the end of the reign of Henry VIII of England, a refugee from Corfu, who was known as Nicander Nucius and fought in a Greek regiment for Henry against the Scots, wrote an account of Britain, Ireland and much of Europe which by no means disgraces its lineage among Greek histories. It records a speech before battle in some dynastic war, by a Greek to Greeks fighting in France, that would not have displeased Thucydides.

Not unnaturally, the best written Greek under the Turks was composed in a popular, direct style, a salted and expressive peasant language. It was the Greece of Edward Lear's watercolors. The memoirs of Makriyannis are the supreme example of how impressive a peasant language can be; he commanded men in the war of independence, and his writings are the first immense achievement of independent Greece. The naive but fresh and very talented paintings of Theophilos of Mytilene in Lesbos, who was still at work in this century, belong spiritually to the same world. But not all Greeks were peasants; an official, classicizing language had survived at Constantinople and through the Church. Its stranglehold on the official life of the country and on its refined literature has only recently been broken. It was a stiff, annoying officialese, but in its more sinuous and subtle spoken form it had its triumphs. In prose it was capable of ironies, and the anonymous, humorous 19th-century memoirs of an Asian Greek called *The Military Life* could not have been written as effectively in any other style.

In verse, this style is an element in the startling originality of Constantine Kavafis (1863–1933), the Alexandrian poet. His family came from Constantinople and it had been rich, but Kavafis worked as a clerk in the irrigation department of the British administration in Egypt. His poetry is often a commentary on stories taken from the late Classical history of the Greeks. He was extremely widely read, homosexual, passionate, and politically very bitter. Among his favorite writings were Oscar Wilde's book on socialism and Gibbon's *Decline and Fall*. As a writer and as a personality he was Greek to the bone; he was also utterly modern. The texture of his language, over which an ironic light plays, is perhaps untranslatable. His rhythms are impossible to imitate and his bite is hard to forget.

But the greatest of modern Greek writers is certainly George Seferis (1900–71), one of the most powerful and most moving and also one of the wisest poets of the 20th century, who ranks with Pasternak. He was born in Smyrna, and came to Athens as a refugee at the time of the Turkish destruction of Greek Asia. His education and reading were immensely wide even for a professional diplomat who was also a great poet. His understanding of the modern Greek language in all its behavior and history was deeper than anyone else's has ever been, but his writing embodied that understanding in ways that are not obvious; it can be sensed only in a complete rightness, an inevitability of words and phrases. In his writings the modern language came of age. It is as strong as it ever was, as capable of discussing anything whatever, as it was in the time of Aristophanes, as fine in its texture, as modern.

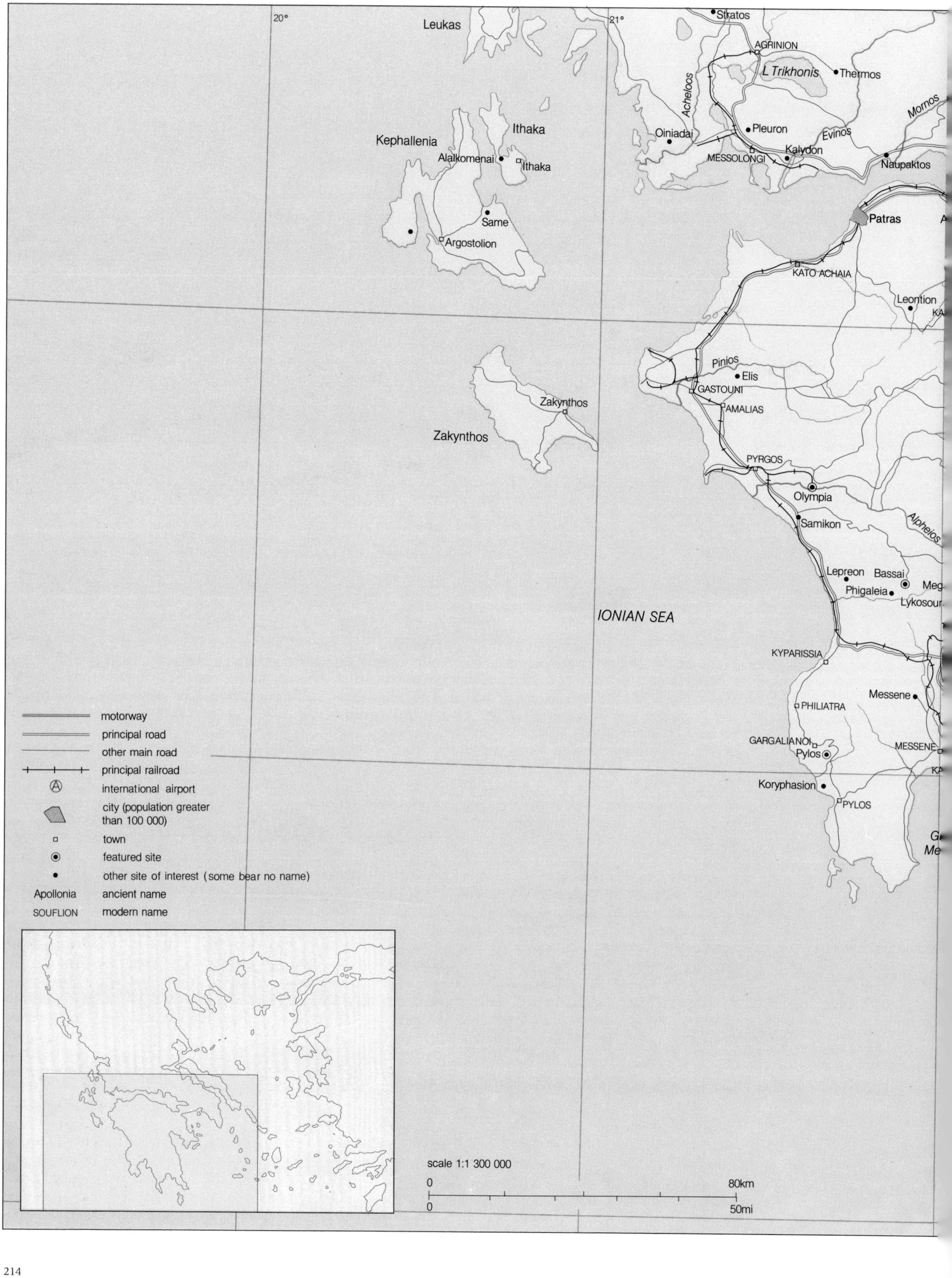

20°   Leukas   21°   • Stratos

                                                    AGRINION
                                                    L Trikhonis   • Thermos

                          Ithaka   Mornos

Kephallenia   Oiniadai   • Pleuron   Evinos
        Alalkomenai   □ Ithaka   Kalydon
                                                 MESSOLONGI   • Naupaktos

                • Same
          □ Argostolion   Patras

                                                 □ KATO ACHAIA

                                                           Leontion

                                        Pinios
                                             • Elis
                          Zakynthos   GASTOUNI
                                       AMALIAS
Zakynthos

                                       PYRGOS
                                             • Olympia

                                       • Samikon   Alpheios

                                       Lepreon Bassai
                                       Phigaleia Meg
                                             Lykosour

              IONIAN SEA

                                       KYPARISSIA

                                       PHILIATRA   Messene

                                       GARGALIANOI
motorway   Pylos   MESSENE
principal road
other main road   Koryphasion
principal railroad   □ PYLOS
international airport
city (population greater   G
than 100 000)   Me
town
featured site
other site of interest (some bear no name)

Apollonia   ancient name
SOUFLION   modern name

scale 1:1 300 000

0   80km

0   50mi

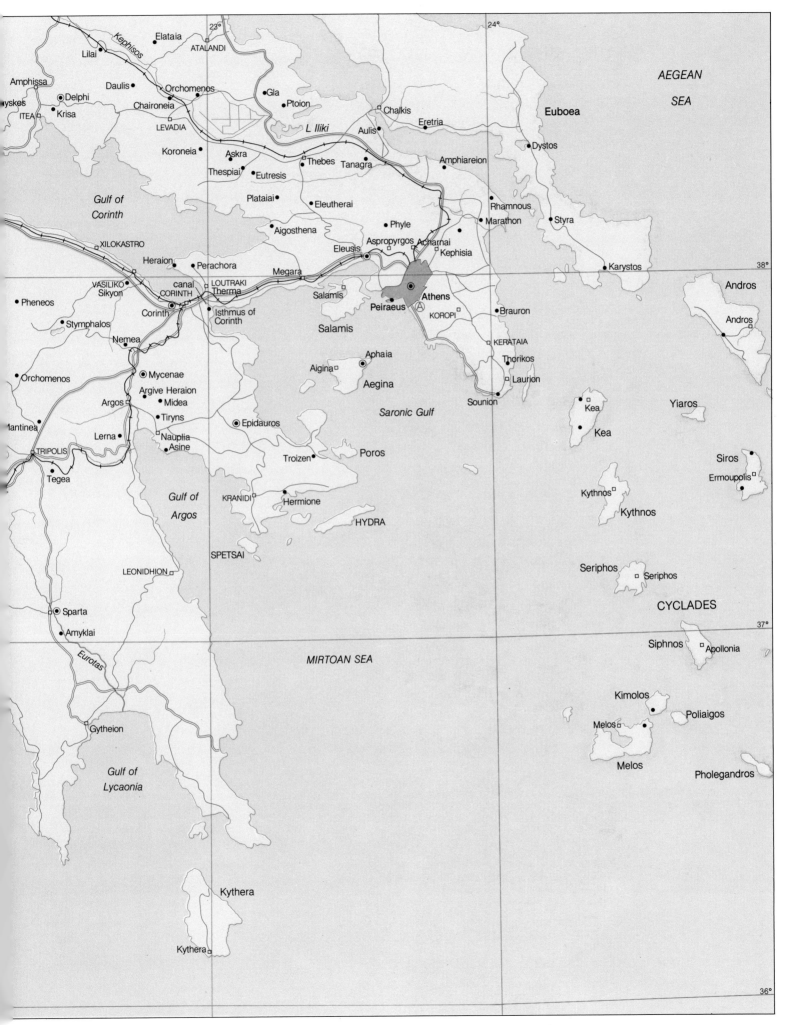

Elataia
Kephisos
Lilai
ATALANDI
Amphissa
Daulis
Orchomenos
·yskes
Delphi
Chaironeia
Gla
ITEA
Krisa
Ptoion
LEVADIA
Chalkis
Euboea
Eretria
Koroneia
Aulis
L Iliki
Dystos
Askra
Thebes
Tanagra
Thespiai
Eutresis
Amphiareion
Gulf of
Corinth
Plataiai
Eleutherai
Rhamnous
Aigosthena
Phyle
Marathon
Styra
Eleusis
Aspropyrgos
Acharnai
XILOKASTRO
Heraion
Perachora
Megara
Kephisia
Karystos
VASILIKO
canal
LOUTRAKI
Salamis
Andros
Sikyon
CORINTH
Therma
Athens
Pheneos
Corinth
Isthmus of
Peiraeus
Andros
Stymphalos
Corinth
Salamis
KOROPI
Brauron
Nemea
Aphaia
KERATAIA
Orchomenos
Mycenae
Aigina
Aegina
Thorikos
Argive Heraion
Laurion
Argos
Midea
Yiaros
Mantinea
Tiryns
Sounion
Kea
Saronic Gulf
Kea
Lerna
Nauplia
TRIPOLIS
Asine
Epidauros
Siros
Tegea
Poros
Ermoupolis
Troizen
Kythnos
Gulf of
KRANIDI
Argos
Hermione
Kythnos
HYDRA
Seriphos
SPETSAI
Seriphos
LEONIDHION
CYCLADES
Sparta
Amyklai
Siphnos
Apollonia
MIRTOAN SEA
Eurotas
Kimolos
Poliaigos
Melos
Gytheion
Melos
Gulf of
Lycaonia
Melos
Pholegandros

Kythera

Kythera

AEGEAN

SEA

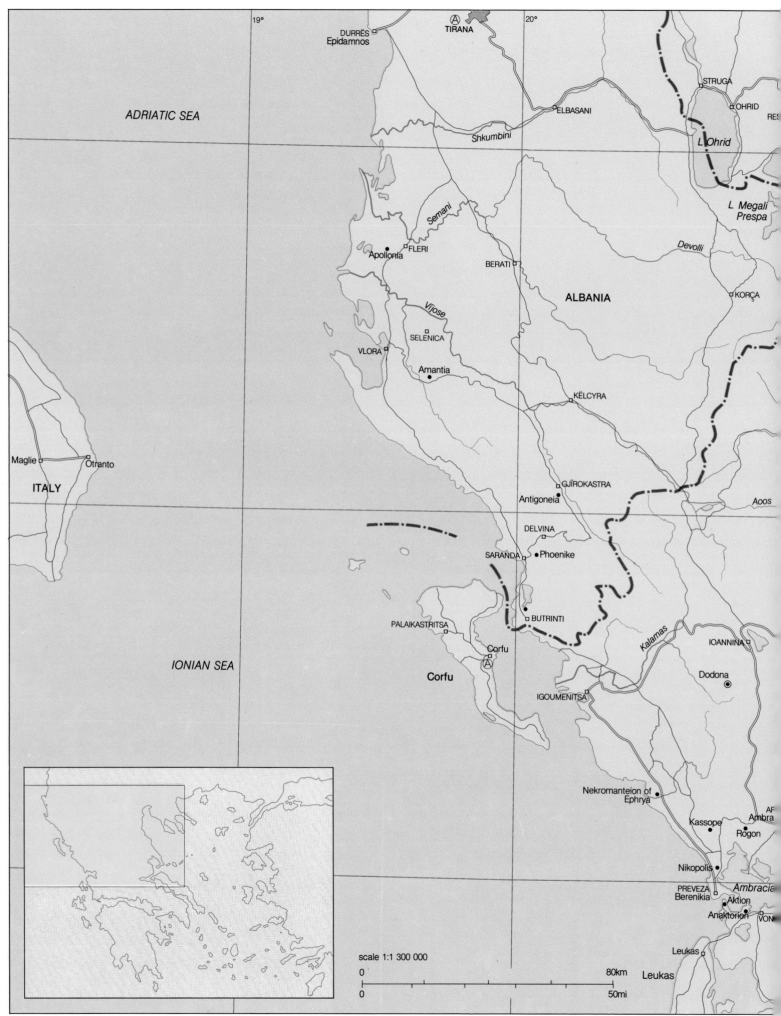

19°

20°

DURRÉS
Epidamnos

TIRANA

STRUGA

OHRID

ELBASANI

RES

Shkumbini

L Ohrid

ADRIATIC SEA

*L Megali
Prespa*

Semani

Devolli

FLERI
Apollonia

BERATI

ALBANIA

KORÇA

Vjose

SELENICA

VLORA

Amantia

KËLCYRA

Maglie
Otranto

ITALY

GJÏROKASTRA

Antigoneia

Aoos

DELVINA

SARANDA
Phoenike

PALAIKASTRITSA

BUTRINTI

Kalamas

IOANNINA

Corfu

IONIAN SEA

Corfu

Dodona

IGOUMENITSA

Nekromanteion of
Ephyra

Kassope
Ambra
Rogon
AF

Nikopolis

PREVEZA
Berenikia

Ambracia

Aktion

Anaktorion
VON

Leukas

scale 1:1 300 000

0   80km

Leukas

0   50mi

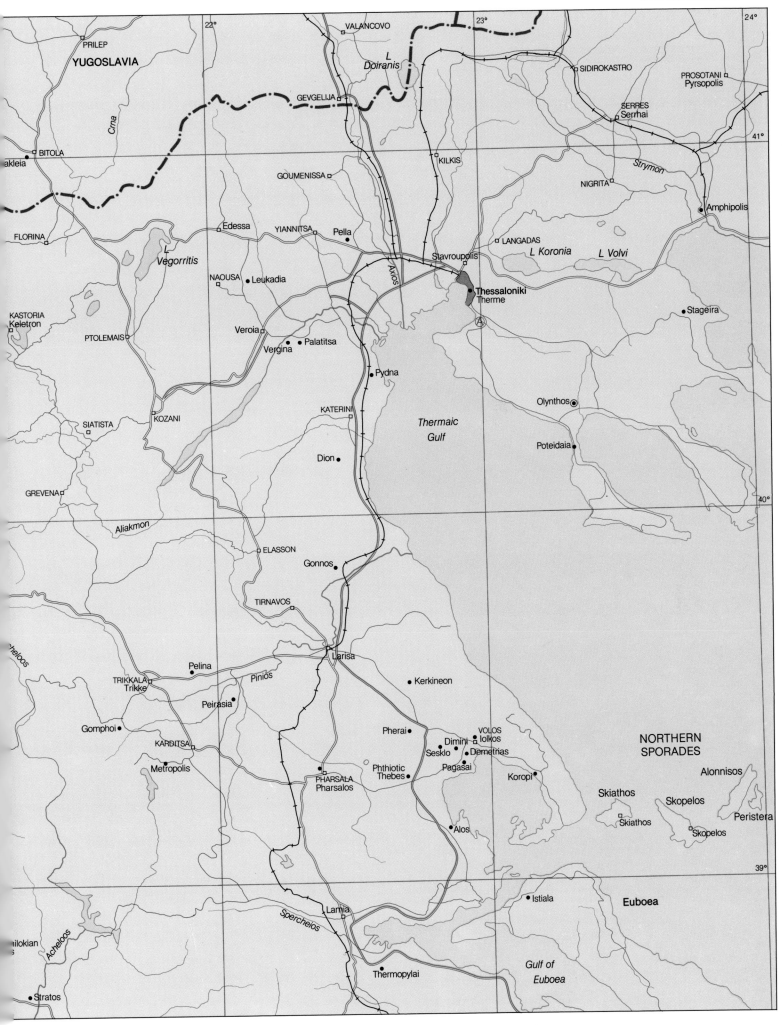

YUGOSLAVIA

PRILEP

VALANCOVO

L Doiranis

GEVGELIJA

SIDIROKASTRO

PROSOTANI
Pyrsopolis

BITOLA

Crna

akleia

KILKIS

SERRES
Serrhai

Strymon

FLORINA

GOUMENISSA

NIGRITA

Amphipolis

Edessa

YIANNITSA

Pella

LANGADAS

L Koronia

L Volvi

L Vegorritis

Stavroupolis

Thessaloniki
Therme

NAOUSA

Leukadia

Axios

Stageira

KASTORIA
Keletron

Veroia

PTOLEMAIS

Vergina

Palatitsa

Olynthos

Pydna

KATERINI

Thermaic Gulf

Poteidaia

SIATISTA

KOZANI

Dion

GREVENA

Aliakmon

ELASSON

Gonnos

TIRNAVOS

Pelina

Larisa

Kerkineon

TRIKKALA
Trikke

Pinios

Peirasia

**NORTHERN
SPORADES**

Gomphoi

Pherai

VOLOS
Iolkos

Alonnisos

KARDITSA

Dimini

Demetrias

Metropolis

Sesklo

Pagasai

Koropi

Skopelos

PHARSALA
Pharsalos

Phthiotic
Thebes

Skiathos

Peristera

Skiathos

Skopelos

Alos

Acheloos

ilokian

Spercheios

Lamia

Istiala

Euboea

Stratos

Thermopylai

*Gulf of
Euboea*

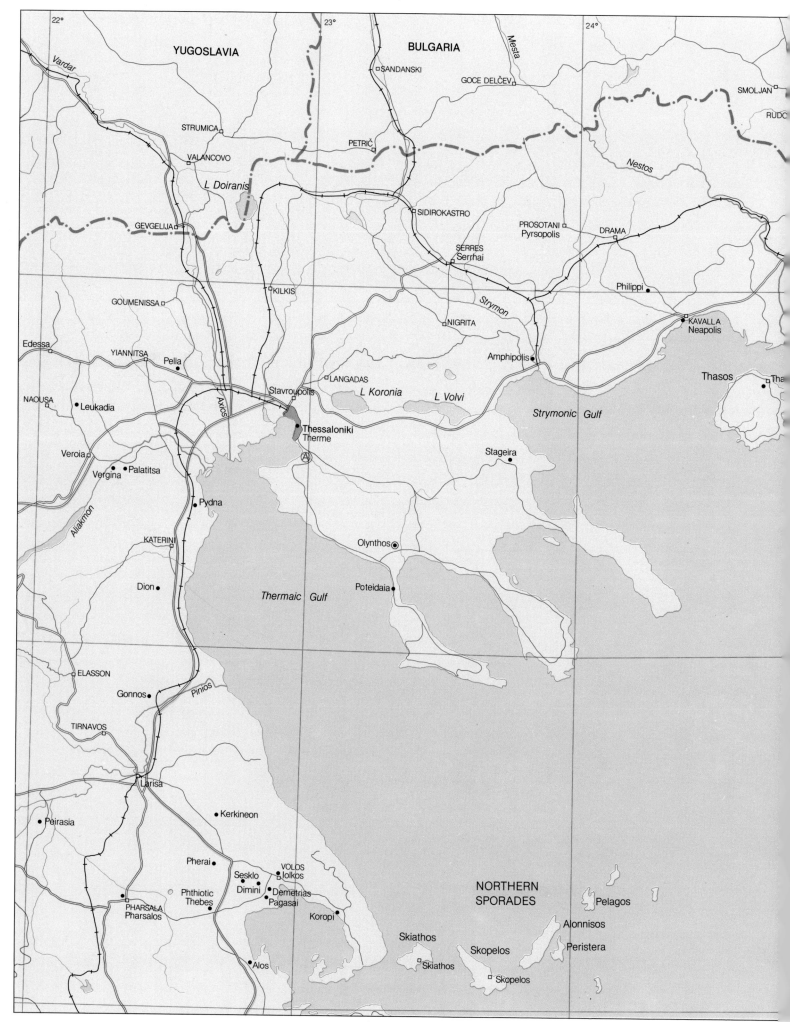

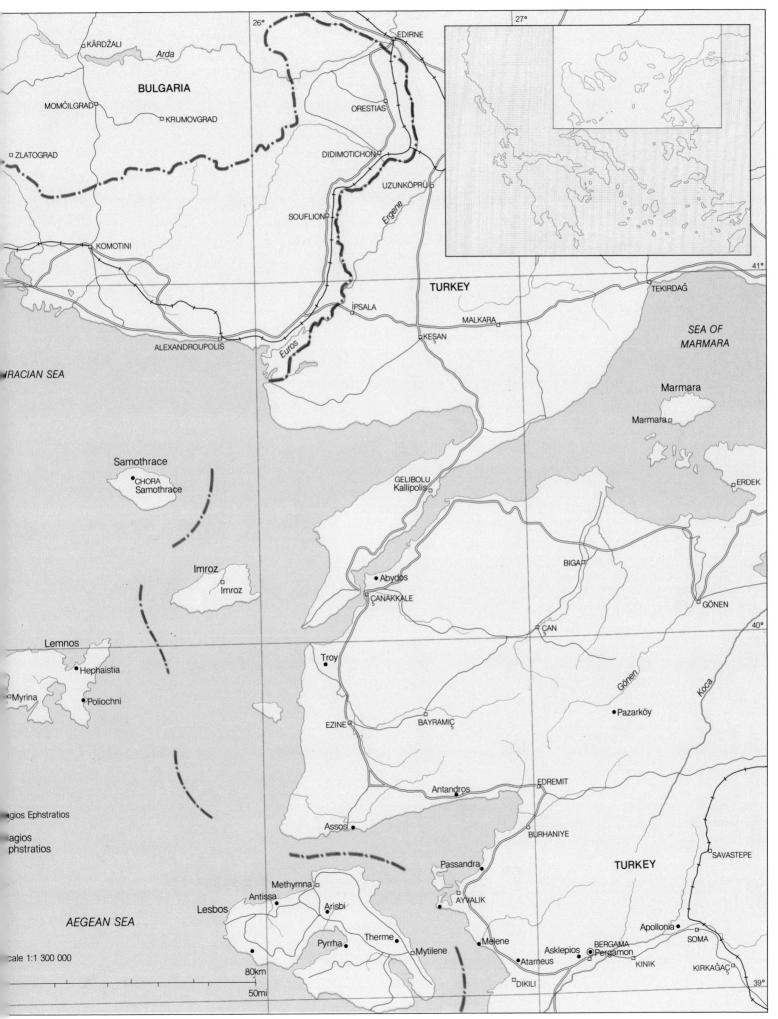

KÂRDŽALI

Arda

BULGARIA

EDIRNE

26°

27°

MOMČILGRAD

ORESTIAS

KRUMOVGRAD

DIDIMOTICHON

ZLATOGRAD

UZUNKÖPRÜ

Ergene

SOUFLION

41°

KOMOTINI

TURKEY

TEKIRDAĞ

İPSALA

SEA OF MARMARA

MALKARA

KEŞAN

ALEXANDROUPOLIS

Euros

THRACIAN SEA

Marmara

Marmara

ERDEK

Samothrace

•CHORA
Samothrace

GELIBOLU
Kallipolis

Imroz

BIGA

•Abydos

GÖNEN

ÇANAKKALE

ÇAN

40°

Imroz

Lemnos

•Hephaistia

Troy

Gönen

Koca

•Myrina

•Poliochni

•Pazarköy

EZINE

BAYRAMIÇ

agios Ephstratios

EDREMIT

agios
phstratios

•Antandros

BURHANIYE

Assos •

•Passandra

SAVASTEPE

Methymna

TURKEY

Antissa

Lesbos

Arisbi

•AYVALIK

AEGEAN SEA

•Melene

Apollonia •

Pyrrha

Therme

Asklepios

SOMA

Mytilene

BERGAMA
Pergamon

Scale 1:1 300 000

•Atarneus

KINIK

KIRKAĞAÇ

80km

DIKILI

39°

50mi

219

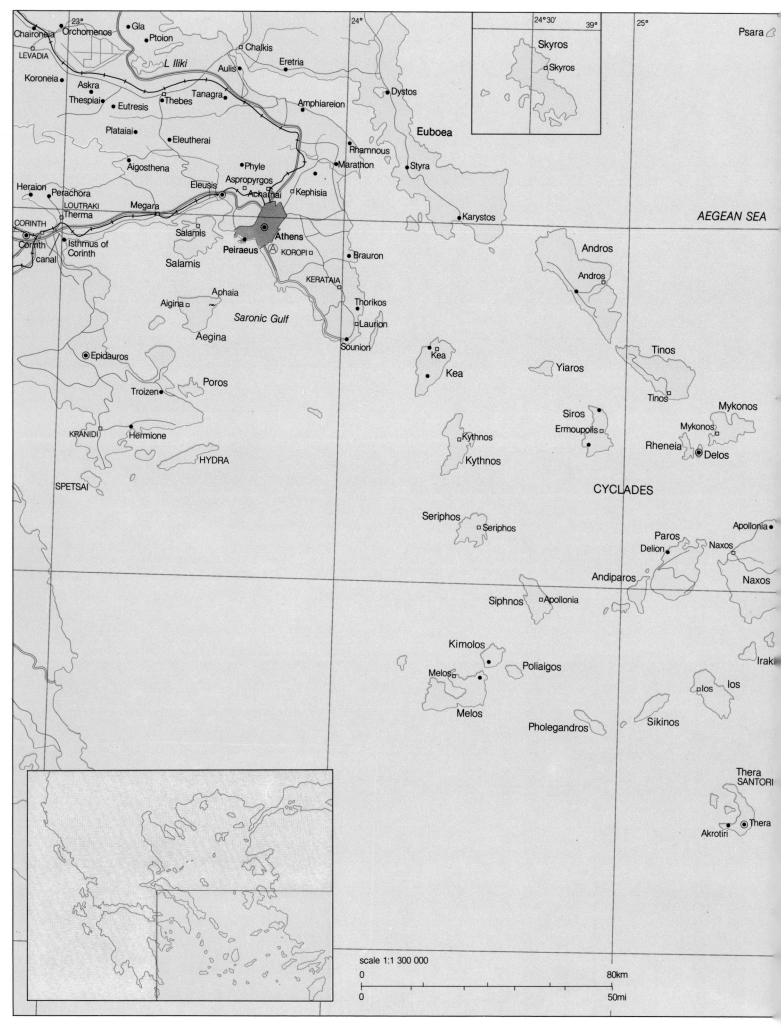

Psara

23°

Chaironeia
Orchomenos
Gla
Ptoion
LEVADIA
L Iliki
Chalkis
Eretria
Koroneia
Askra
Aulis
Thespiai
Eutresis
Tanagra
Thebes
Amphiareion
Plataiai
Eleutherai
Aigosthena
Phyle
Rhamnous
Heraion
Perachora
Eleusis
Aspropyrgos
Marathon
LOUTRAKI
Therma
Megara
Achainai
Kephisia
CORINTH
Salamis
Athens
Brauron
Corinth
Isthmus of
Corinth
KOROPI
canal
Salamis
Peiraeus
KERATAIA
Karystos
Aphaia
Thorikos
Aigina
Aegina
Laurion
Sounion

Euboea
Dystos
Styra

24°

24°30'   39°

Skyros
Skyros

25°

AEGEAN SEA

Andros
Andros

Tinos
Tinos

Epidauros

Poros
Troizen

KRANIDI
Hermione

HYDRA

SPETSAI

Saronic Gulf

Kea
Kea

Yiaros

Siros
Ermoupolis

Kythnos
Kythnos

Mykonos
Mykonos
Rheneia
Delos

CYCLADES

Seriphos
Seriphos

Paros
Delion
Andiparos
Naxos
Naxos

Apollonia

Siphnos
Apollonia

Kimolos
Poliaigos
Melos
Melos
Pholegandros

Iraki

Ios
Ios

Sikinos

Thera
SANTORI
Akrotiri
Thera

scale 1:1 300 000

0   80km

0   50mi

220

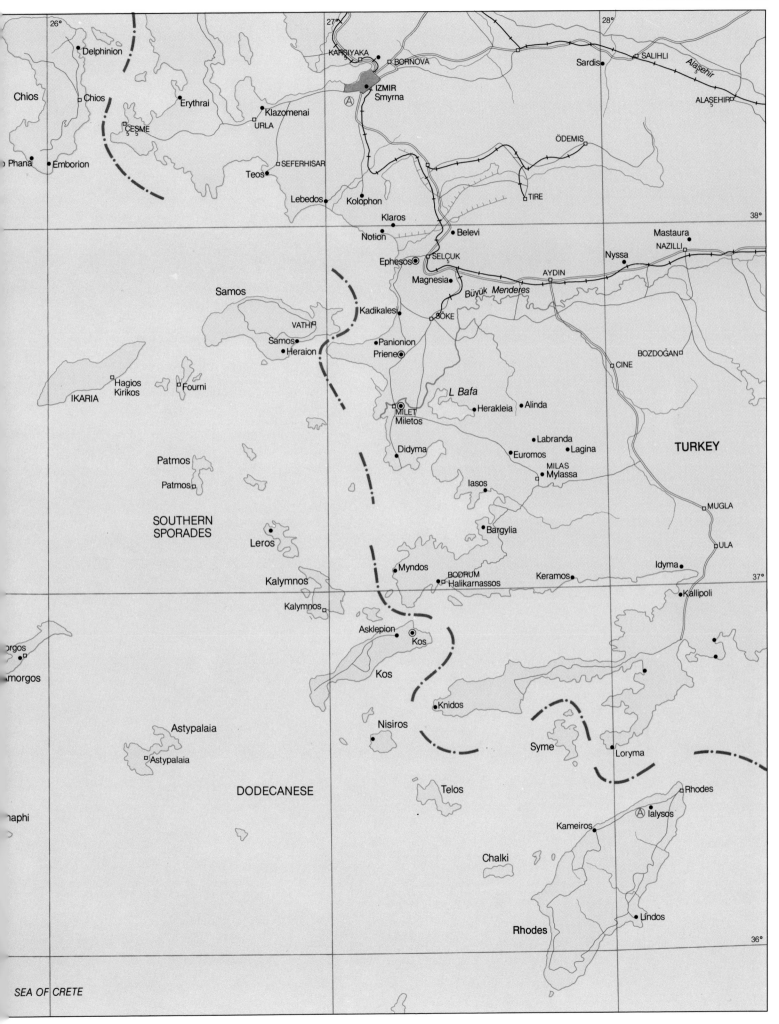

26°

Delphinion

Chios

Chios

Erythrai

Phana Emborion

ÇEŞME
5 5

Klazomenai

URLA

Teos

SEFERHISAR

Lebedos Kolophon

Klaros

Notion

27°

KARŞIYAKA

BORNOVA

IZMIR
Smyrna

Belevi

ÖDEMİŞ

TIRE

28°

Sardis

SALIHLI

Alaşehir

ALAŞEHIR
5

38°

Ephesos SELÇUK

Magnesia

Büyük Menderes

AYDIN

Mastaura

NAZILLI

Nyssa

Samos

Kadikalesi

VATHI

Samos Panionion

Heraion Priene

SÖKE

BOZDOĞAN

CINE

Hagios
Kirikos

Fourni

IKARIA

L Bafa

MILET
Miletos

Herakleia Alinda

Labranda

TURKEY

Patmos

Didyma

Euromos Lagina

MILAS
Mylassa

Patmos

Iasos

SOUTHERN
SPORADES

Leros

Bargylia

MUĞLA

ULA

Myndos

Kalymnos

BODRUM
Halikarnassos

Keramos

Idyma

37°

Kalymnos

Kállipoli

orgos

morgos

Asklepion

Kos

Kos

Knidos

Astypalaia

Nisiros

Syme

Loryma

Astypalaia

DODECANESE

Telos

Rhodes

aphi

Ialysos

Kameiros

Chalki

Lindos

Rhodes

36°

SEA OF CRETE

221

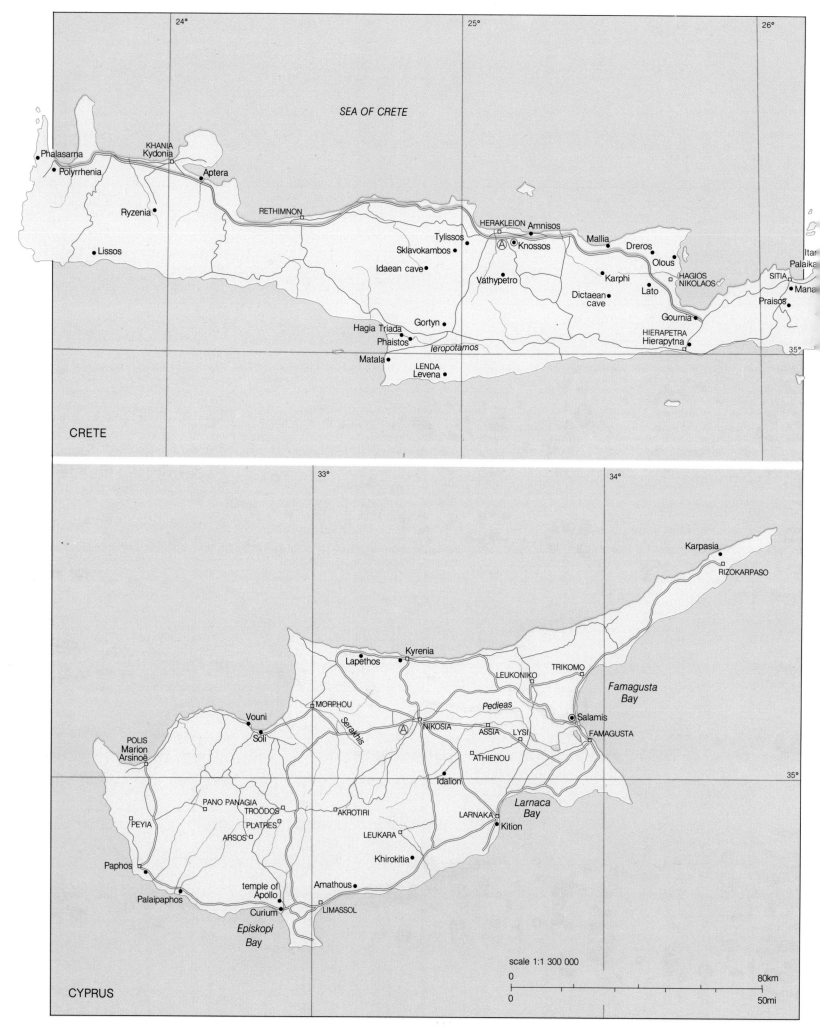

CRETE

Phalasarna
Polyrrhenia
KHANIA
Kydonia
Aptera
Ryzenia
Lissos
SEA OF CRETE
RETHIMNON
Tylissos
Sklavokambos
Idaean cave
HERAKLEION Amnisos
Knossos
Vathypetro
Mallia
Dreros
Olous
Karphi
HAGIOS NIKOLAOS
Dictaean cave
Lato
Gournia
Praisos
SITIA
Mana
Palaika
Itar
HIERAPETRA
Hierapytna
Hagia Triada
Gortyn
Phaistos
Ieropotamos
Matala
LENDA
Levena

CYPRUS

Karpasia
RIZOKARPASO
Lapethos
Kyrenia
TRIKOMO
LEUKONIKO
Famagusta Bay
Vouni
MORPHOU
Pedieas
Serakhis
NIKOSIA
Salamis
ASSIA
LYSI
FAMAGUSTA
POLIS
Marion
Arsinoë
Soli
ATHIENOU
Idalion
Larnaca Bay
PANO PANAGIA
TROÖDOS
AKROTIRI
LARNAKA
PEYIA
PLATRES
LEUKARA
Kition
ARSOS
Khirokitia
Paphos
Amathous
temple of Apollo
Palaipaphos
Curium
LIMASSOL
Episkopi Bay

scale 1:1 300 000
0 .... 80km
0 .... 50mi

GLOSSARY

Wherever possible in this book we have avoided using specialized terms. A certain number, for which there was not sufficient space in the text for an explanation, are treated in this Glossary.

Academy A training ground for naked exercise outside Athens, a pleasant place with grass, trees and decorative and sacred buildings. It was made famous by Sokrates and above all by Plato, whose school of philosophy was centered there. The site has been identified, but is now built over.

Achaemenid empire The classical Persian empire.

agora The central area of a city or small town, usually a square or rectangle, with colonnades, public and sacred buildings. Under the Romans one side was a vast official "basilica" and the rest colonnades. Hence monastic cloisters, college quadrangles, the squares of provincial towns.

akroterion Terracotta or marble ornament on the pinnacle or the edge of the roof of a building.

amphora Two-handled ("two-eared") pot for transporting oil, wine etc. Usually long, often with a sharp end, ideal for tying on a mule's or donkey's back, and easy to handle. The same word is used for smaller, finer vessels of similar shape.

beehive tomb Like a dome or bubble of stone with an alley or approach and great door, in which the rich or noble Bronze Age dead were buried. Sometimes enormous, perfectly proportioned, strangely echoing.

black-figure Pottery with black figures on a tan ground.

caryatid Column to support a porch or a colonnade, in the form of a free-standing woman bearing it on her head.

cavea The semicircle of stone benches rising in tiers in which the audience of an ancient theater sat in the open air.

cella The inner room of a temple where the principal statue stood.

centaur Creature with a human head and arms and upper body and the four legs and lower body of a horse.

city-state A sovereign state with a unified government based on one single town or city, and controlling its surrounding territories, great or small. Such a city or state might be artificially created (Megalopolis in Arcadia or Messene in Messenia) and its territory might be enormous (Attica or Laconia) or small (Plataiai in Greece or Megara Hyblaia in Sicily).

Corinthian column Its capital is carved with an elaborate cluster of stone foliage (Hellenistic). The column is fluted.

Cynics Philosophic deriders of worldly values who cultivated rough dress and poverty. The Christians adopted their arguments against the gods and some of their moral and social attitudes.

deme A community, a village or small town in Attica, was called a deme. *Demos* means people with a capital *P*. The local communities retained a basic political and social importance well into the 5th century.

Dioskouroi The twin brothers Kastor the athlete and Polydeukes the boxer (the Roman Pollux). Their parentage was half-human, half-divine. They were worshiped particularly in Sparta and its African colonies. The name means the youths who are sons of Zeus.

Doric column The plainest of plain capitals, and a simple column.

Eleusinian mysteries A symbolic or sacramental initiation that brought the Athenians, and all Greeks if they underwent it, into a special relation with the gods, and which offered mysterious happiness in the afterlife.

The physical fact at the center of the mysteries was the growth of wheat. Eleusis was a sanctuary of the earth mother as corn goddess. It had a cave which led to the Underworld.

Epicureans The followers of Epicurus, cultivating a philosophy of pleasure, withdrawal from the world, friendship and privacy. By limiting fear, hope and desire a man attains to peace. Christianity owes something to this philosophy.

frieze A long band of relief sculpture decorating the upper stonework of a temple.

geometric A style of decoration with repeated geometric motifs, flourishing in Greece in the 8th century BC and earlier. Horse, bird and man, scenes of burial, processions and battles and shipwrecks were introduced little by little in the centuries of this style, but purely geometric art at its best was almost more impressive. We treat it as a style of decorated pottery, but it was used also for wall-painting and for textiles.

Gorgon A grotesque female figure with snake hair, so horrid that the sight of her might turn a man to stone. Most representations of her are rather jollier than this legend suggests.

Hellespont The narrow sea channel that divides Europe from Asia Minor at the northeast corner of the Mediterranean. Both Troy and Byzantion owed their importance to their situation here at the entrance to the Black Sea.

herm A tall block of stone with the head of a god and an erect sexual organ as its only features.

hydria Water-pot.

Indo-European This word was used in the 19th century of an original common language from which Indian and European languages were descended; then of the people who must have spoken it, and of their "folk-wanderings." Some enthusiastic racialists believed that the Germans and the Afghan Pathans were its purest descendants. Today we are still forced to speak of an Indo-European family of languages, but the historical foundation for their development and separation remains obscure.

Ionic column Elegantly designed column of east Greek origin with capital like a pair of formalized ram's horns.

Isthmus The neck of land that joins southern Greece to the mass of Europe, cut today by the Corinth canal.

kalyx-krater A mixing bowl shaped like a deep cup.

koine The simplified Greek speech, without literary ambition or special dialect, spoken and written all over the ancient world in which Greek became a universal language.

kore The female equivalent of a kouros.

kouros A youth; a male nude statue of a youth, of a formal archaic shape which developed in Greece from the 7th century BC to the 5th. It may represent a god, an athlete, a dead man, or it may be simply an offering to a god.

krater A mixing bowl for wine and water, sometimes fitted with a strainer.

Lapith Member of a mythical tribe of persons, superhuman only by being legendary. They fought a famous fight with the centaurs, who became drunken and lecherous at a Lapith wedding.

lekythos A small Athenian oil-pot used by athletes.

Levant The eastern end of the Mediterranean, where the sun rises; the coast from Byzantion (Istanbul) to Jaffa.

Linear A The earlier of the two Bronze Age Greek scripts, not yet decoded but in some ways similar to Linear B.

Linear B The script of the Mycenaeans in the Bronze Age. It has been decoded and can be read as an early form of the Greek language. The script is not alphabetical but syllabic: that is, each sign denotes not a single sound but a syllable.

metope A single slab of relief sculpture. Used in a series, separated from each other by plainer slabs with a design of vertical lines, around a temple just below its roof.

odeion A concert hall like a covered theater. It always has a roof.

omphalos The navel of the earth, the center of the world, marked by a stone shaped like a Christmas pudding, decorated by a network of woolen ribbons. It was at Delphi.

orchestra The dancing area for the chorus between the stage and the audience in an ancient theater.

Orientalizing The style of Greek art in the early archaic period that adopted innumerable decorative and animal motifs from the east.

ostracism An Athenian system for taking the heat out of politics by a vote of the people whether an exile should take place, and if so, then a second vote of the people to decide who should be exiled.

palaestra An open-air courtyard, surrounded by a colonnade, used as a wrestling school.

palmette A flat, formalized sprouting plant or bud in the shape of a heart upside down.

Panathenaic festival A state festival of Athene at Athens, publicly and lavishly celebrated with a procession, games and prizes and a huge sacrifice with the distribution of the meat.

paraskenia The side wings of the stone embellishments of the stage in a theater.

parodos Actors' entrance in an ancient theater used by the chorus.

peristyle The screen of pillars surrounding a temple, forming colonnades along its sides.

red-figure Pottery with tan figures on a black ground.

satrap The local ruler of a province of the classical Persian empire.

satyr Half-human, half-animal figure with divine powers, from the wilderness at the edges of the world. Satyrs had snub-noses, pricked ears, strong instincts, tails, a pair of legs and nearly perpetual erections.

Seleucid empire The empire in Asia of the family of Seleukos, one of the generals of Alexander the Great and his principal successor in the east.

shaft grave A burial place in a deep narrow pit, used in the early Bronze Age. At Mycenae there was a circle of these graves, marked probably by stone markers.

silk road The overland route to China from the west, following roughly what are now the southern borders of the Soviet Union.

sophists The teachers of persuasive oratory and of paradoxical philosophy who shocked and excited the Athenians in the last 40 years of the 5th century BC and in the 4th.

stoa A colonnade for any civil or commercial purpose, usually with rooms behind it, sometimes with two stories.

Stoics Philosophers of the stiff upper lip and the paradoxical extremes of virtuous atheism. Their logic and their moral arguments are of inspiring interest, but they were irritating people, as Horace makes clear.

temenos The enclosure of a sanctuary, the holy ground belonging to the god and governed by special rules.

LIST OF ILLUSTRATIONS

All site plans by Oxford Illustrators. All maps by Lovell Johns, Oxford. Abbreviations: t = top, tl = top left, tr = top right, c = center, b = bottom etc.; Ash = Ashmolean Museum, Oxford; BM = British Museum, London; DAI = Deutsches Archäologisches Institut; DAFA = Délégation Archéologique Française en Afghanistan; EA = Ekdotike Athenon, Athens; JF = John Fuller, Cambridge; MC = Marion Cox, Abingdon; MH = Michael Holford, Loughton; Nat = National Archaeological Museum, Athens; OI = Oxford Illustrators, Oxford; SH = Sonia Halliday, Weston Turville, Bucks.; ST = Spyros Tsardavoglou, Athens

page
2–5. Title-page freely adapted from vase painting by Hieron: Staatliche Museum, West Berlin. MC.
8–9. Chronological table: JF.
11. Drawing freely adapted from cup by the Ambrosios Painter from Orvieto: Museum of Fine Arts, Boston, Mass., Arts 01.8024. MC.
13t. Greek peasant with sack: Magnum, Paris (photo Constantine Manos).
13b. Map of Europe, Asia and Africa from *Geographia Vetus*, Paris, 1630: Elsevier Archives.
18–19. Landscape with donkey: Magnum, Paris (photo Constantine Manos).
22l. Frieze from propylon of the sanctuary of the Great Gods at Samothrace: Louvre, Paris.
23t. Drawing by Piranesi of temple of "Poseidon" (actually Hera) at Paestum, 1778: Ash.
23b. Drawing by Cyriaco of Ancona (15th century) of frieze from Samothrace: Bodleian Library, Oxford (photo Warburg Institute, London).
25. Drawings from *Antiquities of Athens* by Stuart and Revett, vol. 3. View of the Theseion, elevation of the east front: BM.
26t. Portrait of Sir Arthur Evans by Sir W. B. Richmond, 1907: Ash.
26bl. Heinrich Schliemann: Mansell Collection, London.
26br. Mrs Schliemann: Elsevier Archives.
27. Interior of the treasury of Atreus as seen by Edward Dodwell in *A Classical and Topographical Tour through Greece during 1801, 1805 and 1806*, London, 1819: Ash.
28. Sir Arthur Evans at Knossos with Theodore Fyfe and Duncan Mackenzie during restoration: Ash.
29. Drawing freely adapted from Mycenaean IIIb krater: BM. MC.
30. Alabastron painted with two griffins feeding their young, c. 1150 BC, from Lefkandi: Chalkis Museum (photo British School of Archaeology, Athens, courtesy of M. Popham).
31l and r. Linear A tablets from Hagia Triada, c. 1450 BC: Herakleion Museum (photo EA).
31b. Linear B tablet from Knossos: Hirmer Fotoarchiv, Munich.
32. Marine-style vase from Palaikastro, eastern Crete, c. 1500–1450: Herakleion Museum (JF).
33t. Golden cup from tholos tomb at Vapheio, c. 1500–1450: Nat (photo EA).
33c. Gold ring from Tiryns, c. 15th century BC: Nat (photo EA).
33b. Gaming board from Knossos: Herakleion Museum (photo EA).
34t. Bronze inlaid dagger from Shaft Grave V at Mycenae, 1500–1400 BC: Nat (photo EA).
34b. Snake goddess from Knossos, c. 1600 BC: Herakleion Museum (drawing JF).
35. Aerial view of Mycenae: EA.
36tr. Inlaid bronze dagger hilt from Shaft Grave IV at Mycenae: Nat (photo Robert Harding Associates, London).
36c. Bronze household vessel from shaft grave at Mycenae, c. 1300 BC: Nat (photo Robert Harding Associates, London).
36–37. Gold funeral mask from Shaft Grave V, Circle A, at Mycenae, c. 1550–1500 BC: Nat (photo EA).
Gold cup of Nestor from Shaft Grave IV at Mycenae, 1550–1500 BC: Nat (photo EA).
Wooden hexagonal pyxis with repoussé gold panels from Shaft Grave V at Mycenae: Nat (photo Robert Harding Associates, London).
The lion gate at Mycenae, c. 1250 BC, drawing by Edward Dodwell from *Cyclopean or Pelasgic Remains*,

London, 1834: Ash.
38t. Fresco of bull-leap from east wing of palace of Knossos, 1600–1400 BC: Herakleion Museum (photo EA).
38bl. Palace of Knossos: D.A. Harissiadis, Athens.
38br. Middle Minoan cup from Knossos, 18th century BC: Herakleion Museum (photo Robert Harding Associates, London).
40l. Small terracotta of mourning woman from Thera: DAI, Athens.
40r. Fresco of the fisherman from Thera: Nat (photo Hirmer Fotoarchiv, Munich).
41t. General view of Santorini: Robert Haas, London.
41bl. Excavations at Thera: Hirmer Fotoarchiv, Munich.
41br. Fresco of the antelopes from Thera: Nat (photo Hirmer Fotoarchiv, Munich).
42t. Gallery in the acropolis of Tiryns: EA.
42bl. Ivory figurine with two goddesses and divine child, 13th century BC: Nat (photo EA).
42br. Funeral stele from Shaft Grave V, Circle A, at Mycenae, c. 1550–1500 BC: Nat (JF).
43. Part of the battle fresco from northeast wall of palace of Nestor at Pylos, in M. Lang, *Palace of Nestor at Pylos in Western Messenia*, vol. 2, *The Frescoes*, Princeton, N.J., 1969, and University of Cincinnati: JF.
44. Late Mycenaean vase from Cyprus: Cyprus Museum, Nikosia (photo EA).
46tl. Crawling baby from the Dictaean Cave, Late Minoan I, c. 1600 BC: Ash.
46tr. Head of terracotta statue K3.613 found in the Bronze Age temple at Hagia Irini in Keos: University of Cincinnati Excavations.
46c. Gold ring depicting Mycenaean ship, Late Minoan: Ash.
46b. Graffito of lady in ship from Delos: French School of Archaeology, Athens (photo L. Basch).
47. Terracotta figurine of goddess on horseback: Herakleion Museum (photo EA).
48. Gold necklace with pendant of rock crystal in shape of crescent moon with snakes' head finials from tholos tomb at Khaniale Tekke near Knossos, c. 800 BC: Herakleion Museum (photo EA).
49l. Fresco of the boxers from Thera: Nat (photo EA).
49r. Geometric figures: JF.
50–51. Mother Goddesses: all drawings by JF.
50l. Cycladic female figure from Amorgos, c. 2200–2000 BC: Nat.
50c. Cycladic fiddle idol from Amorgos, c. 2500 BC: BM.
50r. Early Neolithic figurine of woman, sixth millennium BC: Nat.
51tl. Clay figurine of goddess from Gazi, Crete, c. 1400–1100 BC: Herakleion Museum.
51tc. Terracotta figurine from Cyprus, 1450–1225 BC: Louvre, Paris.
51tr. Kourotrophos figurine, c. 1400 BC: Herakleion Museum.
51bl. Clay figurine from Thebes, Boeotia, c. 700 BC: Louvre, Paris.
51cl. Terracotta figurine of goddess from Mycenae, 14th–13th century BC: Nauplion Museum.
51cr. Clay figurine of goddess from Mycenae, 13th century BC: Argos Museum.
51br. Terracotta figurine from Megara Hyblaia, Sicily, c. 560 BC: Archaeological Museum, Syracuse.
52. Hellenistic marble head of Homer: Museum of Fine Arts, Boston, Mass.
53. The apotheosis of Homer from Borillae, 2nd century BC, marble: BM.
54. Red-figure kalyx-krater of the death of Agamemnon, 470–465 BC: Museum of Fine Arts, Boston, Mass.
55t. Scene of Odysseus and his companions attacked by the Laistrygonians from mural paintings of the *Odyssey* in the Esquiline Villa in Rome, 1st century BC: photo Scala, Florence.
55b. Terracotta model tomb from Archanes, Crete, c. 800 BC: Herakleion Museum (photo EA).
56. Navarino bay: EA.
57l. Marble relief depicting scenes from the *Iliad*: Capitoline Museum, Rome (photo Scala, Florence).
57r. Neck of relief pithos found in Mykonos, detail showing Trojan horse, c. 675 BC: Archaeological Museum, Mykonos (photo DAI, Athens).
59. View of Greek islands and sea: D.H. Harissiadis, Athens.
60t. Archaic bronze of Odysseus escaping from the

Cyclops under a ram as described in the *Odyssey*: Olympia Museum (photo EA).
60b. Detail of jug from Aegina showing Odysseus escaping from the Cyclops, mid-7th century BC: DAI, Athens.
61. Drawing freely adapted from Attic geometric krater, mid-8th century BC: Nat. MC.
62. Amphora from Melos depicting Apollo in his chariot, c. 625–620 BC: Nat (photo EA).
63l. Bronze warrior from Dodona, c. 500 BC: Staatliche Museum, West Berlin.
63r. Dodona, the theater: EA.
64t. Geometric vase with prothesis, 8th century BC: Nat (photo Hirmer Fotoarchiv, Munich).
64b. Bronze libation bowl from Olympia, 8th century BC: Ash.
65. Relief of a wheatsheaf, symbol of Demeter, carved on a lintel: Eleusis Museum (photo SH).
68l. Bronze krater from Vix, 6th century BC: Archaeological Museum, Châtillon-sur-Seine (photo Giraudon, Paris).
68c. Glass amphoriskos, 6th century BC: BM, J. Henderson Bequest.
68r. Cloaked warrior from Sparta, c. 500 BC: Wadsworth Atheneum, Hartford, Conn.; J. Pierpont Morgan Collection.
69l. Bronze youth from Peiraeus, c. 520 BC: Nat (photo Scala, Florence).
69br. Black-figure Athenian amphora by the Daybreak Painter, 6th century BC: BM.
69tr. Bronze helmet from Archanes, Crete, c. 600 BC: Schimmel Collection, New York.
70–71. Kouroi and Korai: all drawings by JF.
70bl. Kouros from Melos, 555–540 BC: Nat.
70c. Kouros of Kroisos from Attica, c. 520 BC: Nat.
70r. Kouros from Attica, c. 615–590 BC: Metropolitan Museum, New York.
Rear view of head, ibid.
Close-up of hand, ibid.
71l. Marble kore from Attica, c. 570 BC: Staatliche Museum, West Berlin.
71r. Front and rear view of marble kore from Attica, c. 560 BC: Acropolis Museum, Athens.
71c. Front and rear view of marble kore from near the Erechtheion, c. 530 BC: Acropolis Museum, Athens.
71br. Rear view of Etruscan gypsum kore from Vulci: BM.
72t. Mount Olympos from the sea: R. V. Schoder, S. J., Chicago.
72bl. Small bronze statue of goddess sidesaddle on horseback from Olympia: Olympia Museum (JF).
72br. Bronze tripod leg, Geometric period: Olympia Museum (photo EA).
73. Reconstruction of Delphic victory column in the Hippodrome, Istanbul: Topkapi Museum (photo SH).
74. Two ivory heads from chryselephantine statues at Delphi, 6th century BC: Delphi Museum (photo French School of Archaeology, Athens).
75t. Reconstruction showing decoration on gold plaques found at Delphi, 6th century BC: Delphi Museum (photo French School of Archaeology, Athens).
75b. Detail of one of the gold plaques, ibid.
76tl. Bronze charioteer, 475–470 BC: Delphi Museum (photo Hirmer Fotoarchiv, Munich).
76tr. View over the site of Delphi: A. F. Kersting, London.
76bl. Bronze legs of the charioteer's horse, 475–470 BC: Delphi Museum (photo French School of Archaeology, Athens).
76bc. Tholos on the lower sanctuary terrace, early 4th century BC: Robert Harding Associates, London.
76br. Detail of frieze of Siphnian treasury, c. 525 BC: Delphi Museum (photo Alison Frantz).
77tc. Naxian sphinx, c. 560 BC: Delphi Museum (JF).
77tr. Karyatid from Siphnian treasury, 530–526 BC: Delphi Museum (JF).
78tl. Vase painting depicting Apollo, Hermes and Artemis at omphalos from Athens: BM.
78tr. Engraved lead token used in consulting the oracle at Dodona: Antikenmuseum, West Berlin.
78c. Terracotta representation of omphalos from Delphi: Delphi Museum (photo SH).
78bc. Athenian treasury at Delphi: SH.
79. Attic vase depicting Aigeus consulting the priestess of

BIBLIOGRAPHY

Part One

A. Andrewes, *The Greeks*. London 1967.
J. B. Bury and R. Meiggs, *History of Greece to the Death of Alexander the Great*. 4th ed. London 1975.
Cambridge Ancient History. 3rd ed. Cambridge 1970.
J. K. Campbell, *Honour, Family and Patronage*. Oxford 1964.
M. Cary, *The Geographic Background of Greek and Roman History*. Oxford 1949.
E. Dodwell, *Cyclopean or Pelasgic Remains*. London 1834.
J. du Boulay, *Portrait of a Greek Mountain Village*. Oxford 1974.
N. G. L. Hammond, *History of Greece to 322 BC*. 2nd ed. Oxford 1967.
S. C. Humphreys, *Anthropology and the Greeks*. London 1978.
W. M. Leake, *Travels in the Morea*. 3 vols. London 1830.
—— *Travels in Northern Greece*. 4 vols. London 1835.
A. D. Momigliano, *Alien Wisdom*. Cambridge 1975.
Oxford Classical Dictionary. 2nd ed. Oxford 1970.
Pitton de Tournefort, *Relation d'un voyage du Levant*. Lyon 1717.
H. J. Rose, *A Handbook of Greek Mythology*. 6th ed. London 1958.
R. Stillwell, W. L. MacDonald, and M. A. McAllister, *The Princeton Encyclopedia of Classical Sites*. Princeton, N.J. 1976.
J. Stuart and N. Revett, *The Antiquities of Athens*. 4 vols. London 1762–1816.

Part Two

C. W. Blegen, *Troy and the Trojans*. London 1963.
K. Branigan, *The Foundations of Palatial Crete*. London 1970.
H. -G. Buchholz and V. Karageorghis, *Prehistoric Greece and Cyprus*. London 1973.
J. Chadwick, *The Decipherment of Linear B*. 2nd ed. Cambridge 1968.
—— *The Mycenaean World*. Cambridge 1976.
V. R. d'A. Desborough, *The Last Mycenaeans and their Successors*. Oxford 1964.
—— *The Greek Dark Ages*. London 1972.
Sir Arthur Evans, *The Palace of Minos at Knossos*. Vols. 1–4. London 1921–35. Index volume 1936. Repr. New York 1963.
M. I. Finley, *The World of Odysseus*. 2nd ed. Harmondsworth 1962.
A. Furumark, *The Mycenaean Pottery. Analysis and Classification*. Stockholm 1941. Repr. Stockholm 1972.
—— *The Chronology of Mycenaean Pottery*. Stockholm 1941. Repr. Stockholm 1972.
J. W. Graham, *The Palaces of Crete*. Princeton, N.J. 1962. Repr. 1969.
R. Higgins, *Minoan and Mycenaean Art*. London and New York 1967.
M. S. F. Hood, *The Home of the Heroes. The Aegean before the Greeks*. London 1967.
—— *The Minoans*. London 1971.
R. W. Hutchinson, *Prehistoric Crete*. Harmondsworth Repr. 1968.
G. S. Kirk, *Homer and the Epic*. Cambridge 1965.
—— *Myth, its Meaning and Function*. Cambridge 1970.
A. D. Lacy, *Greek Pottery in the Bronze Age*. London 1967.
J. V. Luce, *The End of Atlantis*. London 1969.
S. Marinatos and M. Hirmer, *Crete and Mycenae*. London 1960.
F. Matz, *Kreta, Mikene, Troja. Die minoische und die homerische Welt*. Stuttgart 1956.
—— *Crete and Early Greece*. London 1962.
O. Murray, *Early Greece and the Near East*. London 1980.
G. Mylonas, *Ancient Mycenae*. London 1957.
—— *Mycenae and the Mycenaean Age*. Princeton, N.J. 1966.
M. P. Nilsson, *The Minoan-Mycenaean Religion and its Survival in Greek Religion*. 2nd ed. Lund 1950.
D. L. Page, *The Homeric Odyssey*. Oxford 1955.
—— *History and the Homeric Iliad*. Berkeley, Ca. 1959.
J. D. S. Pendlebury, *The Archaeology of Crete*. London 1939. Repr. New York 1965.
C. Renfrew, *The Emergence of Civilization. The Cyclades and the Aegean in the Third Millennium BC*. London 1972.
A. E. Samuel, *The Mycenaeans in History*. Englewood Cliffs, N.J. 1966.
N. K. Sandars, *The Sea Peoples*. London 1978.

K. Schefold, *Myth and Legend in Early Greek Art*. London 1966.
H. Schliemann, *Mycenae*. London 1878.
—— *Ilios*. London 1880.
A. M. Snodgrass, *Archaeology and the Rise of the Greek State*. Cambridge 1977.
—— *The Dark Age of Greece*. Edinburgh 1971.
F. H. Stubbings, *Mycenaean Pottery from the Levant*. Cambridge 1951.
—— *Prehistoric Greece*. London 1972.
Lord William Taylour, *Mycenaean Pottery in Italy and Adjacent Areas*. Cambridge 1958.
—— *The Mycenaeans*. London 1964.
G. Thomson, *The Prehistoric Aegean*. London 1978.
M. Ventris and J. Chadwick, *Documents in Mycenaean Greek*. 2nd ed. by J. Chadwick. Cambridge 1973.
E. Vermeule, *Greece in the Bronze Age*. 5th impression. Chicago, Ill., and London 1972.
A. J. B. Wace, *Mycenae. An Archaeological History and Guide*. Princeton, N.J. 1949.
—— and F. H. Stubbings (eds.), *A Companion to Homer*. London 1962.
P. Warren, *The Aegean Civilizations*. Oxford 1975.
C. Zervos, *L'Art de la Crète néolithique et minoenne*. Paris 1956.
—— *L'Art des Cyclades*. Paris 1957.
—— *La Naissance de la civilisation en Grèce*. Vols 1–2. Paris 1962.

Part Three

A. Andrewes, *Greek Tyrants*. London 1956.
J. Boardman, *The Greeks Overseas*. 3rd ed. London 1980.
—— *Preclassical*. Harmondsworth 1967.
—— *Athenian Black Figure Vases*. London 1974.
—— *Athenian Red Figure Vases of the Archaic Period*. London 1975.
—— *Greek Sculpture: the Archaic Period*. London 1978.
R. J. Bonner, *Aspects of Athenian Democracy*. Berkeley, Ca. 1933.
C. M. Bowra, *Greek Lyric Poetry*. 2nd ed. Oxford 1961.
—— *Pindar*. Oxford 1964.
A. R. Burn, *Lyric Age of Greece*. London 1960.
—— *Persia and the Greeks*. London 1962.
P. Cartledge, *Sparta and Lakonia*. London 1979.
M. and V. Charbonneaux, *Archaic Greek Art*. London and New York 1971.
J. N. Coldstream, *Greek Geometric Pottery*. London 1968.
—— *Geometric Greece*. London 1977.
J. K. Davies, *Athenian Propertied Families*. Oxford 1971.
J. de Romilly, *La Loi dans la pensée grecque*. Paris 1971.
V. R. d'A. Desborough, *The Greek Dark Ages*. London 1972.
T. J. Dunbabin, *The Western Greeks*. Oxford 1948.
V. Ehrenberg, *From Solon to Socrates*. 2nd ed. London 1973.
B. Farrington, *Greek Science*. 2nd ed. Harmondsworth 1969.
M. I. Finley, *Ancient Sicily*. London 1968.
W. G. Forrest, *The Emergence of Greek Democracy*. London 1966.
—— *A History of Sparta, 950 BC–192 BC*. London 1968.
H. Fränkel, *Early Greek Poetry and Philosophy*. Oxford 1975.
E. N. Gardiner, *Athletics of the Ancient World*. Oxford 1930.
A. J. Graham, *Colony and Mother City in Ancient Greece*. Manchester 1964.
D. Harden, *The Phoenicians*. Harmondsworth 1971.
H. A. Harris, *Greek Athletes and Athletics*. London 1964.
—— *Sport in Greece and Rome*. London 1972.
A. R. W. Harrison, *The Law of Athens*: vol. 1 *The Family and Property*. Oxford 1968; vol. 2 *Procedure*. 1971.
C. and S. Hawkes (eds.), *Greeks, Celts and Romans*. London 1973.
C. Hignett, *Xerxes' Invasion of Greece*. Oxford 1963.
E. Homann-Wedeking, *Archaic Greece*. London 1968.
E. Hussey, *The Presocratics*. London 1972.
G. L. Huxley, *The Early Ionians*. London 1966.
L. H. Jeffrey, *Archaic Greece*. London 1976.
G. K. Jenkins, *Ancient Greek Coins*. London 1972.
A. Johnston, *The Emergence of Greece*. Oxford 1976.
G. S. Kirk and J. E. Raven, *The Presocratic Philosophers*. Cambridge 1957.
C. M. Kraay, *Archaic and Classical Greek Coins*. London

1976.
—— and M. Hirmer, *Greek Coins*. London 1966.
E. Langlotz and M. Hirmer, *The Art of Magna Graecia*. London 1965.
A. Lesky, *History of Greek Literature*. London 1966.
P. Maas, *Greek Metre*, trans H. Lloyd-Jones. Oxford 1962.
S. Moscati, *The World of the Phoenicians*. London 1968.
M. P. Nilsson, *A History of Greek Religion*. 2nd ed. Oxford 1949.
—— *Greek Popular Religion*. New York 1940.
—— *Greek Piety*. Oxford 1948.
H. W. Parke, *Greek Oracles*. London 1967.
H. Payne, *Necrocorinthia*. Oxford 1931.
S. Piggott, *Ancient Europe*. Edinburgh 1973.
M. J. Price and N. Waggoner, *Archaic Greek Coinage*. London 1976.
D. S. Raven, *Green Metre*. London 1969.
E. Rawson, *The Spartan Tradition in European Thought*. Oxford 1969.
P. J. Rhodes, *The Athenian Boule*. Oxford 1972.
G. M. A. Richter, *Korai: Archaic Greek Maidens*. London 1968.
—— *Kouroi: Archaic Greek Youths*. 3rd ed. London 1970.
S. Sambursky, *The Physical World of the Greeks*. London 1956.
B. Schweitzer, *Greek Geometric Art*. London and New York 1971.
E. Vanderpool, *Ostracism at Athens*. Cincinnati, Ohio 1970.
M. L. West, *Early Greek Philosophy and the Orient*. Oxford 1971.
A. G. Woodhead, *The Greeks in the West*. London 1962.

Part Four

P. E. Arias and M. Hirmer, *A History of Greek Vase Painting*. London 1962.
B. Ashmole, *Architect and Sculptor in Classical Greece*. London 1972.
J. D. Beazley, *Potter and Painter in Ancient Athens*. Oxford 1946.
H. Berve, G. Gruben and M. Hirmer, *Greek Temples, Theatres and Shrines*. London 1963.
M. Bieber, *The History of the Greek and Roman Theater*. 2nd ed. Princeton, N.J. 1961.
C. Blümel, *Greek Sculptors at Work*. 2nd ed. London 1969.
J. Boardman, *Greek Art*. Revised ed. London 1973.
—— *Greek Gems and Finger Rings*. London 1971.
R. S. Buck, *Plato's Phaedo*. London 1955.
R. Carpenter, *The Architects of the Parthenon*. Harmondsworth 1970.
M. Cary and E. H. Warmington, *The Ancient Explorers*. London 1929; paperback revised ed. 1963.
L. Casson, *Ships and Seamanship in the Ancient World*. Princeton, N.J. 1971.
—— *Travel in the Ancient World*. London 1974.
W. R. Connor, *The New Politicians of Fifth Century Athens*. Princeton, N.J. 1971.
R. M. Cook, *Greek Art. Its Development, Character and Influence*. London 1972.
F. M. Cornford, *Before and after Socrates*. Cambridge 1932.
J. J. Coulton, *Greek Architects at Work*. London 1977.
J. K. Davies, *Democracy and Classical Greece*. London 1978.
J. de Romilly, *Thucydides and Athenian Imperialism*. Oxford 1963.
G. E. M. de Ste. Croix, *The Origins of the Peloponnesian War*. London 1972.
W. B. Dinsmoor, *The Architecture of Ancient Greece*. 3rd ed. London and New York 1950.
E. R. Dodds, *The Ancient Concept of Progress*. Oxford 1973.
K. J. Dover, *Aristophanic Comedy*. London 1972.
—— *Greek Popular Morality*. Berkeley, Ca. 1974.
—— *Greek Homosexuality*. London 1978.
V. Ehrenberg, *Sophocles and Pericles*. Oxford 1954.
J. Ellis Jones et al., *An Attic Country House*. London 1974.
J. H. Finley, *Thucydides*. Cambridge, Mass. 1976.
M. I. Finley (ed.), *Slavery in Classical Antiquity*. Cambridge 1960.
R. Flacelière, *Daily Life in Greece at the Time of Pericles*. London 1965.
R. J. Forbes, *Studies in Ancient Technology*. 9 vols. 2nd ed. Leiden 1964–72.

C. W. Fornara, *Herodotus*. Oxford 1971.
A. French, *The Growth of the Athenian Economy*. London 1964.
G. Glotz, *Ancient Greece at Work*. London 1926.
W. C. K. Guthrie, *History of Greek Philosophy*. 5 vols. Cambridge 1962–78.
I. Henderson, "Ancient Greek Music" in *The New Oxford History of Music*, vol. 1: *Ancient and Oriental Music*. Oxford 1957.
R. J. Hopper, *The Acropolis*. London 1971.
—— *Trade and Industry in Classical Greece*. London 1979.
J. Jones, *On Aristotle and Greek Tragedy*. London 1962.
D. Kurtz, *Athenian White Lekythoi*. Oxford 1975.
—— and J. Boardman, *Greek Burial Customs*. London 1971.
W. K. Lacey, *The Family in Classical Greece*. London 1968.
M. L. W. Laistner, *A History of the Greek World from 479 to 323 BC*. 3rd ed. London 1957; paperback ed. 1970.
A. W. Lawrence, *Greek and Roman Sculpture*. London 1972.
—— *Greek Architecture*. 3rd ed. Harmondsworth 1973.
A. Lesky, *Greek Tragedy*. London 1965.
R. J. Ling, *The Greek World*. Oxford 1976.
R. Lullies and M. Hirmer, *Greek Sculpture*. Revised ed. London 1960.
H. -I. Marrou, *A History of Education in Antiquity*. London 1956.
R. Martin, *L'Urbanisme dans la cité grecque*. Paris 1974.
R. Meiggs, *The Athenian Empire*. Oxford 1972.
—— and D. M. Lewis, *Selection of Greek Historical Inscriptions*. Oxford 1969.
H. Michell, *The Economics of Ancient Greece*. Revised ed. Cambridge 1957.
N. R. Murphy, *The Interpretation of Plato's Republic*. Oxford 1951.
H. W. Parke, *Festivals of the Athenians*, London 1977.
—— *Greek Mercenary Soldiers*. Oxford 1933. Repr. 1970.
A. W. Pickard-Cambridge, *The Dramatic Festivals of Athens*. 2nd ed. Oxford 1968.
J. E. Raven, *Plato's Thought in the Making*. Cambridge 1965.
K. Reinhardt, *Sophokles*. 3rd ed. Frankfurt 1947.
G. M. A. Richter, *The Sculpture and Sculptors of the Greeks*. 4th ed. New Haven, Conn. 1970.
—— *Handbook of Greek Art*. 7th ed. London and New York 1974.
—— *Portraits of the Greeks*. London 1966.
D. S. Robertson, *Greek and Roman Architecture*. 2nd ed. Cambridge 1943. Paperback ed. 1969.
M. Robertson, *History of Greek Art*. Cambridge 1976.
D. Ross, *Plato's Theory of Ideas*. Oxford 1951.
A. M. Snodgrass, *Arms and Armour of the Greeks*. London 1967.
E. S. Staveley, *Greek and Roman Voting and Elections*. London 1972.
D. E. Strong, *The Classical World*. London 1965.
A. E. Taylor, *Plato*. London 1926.
J. Travlos, *Pictorial Dictionary of Ancient Athens*. London 1971.
A. D. Trendall and T. B. L. Webster, *Illustrations of Greek Drama*. London 1971.
J. P. Vernant, *Mythe et pensée chez les grecs*. Paris 1965.
—— *Mythe et tragédie en Grèce ancienne*. Paris 1972.
B. Vickers, *Towards Greek Tragedy*. London 1974.

J. Vogt, *Ancient Slavery and the Ideal of Man*. Oxford 1974.
A. J. A. Waldock, *Sophocles the Dramatist*. Cambridge 1966.
T. B. L. Webster, *Athenian Culture and Society*. London 1973.
F. E. Winter, *Greek Fortifications*. London 1971.
A. G. Woodhead, *The Study of Greek Inscriptions*. Cambridge 1959.
R. E. Wycherley, *How the Greeks Built Cities*. 2nd ed. London 1962.
A. E. Zimmern, *The Greek Commonwealth*. 5th ed. Oxford 1947. Paperback ed. 1961.

Part Five
M. Bieber, *The Sculpture of the Hellenistic Age*. New York 1955.
M. Cary, *A History of the Greek World from 323 to 146 BC*. 2nd ed. London 1951.
G. L. Cawkwell, *Philip of Macedon*. London 1978.
K. J. Dover, *Lysias and the Corpus Lysiacum*. Berkeley, Ca. 1968.
J. R. Ellis, *Philip II and Macedonian Imperialism*. London 1976.
P. M. Fraser, *Ptolemaic Alexandria*. 3 vols. Oxford 1972.
G. T. Griffith, *History of Macedonia*, vol. 2. Oxford 1972.
P. Grimal, *Hellenism and the Rise of Rome*. London 1968.
W. Jaeger, *Aristoteles*. Berlin 1955.
G. Kennedy, *The Art of Persuasion in Greece*. London and Princeton, N.J. 1963.
R. Lane Fox, *Alexander the Great*. London 1973.
J. A. O. Larsen, *Greek Federal States*. Oxford 1968.
N. Lewis, *Papyrus in Classical Antiquity*. Oxford 1974.
A. A. Long, *Hellenistic Philosophy*. London 1974.
R. Pfeiffer, *History of Classical Scholarship: from the Beginnings to the End of the Hellenistic Age*. Oxford 1968.
A. W. Pickard-Cambridge, *Demosthenes*. New York 1914.
J. H. Randall Jr., *Aristotle*. New York 1960.
L. D. Reynolds and N. G. Wilson, *Scribes and Scholars*. 2nd ed. Oxford 1974.
L. Robin, *Aristote*. Paris 1944.
W. D. Ross, *Aristotle*. 5th ed. London 1960.
—— *The Development of Aristotle's Thought*. London 1957.
M. I. Rostovtzeff, *Social and Economic History of the Hellenistic World*. 3 vols. Oxford 1941.
W. W. Tarn, *Hellenistic Military and Naval Developments*. Cambridge 1930.
—— *Hellenistic Civilization*. 3rd ed. rev. G. T. Griffith. London 1952.
E. G. Turner, *Greek Papyri: An Introduction*. Oxford 1968.
—— *Greek Manuscripts of the Ancient World*. Oxford 1971.
U. von Wilamowitz-Moellendorff, *Hellenistiche Dichtung*. Berlin 1924. Repr. 1961.
T. B. L. Webster, *Hellenistic Poetry and Art*. London 1964.
H. D. Westlake, *Thessaly in the Fourth Century*. London 1935.

Part Six
P. Brown, *The World of Late Antiquity*. London 1971.
R. Browning, *Medieval and Modern Greek*. London 1969.

E. Fraenkel, *Horace*. Oxford 1957.
R. Heinze, *Virgils epische Technik*. Leipzig and Berlin 1915. Repr. Stuttgart 1965.
L. Politis, *A History of Modern Greek Literature*. Oxford 1973.
S. Runciman, *Mistra*. London 1980.
W. St. Clair, *That Greece might still be Free*. London 1972.
C. A. Trypanis (ed.), *Medieval and Modern Greek Poetry*. Oxford 1951.
G. Williams, *Tradition and Originality in Roman Poetry*. Oxford 1968.

Greek Literature in English Translation
Aischylos, *Oresteia*, tr. D. Young. Oklahoma 1975.
—— *Prometheus and Other Plays*, tr. P. Vellacott. Harmondsworth 1970.
Apollodoros, *The Library*, tr. J. G. Frazer. 2 vols. London 1921.
Apollonios Rhodios, *Argonautica*, tr. E. V. Rieu. Harmondsworth 1959.
Aristophanes, tr. B. B. Rogers. 3 vols. London 1924.
Aristotle, *Ethics*, tr. J. A. K. Thomson. Harmondsworth 1969.
—— *Metaphysics*, tr. J. Warrington. London 1968.
—— *Poetics*, tr. G. F. Else. Michigan 1970.
—— *Politics and Athenian Constitution*, tr. J. Warrington. London 1959.
Demosthenes and Aischines, *Political Speeches*, tr. A. N. W. Saunders. Harmondsworth 1975.
Euripides, tr. G. Murray. London 1976.
Greek Anthology, tr. P. Jay. London 1973.
Herodotos, tr. A. de Sélincourt. Harmondsworth 1954.
Hesiod and Theognis, tr. D. Wender. Harmondsworth 1973.
Hippokrates, tr. W. H. S. Jones and E. T. Withington. 4 vols. London 1923–31.
Homer, tr. A. Pope. 4 vols. London 1967.
Kallimachos, tr. A. W. Mair. London 1955.
C. P. Kavafis, *Poems*, tr. J. Mavrogordato. London 1971.
Lucian, tr. A. M. Harmon, K. Kilburn and M. D. Macleod. 8 vols. London 1913–67.
Menander, *Girl from Samos*, tr. E. G. Turner. London 1972.
Pausanias, tr. P. Levi. 2 vols. Harmondsworth 1971.
Pindar, tr. R. Lattimore. 2nd ed. Chicago, Ill. 1976.
Plato, *Gorgias*, tr. W. Hamilton. Harmondsworth 1971.
—— *Last Days of Socrates*, tr. H. Tredennick. Harmondsworth 1969.
—— *Laws*, tr. T. Saunders. Harmondsworth 1970.
—— *Protagoras and Meno*, tr. W. K. C. Guthrie. Harmondsworth 1970.
—— *Republic*, tr. H. D. P. Lee. Harmondsworth 1970.
—— *Symposium*, tr. W. Hamilton. Harmondsworth 1970.
Plutarch, *Age of Alexander*, tr. I. S. Kilvert. Harmondsworth 1973.
G. Seferis, *Collected Poems*, tr. E. Keeley and P. Sherrard. London 1973.
Sophokles, tr. E. F. Watling. 2 vols. Harmondsworth 1969.
Theokritos, *Greek Pastoral Poetry*, tr. A. Holden. Harmondsworth 1974.
Thucydides, tr. R. Warner. Harmondsworth 1954.
Xenophon, *Persian Expedition*, tr. R. Warner. Harmondsworth 1967.

GAZETTEER

INDEX